S0-BEP-273

BYZANTIUM AND THE RISE OF RUSSIA

BYZANTIUM AND THE RISE OF RUSSIA

A Study of Byzantino-Russian Relations
in the Fourteenth Century

JOHN MEYENDORFF

ST VLADIMIR'S SEMINARY PRESS
Crestwood, New York 10707
1989

First published 1981 by
Cambridge University Press
Copyright © 1980 Cambridge University Press

Reprinted with Permission

Library of Congress Cataloging-in-Publication Data

Meyendorff, John. 1926 -
    Byzantium and the rise of Russia: a study of Byzantino-Russian relations in
the fourteenth century / John Meyendorff.
        p.   cm.
    Reprint. Originally published: Cambridge: New York: Cambridge
University Press, 1981.
    Includes bibliographical references.
    ISBN 0-88141-079-9
    1. Soviet Union--Foreign relations--Byzantine Empire.
2. Byzantine Empire--Foreign relations--Soviet Union. 3. Soviet Union--Foreign
relations--To 1689. 4. Byzantine Empire--Foreign relations--1081-1453. 5.
Soviet Union--History--1237-1480.
I. Title.
[DK67.5.B95M49 1989]
327.47-495--dc20   89-28011
                                                                 CIP

BYZANTIUM AND THE RISE OF RUSSIA

published by

ST VLADIMIR'S SEMINARY PRESS

ISBN 0-88141-079-9

ALL RIGHTS RESERVED

PRINTED IN THE UNITED STATES OF AMERICA

To my Wife

Contents

Contents

Abbreviations used for frequently cited books, articles, series, and periodicals

AAE	*Akty sobrannye v bibliotekakh i arkhivakh Rossiiskoi Imperii Arkheograficheskoyu Ekspeditseyu imperatorskoi Akademii Nauk*, 1, St. Petersburg, 1836.
AI	*Akty istoricheskie*, St Petersburg, 1841–.
Ammann, Abriss	A. Ammann, *Abriss der Ostslavischen Kirchengeschichte*, Vienna, 1950.
Angelov, Iz starata	B. S. Angelov, *Iz starata Bŭlgarska, Russka i Srbska literatura*, Sofia, 1958.
Bank, Iskusstvo	A. V. Bank, *Vizantiiskoe iskusstvo v sobraniyakh sovetskogo soyuza*, Leningrad–Moscow, 1965 (tr. from the Russian by I. Sorokina, Leningrad, 1977).
Barker, Manuel II	J. W. Barker, *Manuel II Palaeologus (1391–1425): a Study in Late Byzantine Statesmanship*, New Brunswick, N. J., 1969.
Beck, Kirche	H.-G. Beck, *Kirche und theologische Literatur im byzantinischen Reich* (Handbuch der Altertumswissenschaft XII, 2, 1: Byzantinisches Handbuch II, 1), Munich, 1959.
Bréhier, Institutions	L. Bréhier, *Les institutions de l'empire byzantin. Le Monde byzantin*, II (L'évolution de l'humanité, 32bis), Paris, 1948.
BZ	*Byzantinische Zeitschrift*, Leipzig, 1892–.
Cherniavsky, 'Khan or basileus'	M. Cherniavsky, '*Khan* or *basileus*: an Aspect of Russian Mediaeval Political Theory', *Journal of History of Ideas*, 20, 1959, pp. 459–76 (repr. in Cherniavsky, M., ed., *The Structure of Russian History. Interpretive Essays*, New York, 1970).
Darrouzès, Documents	J. Darrouzès, *Documents inédits d'ecclésiologie byzantine*, Paris, 1966.
Darrouzès, Recherches	J. Darrouzès, *Recherches sur les 'Οφφίκια de l'église byzantine*, Paris, 1970.
Darrouzès, Régistre	J. Darrouzès, *Le régistre synodal du patriarcat byzantin au XIVe siècle. Etude paléographique et diplomatique*, Paris, 1971.

DATL   H. Leclercq, ed., *Dictionnaire d'archéologie chrétienne et de liturgie*, Paris, 1907–40.

DHGE   *Dictionnaire d'histoire et de géographie ecclésiastiques*, Paris, 1912–.

Dmitriev, 'Rol' i znachenie'   L. A. Dmitriev, 'Rol' i znachenie mitropolita Kipriana v istorii drevne-russkoi literatury', TODRL, xix, 1963, pp. 215–54.

DTC   A. Vacant-E. Mangenot, *Dictionnaire de théologie catholique*, Paris, 1908–72.

Dölger, Regesten   F. Dölger, *Regesten der Kaiserurkunden des oströmischen Reiches (Corpus der griechischen Urkunden des Mittelalters und der neueren Zeit*, Reihe A, Abt. I), I: 565–1025; II: 1025–1204; III: 1204–1282; IV: 1282–1341; V: 1341–1453, Munich and Berlin, 1924, 1925, 1932, 1960, 1965.

DOP   *Dumbarton Oaks Papers*, Washington, 1941–.

Dujčev, 'Tsentry'   I. Dujčev, 'Tsentry vizantiiskoslavyanskogo obshcheniya i sotrudnichestva', TODRL, xix, 1963, pp. 107–129.

Dvornik, The Making   F. Dvornik, *The Making of Central and Eastern Europe*, London, 1949.

D'yakonov, Vlast'   M. D'yakonov, *Vlast' moskovskikh gosudarei. Ocherki iz istorii politicheskikh idei drevnei Rusi*, St Petersburg, 1889.

EO   *Echos d'Orient*, Kadiköe, Paris, 1897–1939.

Erm.   *Ermolinskaya Letopis'*, PSRL, xxiii, St Petersburg, 1910.

Fedotov, Religious Mind   G. Fedotov, *The Russian Religious Mind*, I. *Kievan Christianity*. II. *The Middle Ages, 13th–15th cent.*, Cambridge, Mass., 1946, 1966.

Fennell, Emergence   J. L. I. Fennell, *The Emergence of Moscow, 1304–1359*, Berkeley, Calif., 1968.

Gay, Clément VI   J. Gay, *Le pape Clément VI et les affaires d'Orient*, Paris, 1904.

Gelzer, 'Beiträge'   H. Gelzer, 'Beiträge zur russischen Kirchengeschichte aus griechischen Quellen', *Zeitschrift für Kirchengeschichte*, xiii, 1892, pp. 246–81.

Gelzer, Notitiae   H. Gelzer, *Ungedruckte und ungenügend veröffentlichte Texte der Notitiae episcopatum*, München, K. Akademie der Wissenschaften, Hist. Kl., Abhandlungen, XXI, 1900, Bd. III, Abth.

Golubinsky, Istoriya   E. E. Golubinsky, *Istoriya Russkoi Tserkvi*, I, 1–2, II, 1, Moscow, 1901–.

Grekov, Vostochnaya Europa   I. B. Grekov, *Vostochnaya Evropa i upadok zolotoi ordy (na rubezhe XIV–XV vv.)*, Moscow, 1975.

Grumel-Laurent, *Régestes*	V. Grumel, *Les régestes des Actes du Patriarchat de Constantinople*, Vol. 1: *Les Actes des patriarches*, fasc. I; II; III; IV (by V. Laurent), Paris, 1932, 1936, 1947, 1971.
Halecki, *Empereur*	O. Halecki, *Un empereur de Byzance à Rome. Vingt ans de travail pour l'Union des églises et pour la défense de l'empire d'Orient, 1355–1373*, Warsaw, 1930.
Heyd, *Commerce*	W. Heyd, *Histoire du commerce du Levant au Moyen-Age*, II, Leipzig, 1936.
Hrushevsky, *Istoriya*	M. Hrushevsky, *Istoriya Ukrainy-Rusi*, III, New York, 1954.
Hyp.	*Ipatievskaya Letopis'*, PSRL, II, Moscow, 1962; Engl. tr. by G. Perfecky, Munich, 1973.
Ikonnikov, *O kul'turnom znachenii*	V. Ikonnikov, *O kul'turnom znachenii Vizantii v russkoi istorii*, Kiev, 1869.
Kartashev, *Ocherki*	A. Kartashev, *Ocherki po istorii russkoi tserkvi*, Paris, 1959.
Knoll, *Polish Monarchy*	P. W. Knoll, *The Rise of the Polish Monarchy. Piast Poland in East-Central Europe, 1320–1370*, Chicago, 1972.
Kourouses, Γαβαλᾶς	S. Kourouses, Μανουὴλ Γαβαλᾶς, εἶτα Ματθαῖος μητροπολίτης 'Εφέσου, Α'. – Τὰ βιογραφικά, Athens, 1972.
Lavr.	*Lavrentievskaya Letopis'*, PSRL 1, Moscow, 1962.
Likhachev, 'Nekotorye zadachi'	D. S. Likhachev, 'Nekotorye zadachi izucheniya vtorogo yuzhnoslavyanskogo vliyaniya v Rossii', *Izsledovaniya po slavyanskomu literaturovedeniyu i fol'kloristike sovetskikh uchenykh na IV. mezhdunarodnom s'ezde slavistov*, Moscow, 1960, pp. 95–151.
Lvov.	*L'vovskaya Letopis'*, PSRL, XX, 1, 1910–14.
MM	F. Miklosich and I. Müller, *Acta patriarchatus Constantinopolitani*, Vienna, 1862–.
Makary, *Istoriya*	Makary, mitropolit, *Istoriya russkoi tserkvi*, IV, 1, St Petersburg, 1866.
Maksimovič, *Politička uloga*	L. Maksimović, 'Politička uloga Iovana Kantakuzena posle abdikacii', ZRVI, 9, Belgrade, 1966, pp. 119–93.
Mansvetov, *Kiprian*	I. Mansvetov, *Mitropolit Kiprian v ego liturgicheskoi deyatel'nosti*, Moscow, 1882.
Medvedev, *Gumanizm*	I. P. Medvedev, *Vizantiisky Gumanizm XIV–XV vv.*, Leningrad, 1976.
Mercati, *Notizie*	G. Mercati, *Notizie di Procoro e Demetrio Cidone, Manuele Caleca e Teodoro Meliteniota, ed altri appunti per la storia della teologia e della letteratura bizantina del secolo XIV* (Studi e testi, 56), Vatican, 1931.

Meyendorff, 'Alexis and Roman' — J. Meyendorff, 'Alexis and Roman: a Study in Byzantino-Russian Relations (1352–1354)', BS, XXVIII, 1967, 2, pp. 278–88 (repr. in *St. Vladimir's Theological Quarterly*, 11, 1967, 3, pp. 139–48).

Byzantine Theology — J. Meyendorff, *Byzantine Theology. Historical Trends and Doctrinal Themes*, New York, 1974.

'Ideological crises' — J. Meyendorff, 'Ideological crises, 1071–1261', *XVe Congrès International des études byzantines. Rapports et co-Rapports*, IV. *Pensée, philosophie, histoire des idées*, I. *Crises idéologiques*, Athens, 1976.

Introduction — J. Meyendorff, *Introduction à l'étude de Grégoire Palamas*, Paris, 1959 (Engl. tr., *A Study of Gregory Palamas*, London, 1964).

'O vizantiiskom isikhazme' — J. Meyendorff, 'O vizantiiskom isikhazme i ego roli v kul'turnom i istoricheskom razvitii Vostochnoi Evropy v XIV-m veke', TODRL, XXIX, 1974, pp. 291–305.

'Projets' — J. Meyendorff, 'Projets de Concile oecuménique en 1367', DOP 14, 1960, pp. 147–77.

'Spiritual trends' — J. Meyendorff, 'Spiritual trends in Byzantium in the late thirteenth and early fourteenth centuries', *Art et Société à Byzance sous les Paléologues*, Venice, 1971 (also in P. Underwood, *The Kariye Djami*, vol. 4, Princeton, N. J., 1975, pp. 93–106).

MGH — *Monumenta Germaniae Historica*, G. H. Pertz, et al., edds., Hanover, 1826–.

Moshin, 'O periodizatsii' — V. Moshin, 'O periodizatsii russko-yuzhnoslavyanskikh literaturnykh svyazei', TODRL, XIX, 1963, pp. 28–106.

Mosk. — *Moskovsky Letopisny Svod*, PSRL, XXV, 1949.

Nasonov, *Mongoly i Rus'* — A. N. Nasonov, *Mongoly i Rus'. Istoriya tatarskoi politiki na Rusi*, Moscow–Leningrad, 1940 (repr. Mouton, 1969).

Nicol, *The Last Centuries* — D. M. Nicol, *The Last Centuries of Byzantium, 1261–1453*, London, 1972.

Nik. — *Nikonovskaya Letopis'*, PSRL, X–XI, St Petersburg, 1862, 1897.

Novg. — *Novgorodskaya Pervaya Letopis' Starshego i Mladshego izvodov*, ed. A. Nasonov, Moscow–Leningrad, 1950; Engl. tr. R. Michell and N. Forbes, *The Chronicle of Novgorod*, Hattiesburg, Miss., 1970.

Obolensky, 'Byzantium, Kiev and Moscow' — D. Obolensky, 'Byzantium, Kiev and Moscow: a Study of Ecclesiastical Relations', DOP, XI, 1957, pp. 23–78 (repr. in D. Obolensky, *Byzantium and the Slavs. Collected Studies*, Variorum, London, 1971).

Abbreviations

Commonwealth	D. Obolensky, *The Byzantine Commonwealth*, London, 1971.
'Late Byzantine Culture'	D. Obolensky, 'Late Byzantine Culture and the Slavs: a Study in Acculturation', *XVe Congrès International d'Etudes Byzantines. Rapports et co-Rapports*, Athens, 1976.
Philorhomaios	D. Obolensky, 'A *Philorhomaios anthrōpos*: Metropolitan Cyprian of Kiev and all Russia', DOP, 32, 1979, pp. 79–98.
OCP	*Orientalia Christiana Periodica*, Rome, 1935–.
Ostrogorsky, History	G. Ostrogorsky, *History of the Byzantine State*, 2nd ed., Rutgers University Press, New Brunswick, N. J., 1969.
Pashuto, Ocherki	V. T. Pashuto, *Ocherki po istorii Galitsko-Volynskoı Rusi*, Moscow, 1950.
Obrazovanie	V. T. Pashuto, *Obrazovanie Litovskogo Gosudarstva*, Moscow, 1959.
Pavlov, 'O nachale'	A. S. Pavlov, 'O nachale Galitskoi i Litovskoi mitropolii i o pervykh tamoshnikh mitropolitakh po vizantiiskim documental'nym istochnikam XIV-go veka', *Russkoe Obozrenie*, 1894, III, May, pp. 214–51.
Opyty	A. S. Pavlov, *Kriticheskie opyty po istorii drevneishei greko-russkoi polemiki protiv Latinyan*, St Petersburg, 1878.
Pelliot, Mongols et papes	P. Pelliot, *Mongols et papes aux XIIIe et XIVe siècles*, Paris, 1922.
PG	J. P. Migne, *Patrologiae cursus completus*, series Graeco-latina, Paris, 1857–.
Podskalsky, Theologie	G. Podskalsky, *Theologie und Philosophie in Byzanz. Der Streit und die theologische Methodik in der spätbyzantinischen Geistesgeschichte (14./15.Jh.), seine systematischen Grundlagen und seine historische Entwicklung*, Munich, 1977 (Byzantinisches Archiv, Heft 15).
Popov, Obzor	A. Popov, *Istoriko-literaturny obzor drevne-russkikh polemicheskikh sochinenii protiv Latinyan (XI–XV v.)*, Moscow, 1875 (repr. Variorum, London, 1972).
Poppe, Państwo i Kościół	A. Poppe, *Państwo i Kościół na Rusi w XI wieku*, Warsaw, 1968.
Pothast, Regesta	A. Pothast, ed., *Regesta Pontificum Romanorum*, II (Berlin, 1875).
PPS	*Pravoslavnyi Palestinsky Sbornik*, St Petersburg, 1881–1917.
Primary Chronicle	*Povest' vremennykh let*, D. S. Likhachev et al., Moscow–Leningrad, 1950, I–II; tr. S. H. Cross

xiii

and O. P. Sherbowitz-Wetzor, *The Russian Primary Chronicle*, Cambridge, Mass., 1953.

Priselkov,   M. D. Priselkov, *Istoriya russkogo letopisaniya*,
Letopisanie   Leningrad, 1940

'Yarlyki'   M. D. Priselkov, 'Khanskie yarlyki russkim mitropolitam', in *Petrograd, Universitet, Istorikofilologichesky fakul'tet, Zapiski*, 133, Petrograd, 1916.

Priselkov-Fasmer,   M. D. Priselkov and M. R. Fasmer, 'Otryvki V. I.
'Otryvki'   Beneshevicha po istorii russkoi tserkvi', *Akademiya Nauk, Otd. russkogo yazyka i slovesnosti, Izvestiya*, xxi, 1916, pp. 48–70.

Prokhorov,   G. M. Prokhorov, 'Etnicheskaya Integratsiya v
'Etnicheskaya   Vostochnoi Evrope v XIV v. (Ot isikhastskikh
Integratsiya'   sporov do Kulikovskoi bitvy)', *Doklady otdeleniya etnografii, vyp. 2, Geograficheskoe obshchestvo SSSR*, Leningrad, 1966. pp. 81–110.

'Gimny'   G. M. Prokhorov, 'K istorii liturgicheskoi poezii. Gimny i molitvy Filofeya Kokkina', TODRL, xxvii, 1973, pp. 120–49.

'Keleinaya   G. M. Prokhorov, 'Keleinaya isikhastskaya
literatura'   literatura v biblioteke Troitse-Sergievoi lavry s XIV-go po XVII v.', TODRL, xxviii, 1974, pp. 317–24.

'Letopisnaya'   G. M. Prokhorov, 'Letopisnaya Povest' o Mityae', TODRL, xxx, 1976, pp. 238–54.

Povest'   G. M. Prokhorov, *Povest' o Mityae, Rus' i Vizantiya v epokhu kulikovskoi bitvy*, Leningrad, 1978.

PS   *Pravoslavny Sobesednik*, Kazan', 1855–1917.

PSRL   *Polnoe Sobranie Russkikh Letopisei*, St Petersburg–Moscow.

Regel,   W. Regel, *Analecta Byzantino-Russica*, St Peters
Analecta   burg–Leipzig, 1891.

Rhalles-Potles   Γ. Α. Ῥάλλη-Μ. Ποτλῆ, Σύνταγμα τῶν θείων καὶ ἱερῶν κανόνων, i–v, Athens, 1852.

REB   *Revue des études byzantines*, Bucharest, 1947–1948; Paris, 1949–.

RIB   *Pamyatniki drevne-russkago kanonicheskago prava*, i [A. S. Pavlov, ed.], *Russkaya Istoricheskaya Biblioteka*, vi, St Petersburg, 1880.

Rog.   *Rogozhsky Letopisets*, PSRL, xv, Moscow, 1965.

Ševčenko,   I. Ševčenko, 'The decline of Byzantium seen
'The decline'   through the eyes of its intellectuals', DOP, 15, 1961, pp. 169–86.

Sobolevsky,   A. I. Sobolevsky, *Yuzhnoslavyanskoe vliyanie na
Yuzhnoslavyanskoe   russkuyu pis'mennost' v XIV–XV vv.*, St Petersburg,

vliyanie	1894 (also published by the author as a part of his book *Perevodnaya literatura Moskovskoi Rusi XIV–XVII vv.*, St Petersburg, 1903).
Sokolov, *Arkhierei*	P. Sokolov, *Russky arkhierei iz Vizantii i pravo ego naznacheniya do nachala XV-go veka*, Kiev, 1913.
Speransky, *Iz istorii*	M. N. Speransky, *Iz istorii russko-slavyanskikh literaturnykh svyazei*, Moscow, 1960.
Spuler, *Goldene Horde*	B. Spuler, *Die Goldene Horde. Die Mongolen in Russland, 1223–1502*. 2. Aufl., Wiesbaden, 1965.
Syrku, *K istorii ispravleniya*	P. Syrku, *K istorii ispravleniya knig v Bolgarii v XIV-m veke*, I. *Vremya i zhizn' patriarkha Evthimiya Ternovskago*, St Petersburg, 1890; vyp. II. *Teksty*, St Petersburg, 1890.
Tachiaos, Ἐπιδράσεις	A. Tachiaos, Ἐπιδράσεις τοῦ ἡσυχασμοῦ εἰς τὴν ἐκκλησιαστικὴν πολιτικὴν ἐν Ῥωσίᾳ, 1328–1406, Thessaloniki, 1962.
Κυπριανός	A. Tachiaos, "Ὁ μητροπολίτης Ῥωσίας Κυπριανὸς Τσαμπλάκ", Ἐπιστημονικὴ Ἐπετηρὶς Θεολογικῆς Σχολῆς, VI, Thessaloniki, 1961, pp. 163–241.
Theiner, *Hung.*	Theiner, A., ed., *Vetera Monumenta historica Hungariam sacram illustrantia* . . . , Rome, 1859–60, I.
Pol. Lit.	Theiner, A., ed., *Vetera Monumenta Poloniae et Lithuaniae gentiumque finitimarum historiam illustrantia* . . . , I, Rome, 1860.
Tikhomirov, *Galitskaya Mitropoliya*	N. D. Tikhomirov, *Galitskaya Mitropoliya. Tserkovnoistoricheskoe issledovanie*, St Petersburg, 1895 (repr. from *Blagovest*, 1895, I–II).
'Puti'	M. N. Tikhomirov, 'Puti iz Rossii v Vizantiyu v XIV–XV vv.', *Vizantiiskie Ocherki*, Moscow, 1961, pp. 3–33.
Svayazi	M. N. Tikhomirov, *Istoricheskie svyazi Rossii so slavyanskimi stranami i Vizantiei*, Moscow, 1969.
Tinnefeld, 'Kirchenpolitik'	F. Tinnefeld, 'Byzantinisch-Russische Kirchenpolitik im 14. Jahrhundert', BZ, 67, 1974, pp. 359–83.
TODRL	*SSSR, Akademiya Nauk, Otdel drevne-russkoy literatury, Trudy*, Leningrad, 1934—.
Troits.	*Troitskaya Letopis'. Rekonstruktsiya teksta*, ed. M. D. Priselkov, Moscow–Leningrad, 1950.
Tver.	*Tverskaya Letopis'*, PSRL, XV, 1863.
Val'denberg, *Drevnerusskiya ucheniya*	V. Val'denberg, *Drevnerusskiya ucheniya o predelakh Tsarskoi vlasti*, Petrograd, 1915.
Vernadsky, *Mongols*	G. Vernadsky, *A History of Russia.* III. *The Mongols in Russia*, New Haven, Conn., 1953.

VMC	Makary, Metropolitan, *Velikiya Minei Chet'i*, Moscow, 1868–.
Voskr.	*Voskresenskaya Letopis'*, PSRL, vii, St Petersburg, 1856.
VV	*Vizantiiskii Vremennik*, 1894–.
Vzdornov, 'Rol' masterskikh'	G. I. Vzdornov, 'Rol' slavyanskikh monastyrskikh masterskikh pis'ma Konstantinopolya i Afona v razvitii knigopisaniya i khudozhestvennogo oformleniya russkikh rukopisei na rubezhe XIV–XV vv', TODRL, xxiii, 1968, pp. 171–98.
Zachariae, *Jus*	K. E. Zachariae a Lingenthal, *Jus graecoromanum*, 7 vols., Leipzig, 1856–84.
ZhMNP	*Zhurnal Ministerstva Narodnago Prosveshcheniya*, St Petersburg, 1834–.
ZRVI	*Zbornik radova Vizantološkog instituta*, Belgrade, 1952–.
Žužek, *Kormchaya*	I. Žužek, *Kormchaya Kniga. Studies on the Chief Code of Russian Canon Law* (Orientalia Christiana Analecta, 168), Rome, 1964.

Acknowledgements

The completion of this book has been made possible by a grant of the United States National Endowment for the Humanities. Also, during the academic year of 1977–8, the Center for Byzantine Studies at Dumbarton Oaks, Washington, D.C. offered me its remarkable resources and facilities. I am grateful to Mrs Mary-Lou Masey of Dumbarton Oaks, to Mr Iain White, subeditor at the Cambridge University Press, for their contribution in editing the manuscript and to Miss Rasa Mažeika for having prepared the Index. Professor George Majeska, of the University of Maryland, has graciously read several chapters, making helpful suggestions.

Sir Steven Runciman, by his encouragement and interest has made the publication of my work possible. But more than to anyone, I am grateful to Professor Dimitri Obolensky, of Oxford, who used his time and extraordinary competence very generously in improving and correcting my text. It is obvious, however, that I alone am responsible for the shortcomings and inaccuracies of the book.

J.M.

Note on proper names

No deliberate effort was made to introduce rigorous consistency in the transcription of Greek and Slavic proper names. Whereas original spellings and endings were preserved in some cases (Philotheos, Theognostos, Ivan), the usual English forms were prefered in others (Maximus, Gregory, Michael). We apologize to those of our readers who would have prefered more philological accuracy.

J. M.

EASTERN EUROPE c.1390

.... Muscovite territories
/////// Grand Principality of Lithuania

| 0 | km | 300 |
| 0 | miles | 200 |

Introduction

Historians of Russia have frequently described the great variety of cultural, political, religious, economic and geographical factors which allowed the originally insignificant principality of Moscow to become in the fourteenth century the capital of a nation and, eventually, to build an empire. Having been a faithful vassal of the Mongol khans and an executioner for their lordship over Russia, the Muscovite prince, by turning against the hated conquerors at the Battle of Kulikovo (1380), acquired sudden credibility for his position of leadership. His successors in the following two centuries would build on the foundations laid by him and would expand Moscow's power into one of the most powerful and lasting empires of European history.

The purpose of this book is not to describe again the emergence of Muscovite Russia, but to examine the cultural, spiritual and political roots of the events of the fourteenth century which gave Moscow the possibility of rising to the position which it came to occupy for so long. The role played in this process by the then already moribund Byzantine empire has to be considered as one of the most important – if not the most important – aspect of Byzantium's contribution to the history of modern Europe.

The 'gathering of Russian lands' around Moscow, the competition between Moscow and Tver, the role of the Golden Horde (the residence of the Mongol khans on the lower Volga river), the military struggle with Lithuania, all these aspects of the rise of Moscow in the fourteenth century have been described in detail, and sometimes brilliantly, by historians of Russia. All of them, however, have limited themselves, almost exclusively, to consulting Russian sources and visualizing the facts as episodes of Russian national history only.

In the present book an attempt is made at widening the perspective and envisaging the birth of the Russian empire in a broader setting: that of Eastern Europe as a whole, and particularly of Byzantine imperial diplomacy, and including also such factors as

the commercial activities of the Italian merchant-city-republics –
Genoa and Venice – which controlled the commercial routes leading from the Mediterranean to China through the Black Sea.

Our approach to the history of Eastern Europe in the fourteenth
century is made possible not only through the availability of
Byzantine diplomatic sources (which are very insufficiently used
by historians of the period), but also thanks to recent research
accomplished by both Western and Russian historians, to whom
credit will be given, as we attempt to synthesize the results of their
work.

The Byzantine ecclesiastical and imperial diplomacy of the
fourteenth century in Eastern Europe is better known to us than
that of other periods of Byzantine history. While practically all the
archives of the imperial and patriarchal chanceries of Byzantium
perished either in 1204, when the city was sacked by the Crusaders,
or in 1453, when it fell under the Turks, two volumes of official
documents of the patriarchate, containing patriarchal (and some
imperial) decisions taken between 1315 and 1402 are preserved in
two Vienna manuscripts. What appears when these documents
are interpreted in the light of the contemporary political and
intellectual history of Byzantium and confronted with the evidence
available in other Byzantine South-Slavic and Russian sources, is
a continuous administrative activity in areas directly dependent
upon the ecclesiastical jurisdiction of the Byzantine patriarchate,
and particularly the territories of the former Kievan state, by now
politically divided between Poland, the Grand-duchy of Lithuania
and the Mongol empire. This activity involves not only ecclesiastical affairs, but also purely political issues, which directly concern
the person and the power of the 'Metropolitan of Kiev and all
Russia', an appointee of Byzantium, residing permanently in
Moscow since 1308.

The documents contained in the Vienna manuscripts and published as early as 1860 have of course been known to historians of
Byzantium and Russia ever since. These historians, however, still
underestimate the impact of Byzantine diplomacy in Russia,
mainly because they tend to ignore the reality of what Dimitri
Obolensky, in a remarkable recent book, called the 'Byzantine
Commonwealth', i.e., the supra-national idea of an association of
Christian peoples, to which the emperor and the 'ecumenical
patriarch' of Constantinople provided a symbolic leadership –
even if each of these peoples was fully independent politically and
economically. In this book, we will try to show that it is not only

possible, but also historically necessary for historians of Byzantium, of the Southern Slavic nations, and of Russia, to envisage the major events of fourteenth-century East European history as politically and ideologically correlated. Byzantium did in fact exercise, in the framework of its 'Commonwealth', the role of a universal centre, parallel to that of Rome in the Latin West. But while the innumerable papal letters and other documents of the papal curia are still preserved and available to scholars, the violent end which Byzantium suffered in 1453 has suppressed scholarly access to Byzantium's past. Its historic role was thus largely obscured, not only through the well-known anti-Byzantine prejudice of Western historians, but also through lack of objective evidence. It is time that the picture be corrected at least in those areas where evidence is available: the direct administrative power exercised by the Byzantine patriarchate over the Russian Church, which represented the only structure holding together the various Russian principalities, and the continuous spiritual and intellectual impact of Byzantium upon the Slavic countries. In both these areas, in the fourteenth century, Byzantine influence was paradoxically in the ascendant, in spite of the extreme political weakness of the Byzantine empire: the monastic revival in the Byzantine world and its impact upon the activities of the patriarchate contributed to this extraordinary new energy of the Byzantine Church, which was also communicated to the other centres of the 'Byzantine Commonwealth'.

Geography and economy made contacts inevitable between Russians and Byzantines since the very inception of Russia as a state, and of the people called *Rus'* as a nation. The original Russian state, which appeared in the ninth century under the leadership of a dynasty of Varangian, or Scandinavian origin, used as its economic, political and military base the trade route 'from the Varangians to the Greeks' which linked the Baltic and the Black Seas. It was essentially a river-route, following the course of the Neva, the Volkhov, the Lovat' and the Dnieper. The Russian fortress-cities of Novgorod and Kiev controlled the route. The importance of the route – hence the economic prosperity of the Kievan state – was linked to the Arab control of the Mediterranean: the northern passage had become an essential connection between Byzantium and Western Europe.

Having successfully contained the Arab and Bulgarian conquerors and surmounted the internal crisis of iconoclasm, the

Byzantine empire under its glorious Macedonian dynasty (867–1056) entered a period of consolidation and spectacular expansion. In the Middle East, the Balkans and Italy, this expansion took the form of direct military reoccupation of former Roman territories. In Central Europe and in Russia, Byzantine civilization penetrated as the vehicle of Christian mission. In 867, Patriarch Photius announced to the world that the 'Rus" (οἱ 'Ρῶς), who had recently launched a fierce attack at Constantinople itself, had accepted a Christian bishop from Byzantium; but we know nothing more about the organization of the Church in Russia at that early period.

During the following century, Russia remained, for Byzantium, a basic source of many essential raw materials – furs, wax, honey, slaves – and thus the object of continuous diplomatic concern, well described by Emperor Constantine VII Porphyrogenetos in his *De administrando imperio*. However, peaceful diplomacy was not sufficient to maintain the commercial route open and the materials coming: the Russians were frequently able to impose their conditions by force and, at times, menaced Constantinople. The Russian prince Svyatoslav could be contained only by the long and bloody military campaign of Emperor John Tzimisces (969–76).

But Constantinople was not, for the Russians, an object of military blackmail and economic greed only. In the tenth century, it reached the height of its cultural and political development. The 'New Rome' on the Bosphorus was the unquestionable centre of the civilized Christian world. With a population close to a million, with its imperial palaces and hippodrome and, above all, its 'Great Church' of St Sophia – by far the biggest and most magnificent religious building in the early medieval world – Byzantium exercised on all the Slavic 'barbarians' a fascination with which no Christian centre of the West could compete. Thus, it was able to win their allegiance not only by the force of arms, but by making them acknowledge the superiority of its Christian civilization.

The Kievan princess Olga, the mother of Svyatoslav, personally adopted Christianity. During a visit to Constantinople, she was received with honour by Emperor Constantine VII (957). Her grandson Vladimir, son of Svyatoslav, followed her example: he not only personally received baptism, but also made Christianity Russia's state religion. After successfully intervening in a Byzantine civil war, he even became brother-in-law of the greatest of all emperors of the Macedonian dynasty, Basil II himself, by marrying the emperor's sister (989). Christian scriptures and Byzantine liturgy were already available in the Slavic language. The transla-

4

tions were made in Moravia by St Cyril and St Methodius (863) and perfected in Orthodox Bulgaria: the Russians faced no language barrier in adopting the new religion. Neither were they facing the danger of Byzantine political domination, which was so heavily felt by the Southern Slavs in the eleventh and twelfth centuries: distance made Russia virtually inaccessible to Byzantine conquest. The adoption of Byzantine Christianity was in fact a free choice of the Russians and they always remembered it as such. In the Russian 'Primary Chronicle', written in Kiev in the eleventh century, and which served as a preface to all subsequent records of Russia's existence as a nation, generations of Russians read the account of Vladimir's envoys to Constantinople, after their witnessing of the Byzantine liturgy in Haghia Sophia: 'They led us to the edifices where they worship their God, and we knew not whether we were in heaven, or on earth. For on earth there is no such splendour or such beauty, and we are at a loss how to describe it. We only know that there God dwells among men.'[1] This famous episode illustrates the universalism and missionary impact of Byzantine Christianity.

After the Muslim conquest of the entire Middle East with its ancient non-Greek Eastern communities, it would appear that the Byzantine Church, splendidly isolated in the Greek-speaking territories controlled by the Empire, could have simply become the national Church of the Greeks, as did, for example, the Armenian Church, which remained forever bound by the limits of Armenian culture. But the missionary movement of the ninth and tenth centuries, which expanded the reach of Byzantine Christianity not only throughout the Balkans, but also throughout Eastern Europe up to the Arctic Ocean, has preserved the universal, or 'catholic' vocation of the Orthodox Church, as well as the worldwide significance of Byzantine Christian civilization.

For the Byzantines, the 'baptism of the Russians' signified their integration into the empire itself. And, in a sense, the Russians certainly accepted the principle of imperial supremacy over the whole Christian world. However, the Byzantines and their Slavic converts did not always agree on the practical implications of this common belonging to a universal Christian structure. As compared to the other Orthodox Slavs – Bulgarians and Serbs – the Russians were more loyal to Byzantium. Until the dramatic shift following

---

[1] *Povest' vremennykh let*, ed. D. S. Likhachev and B. A. Romanov, Moscow–Leningrad, 1950, I, p. 75; S. H. Cross, and O. P. Sherbowitz-Wetzor, transl., *The Russian Primary Chronicle*, Cambridge, Mass., 1953, p. 111.

upon the council of Florence (1438), they generally nourished feelings of respect towards Constantinople and its patriarchate, recognizing in it the source of their religious faith and the centre of a superior civilization. This respect was moderated only by occasional apprehension of Greek 'trickery' which appears in the chronicles and other sources.

Under Vladimir and, especially his son Yaroslav, Kiev, the capital of Russia, rapidly adopted Byzantine civilization as the main criterion of its own cultural development. The cathedral church, built by Yaroslav, was dedicated to 'St Sophia', the Divine Wisdom, and decorated with mosaics by the best Greek masters available (1037–46). The monastery 'of the Caves' (Pechersky) in Kiev adopted the rule of the Studios monastery of Constantinople. Byzantine legal, historical and theological literature, whenever it was not already available in translations made in Bulgaria, was translated anew.

This cultural and religious dependence upon Constantinople, which implied the recognition of the Byzantine emperor as the head of the Christian 'inhabited earth' (*oikouméne*), did not prevent, in the early period, occasional military confrontations with Byzantium. In 1043, at the very time when St Sophia in Kiev was being decorated by Greek mosaicists and painters, a Russian fleet attacked Constantinople, as it had done in the past, when Kievan Rus' was still headed by pagan Varangian princes. War had apparently started by a conflict of commercial interests. Defeated by the Greeks, the Rus' retreated, and the confrontation ended with a younger son of Yaroslav marrying a Byzantine princess, probably the daughter of Constantine IX Monomachus (1046). A son, Vladimir, born of this marriage and surnamed *Monomakh*, will play an eminent political role in Kiev and, eventually, become a symbol of Byzantine imperial inheritance in Russia.

After Yaroslav's attempt, no direct Russian offensive on Constantinople was ever repeated, perhaps because Kievan Russia, after Yaroslav's death (1054), lost its political unity. The country became further and further divided into independent principalities (*udely*), each ruled by a descendant of Vladimir and Yaroslav, but paying only nominal allegiance to the 'Grand-prince' of Kiev. Various principalities occasionally joined different foreign alliances and fought against each other. Relations with Constantinople became more difficult when, in the twelfth century, new nomadic invaders, the Cumans, conquered much of the southern Russian steppe and disrupted the Black Sea trade. Three separate political centres – anticipating the polarizations of the fourteenth century, which we will discuss later – emerged in what was the unified Russia of Vladimir and Yaroslav: the Grand-principality of Kiev (gradually losing its ancient prestige), the north-eastern principality of Suzdal and the south-western principality of Galicia. It is noteworthy that during the 1140s and 1150s, in the reign of Byzantine Emperor Manuel I Comnenos, both Kiev and Galicia vacillated in their solidarity with Byzantium and, at times, allied themselves with Hungary, then a fierce enemy of the empire of Constantinople. The status of north-eastern Russia as the faithful ally of the Byzantine emperor during these events was noticed by Byzantine historians and may have been an anticipation of the understanding and mutual support which existed also later, in the fourteenth century, between the empire and the leader of the north-eastern principalities – successor of the Suzdalian princes – the Grand-prince of Moscow.

Eventually, the shrewd diplomacy of Manuel I and the sense of belonging to a single Christian Commonwealth prevailed in Kiev, and Galicia as well, but neither the Byzantines nor the Russians could foresee the forthcoming catastrophes which were to befall the entire realm of Byzantine Christendom in the thirteenth century.

We will come back to the consequence of these tragic events: the sack of Constantinople by the Crusaders in 1204 and the conquest of Russia by the Mongols, which started in 1223 and was practically completed with the fall of Kiev in 1240. With independent Bulgaria and Serbia both toying – at least until 1220 – with the possibility of allying themselves with the triumphant Western papacy, it appeared that the Byzantine Orthodox world had finally collapsed. These events of the thirteenth century will be described only to illustrate the remarkable continuity of cultural and political solidarity of the Orthodox world which survived the cataclysms and faced the events of the fourteenth century with a new dynamism.

In 1261, Michael VIII Palaeologus put an end to the parasitical existence of the Latin empire in Constantinople. He did not succeed, however, in restoring fully the former power of the Eastern Roman emperors. His successors on the throne of Constantinople were to be preoccupied with survival, not expansion. And mere survival would be possible only through a combination of diplomatic strategems and pure luck, until finally the end came in 1453.

7

A shadow of its glorious past, with its territory gradually reduced to the city of Constantinople itself and its suburbs, the Byzantine empire still retained prestige and influence in the Slavic lands, and particularly in Russia. In the fourteenth century the former Kievan realm was divided as in the past between princes of the 'Rurikide' dynasty, but these were also obliged to pay allegiance to powerful foreign overlords: the Mongol khan of the Golden Horde, the Grand-prince of Lithuania, and, in Galicia (after 1340), the king of Poland. The major topics of our study will concern: the gradual rise of the principality of Moscow from the position of a small vassal of the Tatar khan to that of a potential leader of the Byzantine Orthodox world; the contribution of Byzantium to that development, exercised primarily through the activity of the 'Metropolitan of Kiev and all Russia', a Byzantine appointee, who – by deliberate choice of the patriarchate of Constantinople and the Byzantine government – resided not in Kiev, but in Moscow, and, as head of the Russian Church, controlled the only administrative structure which encompassed *all* of Russia; the problem of the distinct political and cultural development in north-eastern Russia and the southern and western parts of the former Kievan realm, a development which eventually led to the emergence of distinct 'Great Russian', 'Ukrainian' and 'Byelorussian' national groups; the extent of the Byzantine cultural and religious influence, dominated by the monastic (or 'hesychast') revival in Byzantium, and which generally tended to transcend local, national and political divisions; the nature of the religious 'zealotism', coming from Byzantium and the South-Slavic countries, which exercised a decisive influence upon culture, literature and art in all the countries of the 'Byzantine Commonwealth', and its relation to other cultural influences coming from other sources; the question whether the Muscovite empire did eventually fulfil the expectations of the religious and intellectual leaders of the fourteenth century, or whether it adopted ideologies significantly distinct from the Byzantine inheritance.

It is our hope that bringing together all these issues will contribute to a more comprehensive picture of the history of Eastern Europe during the late Middle Ages and thus lead to a better understanding of this area of the world, whose impact upon the history of mankind is a fact of the present, as well as of the past.

I

Byzantine civilization in Russia

Since the time when, *ca.* 838, an embassy of the people named *Rhōs* (οἱ 'Ρῶς) was received in Constantinople,[1] the Byzantine government placed the activities of these northern barbarians and their relations with the Empire on a high-priority list in its foreign policy. The reasons were obvious: the *Rhōs* controlled the commercial route between the Black and the Baltic Seas (an important connection with northern and western Europe since the presence of Arab fleets had made the Mediterranean insecure); they were natural competitors of the Asiatic nomads (Pechenegs, Cumans) who roamed the east European plains and, therefore, could serve as useful allies of Byzantium; and finally, whenever their feelings towards the Empire were not friendly, they were able to attack Constantinople in quick raids across the Black Sea. Whereas the exact origins of the name *Rhōs* are obscure, it is undoubtedly connected with the Varangian (Scandinavian) military clans, which ruled the Slavic populations in eastern Europe, and introduced the well-known strategy of Norman warfare in the area of the Black Sea, menacing the capital itself.[2]

The Greek term *Rhōs* which appears in the early Byzantine texts corresponds to the Slavic *Rus'*. It designates *a people*, and not a country. The original Slavic name for the territory inhabited by the *Rus'* was *Russkaya zemlya* ('the land of the *Rus"*). However, starting in the tenth century, Byzantine texts (cf. in particular Constantine Porphyrogenetos) speak of 'Ρωσία, as the country of the *Rhōs*, which included the vast territories from the Carpathian

[1] Dölger, *Regesten*, I, No. 438.
[2] Aside from many mentions of the *Rhōs* in Byzantine, Latin, and Arab sources of the ninth to twelfth centuries, the most important texts about Byzantino-Russian relations in that period are (a) The writings of Patriarch Photius (two homilies 'On the attack of the *Rhōs*', ed. S. Aristarches, Φωτίου λόγοι καὶ ὁμιλίαι, II, Constantinople, 1900, pp. 5–57; Eng. tr. C. Mango, *The Homilies of Photius*, Cambridge, Mass., 1958, pp. 82–110. *Encyclical* of 866, PG CII, col. 736–7). (b) The Treatise *De Administrando Imperio* by Emperor Constantine VII Porphyrogenetos (ed. R. J. H. Jenkins, Dumbarton Oaks Texts, I–II, with a detailed commentary by D. Obolensky). (c) *The Russian Primary Chronicle*, ed. et tr. cit.

mountains to Rostov and Suzdal' in the north-east. The Latin equivalent of 'Ρωσία is, of course, *Russia*. The very vastness of the territory of the *Rhōs* is reflected in some texts which speak of it as μεγάλη 'Ρωσία, 'great Russia'.[3] The term *Rhōsia* is therefore the standard Byzantine name for 'the land of the *Rus*''. In Russia itself, however, the terms *Rus'* and *Russkaya zemlya* were the only ones used until the fourteenth century. The Greek form *Rhōsia* and its Latin equivalent, *Russia*, were accepted in the fifteenth century both in Muscovy and in Galicia-Volhynia (later known as 'Ukraine') to designate the entire territory of the ancient country of the *Rus'*.[4] The ancient term *Rus'* itself regained popularity only with the romantic and Slavophile trends in the nineteenth century, and was then generally applied to the country, rather than to the people inhabiting it.

Since the adoption of Christianity as the state religion of the Kievan principality (988), the influence of Byzantine civilization upon Russia became the determining factor of Russian civilization. The very extent and character of that influence should be understood in the light of the three main elements whose combination determined the life of Byzantine society: the Roman political tradition, the Greek literary heritage, and the Orthodox Christian faith. 'Without all three the Byzantine way of life would have been inconceivable', writes G. Ostrogorsky.[5]

Obviously, these three essential components of Byzantine civilization could not be simply 'exported' to Russia. Their inter-relation, on Russian soil, was quite different and they had to compete with other influences, determined either by local conditions, or by contacts with other foreign civilizations. In any case, the political, economic and military connections with Russia, which existed before 988 and are so vividly described by the Emperor Constantine Porphyrogenetos in his *De Administrando Imperio*, acquired a totally new significance when Russia accepted from Byzantium its religious faith, its ecclesiastical hierarchy, its literature in translation, its art, its political ideology.

---

[3] Neilos Doxopatris, *Notitia patriarchatum*, PG, CXXXII, col. 1105.
[4] See A. V. Soloviev, 'Le nom byzantin de la Russie' in *Musagetes, Contributions to the History of Slavic Literature and Culture*, ed. by D. Čiževskij, s'-Gravenhage, 1957; see also, by the same author '*Reges* et *Regnum Russiae* au Moyen-Age', *Byzantion*, 36, 1966, pp. 144–73.
[5] *History*, p. 27.

I. THE ROMAN POLITICAL TRADITION

From ancient Rome, Byzantium had inherited an ideal and a goal: the establishment of a universal empire, which would supersede the disorderly competition between nations and establish world peace. This ideal of the *pax romana* merged with the Christian aspiration for Christ's universal kingdom. Certainly the Byzantines were always able to make the necessary theological distinctions: the Roman empire, though Christian, was not yet the Kingdom of God. Nevertheless, the Christian emperor was called to somewhat anticipate the reign of Christ and, even, to represent Christ vicariously in his government of the present, still untransformed, sinful and imperfect world, whereas the eucharistic liturgy of the Church (and the hierarchy presupposed by it) was able to provide an experience of the Kingdom itself. Actually, the first duty of the emperor consisted in protecting and sheltering the Church, which alone could give legitimacy to his imperial claims and reality to his responsibilities, as the promoter of the apostolic faith and the guardian of Christian truth in the life of human society. Inexpressible in purely legal terms, the Byzantine theory of Church and State found its ultimate pattern in the idealistic concept of 'symphony', used by the Emperor Justinian. Official and legal texts abound in references to the ideally universal power of the emperor, coinciding with an equally universal expansion of the Church. Symbolically quite important was the proclamation of the unique power of the emperor of 'New Rome' in the liturgy of the Church. In a hymn sung on Christmas day, the providential significance of the universal *pax romana* was acknowledged not only by the Byzantines themselves, but also by all the Slavs:

> When Augustus reigned alone upon earth, the many kingdoms
> of man came to an end . . .
> The cities of the world passed under one single rule;
> And the nations came to believe in one sovereign Godhead.
> The peoples were enrolled by the decree of Caesar;
> And we, the faithful, were enrolled in the Name of the Godhead.[6]

Significantly, the name of the Byzantine emperor was commemorated in the offices of the Church, in Byzantium as well as in

---

[6] *The Festal Menaion*, Mother Mary and K. Ware, trans., London, Faber and Faber, 1969, p. 254. The authorship of this hymn is traditionally attributed to Emperor Leo VI (886–912), but the ideas go back to the famous *Life* of Constantine the Great by Eusebius of Caesarea.

Kievan Russia. As Patriarch Anthony wrote to Grand Prince Basil of Moscow in 1397, 'it is not possible for Christians to have the Church and not to have the empire . . .; it is not possible for them to be separated from one another'.[7] It is therefore not astonishing to find in a text of Patriarch Photius a reference to the Russians as 'subjects' (ὑπήκοοι) of the Empire.[8] Even in Muslim accounts, one finds the idea that the emperor of Constantinople is the sovereign of many nations including Macedonians, Greeks, Bulgarians, Vlakhs, Alans, *Russians*, Iberians (=Georgians) and Turks (=Hungarians).[9]

These texts were sometimes interpreted in the context of Western political ideas, such as suzerainty and vassaldom,[10] or simply disregarded as obviously irrelevant to a concept of history where political reality is seen only in terms of nation-states. In neither case does one really do justice to the idea of the Byzantine 'Commonwealth' of which the emperor was the recognized head and whose existence the Slavic Orthodox nations never challenged, even if occasionally Bulgarians and Serbs attempted to assume its leadership themselves.

In its original version, Roman (and Byzantine) political ideology was fully 'imperial': it implied the direct administration by the emperor of all his subjects. Justinian, in reconquering Italy, or Basil II, in destroying the Bulgarian empire and re-establishing the old Roman *limes* on the Danube, were in a position to reaffirm this imperial tradition, because they disposed of the means necessary for a direct and methodical affirmation of Roman power. However, with the shrinking of the empire's military might, this approach became increasingly unrealistic. It is then that the alliance between the two universalisms of Rome and of the Christian Church served as inspiration for an alternative solution which had already been practised from the fifth to the sixth centuries in the relations between the emperors of Constantinople and the barbarian kingdoms of the West. The latter, after adopting Christianity, recognized at least nominally the universal leadership of the emperor, gladly accepted court titles bestowed by him,

---

[7] MM, II, 188–92. The problem of the liturgical commemoration of Byzantine emperors in Russia will be discussed below (chapter 10, pp. 254–7). It was certainly made by Greek clergy, coming from Constantinople in the tenth century, but may have been omitted later.

[8] Photius, *Epistolae*, PG, CII, 736–7.

[9] Letter of the Sultan of Egypt to Andronicus II, fragment in Regel, *Analecta*, pp. 57–8; cf. references to a number of similar texts in M. D'yakonov, *Vlast'*, pp. 13–29.

[10] A. A. Vasiliev, 'Was Old Russia a Vassal State of Byzantium?' in *Speculum*, VII, 1932, pp. 350–60.

strove to pattern their own court upon the Constantinopolitan model and followed the artistic taste of the imperial capital (cf. the kingdom of Theodoric in Italy). All this implied no direct administrative dependence, but only the acceptance of a principle, that of a unique and universal Christian empire. If this ideal principle had any practical significance, it was primarily through the agency of the Church: faithfully accepting imperial ideology (even if they occasionally confronted emperors, especially when the latter fell into heresy), the Roman popes acted in the West as imperial representatives and as efficient spokesmen for the unity of the *oikouméne*. Among many other documents, the correspondence of Pope Gregory I (590–604) contains numerous examples of such loyalty to the imperial idea, even when concrete cases of imperial policy were disapproved by the pontiff. Addressing a Constantinopolitan official about a decree received from Emperor Maurice which prohibited civil servants to enter on a monastic life, the pope writes: 'In obedience to your commands, I have caused this law to be transmitted to the different countries. I have also informed my Most Serene Sovereigns by this letter that the law is certainly not in accordance with the will of God. I have thus done my duty on both sides. I have obeyed the emperor, and yet have not kept back what I felt ought to be said on behalf of God.'[11]

The history of the relationship between Byzantium and the western Germanic kingdoms of the early Middle Ages – relations which were brutally modified by the imperial coronation of Charlemagne in 800 – provides an almost exact model for the bonds which united the Byzantine 'Commonwealth' in Eastern Europe after the conversion of Slavic nations to Christianity. In the case of Bulgaria, for example, the various dramatic events which occurred between 865 and 1015 are all to be understood in the ideological framework which was basically familiar. By accepting baptism from Byzantium in 865 and by becoming the spiritual son of Emperor Michael III, Khan Boris accepted the ideal system of the universal empire. His son Symeon, and also the West-Bulgarian Tsar Samuel, fought against Byzantium not in order to destroy the empire, *but in order to claim it for themselves*,[12] following the example of the Carolingians. The Byzantine emperors of the tenth century were able to end the Bulgarian usurpation by force,

[11] *Ep.* III, 61, MGH, *Epistolae* I, Berlin, 1891, p. 222; Engl. tr. in F. H. Dudden, *Gregory the Great*, vol. II, London, 1905, p. 184.
[12] Cf. F. Dölger, *Byzanz und die europäische Staatenwelt*, Ettal, 1953, p. 140ff.; also G. Ostrogorsky, 'The Byzantine Emperor and the Hierarchical World Order' in *The Slavonic and East-European Review*, XXXV, 1956–7, p. 7.

Byzantium and the Rise of Russia

restoring, for a time, in the Balkans the traditional form of Roman military and administrative domination. Military impossibility, but certainly not ideology, prevented them from treating the Western, Carolingian usurpation in the same manner. The same military and geographical factors forced them into diplomatic dealings – complicated by the religious conflict with the now German-dominated papacy – but never into a recognition of the Western imperial claims.

Geographically, Russia was also out of reach for military conquest and its territory was never a part of the Roman empire. Its acceptance of the Byzantine political world-view and of Constantinople's cultural leadership represents the greatest of all spiritual conquests of the Byzantine empire. This conquest is so much more extraordinary that it never involved direct political dependence and was therefore accomplished almost exclusively by the Church. Of course, some Soviet historians are reluctant to admit this historical significance of the Church in Russia.[13] They point to economic, military and political contacts between the two countries and stress their importance. But it remains true that the only Byzantine official in Russia with any position of power – very considerable power indeed – was the metropolitan of Kiev, since he controlled the only administrative structure, dependent upon Byzantium, which encompassed the whole of Russia in the period between 989 and 1448. Clearly, the cultural, religious and political consequences of that fact were considerable.

Byzantine political ideology, promoted in Russia by the Church with no less zeal than in Western 'barbarian' Europe, did not produce (as it did in the West with Charlemagne, and, in the Balkans, with Symeon and Samuel of Bulgaria and later Stefan Dušan of Serbia) any attempts to usurp the empire. If Prince Vladimir did really assume the title of βασιλεύς, it was through subordinate association with the legitimate emperor, Basil II, his brother-in-law, not through any *translatio imperii*.[14] His son Yaroslav, however, may have been close to the idea of imitating the Bulgarian assump-

---

[13] See G. G. Litavrin, A. P. Kazhdan, 'Ekonomicheskie i politicheskie otnosheniya drevnei Rusi i Vizantii', *Proceedings of the XIIIth International Congress of Byzantine Studies*, London, 1967, p. 71. For a general review of Soviet historiography on the role of Byzantium in Russian history, see J. Meyendorff, 'The Byzantine impact on Russian civilization', S. H. Baron, Nancy W. Heer, eds., *Windows on the Russian Past. Essays on Soviet Historiography since Stalin*, AAASS, Columbus, Ohio, 1977, pp. 45–6.

[14] Cf. D. Obolensky, 'Byzance et la Russie de Kiev', *Messager de l'Exarchat du Patriarche russe en Europe occidentale*, XXIX, Paris, 1959 (repr. in *Byzantium and the Slavs*, London, 1971, IV), pp. 20–35.

tion of the *imperium*. After building in Kiev a cathedral dedicated
to 'St Sophia' (after 1037), in obvious imitation of the famous
'Great Church' of Constantinople, but also of the Bulgarian St
Sophia in Ohrid, he fought a bloody war against Byzantium (1043)
and appointed a Russian, Hilarion, as metropolitan of Kiev
(1051). However, he never took the step of proclaiming himself
emperor, and preferred to enjoy full membership in the pan-
European family of Christian princes, marrying his children to the
kings and princes of Norway, France, Hungary, Poland, and
Germany.[15] After his death (1054), the division of the whole territory of Kievan Russia into appanages, distributed between
members of the princely family, prevented for centuries the emergence of a centralized state with imperial ambitions.

This political phenomenon – the appanage system of Kievan
Russia – presents the most vivid contrast with the Byzantine tradition, and also with Bulgarian society, since both the 'proto-
Bulgarian' and the Byzantine model favoured the idea of a unified
monarchy. In Russia, however, after a relatively brief historical
interval, when power over the whole country was concentrated in
the hands of the Grand-prince of Kiev, Vladimir (d. 1015) and his
second son Yaroslav (1036–54), the Byzantine imperial tradition
did not take root as the actual political ideology of the country.
Whereas the universal supremacy of the emperor of Constantinople
over the entire Christendom became an indelible part of the Russian world-view, since it was affirmed in Church hymnology
and in the legal texts translated from the Greek, Russia itself
came to be divided by Yaroslav into appanages (*udely*) distributed
between his five sons.[16] The princely clan was apparently supposed
to maintain the unity of the country under the leadership of their
senior, who held the 'Grand-principality' of Kiev. However, the
country was soon torn apart by innumerable struggles for power,
in spite of the fact that the principle of a father–son succession, was
adopted at a family meeting of the princely clan held in Lyubech
(1097). Historians debate the origin of the appanage system in
Russia. Parallels can be found, but elsewhere than in Byzantium.[17]

15 For a full list of these foreign marriages of the descendants of Yaroslav see V. S.
Ikonnikov, *Opyt russkoi istoriografii*, II, 1 (repr. Osnabrück, 1966), pp. 143ff.; see also
B. Leib, *Rome, Kiev et Byzance à la fin du XIᵉ siècle*, Paris, 1924, pp. 143–78; and G.
Vernadsky, *A History of Russia*. II. *Kievan Russia*, New Haven, 1948, pp. 317–48.
16 See the excellent description of the political system in Russia, seen from the
vantage-point of Byzantium, in Obolensky, *Commonwealth*, pp. 223–32.
17 These parallels include the Mongolian empire of the thirteenth to fourteenth
centuries, which was divided into separate sections, each governed by a representative
of Chingis Khan's clan.

In any case, this radical difference in internal political structure was certainly a factor which contributed to prevent Russia from rivalling Byzantium's imperial claims. It also kept it with an ideal, almost mystical conception of the Byzantine Commonwealth: the emperor of Constantinople was, for the Russians, the symbol of world Christian unity, but did not exercise actual power over them.

Political disunity, as well as obvious geographic factors, made Russia vulnerable to the incursions of Asiatic nomads – Pechenegs and Cumans – and weakened, in the Kievan realm, the economic prosperity originally based upon the relatively secure commercial route 'from the Varangians to the Greeks' through Novgorod and Kiev.[18] Economic ties between Russia and Byzantium were also loosened in the twelfth century, and they even further changed in character when, in the thirteenth century, Constantinople was occupied by the Crusaders (1204) and Russia became part of the Mongol empire (1237–41).

As Russian principalities became more numerous and smaller, with a constant increase in the number of Rurikid princes, they were led to form groups and alliances, following geographic and economic patterns. The Grand principality of Kiev gradually lost its original power. After the tenure of the last outstanding Kievan grand-prince, Vladimir Monomakh (1113–25), a grandson of Yaroslav and probably, through his mother, of the Byzantine Emperor Constantine IX Monomachus, new centres overshadowed the old capital. In 1169 Prince Andrew Bogolyubsky of Rostov-Suzdal sacked Kiev and, assuming the title of grand-prince, transferred his residence to Vladimir in the north-east of the country, a region recently colonized and largely immune to the nomads' incursions. The result was that the south-western principalities, particularly Galicia and Volhynia, became independent of the grand-prince and began to solve their own problems, especially in relation to their Polish and Hungarian neighbours, without great concern for the rest of Russia. Finally, the prosperous commercial city of Novgorod, economically tied to the Baltic region and exploiting the riches of the northern forest, while nominally dependent upon the Grand-principality of Vladimir, was also able to develop its own strong political tradition and foreign ties.

However, during the twelfth century, in spite of all the internecine struggles of the princes, a cultural unity was maintained

[18] See Obolensky, *Commonwealth*, pp. 39–40, 223–4.

between the principalities. In the absence of any unquestionable
political centre in Russia, the unity of the nation was largely maintained through the agency of the Church. The national unity of
Russia was, in fact, inseparable from the nation's ties with
Christian universalism, represented by a metropolitan appointed
from Byzantium.[19]

2. TRANSLATIONS FROM THE GREEK

Committed to the Greek language, as the essential vehicle of
civilization, the Byzantine empire was not a nation-state in the
modern sense, even if Slavic texts invariably designate it as the
land of the 'Greeks'. Non-Greeks – provided they accepted the
imperial 'system' and ideology – could easily rise in the *cursus
honorum* of the state and of the Church. 'Without emperors who
knew how to honour and draw to themselves gifted Armenians,
Slavs and other foreigners, the Byzantine empire, if it had followed
a purely nationalistic Greek policy, would have certainly fallen
much earlier than the middle of the fifteenth century, not under
the assaults of Turks, but under those of its own subjects, especially
Slavs and Armenians.'[20]

If the Byzantines knew how to maintain reasonable cultural
pluralism within the Empire's borders, they had no choice but to
practise even greater tolerance in the framework of their wider
Commonwealth. Here also the tradition of cultural pluralism –
which was basically Roman – allied itself with the needs of the
universal Christian mission. In the tenth century, when Byzantine
Christianity was formally adopted in Russia, a great number of
scriptural, liturgical, theological, and historical texts existed
already in Slavic translation, prepared either during the Cyrillo-
Methodian mission in Moravia, or later in Bulgaria. The cultural
connection between Russia, the Cyrillo-Methodian mission and
Bulgaria is recognized by the Russian 'Primary Chronicle', whose
text, repeated in all later chronicles, includes an account of the
conversion of Bulgarians and Moravians and emphasizes that the

---

[19] Under Manuel Comnenus, new bishops – including the metropolitan of Kiev –
were required to take an oath of allegiance to the emperor (see A. Pavlov, 'Sinodal'
nyi akt Konstantinopol 'skago patriarkha Mikhaila Ankhiala 1171-go goda o privode
arkhiereev k prisyage', VV, II, 1895, pp. 388–93.) The requirement eventually
disappeared, but the role of the emperor in appointing Russian metropolitans is
well documented until the fifteenth century,

[20] V. I. Lamansky, 'Vidnye deyateli zapadno-slavyanskoi obrazovannosti', *Slavyansky
Sbornik*, I, St Petersburg, 1875, p. 21.

language used by Byzantine missionaries in Moravia 'prevails also among the Rus' and the Danubian Bulgarians'.[21] We also know that new translations from the Greek were made available and copied in Kiev.[22] It is difficult to determine which translations were imported from abroad and which were made in Russia. In any case, there is no doubt that the immediate needs of the Church were satisfied as a first priority: the entire New Testament, passages of the Old Testament which are a part of the liturgical cycles (particularly the *Psalms*), the texts of the Eucharist and the sacraments, as well as the immense corpus of Byzantine hymnography[23] were already accessible in Kievan Russia in the tenth and eleventh centuries. In addition to these texts, which were necessary on a daily basis, a number of hagiographic texts – required as readings in monastic communities – monastic rules and some encyclopedic reference books, such as chronicles, the *Topography* of Cosmas Indicopleustes, and the *Physiologus* – were also translated.[24]

Equally significant is the translation, initiated in Bulgaria, of Byzantine legal texts. The *Ecloga* of the Isaurian emperors was adapted to Slavic use in Bulgaria under the title of *Zakon sudnyi lyudem*. This, and other texts of ecclesiastical and civil law, including the original text of the *Ecloga*, the *Procheiron*, the *Nomos georgikos* and the two main versions of the *Nomocanon* (a Byzantine collection of civil and ecclesiastical laws), were available in Slavic translation made in Bulgaria or Serbia.[25] In 1274 Metropolitan Cyril introduced to Russia the *Kormchaya Kniga*, the Slavic translation of the *Nomocanon* made by St Sava of Serbia.[26]

---

[21] *Primary Chronicle*, a. 898, I, p. 21; tr., p. 62; on this question, see particularly Moshin, 'O periodizatsii', pp. 38–43, 59–85.

[22] Prince Yaroslav, son of Vladimir, 'assembled many scribes and had them translate from Greek into the Slavic language. And they wrote many books.' *Primary Chronicle*, I, p. 102; tr., p. 137.

[23] The *Primary Chronicle* mentions particularly the entire New Testament (*Apostol i Evangelie*, inaccurately translated by Cross as 'the *Acts* and the Gospel'), the Psalter and the *Oktoechos*; the latter book contains the hymnographic proper for the repeatable cycle of eight weeks (ed. cit., p. 22; tr. pp. 62–3).

[24] A. I. Sobolevsky, 'Materialy i issledovaniya v oblasti slavyanskoi filologii i arkheologii', in *Akademia Nauk, otd. russkogo yazyka i slovesnosti, Sbornik*, LXXXVIII, 1910, n. 3, pp. 162–77; D. Obolensky, 'The Cyrillo-Methodian Heritage in Russia' DOP, XIX, 1965, pp. 60–1 (repr. in Obolensky, D., *Byzantium and the Slavs: Collected Studies*, London, 1971); on the translation of Byzantine chronicles, see also I. Sorlin, 'La diffusion et la transmission de la littérature Byzantine en Russie prémongole', *Travaux et Mémoires*, 5, Paris, 1973, pp. 385–408.

[25] See A. Pavlov, 'Knigi zakonnye, soderzhashchie v sebe, v drevne-russkom perevode, vizantiiskie zakony zemledel'cheskie, ugolovnye, brachnye, i sudebnye', in *Akademiya Nauk, otd. russkago yazyka i slovesnosti, Sbornik*, XXXVIII, No. 3, St Petersburg, 1885, pp. 1–92.

[26] Cf. Žužek, *Kormchaya*.

However, legal texts and historiography are the two areas where Russians showed greater independence from their Byzantine tutors. Both the *Pravda Russkaya* and the so-called *Statute of St Vladimir*, while showing some awareness of the Byzantine legal traditions, are independent legislations. This independence may, however, be interpreted as indicating that the Byzantine legislation was taken for granted and needed only to be supplemented with regulations directly relevant for Rus'. Even more striking is the originality and richness of the Russian Chronicles. Their compilers, while making explicit use of Greek models, provide an independent, extremely varied and historically informative picture of the country's history. The quality of their work is vastly superior to any historiographical texts produced in other Slavic countries. Russians were geographically too far from Constantinople and their country had never been administratively part of the empire, so that they could not be satisfied with translated Byzantine historiography. The chronicles reflect Russia's sense of national identity and unity independently of Byzantium. However, these accounts, produced either at the metropolitan's court or at other ecclesiastical establishments, still never lose sight of the Byzantine Orthodox *oikouméne*, of which Russia is always seen as a part.

Byzantine art was generously imported to Russia immediately after 988. The churches erected in Kiev by Vladimir and Yaroslav were built and decorated by Greek artists. The cathedral of St Sophia in Kiev preserves, even today, some of the best Byzantine mosaic decoration of the eleventh century. It apparently took Russia at least a century to conceive new styles in art and architecture, within the framework of Byzantine tradition. The great monuments of Novgorod and the north-eastern principalities are examples of this new development, which was to receive a new impetus in the fourteenth century.

But the impact of Byzantine Greek civilization was not restricted to the translation of texts and transmission of artistic patterns. A great number of Greeks came to Russia in person and occupied influential positions, particularly in the Church. Out of twenty-three metropolitans mentioned in the chronicles for the pre-Mongolian period, seventeen were certainly Greeks, while only two were Russians (the nationality of the remaining four is unknown). It appears that the majority of the diocesan bishops were recruited among the local clergy, but some were certainly Greeks. Our sources also mention the presence of Greek teachers and

Greek books in many parts of Russia.[27] The administrative control of the Russian Church by Greek ecclesiastics undoubtedly contributed to the literal compliance of Russian liturgical texts and customs with those of Constantinople, and provides at least a partial explanation of why more initiative and originality appears in secular (i.e. legal) aspects of Russian culture than in the ecclesiastical. Even when Russia acquired its ecclesiastical independence, the conservative instinct of remaining faithful to the 'Greek books' continued to be a pattern of Russian medieval civilization.

Naturally this desire to imitate Greek models appears in the earliest examples of local Russian literature. Even the two Russians who, supported by powerful Kievan princes, became primates of Russia, breaking with the established procedure of appointing metropolitans from Constantinople – Hilarion (1051) and Clement (1147–55) – were themselves models of a purely Byzantine tradition in theology, exegesis and rhetoric. Clearly their qualifications to assume the position and status of metropolitan had been measured according to patterns received from Byzantium: Russian incumbents were not to be inferior to their Greek predecessors. The same can be said of Cyril of Turov (mid-twelfth century), the author of the first Russian collection of exegetical sermons.[28] Similarly, when the Grand-prince Andrew Bogolyubsky of Vladimir (1157–74) wanted to assert his predominance in Russian lands and the ecclesiastical independence of his Grand-principality from the metropolitan of Kiev, he used Byzantine devotional and hagiographical traditions (the icon of Our Lady of Vladimir, the feast of *Pokrov*) and recalled to memory the Greek origin of the local saint, Leonty of Rostov.[29] By this he intended

---

[27] See V. Ikonnikov, *O kul'turnom znachenii*, pp. 52–4.
[28] On the Byzantine tradition expressed by these three authors, see G. Fedotov, *Religious Mind*, I, pp. 63–93 (the contrast between 'Byzantinism' and 'Russian Kenoticism' accepted by Fedotov is, however, hardly justified); see also L. Müller, *Des Metropoliten Ilarion Lobrede auf Vladimir den Heiligen*, Slavistische Studienbücher, II, 1962.
[29] *Pokrov* is the Slavic term designating the veil (μαφόριον) of the Virgin, a major relic to which the Byzantines attributed the salvation of Constantinople from the Persians, the Arabs and the Bulgarians. It was kept in the church of the Blachernai. According to his Greek *Vita*, St Andrew *Salos* – the patron-saint of Andrew Bogolyubsky – had a vision of the Virgin holding her *maphorion* over the city. It is this vision which is commemorated by the feast of Pokrov, instituted by Andrew for celebration on 1 October. (On the origin of the Feast, see [A. Ostroumov], 'Proiskhozhdenie prazdnika Pokrova', in *Prikhodskoi Listok* (*prilozhenie k 'Tserkovnym Vedomostyam'*), 1911, No. 11; Th. Spassky, 'K proiskhozhdeniyu ikony i prazdnika Pokrova', *Pravoslavnaya Mysl'*, IX, Paris, 1953, pp. 138–51; cf. also N. N. Voronin,

to enhance the prestige of his capital, Vladimir.[30] As the Bulgarians of the tenth century, so did the Russians, even when they showed sporadic opposition to the imperial and ecclesiastical control of Byzantium, refer to cultural and religious categories adopted from the Byzantines and made available to them in Slavic translation of Greek texts.

Of course, in addition to churchmen and ecclesiastics, Greek diplomats, merchants, craftsmen and artists also travelled to Russia, whereas Russians served in the Byzantine army. Russian princes themselves occasionally visited Constantinople and intermarried with Greeks. In Constantinople, an area of the city became the normal residence for Russian visitors. Russian monks settled on Mount Athos and other monasteries in the Middle East, and a steady flow of Russian pilgrims passed through the Byzantine capital on their way to the Holy Land.[31]

Was the knowledge of the Greek language very widespread among the Russians? This does not seem to be the case: the few existing (and little studied) Greek–Russian glossaries seem to reflect the commendable efforts of some conscientious or interested students, but also their disenchantment with the difficulties they encountered.[32] Studies of Greek were probably concentrated in a few centres such as Vladimir, where the Grand-prince's library included a number of Greek books,[33] or Rostov, where the bishop was normally a Greek and where Greek was used in liturgical service along with Slavonic.[34] Ethnic Greeks, living in Russia, were not particularly popular with the local population. The Chronicles frequently accuse them of being deceitful,[35] but generally recognize their 'wisdom' (*mudrost'*) and refinement (*khitrost'*), the signs of a culturally superior civilization. Several Greek bishops

---

'Andrei Bogolyubsky i Luka Khrizoverg', *VV*, XXI, 1962, pp. 29–50; 'Zhitie Leontiya Rostovskogo i vizantiisko-russkie otnosheniya vtoroi poloviny XII v', *VV*, XXIII, 1963, pp. 23–46.

[30] Cf. I. Ševčenko, 'Russo-Byzantine Relations after the Eleventh Century', *Proceedings of the XIIIth International Congress of Byzantine Studies*, London, 1967, p. 95.

[31] Cf. G. G. Litavrin, A. P. Kazhdan, 'Ekonomicheskie i politicheskie otnosheniya drevnei Rusi i Vizantii', *Proceedings of the XIIIth International Congress of Byzantine Studies*, London, 1967, pp. 69–81.

[32] Cf. the edition of the *Rech tonkosloviya grecheskogo*, a fifteenth-century Greek textbook, by M. Vasmer, *Ein russisch-byzantinisches Gesprächsbuch*, Leipzig, 1922; cf. also I. Ševčenko, *ibid.*, p. 98.

[33] V. Ikonnikov, *op. cit.*, p. 53.

[34] Golubinsky, *Istoriya*, I, 1, p. 359–60.

[35] Reporting the breaking of an oath by the bishop of Chernigov, Anthony, in 1164, the chronicler comments: 'In himself he held deceit, because Greek by birth' (PSRL, II, St Petersburg, 1908, col. 523).

and monks found their way into the Russian catalogue of saints. So neither temperamental nor cultural differences, nor even political interests, were able to break the bonds – based on the Orthodox faith and the traditions of Romano-Byzantine universalism – which connected Russia and Byzantium.

But one can safely say that, precisely because Byzantine culture came to Russia in *translation*, Hellenism was never bequeathed to Russia in its intellectual and creative dimension. The Byzantines preserved the inheritance of ancient Greek philosophy and thought. Byzantine intellectuals were able, until the very end of the Empire, to appreciate and interpret this inheritance. However, the cultivation of the secular culture of Antiquity was generally frowned upon by the Church and, particularly, by the monks, i.e., by those elements of Byzantine society which were directly responsible for the transmission of Byzantine civilization to the Slavs. If SS. Methodius and Cyril (the latter was also known under his secular name of Constantine the 'philosopher', and was a man well-versed in secular culture) would perhaps not have been opposed in principle to translating ancient Greek authors into Slavic if they had had the time to do so, they certainly did not consider it a high priority. Their successors, Greeks or Slavs, who worked for the expansion of Christianity in Slavic lands, found it neither desirable nor realistic to initiate the Slavs to anything but Christianity itself, its scriptures and liturgies. As it was rightly emphasized by G. P. Fedotov, there is a vital contrast between the evangelization of Western, Germanic barbarians, and the adoption of Byzantine Christianity by the Slavs: the Eastern 'barbarians' received the Christian faith in their own Slavic language, whereas their Western cousins were called to study Latin to achieve the saving knowledge of the faith. Rapidly and successfully 'indigenized' in Slavic lands, Christianity never became a vehicle of secular learning, whereas in the West – though restricted to only a few and monopolized by Latin-trained clergy – Christian knowledge involved access to Latin poetry and rhetoric.[36] In principle, Christian Byzantium avoided hellenizing its converts. It did not impose upon them the study of a foreign language.[37] This generous –

[36] Fedotov, *Religious Mind*, pp. 39–40.

[37] There were some exceptions to this rule, but the purported Hellenization of Bulgaria after the Byzantine conquest in the eleventh century has been exaggerated by historians (see particularly V. N. Zlatarski, *Istoriya na Bulgarska durzhava*, II, Sofia, 1927, p. 57ff.; also I. Ševčenko, 'Three paradoxes of the Cyrillo-Methodian Mission', *Slavic Review*, XXIII, 1964, No. 2, pp. 226–8). There were cases of snobbishness expressed by educated Byzantines (e.g. Theophylact of Bulgaria) concerning

'Cyrillo-Methodian' – approach involved important consequences as to how the Christian faith, made available essentially in *translation* and not in the original Greek, would be accepted and interpreted on Slavic, and particularly Russian, soil. As we have seen in the preceding section, Russia, upon its conversion, joined a political and ecclesiastical structure which reflected Christian and Roman universalism. But culturally, its initiation to the foreign Byzantine civilization was limited by the language barrier, so that new developments depended to a great measure upon indigenous talents, able to use local resources. Some of these men appeared early (e.g. Hilarion of Kiev), but independent creativity in a purely intellectual field had to wait several centuries. Even in the fourteenth century, when the volume of translations from the Greek increased very substantially, the Russians became worthy disciples of Byzantium in the fields of religious art, Orthodox spirituality, hagiography and issues involving personal and social ethics, but the speculative, theological and philosophical achievements of Byzantine Christian Hellenism were accepted only passively and on a very limited scale.

3. THE ORTHODOX FAITH

The transmission of Orthodox Christianity from Byzantium to Russia has never yet been discussed with full awareness of the various factors involved. Aside from the standard histories of Russia, and of the Russian Church (Makary, Golubinsky, Kartashev), the purely religious aspects of the issue were treated in two monumental works: G. Florovsky's *Ways of Russian Theology* (*Puti Russkago bogosloviya*, Paris, 1937), and G. P. Fedotov, *The Russian Religious Mind*, I–II (Cambridge, Mass., 1946–66). Both these authors suggest a contrast between Byzantium and Russia, but their approach to the problem is strikingly different. Florovsky writes about theology and theologians. Very few of the Russian religious authors, whose written works the author reviews with great erudition, meet the patristic intellectual criteria which he accepts as a pattern. In fact Florovsky's book is written to show that in Russia there were no theologians at all until the nineteenth century, and that the entire medieval Russian religious literature was at best a pale imitation of Byzantine models and at worst an

'barbarian' languages. However, the *fact* of liturgical multilinguism was universal in the Byzantine world and its legitimacy in principle was denied by no one (cf. the balanced view on the issue by Obolensky, *Commonwealth*, pp. 151–3).

uncritical copying of Western, heterodox prototypes. The author deliberately avoids discussing forms of religious experience other than purely 'theological', for example the fields of art, liturgy and spirituality. Fedotov, on the contrary, has not much use for doctrines and dogmas. He believes that Byzantine Christianity was 'monophysitic' (i.e. forgetful of the humanity of Jesus), 'Hellenized' ('The Gospels became a book of mysteries . . . , a source of theological speculations') and 'orientalized' (practising 'ethics of slavery, in the disguise of Christian humility'), and discovers a more authentically 'Christian' experience of the suffering, human 'kenotic' Christ in 'Russian' Orthodoxy.

It appears to us that no general understanding of the issue is possible on the basis of preconceived schemes and contrasts. Orthodox Christianity in the Byzantine Empire was a varied and complex phenomenon. To newly baptized Russians, its more intellectual aspects were clearly inaccessible, but Russians rapidly became good pupils in those aspects of the Christian faith which demand an intuitive experience of truth and beauty. In the eleventh century already St Anthony of Kiev learned the traditions of Athonite monasticism and St Theodosius introduced into Russia the monastic *Rule* of St Theodore of Studios. The Russians were immediately taken up by the beauty of the Byzantine liturgy and soon learned the arts of mosaic, fresco, and manuscript illumination. The Greek artists invited to Russia were the best available and their Russian pupils were soon to reach the perfection of their masters. And since, in Eastern Christianity, icon-painting and icon-veneration involved the theology of the Incarnation, this successful importation of Byzantine art had more than an aesthetic significance: it also taught the content of the faith. With the language of its liturgy and its art, with the cosmic significance of its various sacraments and sacramentals (blessings of the water, of the harvest, of fruits, of houses and boats), which affirmed that all the forms of individual and social life, in all their dimensions, could be assumed into the Kingdom of God, the Orthodox faith of Byzantium was accessible and flexible enough to become 'culture', understood by the learned and the simple alike in Russia.

This is why *continuity* between Byzantium and Russia should probably be emphasized more than the inevitable discontinuities of a historical process which witnessed the acceptance, by a 'barbarian' nation which hardly possessed any literature, of the most elaborate, most sophisticated and centuries-old tradition of Christianity. This is particularly clear in the area of hagiography.

One can readily agree with Fedotov that the intensity with which SS Boris and Gleb – two sons of St Vladimir, murdered by their brother Svyatopolk – were venerated in Russia, as symbols of Christian humility and non-violence, helps our understanding of early Christianity in Kiev. But was not the cult of martyrs of early Christianity and of later periods imported from Byzantium, where it occupied a central place in the *Oktoechos* (a liturgical book for daily use, translated by St Methodius into Slavic), the *Menaion*, and the various *Synaxaria*? Similarly, the holiness of Russian monks represented a spirituality basically identical with that of the Greek or Syrian Fathers. On the other hand, Vladimir's image was patterned after Constantine's already by Hilarion of Kiev, and the holy princes (some of them martyred by Tatars) had models in the well-known Greek military saints. Between 'Greek' and 'Russian' Orthodoxy there were occasional differences in accent and style, but these differences were remarkably slight, if one considers the basic identity of approach and intuition, which remained intact in spite of the vast historical and cultural gaps between the two countries. Throughout the Middle Ages the Orthodox faith always served as a unifying factor between them.

If there is a feature of 'Russian' Orthodoxy which can be seen as a contrast to the Byzantine perception of Christianity, it is the nervous concern of the Russians in preserving the *very letter* of tradition received 'from the Greeks'. This concern caused an ecclesiastical crisis in Moscovy, when, in the sixteenth and seventeenth centuries, the problem of which 'books' were 'correct' came to the fore. However, the issue goes back to the very origins of Russian Christianity, when an immense and sophisticated mass of written material, produced by centuries of cultural and intellectual development, was translated and offered to the Russians as the unique *source* of religious knowledge. Clearly, Russian Christians could not fully understand, let alone appreciate or criticize, the iambic meters of the Byzantine *canons* for the great feasts, the legal sophistication of Greek canonists, or the trinitarian and christological distinctions found in the *Theotokia* of the Resurrection Vespers in the *Oktoechos*.[38] Some of the more difficult texts remained for ever unintelligible in Slavic translation and, surely, the poetic dimension of some hymns was sometimes completely

---

[38] Some familiarity with the Byzantine theological heritage makes one understand better the full dimensions of the problem. On this see Meyendorff, *Byzantine Theology*; also *Christ in Eastern Christian Thought*, Washington, D.C., 1969 (second ed., New York, 1975).

lost, in spite of the remarkable intrinsic potential of the Slavic tongue and the many strokes of real genius in the translators' work. At all times, in Russia, there was a certain unconscious awareness that Christianity had been 'imported'. This awareness prompted Russian – particularly Muscovite – churchmen towards a conservative devotion for the imported 'books' whose content often appeared mysterious, but which remained the only authentic criterion of Orthodoxy originally received from Byzantium. Any significant departure from this written deposit in words or thoughts was seen as potential heresy.

This devotion to the Byzantine religious inheritance was also decisive for Russia's relations with Western Christendom. There is every reason to believe that from the very time of the baptism of Vladimir the Kievan Church, in its attitude towards both Rome and Germanic Christianity, it followed Constantinople in every respect. Some historians have postulated an independent connection between the metropolitanate of Kiev and Rome.[39] Others have attributed to the Greek leadership of the Church a pronounced anti-Latin campaign, which put an end to an otherwise pro-Western Russian attitude.[40] Such views could possess a semblance of credibility only on the assumption – which was widely held until very recently – that the incident of 1054 between the patriarch of Constantinople, Michael Keroullarios, and the legates of Pope Leo IX was to be understood as the final and definitive schism between the churches of Rome and Byzantium. If this had been the case, such facts as the presence of some Western saints in Russian prayers and calendars or the solemn celebration by the Russian Church of the transfer of the relics of St Nicholas from Myra to Bari in Italy (1087),[41] could be considered as signs that the Russians were disloyal to Constantinople and entertained independent relations with the Latin Church. In reality, however, the events of 1054 were seen in Constantinople itself as nothing more than another incident between patriarchates and no formal canonical sanction was taken against either

---

[39] Cf. particularly N. de Baumgarten, *Saint Vladimir et la conversion de la Russie*, Orientalia Christiana 27, 1, No. 72, 1932. This view recurs also in more recent Roman Catholic publications, for example, V. Meysztowicz, 'L'union de Kiev avec Rome sous Grégoire VII', *Studi Gregoriani*, 5, 1956, pp. 83–108.

[40] A. I. Sobolevsky, 'Otnoshenie drevnei Rusi k razdeleniyu tserkvei', *Akademiya Nauk, Izvestiya*, VI seriya, VIII, 1914, No. 2, pp. 95–102.

[41] Cf. E. Golubinsky, *Istoriya*, I, 1, pp. 773–5; B. Leib, *Rome, Kiev et Byzance à la fin du XIe siècle*, Paris, 1924, pp. 51–74; A. P. Vlasto, *The Entry of the Slavs into Christendom. An introduction to the Medieval History of the Slavs*, Cambridge, 1970, pp. 290–2; F. Dvornik, *The Making*, pp. 242–7; V. Moshin, 'O periodizatsii', pp. 44–5.

the papacy, or the Latin Church as a whole.[42] Contacts with the West which were initiated in Russia, paralleled similar and numerous contacts in Constantinople itself and were not necessarily opposed by the Greek clergy. In fact the correspondence, admittedly polemical, which took place between the Antipope Clement III (1080–1100) and the Greek metropolitan of Kiev, John II, was transmitted by Theodore, 'a Greek member of the metropolitan's court', who also 'brought from Rome, from the Pope many relics of saints'.[43] There is no evidence, therefore, that the Greek clergy promoted in Russia a particularly anti-Latin spirit. One should rather assume that the metropolitanate of Kiev, represented both by its Greek leadership and the mass of its Russian flock, participated, together with the other provinces of the patriarchate of Constantinople, in the creeping estrangement between the Churches, which developed gradually in the eleventh and the twelfth centuries.[44] The fact that, during that period, Greek and Latin polemicists were more involved in ritual and disciplinary issues – and did not confine themselves (as was the case in the age of Photius) to the basic trinitarian problem of the *Filioque* – made these polemics more readily accessible to the Russians. Characteristically, in the Russian *Primary Chronicle's* account of Vladimir's conversion the principal 'heresy' of the Latins is seen in their use of unleavened bread for the Eucharist, in their irreverence towards the holy images and other ritual inadequacies.[45] Ritual issues predominate in those Byzantine anti-Latin treatises which found their way into Russia.[46] In this area, as in others, the Russians were faithful disciples of the Greeks, but selected those elements in Greek theological literature which were

---

[42] For a view of the events of 1054 generally accepted by historians today, see G. Every, *The Byzantine Patriarchate, 451–1204*, 2nd ed., London, 1962, pp. 150–2. Convincing in this regard are documents pertaining to the contacts established between Constantinople and Rome in 1089, when Emperor Alexis I officially requested evidence pertaining to the schism. None was found at the patriarchate. In fact, since the early eleventh century, the Churches were in a state of *de facto* estrangement, but no formal break had occurred (see particularly W. Holtzmann, 'Unionsverhandlungen zwischen Kaiser Alexios I. and Papst Urban II. im Jahre 1089', *BZ*, 28, 1928, pp. 38–67; also B. Leib, *op. cit.*, pp. 19–26).

[43] *Nik.* p. 116.

[44] Cf. A. Poppe, 'Le traité des azymes Λέοντος τῆς ἐν 'Ρωσία Πρεσλάβας: quand, où et par qui a-t-il été écrit?', *Byzantion*, 35, 1965, pp. 504–27.

[45] *Primary Chronicle*, pp. 61, 79–80; tr., p. 98, 115. The chronicle was compiled at least one century after the events of 988. It reflects the polemics between Greeks and Latins which are characteristic of the eleventh century.

[46] See Popov, *Obzor*. Popov's monograph is complemented and, in part, superseded by A. Pavlov, *Opyty*.

27

more easily understandable and more immediately relevant to the practical concerns of the young Church of Russia.

Accepting Byzantine Orthodoxy, the Russians took for granted its doctrines and canons, but they also learned from the Greeks that doctrines could be expressed in liturgical beauty, in music, in the visual arts and in patterns of ascetic behaviour. These aspects of Christianity they loved most and developed very early in their own indigenous ways. The internal coherence of this Byzantine inheritance thus allowed, in the fourteenth century, the organic acceptance by Russians of the hesychast revival and of the artistic Renaissance of the Palaeologan period.

2

The catastrophes of the thirteenth century

In 1204, for the first time in its history of nine hundred years, after having withstood sieges by Persians, Avars, Slavs, Arabs and Turks, Constantinople was finally overwhelmed and sacked by Western Crusaders. The fact that these enemies were Latin Christians and that, after capturing the city, they established their own empire and their own patriarchate on the Bosphorus, profoundly influenced the relations between Latin and Byzantine Christendoms in the following centuries.

Twenty years later, in 1223, a coalition of Russian and Cuman princes was defeated by the armies of Chingis Khan, who had crossed the Caucasus after conquering Persia. The battle took place on the river Kalka, to the north of the Sea of Azov. A decade later, Batu, Chingis Khan's grandson, erupted into the Russian plain from the north-east, crossing the Urals, and proceeded with the systematic conquest and plundering of the entire territory of the Rus'. Kiev was captured and destroyed in 1240.

These two catastrophic events changed the whole political structure of eastern Europe and of the Mediterranean world. The traditional polarization between the Eastern Roman Empire and the western imperial system – a polarization which had been revived by the dramatic confrontation between Manuel I Comnenus (1143–80) and Frederick I Barbarossa (1152–90) – now ended. Latin Christendon, formally headed by the pope, had suppressed its rival. In fact, Western Christendom was far from monolithic, with a number of nation-states competing for leadership, but, in the eyes of Greeks and Slavs it appeared as if the papacy was to become the only heir of the Roman *imperium*. The other world power, that of the Mongols, extended from the Danube to the Pacific ocean, and offered (at least to the Russians) an alternative centre of allegiance. However, no major military confrontation ever occurred between the Tatars and Western Christendon, and diplomatic and commercial ties were soon established between them, with the popes cherishing the possibility of a missionary expansion in Asia.[1]

Between the two new empires, a number of smaller nation-states – pagan Lithuania, the Galician-Volhynian principality, Bulgaria, and Serbia – the latter three religiously and culturally dependent upon the Byzantine heritage – succeeded in assuring their independence by successively appeasing either the Mongols, or the Western powers. The first goal could be achieved by tribute paid to the Golden Horde, the second by recognizing, at least nominally, the pope's supremacy.

In the first decades of the thirteenth century it appeared that Byzantium was dead, both as 'Empire' and as 'Commonwealth', that Latin Christendom had become coextensive with European civilization itself, and that soon it would have to face a confrontation with Asia. In fact, however, neither the Latin presence in the eastern Mediterranean nor the Mongol conquest of Russia proved as destructive as it had originally seemed. Maintained primarily by the Church, the religious, cultural and even political, bonds of the Byzantine Commonwealth survived the catastrophes and eventually made possible a revival in the late thirteenth and fourteenth centuries.

I. BYZANTIUM: DEATH AND RESURRECTION

The sack of Constantinople by the Crusaders in 1204 was an event of major significance, but it did not come as a sudden and unpredictable surprise. Ideologically, politically and economically, the successive Crusades were in too obvious a conflict with Byzantium to allow for a system of peaceful coexistence in the Middle East.

Ideologically, the emergence of the Holy Roman Empire of the West and the reforms of the papacy, which affirmed the universal jurisdiction of the popes as heads of the Christian world, were obviously incompatible with the Byzantine idea of the Empire, as it had been defined in the times of Constantine and Justinian: for the Byzantines, Constantinople was the only 'new Rome'; its emperor was the only '*autocrator* of the Romans' and the Church was governed by a consensus of the five patriarchs – Rome, Constantinople, Alexandria, Antioch and Jerusalem – a consensus which had been institutionally and doctrinally broken by the

---

[1] See particularly Pelliot, *Mongols et papes*; Gay, *Clément VI*.

Roman pope. The unity of Christians could be achieved only by a return to the old pattern. Of course, the Byzantine knew very well how to reconcile ideological consistency with practical compromise: Emperors John II (1118–43) and Manuel I (1143–80) Comneni occasionally envisaged a practical understanding with the German empire. However, Manuel was soon confronted with the universal imperial claims of Frederick I Barbarossa, who could formally, in a letter to the Byzantine emperor, demand that the 'Greek king' pay allegiance to him, as the true emperor.[2] The union of the German empire with the Norman Kingdom of Sicily, under Barbarossa's successor Conrad IV, created, in the late twelfth century, a direct menace to Byzantium, which was openly considered as a major obstacle to Western interests.

Politically, the creation of Latin principalities in Palestine and Syria, which the Byzantines considered their own territory, temporarily conquered by the Arabs, created a permanent state of conflict between Greeks and Latins. If the great Comnenian emperors, Alexis, John and Manuel, succeeded in channelling the Crusaders' movement and occasionally obtained from them statements of allegiance, the weak emperors of the family of Angeloi (1185–1204) appeared as easy prey for their Western enemies, who had been shocked by the fierce anti-Latin popular outbursts under Alexis II (1180–3) and Andronicus I (1183–5), resulting in a brutal massacre of the Latins in Constantinople in 1183.

Economically, the main thrust was coming from the Italian city-republic of Venice, a major naval power, whose ambition was to control the commercial routes between Western Europe and the East: here also Byzantium stood in the way.

The internal policy of the Byzantine empire during the Comnenian period had encouraged the growth of large estates, which were monopolized by a class of military magnates. As long as the imperial power was strong enough to control this Byzantine form of feudalism, the empire continued to present a united appearance. After 1180, however, the quick changes of personalities on the throne and their unpreparedness to face the issues destroyed the façade of Byzantine power. The weakness of the empire was particularly apparent in the Balkans. By 1183, the Serbian Župan Stephen Nemanja, with active Hungarian help, was able to establish a permanently independent country. Almost simultaneously, a Bulgarian revolt, south of the Danube and led by the

---

[2] Cf. Ostrogorsky, *History*, p. 391.

two brothers Peter and Asen, provoked bloody fighting with Byzantine armies which eventually resulted in a *de facto* recognition by Byzantium of an independent Bulgaria with a capital in Trnovo. Under Kalojan (1197–1207), the youngest brother of Peter and Asen, Bulgaria became the major power in the Balkans.

General disintegration affected such outlying provinces as Cyprus, where Isaac Comnenus assumed the imperial title in the last years of the thirteenth century, and Trebizond, where two grandsons of Andronicus I, Alexis and David, with the help of the Georgian Queen Thamar, established a separate empire (1204).

Thus when the Crusaders captured 'the queen of cities' (1204), several elements of a new political structure were already in existence on the territory of the old empire: Trebizond in the east, and the young Slavic states of Serbia and Bulgaria in the Balkans. But the founding of a Latin Empire in Constantinople itself, with a Venetian patriarch occupying the throne of John Chrysostom and of Photius at St Sophia, was an event of extraordinary symbolic significance: not only did it provoke an understandable patriotic reaction on the part of the Greeks, but also, for the first time, Greek theologians and ecclesiastics realized all the seriousness of the papal claims. Before 1204 Byzantine anti-Latin polemics centred upon the Latin addition of the *Filioque* to the creed, and upon questions of liturgy and discipline which were generally seen as serious, but remediable mistakes: now, after the appointment of Thomas Morosini as patriarch by Pope Innocent III, most Byzantines realized that Western Christendom really believed in the exclusive and universal rights of the pope, as successor of Peter, and thus held an understanding of the Church, quite different from their own.[3]

But it soon also became clear that the leaders of the Crusade possessed neither the military power nor the inner cohesion to suppress Byzantine resistance completely. Two Greek states, each pretending to the legitimate succession of the Empire, were formed in the months which followed the fall of the city: Epirus and Nicaea. Michael Doukas, leading a coalition of local Greek aristocracy, assumed the title of 'despot' in Epirus, with its capital in Arta. In 1224, he recaptured Thessalonica from the Latins and was proclaimed 'emperor of the Romans'. Meanwhile, Theodore Lascaris, a son-in-law of Emperor Alexis III, gathered around

[3] See J. Meyendorff, 'St. Peter in Byzantine Theology', in J. Meyendorff, et al., *The Primacy of Peter in the Orthodox Church*, London, 1963.

his capital in Nicaea the important territories of Western Asia Minor. In 1208, he also assumed the imperial title.

An extraordinary mushrooming of 'imperial' centres – Trebizond, Nicaea, Thessalonica, Cyprus, and, soon, Bulgaria – in addition to the Latin empire in Constantinople itself, with each of the leaders of these areas claiming to be 'emperor of the Romans', followed the Latin capture of Constantinople. It was certainly a disintegration of the imperial reality, but also, paradoxically, it was a sign of survival, in the political consciousness of most contemporaries, of the imperial idea itself: no one, not even the Balkan Slavs, were satisfied with simply becoming nation-states. They either continued to pledge a nominal allegiance to a universal body (with the papacy sometimes replacing Constantinople as the carrier of universal imperial legitimacy), or proclaimed the transfer of the empire (*translatio imperii*) to the capital of their own domain. The logic which justified this phenomenon will be used – quite belatedly – in Muscovite Russia, in the fifteenth and sixteenth centuries, with the ideology of 'Moscow – the third Rome'.

In the thirteenth century, however, there remained one important institution which did not succumb to the general trend of disintegration and remained as a powerful bond of unity: this was the Orthodox patriarchate of Constantinople. In 1204, the reigning patriarch John X Kamateros, when the Crusaders entered the city on 13 April, found refuge in Didymotichus, in Thrace,[4] where Latin suzerainty was soon challenged by local Greek aristocracy, which appealed for the protection of the Bulgarians. On 14 April 1205, the Bulgarian tsar Kalojan routed the Latin army in Adrianople. A fierce enemy of the new rulers of Constantinople, Kalojan nevertheless nominally recognized the spiritual leadership of the pope: on 7 November 1204, a Roman cardinal consecrated the Bulgarian Archbishop Basil in Trnovo and Kalojan received a royal crown. It is doubtful that the exiled patriarch John – now a refugee in Bulgaria – viewed these developments with favour. The political opportunism of Kalojan may have even been one of the determining factors, which pushed the Byzantine Church to switch the basis for its survival from Europe to Asia. After the death of John Kamateros (1206) and a vacancy of almost two years, a new patriarchal election, that of Michael Autoreianos, took place not in Bulgaria, but *in Nicaea* (1208) and was

---

[4] Nicetas Choniates, *Hist.*, ed. Bonn, pp. 784, 837.

followed by the imperial coronation of the Nicaean 'despot' Theodore Lascaris.[5]

This event was to carry decisive consequences: coronation by a reigning patriarch was considered essential for the recognition of imperial legitimacy.[6] In choosing Nicaea as the residence of the exiled patriarchate, the leadership of the Church – which was certainly solicited from at least two other sides, Epirus and Bulgaria – was in fact determining the future fate of Byzantine civilization.

Thus the coronation of Theodore Angelos of Epirus by the Archbishop of Ohrid, after his capture of Thessalonica from the Latins (1224), lacked the prestige of legitimacy enjoyed by the Emperor of Nicaea. This role in the survival of imperial continuity will be a very important factor throughout the history of the fourteenth century in Byzantium, and, also, in Russia.

We do not possess enough information about the procedure of the patriarchal election which took place in Nicaea in 1208. The political ability of Theodore Lascaris must have played an important role. In any case, the election received wide ecclesiastical support and recognition outside of the territories controlled by Nicaea. The new patriarch took immediate control of the entire administrative apparatus and power of his predecessors, including the control of distant metropolitanates, which belonged to its jurisdiction, in Trebizond, the Caucasus, Russia and the Balkans. The weakness of his political basis in Nicaea was compensated for by his diplomatic flexibility. For instance, the patriarchate realized that direct administrative control of the Bulgarians and the Serbians had become impossible since the collapse of Byzantine military control of the Balkans. Both the Bulgarian and the Serbian rulers were in a strong position to bargain for ecclesiastical independence with the Greeks and, eventually, the pope. Recognizing the inevitable, the patriarchate of Nicaea consecrated St Sava as autocephalous archbishop of Serbia (1219) and, in 1235, recognized the Bulgarian patriarchate of Trnovo. In earlier times, the Byzantine would have never granted these concessions willingly, but the exiled empire of Nicaea had no other choice. Actually, it was also obtaining, through these generous gestures, substantial advantages: the recognition of its own canonical legitimacy and honorary primacy by the Bulgarians and the Serbs,

---

[5] A. Heisenberg, 'Neue Quellen zur Geschichte des Lateinischen Kaisertums und der Kirchenunion' in *Bayerischen Akademie der Wissenschaften, Philos.- philol. und hist. Klasse,* 1923, 2, Abt., Munich, 1923, pp. 5–11, 28, 35.

[6] Cf. J. Meyendorff, 'Ideological crises'.

and the severance of the ambiguous relations of the two Slavic Orthodox nations with the Roman pope. We will see below that equally flexible ecclesiastical policies in Russia will also bring equally positive results.

The political and economic strengthening of the Nicaean empire by its very distinguished leaders has been well described by historians. It will lead to the recapture of Constantinople in 1261. But this restoration would not have been possible, if during the years of imperial collapse (1204–61), the Byzantine 'Commonwealth' had not possessed a mechanism of survival, based on strong religious and cultural ties and, also on institutional flexibility.

The Emperor Michael VIII Paleologus (1259–82) who, after reaching the throne in Nicaea by usurpation, had the luck of being also crowned a second time in St Sophia, after the recapture of Constantinople by the Greeks (1261), became the prime mover and also the victim of a brilliant, but often contradictory and self-defeating game of diplomacy involving powers of the West and the East, and aiming at the survival of the newly regained city. In order to face the challenge of Charles of Anjou, Norman king of Sicily, who actively planned the restoration of Latin power on the Bosphorus, he negotiated with the papacy the union of the churches, which would make a new Latin Crusade against Constantinople unjustifiable. To reach this goal he first accepted the Roman faith, in a personal confession drafted by Latin theologians, then had his delegates sign the decrees, issued by the Council of Lyons (1274). Finally, he installed John Beccos, a partisan of the union, as patriarch. This created fierce internal conflict in Byzantium, but did not prevent Charles of Anjou from plotting the Latin revenge. The Sicilian menace was eventually to be neutralized not by the papacy, but by another ally of Michael, King Peter of Aragon, and the rebellious people of Sicily, who massacred their Norman overlords during the famous 'Sicilian Vespers' (1282).

Similar tactics – finding allies and creating 'second fronts' in the back of one's enemies[7] – led to agreements between Michael and Khan Hulagu and his son Abaga, the Mongol rulers in Persia and Iraq, who had humbled the Seljuq Turks of Asia Minor and prevented their being a danger to either Nicaea, or to the restored Empire of Constantinople. Abaga even married Michael's illegiti-

---

[7] 'Michael VIII encircled the ring of powers hostile to Byzantium with a further ring intended to hold the enemies of the Empire in check', Ostrogorsky, *History*, p. 459.

mate daughter Maria (1265), and expressed interest in Christianity. His contacts with the papacy[8] show that the Persian alliance fitted perfectly with Michael's own policy of union with Rome: one version of his plans for survival was therefore based on an axis Rome–Constantinople–Persia, which was directed against both Charles of Anjou and the Seljuqs.

This formula did however have disadvantages. In the second half of the thirteenth century, the Mongol empire created by Chingis Khan was already divided between several competing centres. The khans of the Golden Horde, who ruled Russia and were allied with the Mamluks of Egypt, competed fiercely with Hulagu and Abaga. They repeatedly raided Byzantine territories, because Michael was a friend of their rivals. In order to appease them, the Byzantine emperor made another of his illegitimate daughters, Euphrosyne, marry Nogay, an eminent Mongol in the region of the Black Sea.[9] Since Michael, in his struggle against Venice, which supported the Angevins, was also largely dependent upon Genoa and had granted the Genoese important commercial privileges in the Black Sea, and since the Genoese commercial interests on the Crimea and the lower Don were dependent upon the goodwill of the Golden Horde, another competing political axis, including Genoa, Constantinople and the Golden Horde, hostile to the papacy (which had excommunicated Genoa for its alliance with Michael), became an alternate diplomatic and military tool in the hands of Michael. In 1282, the emperor died, while leading an army of 4000 Tatars, sent by his son-in-law Nogay, against the rebellious John Doukas of Thessaly. He would probably have broken his religious allegiance to the pope, if he had had the time, since this tie became politically useless after the Sicilian Vespers.

The alliance with Genoa and the Golden Horde proved to be Michael's inheritance to his successors. It was to play a significant role in Byzantium's Russian policies in the fourteenth century also.

2. THE MONGOLS IN THE MIDDLE EAST AND IN EUROPE

One of the most extraordinary events of history, the creation of the Mongol empire which, by 1300, extended from the Balkans

[8] See P. Pelliot, *Mongols et papes*, pp. 11–12.
[9] See A. N. Nasonov, *Mongoly i Rus'*, pp. 41–4; on Michael's Western policies, see D. J. Geanakoplos, *Emperor Michael Palaeologus and the West*, Cambridge, Mass., 1959; and K. M. Setton, *The Papacy and the Levant (1204–1571)*, I, Philadelphia, Pa., 1976.

and the Carpathian mountains to the Pacific Ocean, and from the northern-Russian forests to Mesopotamia, profoundly influenced the history of Eastern Europe. By checking the power of the Turks in Asia Minor, it delayed the fall of Byzantium for two hundred years, but it also eventually pushed some of the Turkish tribes westwards and indirectly contributed to their advances on imperial territories in the late fourteenth century. In Russia, the Mongol yoke was a determining factor of political and cultural life until the late fifteenth century: a devastated country survived by creating new centres of power and civilization, and thus shaped its future in a totally new way. The role of Byzantine diplomacy and cultural traditions in the creation of this new political geography will be studied in this book.

In 1206, an assembly of tribal leaders, in the eastern parts of the great Eurasian plain, took the decisive step of electing the young leader of a local clan as 'emperor' (*kagan, khan* or *kaan*). His name was Temuchin, but he received the surname, or title, of Chingis.[10] Temuchin's own clan belonged to the tribe of the 'Mongols'. One of the other tribes which joined the coalition was that of the 'Tatars'. Eventually, this latter name became more popular in designating the empire of Chingis Khan, especially in its western corrupted form of 'Tartar' (by phonetic similarity with the mythical 'Tartarus'). The submission of Central Asia, Persia and Northern China, including Peking, to Mongol rule was completed by 1225. In June 1223, the two Mongol generals Jebe and Subudey, having crossed the Caucasus from Persia, inflicted a crushing defeat upon a coalition of Russian and Cuman armies on the river Kalka, but soon returned to Asia. Before his death (1226), Chingis Khan divided his huge empire among his four sons. The north-western area, including Kazakhstan and the region of the Urals, went to his oldest son Juchi. Since Juchi died a few months before his father, his son Batu, Temuchin's grandson, inherited the north-western *ulus*, as the areas of the now divided empire were called. In 1229, the assembly of Mongol tribal leaders elected Ugudey, the third son of Chingis Khan, as Great Khan with residence in Karakorum. To him the local khans, including Batu, paid allegiance.

The armies of Batu, under the very capable leadership of Subudey – the Mongol general who headed the brief incursion

[10] There is no scholarly consensus as to the exact meaning of this title, but it was certainly meant to express Temuchin's 'greatness', 'strength' and power over the clans: cf. Vernadsky, *Mongols*, pp. 17–18.

into southern Russia in 1221-3 – established the power of the Great Khan over the whole of Russia during a four-year campaign (1237-42). Destroying the cities which attempted to resist, and massacring their population, but leaving intact the political structures of the country as a whole, the Mongols established a rule based on a tribute, which local princes were obliged to pay under the menace of a new onslaught. Central Russia fell first with the city of Ryazan taken in 1237. Vladimir, the residence of the north-eastern Grand-prince, was burned in 1238. After a respite taken during 1239, the Mongol armies moved south and, in 1240, conquered the great centres of Kievan Russia: Pereyaslavl', Chernigov and Kiev itself.

Moving further west in 1241, they destroyed the principality of Galicia, subdued Hungary, invaded Croatia and reached the Adriatic Sea at Dubrovnik (Ragusa). A separate Mongolian army crossed Poland, Silesia and Moravia. In the spring of 1242, however, receiving the news of Ugudey's death and foreseeing a struggle for power at home, Batu left for Asia. He kept the direct administration of Russia proper in the framework of a vast area known as Kypchak. His permanent residence was on the lower Volga and became known as the Golden Horde, which grew into a new city, Sarai. Russian princes were forced to receive their investiture by travelling there, in order to pledge allegiance to the khan of Kypchak. Some were even obliged to make the long voyage to Karakorum to honour the Great Khan.[11]

The Mongol conquest was undoubtedly a national and cultural disaster for Russia, a political humiliation for its princes and an economic catastrophe for its entire population, even if the khans left the political structure of the country practically intact. However, as all historians of the period point out, the Church received privileged treatment from the conquerors and was exempt from the taxes imposed on the country as a whole.[12] This policy of the Mongols was motivated not only by principles of religious tolerance, which was indeed one of the characteristics of the Mongol empire, but also by considerations of international politics: the Church in Russia was headed by an appointee from Byzantium and could be used as a channel for important international con-

---

[11] The travels to Karakorum ceased after 1279, when Khan Kubilay conquered the whole of China and became emperor in Peking.

[12] The privileges were granted at the outset of the conquest by Batu himself, and extended by his successors. A decree of Mengu-Temir, issued in 1267, refers to these previous measures taken by Batu (see Vernadsky, *Mongols*, pp. 165-6).

tacts. At a result of this toleration, the Church became the main guardian of Byzantine cultural values and the Byzantine world-view in Russia, consciously using the opportunity offered to it by the new political situation in Eastern Europe. The Byzantine government of Nicaea, on the other hand, showed great wisdom and flexibility in handling the Russian situation and, thus, pre-served in modified form the inheritance of old *oikouméne* in spite of the onslaught of Crusaders coming from the West and the seem-ingly unlimited power of the Mongol empire.

The violent and bloody conquest of the north-eastern Russian principalities by the Mongols and the fall of Kiev in 1240, had left one area of the ancient Kievan realm in a relatively privileged position: the western principalities of Volhynia and Galicia, headed by the Grand-prince, Daniel Romanovich (1221–64). The armies of Khan Batu had only crossed the country, during the winter of 1240–1, destroying cities and formally conquering the area. At that time, Daniel was absent, seeking help in neighbour-ing Hungary and Poland. As Batu pursued his march westward, the prince was able to return home and undertake a series of skilful diplomatic manoeuvres, asserting for his principality an independent position as one of the buffer states between East and West.

Firstly, he assumed leadership in the affairs of the Church. The office of 'Metropolitan of Kiev and all Russia' had been vacant since its holder, the Greek Joseph, had disappeared from the scene, probably returning home, as the Mongols were sacking Kiev in 1240. The patriarchate, in its Nicaean exile, was obviously unable to take immediate measures to fill the office, leaving possibilities open for usurpations. We know of one such usurpation in the case of Joasaph, bishop of Ugrovsk, who assumed the title of metro-politan, only to be deposed by Daniel. The exact chronology of that event is uncertain.[13] It is unclear whether Joasaph assumed the position of 'Metropolitan of Kiev and all Russia', or only 'of Galicia': in the latter case, he would be an early precursor of later similar attempts at Galician ecclesiastical autonomy. In any case, Daniel's negative reaction shows the Grand-prince's ambition to influence the fate of the whole Russian Church and not only that of his own principality. Upon returning from exile, he established

[13] It is reported by the Hypatian chronicle under the year 1224 (PSRL, II, Moscow, 1962, col. 740), but several historians (Golubinsky, *Istoriya*, p. 52; V. T. Pashuto, *Ocherki*, p. 228) consider that Joasaph's usurpation took place in 1241, after the fall of Kiev.

his candidate, Cyril, as 'Metropolitan of Kiev and of all Russia'.[14] Metropolitan Cyril, a native Russian taking a position previously occupied, almost exclusively, by Greeks, was to have an extraordinarily long and productive tenure (1242–81) as primate of the Church in Russia.

The peculiarity of Cyril's appointment as metropolitan is that six years at least elapsed between his establishment by Grandprince Daniel (1242) and his trip to Nicaea in order to obtain the traditional and canonically required patriarchal confirmation (1248–9). Was he, during that period, only a metropolitan-elect,[15] or had he been consecrated by Russian bishops, following the two precedents of metropolitans Hilarion (1051) and Clement (1147)? The absence in our sources of any known protest by the Nicaean patriarch against a consecration by Russian bishops can be easily explained in the context of the great confusion of those days and the flight of the Nicaea-appointed metropolitan Joseph. The generosity of the enfeebled Byzantine authorities of the day towards their Slavic daughter-churches could have been extended to Russia: was not the originally usurped Bulgarian patriarchate of Trnovo recognized by the exiled ecumenical patriarchate (1235), which also established an independent Serbian church (1219)? In any case, in 1246, even before establishing official ties with the Greek patriarch, Metropolitan Cyril acted authoritatively as Daniel's envoy to Hungary, where he even presided over the marriage of Daniel's son Leo to the daughter of Hungary's King Bela IV.[16]

Our sources are unanimous in affirming that Cyril, some time in 1248–9, eventually performed the required voyage to the patriarchate. He returned as 'Metropolitan of Kiev and all Russia', and as the only canonical heir of his Greek predecessors. This voyage and official ties with the patriarchate implied highly significant options not only for Cyril himself, but also for his sponsor, Grandprince Daniel, and, undoubtedly, for the whole of Russia. Having desperately, but unsuccessfully, called for Hungarian and Polish help against the Mongols, Daniel, in 1245–6, himself made a trip to the Golden Horde and paid obeisance to Khan Batu. This voyage certainly had ecclesiastical repercussions. The authority of Daniel's candidate for the metropolitan see, as the head of the

---

[14] For the date, see E. Golubinsky, *Istoriya*, p. 53.
[15] This view is taken for granted by historians of the Russian church Makary (*Istoriya* p. 8) and A. Kartashev (*Ocherki*, pp. 290–1).
[16] *Hyp.*, col. 809; Engl. tr. p. 59.

whole Church of Russia, depended politically upon his recognition of the Mongol rule, which extended over the rest of Russia, and, ecclesiastically, upon the ecumenical patriarch's approval. It is the fulfilment of these two mutually related conditions which allowed Cyril to win universal recognition as the sole legitimate head of the Church in Russia.[17]

But submission to the Tatars was not the last resort of the still powerful and diplomatically imaginative Daniel of Galicia. His continuous contacts with Hungary, Austria and the papacy are well-recorded in Russian and Western sources, and Metropolitan Cyril himself, as we have seen above, cooperated with some of his initiatives. In 1245, Daniel welcomed the visit of papal legate John of Pian de Carpini, who on his way to the Great Khan visited Russia. Papal appeals to ecclesiastical unity[18] and exchanges of embassies led to an offer by Pope Innocent IV of a king's crown to Daniel in 1248. A similar privilege had been accepted by Bulgarian and Serbian Orthodox rulers. Daniel, however, rejected the offer, specifically pointing to the fact that the pope was not in a position to protect him effectively against the Mongol armies.[19] His contacts with the pope had obtained for him, however, some immediate political and military advantages in his relations with his Hungarian, Polish and Lithuanian neighbours and the Teutonic Knights. Significantly, after his refusal of the papal offer, Metropolitan Cyril left for Nicaea, seeking his canonical confirmation by the Orthodox exiled patriarch.

In the following years, the contacts between Daniel and the papacy were resumed and led to his eventual acceptance of a king's crown (1253). We have no information as to whether Metropolitan Cyril was ever personally involved in negotiations with the pope. When papal envoy John of Pian de Carpini affirmed that in June 1247 Grand-prince Daniel and his brother Basil, 'with their bishops and other men of account', accepted to 'hold the pope for their special lord and father, and the Church of

---

[17] Besides Joasaph of Ugrovsk, who was rejected by Daniel, another competitor for the position of metropolitan emerged in the person of a Peter Akerovich, who attended the council of Lyons in 1245. Identified as *Archiepiscopus Ruthenus*, or *de Russia* (*Ann. Burt.*, MGH, *Scriptores*, Leipzig, 1925, 27, pp. 474), he is generally believed to be an appointee of Prince Michael of Chernigov, who was then in nominal control of Kiev and attempted (as Daniel of Galicia was also doing) to find friends in the West (cf. St. Tomashivsky, 'Predtecha Isidora Petro Akerovich, neznany mitropolit rus'kii', in *Annales ordinis S. Basilii Magni*, Jovkva, 1927, II, 3–4, pp. 221–313; also V. T. Pashuto, *Ocherki*, pp. 59–60).

[18] Pothast, *Regesta*, 12 094–12 098.

[19] *Hyp.*, cols. 826–7; Engl. tr. p. 67 (for chronology, see Pashuto, *op. cit.*, pp. 252–4)

Rome for their lady and mistress',[20] one should take his information with caution: nowhere else is there any evidence that Galicians and Volhynians or their Orthodox bishops were at that time ready to accept the faith of the Roman church. Rather, just as the Bulgarians and the Serbians did earlier in the century, they were interpreting papal jurisdiction in political terms, as a substitute for the apparently collapsing Byzantine *imperium*.[21] Already, in 1257, Pope Alexander IV (1254–61) was calling for a Crusade in Central Europe, including the Lithuanian 'pagans' and the Russian 'schismatics' among the enemies of the Cross and condemning Daniel for his 'betrayal' of the faith.[22] Clearly, the misunderstanding – if there ever was one, as to Daniel's religious allegiance – had been already dispelled and the canonical and ecclesiastical implications which the papacy required from the western Russian principalities had been rejected by the Russians.

Upon his confirmation by the patriarch, Metropolitan Cyril assumed, for over thirty years, the role which was that of his Greek predecessors: as head of the Church, he controlled the only administrative structure which covered the whole of Russia, from the Carpathian mountains to the upper Volga and from Novgorod to the Golden Horde. Being an appointee of Daniel of Galicia, he did not feel bound by the policies of his princely sponsor. Immediately upon his return from Nicaea, he travelled to Vladimir in the north-east (1250) and celebrated the marriage of Daniel's daughter with Andrew, Grand-prince of Vladimir. He visited Novgorod the next year (1251). His presence in northern Russia is mentioned so often in the chronicles, that he undoubtedly sojourned there for several consecutive years, establishing close ties with the leading political personality of the area, Alexander Yaroslavich 'Nevsky', who occupied successively the positions of prince of Novgorod (1240–52) and Grand-prince of Vladimir (1252–63). Metropolitan Cyril presided over Alexander's funeral in Vladimir (1263) and himself died in Pereyaslavl'-Zalessky in northern Russia (1281), after having held, also in Vladimir, an important council of all the Russian bishops (1274).[23] In fact,

---

[20] *Historia Mongolorum*, ed. Giorgio Pullé, Florence, 1913, p. 119; Engl. tr. in M. Komroff, *Contemporaries of Marco Polo*, New York, 1928, p. 50.

[21] See a good comparative discussion of the attitude of the various Eastern European nations in Obolensky, *Commonwealth*, pp. 240–1.

[22] Cf. N. Dashkevich, 'Peregovory papy s Daniilom Galitskim ob unii Yugo-zapadnoy Rusi s katolichestvom', in *Kiev, Universitet, Izvestiya*, 8, 1884, p. 175; cf. Pothast, *Regesta*, 16 700, 16 731.

[23] Cf. the dates of the major events of Cyril's tenure as metropolitan in E. Golubinsky, *Istoriya*, p. 57.

Cyril had transferred the centre of his activities as metropolitan to the north-east, an area under immediate Tatar suzerainty, and to Novgorod, which had just repulsed, under the leadership of Alexander Nevsky, the assault of the Teutonic Knights and the Swedes. The latter, in the name of Latin Christendom, had been crusading against the only areas of Russia which had remained free from Mongol control.

This decisive shift undertaken by Metropolitan Cyril could not possibly be a purely personal decision. Neither can it be said that the metropolitan was betraying the Galician Grand-prince, since he promoted the unity of the two princely families through matrimonial ties. A simple reference to the 'anti-Western' sympathies of Cyril is also insufficient. There is no evidence that he was systematically anti-Latin. Both in Byzantium and in Russia, the ecclesiastical leadership was never totally closed to negotiations with the papacy, although it was generally aware of the ephemeral and political character of unionist initiatives undertaken by East European emperors and princes. Cyril himself may have taken part in some of them, while he was still in Galicia. On the other hand, he kept a position of non-involvement at the time when, during his tenure as Metropolitan of Kiev and all Russia, his own ecclesiastical superior in Constantinople was the *Uniate* patriarch John Beccos (1275–82), an appointee of Emperor Michael VIII Palaeologus, who had accepted and enforced the Union of Lyons (1274) with Rome. During that period, the Russian metropolitanate kept normal relations with the patriarchate. In 1276, the bishop of Sarai, Theognostos, a suffragan of Metropolitan Cyril, was present at a meeting of the patriarchal synod presided over by John Beccos, and received official synodal answers to canonical and disciplinary questions raised in Russia without any reference to the patriarch's relations with the papacy.[24] However, the Russians did receive information about the events in Constantinople. In 1283, on the occasion of the election, in Constantinople, of Cyril's successor Maximus, the patriarch of Alexandria Athanasius II (who at that time was residing in Byzantium) wrote a solemn letter to Russia, reaffirming the orthodoxy of the patriarchate. Clearly, the appointment of Maximus was challenged on the grounds that the Greek Church was doctrinally insecure and

---

[24] The *Answers* of the Synod exist both in the Greek original (RIB, vi, *Prilozheniya*, 1, cols. 5–12) and in a Slavic version (ibid., 12, col. 129–40); cf. Grumel-Laurent, *Régestes*, i, fasc. IV, Paris, 1971, N. 1427, no. 213–15 (Sarai is erroneously located in the Crimea).

internally divided,[25] but since these protests had lost ground after the death of Emperor Michael VIII (1281), one can assume that the assurances given – in his capacity of an uninvolved third party – by the patriarch of Alexandria were amply sufficient to alleviate the Russian fears. Maximus assumed his position peacefully.

Clearly, in the case of Cyril, as in that of Grand-prince Alexander Nevsky, wider and long-term considerations of *Realpolitik* were decisive for the options they took in the second half of the thirteenth century. As a prince in Novgorod, Alexander led his armies in two decisive victories against Western Crusaders: the Swedes on the river Neva (1240) and the Teutonic Knights on Lake Chud' (Lake Peipus) (1242). Having been confirmed by Khan Batu to replace his father and his brother Andrew, as Grand-prince in Vladimir, he affirmed his loyalty to the Mongol ruler, who, unlike the Latin Crusaders, was fully tolerant of the religious inheritance of Russia and, more generally, of the cultural 'Commonwealth' of Byzantium, to which Russia belonged. As some modern historians have perceptively noted, Alexander's interests and policies were also those of the Nicaean empire, after it gained more strength and self-assurance under Emperor John Vatatzes. These policies were based on the following facts: the Mongol empire was there to stay; it had helpfully weakened the power of the Seljuq Turks, menacing Nicaea and Constantinople; it could be counted on, as a support against Western expansionism; it controlled the communication route between Byzantium and Russia; it was basically tolerant of the Orthodox Church. If Daniel of Galicia could be tempted by Western alliances, Alexander was geographically cut away from any power except that of the Golden Horde. As to Metropolitan Cyril, he was responsible for a flock whose vast majority was now on Alexander's (and the Golden Horde's) territories. The tradition and canonical ties between Byzantium and Russia, whose governments had parallel interest, could only be enhanced by a policy of loyalty to the Mongol empire.[26]

The Nicaean emperors had repeatedly made diplomatic attempts at reaching understanding with Western powers, i.e. primarily Emperor Frederick II and the papacy. But the Western struggle between the empire and the priesthood, as well as the ecclesiastically uncompromising stand of the papacy ruined the

---

[25] A. Failler, 'Le séjour d'Athanase II d'Alexandrie à Constantinople', REB, 35, 1977, pp. 43–71 (text of the letter of Athanasius II, pp. 59–63).

[26] The connection between the empire of Nicaea and Alexander Nevsky, realized primarily through the Church, was well seen by Priselkov, *Letopisanie*, pp. 104–5.

unionistic hopes of the exiled Byzantine court. In 1256, a round of negotiations between Pope Alexander IV and Emperor Theodore II Lascaris ended in failure,[27] and the Nicaean government moved in the direction of the alternate political option: agreement with the Mongols. A high level Tatar embassy was received by the emperor in Magnesia in 1257 and a Byzantine embassy went, almost immediately, to the Golden Horde.[28] The most obvious consequences of the negotiations occurred in Russia. The Mongol rule was consolidated and extended. It now included Novgorod (which had never been militarily occupied) and Galicia-Volhynia (where Grand-prince Daniel was forced to break his Western contacts). One cannot imagine that these developments took place without the active participation of Alexander Nevsky and Metropolitan Cyril.

The population of northern Russia was subjected to a Mongol census, with taxation in mind, but the Chronicle specifically affirms that 'abbots, monks, priests, members of the clergy and those who vow loyalty to the Holy Mother of God and the bishop' were not counted.[29] Ten years later, the new khan Mengu-Temir issued a decree (*yarlyk*), addressed to Metropolitan Cyril, which extended exemptions from taxation and granted other economic guarantees to the Church.[30] Furthermore, in 1261, a bishop suffragan of the metropolitan was appointed to Sarai itself, presiding over a community of the many Russians who lived at the khan's court, of Greek diplomats and merchants who travelled there frequently, and of other Orthodox Christian visitors to the court of the Golden Horde.[31]

In the light of these developments in Russia, one can even better understand the policies of Byzantine Emperor Michael Palaeologus in the latter part of his reign, when he became disillusioned with the possible results of his union with the pope in Lyons (1274) and turned to an alliance with the Mongols and

[27] V. Laurent, 'Le pape Alexandre IV (1254–1261) et l'empire de Nicée', EO, XXXIV, 1935, pp. 26–55.
[28] See M. A. Andreeva, 'Priem tatarskikh poslov pri Nikeiskom dvore', in *Sbornik statei posvyashchennykh pamyati N. P. Kondakova*, Prague, 1926, pp. 187–200.
[29] *Lavr.* 1257, PSRL, I, Moscow, 1962, col. 475.
[30] Priselkov, 'Yarlyki', p. 83 (text of the *yarlyk, ibid.*, pp. 96–8); cf. A. N. Nasonov, *Mongoly i Rus'*, 14–15; G. A. Fedorov-Davydov, *Obshchestvenyi stroi Zolotoi ordy*, Moscow, 1973, pp. 34–5.
[31] *Lavr*, col. 476; cf. a list of subsequent bishops of Sarai in Spuler, *Die Goldene Horde*, p. 231. On the international character of the diocese, see the *Answers* of the Synod of Constantinople to Theognostus of Sarai (1276) in RIB, VI, *Prilozheniya*, I, col. 10 (Visitors from Alania and Zecchia).

Genoa (see above, p. 36). We have seen above that the leadership of the Russian metropolitanate had ignored Michael's 'uniatism' and was following, even after the death of Grand-prince Alexander Nevsky (1263) a policy of loyalty to the Tatars and defensiveness against Western inroads. It may have played a role in exercising pressure upon Byzantium – on behalf of the khan – to turn the empire away from the papal alliance. The role of the bishop of Sarai (who may have been a Greek) and of the Russian metropolitan, in establishing diplomatic contacts between Byzantium and the Golden Horde is attested by the Russian sources. According to the 'Chronicle of Nikon', the bishop of Sarai Theognostos, was sent to Constantinople 'by the most holy Cyril, Metropolitan of Kiev and all the Rus', and by the khan [*tsar' Ordynsky*] Mengu-Temir, to the patriarch and to the Emperor Michael Palaeologus of Greece'. He was carrying 'letters' and 'gifts' both from the metropolitan and the khan.[32] There can be hardly any doubt that these letters were related to the support given to Michael by the Mongols against his Angevin and Venetian enemies. Upon the emperor's death in December 1282, union with Rome was immediately disavowed and the patriarchate of Constantinople returned to Orthodoxy. Cyril's successor, Maximus, a Greek, travelled to the Horde immediately upon his accession to the position of metropolitan in 1283.

In the year 1300, the same metropolitan, keeping the traditional title of 'Kiev and all the Rus'' established his permanent residence in Vladimir, in northern Russia,[33] where he died in 1305. This event – already prepared by the activity of Cyril – was the source of future and important developments which were to mark the fourteenth century.

The establishment of the Latin empire in 1204 and the Mongol invasion of Eastern Europe signalled the end of Byzantium as a political, economic and military power. Even after the recapture of Constantinople by Michael Palaeologus in 1261, the empire was to remain a minor state with its commerce monopolized by the Genoese and with the new nation-states of Serbia and Bulgaria, as well as Latin principalities, established on its former territories in

---

[32] PSRL, x, Moscow, 1965, p. 157; on the important role of the metropolitanate as a channel of communication between the Golden Horde and Byzantium, see A. N. Nasonov, *op. cit.*, pp. 39, 45.

[33] *Lavr.*, PSRL, I, col. 485. The Chronicle specifies that the travel of the metropolitan to Northern Russia was not a simple pastoral visitation, as in the case of Cyril, but that Tatar devastations made his sojourn in Kiev impossible and that he moved to Vladimir 'with his entire court' ('*so vsem svoim zhitiem*').

the Balkans. Byzantine influence now depended only on the traditional prestige of the 'imperial city', and on its artistic and cultural creativity, which the Slavic nations continued to recognize and admire above any other. However, there cannot be any doubt that the Church was the major channel of the spiritual and cultural ties uniting Constantinople, the Balkan nations and Russia. The history of the 'Metropolitanate of the Rus″', which continued to exercise its jurisdiction over the whole of Russia and obtained a unique position vis-à-vis the Golden Horde, strikingly demonstrates that religious and cultural values, carried through Byzantium, possessed a strong capacity for survival. It also prefigures, already in the thirteenth century, the Byzantine ecclesiastical policies of the fourteenth: while frequently probing opportunities for Church union with the papacy and for political alliances in the West, Byzantium – and especially Byzantine churchmen – tended to prefer a long-term policy of spiritual independence from the West. Culturally and religiously, they felt less threatened by Mongols and Turks than by the papacy, the Teutonic Knights and the monarchies of Central Europe.

3

The Mongols, their Western neighbours
and Russian subjects

By 1300, the Mongol khanate of Kypchak, with its capital in Sarai on the lower Volga (also known as 'Golden Horde') stood firmly in control of what today is European Russia. The presence of its power on the eastern, northern and north-western shores of the Black Sea placed the Mongols in direct contact with Byzantium and the Italian city-republics of Genoa and Venice, which had established prosperous trading centres in the Crimea. The Crimean peninsula itself was governed by a Tatar emir, residing in Solgat, or Krim (east of Caffa). The western borders of the Tatar empire were not very precise: Bulgaria, Hungary, Poland and Lithuania had either experienced, for various lengths of time, the Mongol conquest, or paid tribute to the khans, but the stabilized situation, which prevailed in the early fourteenth century, left these countries in an attitude of apprehensive independence. The western Russian principalities were drawn into the orbit of Poland or Lithuania, as an alternative to the Tatar yoke. The presence, in the Baltic region, of territories under the control of Teutonic Knights was another disturbing factor, which was to play a significant role in Lithuanian, Polish and Russian political and religious attitudes. We shall briefly discuss the factors which, in each of these regions, were particularly significant in determining the fate of Byzantino-Russian relations.

I. THE AREA OF THE BLACK SEA

A grandson of Batu, Khan Mengu-Temir (Mongka-Temür) assumed power in the Golden Horde in 1266. In Russia, he was faced with no opposition and could afford to be liberal: the Chronicle signals that, upon his accession, 'the Rus' received relief from oppression by the impious'.[1] The new khan also took

[1] *Troits.*, p. 329.

constructive measures to assure economic prosperity, which, for the Golden Horde, was largely based on trade. The commercial city of Novgorod, which assured a connection with the Baltic and which was never militarily occupied by the Mongols, but whose princes were appointed with the khan's confirmation, received guarantees of its freedoms and privileges.[2] Mengu-Temir was also concerned with the trade route to the Mediterranean, which passed through the Black Sea and Byzantium. In March 1261, by the treaty of Nymphaeum, the Genoese had received a privileged position in Constantinople, soon to be recovered by Emperor Michael VIII[3] and, in spite of the vicissitudes of their relations with the Byzantines and the fierce competition of the Venetians, succeeded in preserving effective predominance in the Black Sea throughout most of the fourteenth century. Some time after his accession, in 1266, Mengu-Temir granted permission to establish in the Crimea the famous Genoese trading post of Caffa.[4] However, the main commercial contacts between the Italian merchants, the Byzantines and the Mongol empire continued through the nearby Crimean commercial port of Sougdaia (Ital.: Soldaia; Russian: Surozh; Mongol: Sudak), an ancient Greek settlement with Greek, Russian and Armenian population, controlled by the Tatars since 1223.[5]

The predominance of the Genoese over the Black Sea trade in slaves, wheat and products of India, Persia and China, brought by caravans through Sarai, was assured, on the one hand, by their permanent holding of Galata, the area beyond the Golden Horn, in Constantinople itself, which was ceded to them by Emperor Michael VIII, and on the other hand, by the Mongol military control of the trade routes. Genoese power was, therefore, based on the double alliance with Byzantium and the Tatars and gave Genoa the control of the Black Sea which had become (after the closing of other commercial routes towards the East) the nerve centre of the European economic system of trade.

In the case of Byzantium, the alliance looked more like a unilateral dependence of an enfeebled empire upon the powerful

---

[2] Vernadsky, *Mongols.*, pp. 170–1.
[3] Dölger, *Regesten*, I, 3, No. 1889, pp. 36–8.
[4] The grant is mentioned by Nicephorus Gregoras, *Hist.*, ed. Bonn, II, pp. 683–4; for the probable date, see Heyd, *Commerce*, pp. 158–63; also M. Nystazopoulou, 'Ἡ ἐν τῇ ταυρικῇ Χερσονήσῳ πόλις Σουγδαίας ἀπὸ τοῦ ΙΓ μέχρι τοῦ ΙΕ αἰώνος, Athens, 1965, pp. 30–1.
[5] Cf. G. I. Bratianu, *Recherches sur le commerce génois dans la Mer Noire au XIIIe siècle*, Paris, 1929, pp. 200–205; M. Nystazopoulou, *op. cit.*, 29–40.

Italian merchants. However, in the framework of his infinitely subtle and complicated diplomatic game, Michael VIII – who himself had been obliged to assign the trade monopoly to the Genoese, in order to obtain this support against the Latin empire, supported by Venice – tried to disengage himself from the Genoese grip after his recapture of Constantinople. In 1265, he opened the Black Sea to the Venetians in a formal treaty (contradicting his former commitment to the Genoese). Venice profited much from the arrangement, but had to face an armed conflict with Genoa. In 1296, the Venetian fleet was able to capture Caffa and hold it for three years.[6] It never gave up its interests in the region and obtained, from Khan Uzbek, the concession of a special quarter in the commercial city of Tana, the modern Azov, at the mouth of the river Don (1332). In the same year, the city of Vosporo, on the 'Cimmerian Bosphorus' (on the eastern tip of the Crimean peninsula) was also ceded to the Venetians who needed it as an outpost of Tana.[7] Venetians and Genoese fought repeatedly against each other (in 1352–5, and again in 1376–81), and their ruthless competition had immediate repercussions in Byzantine internal policies and dynastic struggles, since both Italian republics strived to obtain the support of the Byzantine court. Often, the only real political leverage left to the Byzantine government was to play the Italians against each other. Practically, however, at least until the peace of Turin (1381), the Genoese kept the upper hand in this competition and succeeded in keeping their fortified posts in Galata until the Turkish conquest (1453), and Caffa until 1475.[8]

The attitude of the Mongols towards the Italian settlement was not always consistent. In the late thirteenth century, the powerful Khan Nogay, who was technically dependent upon the khans of Kypchak (Sarai), but who, in fact, ruled an independent empire on the northern shores of the Black Sea and had an independent foreign policy, supported the Venetians against the Genoese allies of Sarai, until his armies were defeated by Khan Tokhta (1299–1300).[9] But the victorious Tokhta, suddenly angry at the slave trade practised by the Genoese and which certainly involved his own subjects being sold in the Middle East markets, arrested the Genoese merchants in Sarai (1307) and burnt down Caffa (1308). The city was rebuilt by the Genoese under Tokhta's successor

[6] Heyd, *op. cit.*, pp. 168–70.   [7] *Ibid.*, p. 184.
[8] E. Ch. Skrzhinskaya, 'Genueztsy v Konstantinople v XIV-m veke', VV I (XXVI), 1947, p. 233.
[9] Vernadsky, *op. cit.*, pp. 188–9.

Uzbek. In 1343, the murder of a Tatar official in Tana provoked reprisals on the part of Khan Djanibek, who expelled the Italians from Tana and besieged Caffa. The siege, however, ended in failure. Eventually, the alliance between the Mongols and the Genoese, based on obvious common interest, was restored, but the loss of Tana had long lasting economic effects in Western Europe.[10]

The establishment of the Italian colonies in the Black Sea involved also the presence of Latin ecclesiastics and missionaries in the area.[11] Just as the numerous papal missions to the Mongols pursued simultaneously diplomatic and missionary goals, the appointment of ecclesiastical officials for the Italian settlements responded both to concrete pastoral needs and to wider considerations of ecclesiastical diplomacy. In the Crimean peninsula, whereas Sougdaia (Soldaia, Surozh) remained the seat of a Greek Orthodox metropolitan, a bull of Pope John XXII, dated 1318, mentions the establishment of a Latin bishop in Caffa and later (1322) extends his jurisdiction to a vast territory extending from Sarai to Varna in Bulgaria. The first incumbent was a Franciscan monk, Jerome.[12] The same pope John XXII, in the very year when the Venetians obtained their concession in the Eastern Crimea (1333), set up a metropolitanate in 'Vosporo' (the 'Cimmerian Bosphorus').[13] In the same year, the presence of the Englishman Geraldus, as bishop in Sebastopolis, on the eastern coast of the Black Sea,[14] in the vicinity of the Byzantine metropolitanates of Zecchia and Alania, shows how closely interconnected were the Byzantine and Latin establishments in the area. In 1357 and 1365 respectively, the cities of Cembalo (Συμβόλων λιμήν) and Sougdaia were taken by the Genoese and Latin bishoprics were established there also.

In terms of the relations between Byzantium and Russia, the Italian settlements on the shores of the Black Sea are of central importance for geographical, economical, political and religious reasons. Throughout the fourteenth century, merchants, ambassadors, ecclesiastical officials and pilgrims travelling between Constantinople and northern Russia almost inevitably took the route through Sarai, Tana, Caffa and Sougdaia: their accounts constitute one of the major sources for the period. On the other hand,

---

[10] Heyd, *op. cit.*, pp. 187–8.
[11] On these ecclesiastical settlements, see primarily R. Loenertz, *La Société des frères pérégrinants. Etudes sur l'Orient dominicain*, I, Rome, 1937, pp. 88–134.
[12] Heyd, *op. cit.*, pp. 172–3.   [13] Raynaldi, *Annales*, 1333, No. 17, 36, 37.
[14] Raynaldi, *Annales*, 1330, No. 57.

the economic and political ties, which linked the khanate of Kypchak with the Genoese – who also exercised practical control on the economic life of the Byzantine empire – had inevitable repercussions in both Byzantium and Russia, since the Genoese were in a powerful position to pursue their interests both in Constantinople and in Sarai. The ecclesiastical officials sent by the pope to the East maintained channels of communications in the ever recurring union negotiations between Byzantium and Rome. Whereas, since the fall of the Latin empire, papal representatives exercised no direct power over Eastern Christians, they more often gave Byzantine ecclesiastics and theologians a more intellectual image of the Latin West. The Dominican order, particularly, with its Thomistic tradition, led the Latin side in theological debates with the Greeks. In 1334, during a stay in Constantinople, the Dominican Francesco da Cammerino, appointed by Pope John XXII to the newly erected metropolitanate of the 'Bosphorus' (Vosporo, the contemporary Kerch), together with another Dominican, Richard of England, bishop of Kherson or 'Khersonesos'[15] conducted lengthy debates with Nicephorus Gregoras and Barlaam the Calabrian, successively appointed spokesmen for the Greek side.[16] The Dominican convent of Genoese Galata also served as a school of Latin language and theology to a young Byzantine diplomat and intellectual, Demetrios Kydones, who soon voiced his astonishment at the discovery that, among Latins, one can find not only ruthless warriors (like the Frankish Crusaders), or ingenious merchants (like the Italian traders), but also learned people, able to appreciate, better than the Byzantines themselves, the refinements of ancient Greek philosophy.[17] The emergence in Byzantium of an articulate and convinced party of 'latinophrones', favouring union with Rome, was closely connected with the presence of Italian merchants in the area and represented a substantial factor in Byzantine history, making possible the conversion of Emperor John V (1369) and, eventually, the council of Florence with its well-known impact on Byzantino-Russian relations.

[15] Cf. R. Loenertz, *op. cit.*, pp. 128–30; also C. Gianelli, 'È Francesco Petrarca e un altro Francesco, e quale, il destinatorio del "De primatu papae" di Barlaam Calabro?' in *Scripta minora* (*Studi bizantini e neoellenici*, 10), Rome, 1963, pp. 189–201.
[16] On these debates see Gregoras, *Hist.*, ed. Bonn, I, 501–4; M. Jugie, 'Barlaam de Seminaria', DHGE, VI, 817–34; J. Meyendorff, 'Un mauvais théologien de l'unité: Barlaam le Calabrais', in *1054–1954: L'Eglise et les églises*, Chévetogne, 1955 (repr. in J. Meyendorff, *Byzantine Hesychasm*, Variorum, London, 1974).
[17] *Apologia* I, in Mercati, *Notizie*, p. 365.

This 'opening to the West' spurred in Byzantium by the presence of constant economic and intellectual ties with the Italians, had no parallel in Russia, which had been cut off from the West by the Tatar yoke. We shall also see that, throughout the fourteenth century, the Genoese, allied to the khanate of Kypchak, were to be interested in perpetuating Mongol control over Russia and, indirectly, discouraging pro-Western tendencies.

2. GERMAN KNIGHTS ON THE BALTIC

The Eastern shores of the Baltic Sea were the last region of Europe to accept Christianization. The peoples of the area belonged neither to the Germanic, nor to the Slavic linguistic groups. The Prussians, Lithuanians and Letts formed a separate Indo-European group, whereas the Ests and Finns spoke a 'Finnougric' (therefore Turkic, or Mongolian) language. It appears that Eastern Christianity, coming from the prosperous centre of Novgorod, had penetrated the region, especially in Eastern Finland (Karelia) and Estonia since the eleventh century.[18] However, in the late twelfth and, particularly the thirteenth centuries, a large-scale offensive, both religious and military, sponsored by the papacy, but also actively supported by the kingdoms of Sweden, Denmark, and Germany, extended Latin Christendom to the Baltic region. The brutal military force used to affirm the supremacy of Western Christianity – which paralleled exactly the Crusaders' conquests in the Middle East and the capture of Constantinople in 1204 – provoked a long-lasting reaction among both the pagan populations of the area (which survived for two more centuries) and the Eastern Orthodox.

In Finland, Christianization meant forceful incorporation – both political and cultural – into the kingdom of Sweden. This was effected militarily in the thirteenth century. In the regions lying to the south of the Gulf of Finland, the initiative belonged to the Germans. The city of Riga, founded around 1198 by merchants from Bremen, became the centre of missionary expansion. Heading a Crusading army of Germans and Danes, the German bishop Albert landed there[19] and, in 1207, was recognized by the

---

[18] Cf. Heiki Kirkinen, *Karjala idän kulttuuripiirissä*, Kirjayhtymä, Helsinki, 1963, p. 71. (I am indebted to Professor Kirkinen and to Mr Rauno Pietarinen for this reference.)

[19] Cf. G. Gnegel-Waitschies, *Bischof Albert von Riga. Ein Brenner Domherr als Kirchenfürst im Osten*, Hamburg, 1958.

Hohenstaufen as feudal prince over the whole of Latvia. In order to expand his power, he founded a new religious and military order, the Knights of the Sword, also known as Livonian Knights, dedicated to the conversion of the pagans. Disquieted by Albert's connection with the Hohenstaufen, Pope Innocent III separated the diocese of Riga from the metropolitanate of Bremen and submitted it directly to Rome. He also established his direct control over the Knights (1204). In Estonia also, the originally Russian city of Yuryev (Dorpat, Derpt – the modern Tartu), became the seat of a German bishop.

The subsequent and long history of the German Knights who came to exercise, in the Baltic region, a power largely independent from the local Latin ecclesiastical hierarchy and indiscriminately hostile to both local paganism and Eastern Orthodoxy, became a decisive element in the political and religious history of Russia, as well.

The original Livonian Order, formed in Riga, was eventually strengthened by powerful newcomers: the Teutonic Knights. Originated by German nobles fighting in Palestine (1191–8), the Order created a number of chapters in Germany and, in 1226, was invited by the Polish Duke Conrad of Mazovia to fight against the Prussians, a Baltic nation, neighbouring Catholic Poland. Having accepted the invitation, the Knights proceeded with the conquest of Prussia. By 1249, the land of the subjugated Prussians became the property of the Order. At that time, under the patronage of the Roman Curia, the Teutonic Order merged with the Knights of the Sword, so that the entire Baltic region, from Pomerania to Estonia, came under the control of a single Order of Knights, who were followed by German colonists. From their fortified towns and military posts, the Knights ruled the indigenous, formally Christianized population and waged constant warfare against their neighbours, particularly the Orthodox Russians and the pagan Lithuanians. We have noted earlier how this Crusade against the East was met by the Novgorodian Grand-prince Alexander 'Nevsky', who stopped the Swedes on the river Neva (1240) and won a second victory over the Knights on Lake Peipus, or Chud' (1242). As Grand-prince of Vladimir, Alexander had no real political alternative than loyalty to the khan of Kypchak, however unattractive the Tatar yoke may have been for the Russians. The Crusading spirit of the Swedes and, particularly, the German Knights had thus provoked, on the part of the Russians, a reaction in all things similar to the reaction of the

Greeks to the sack of Constantinople: Western Latin Christianity became identified with conquest by Crusading armies and forceful integration in a foreign civilization.[20] It is significant to note that those Orthodox countries which avoided facing direct conquest by the Crusaders – Bulgaria, Serbia and Galicia-Volhynia – were much more open to Western contacts and, all of them, even accepted (however briefly) the political overlordship of the papacy.[21] Here lies one of the keys to the understanding of the relations between Byzantium and Moscow in the fourteenth century, as opposed to the more cautious attitude of Orthodox Byzantium towards western Russian principalities of that period. The assumption by the medieval papacy, after its victory over the *imperium*, of political leadership in Latin Christendom, and, therefore, the endorsement by the pope of military conquest, as legitimate tool of Christian 'mission' among the Muslims and pagans, and of Latin expansion among Eastern Christians, ruined existing opportunities for rapprochement. The papal appeals for a Christian alliance against the Mongols, however sincere, sounded unconvincing, particularly in the Baltic region, where papal endorsements and encouragements went to the brutal imperialism of German knights and colonists in their struggle against local pagans and Orthodox Russians.

Reaction against the Knights' offensive came not only from the northern Russian principalities, but also from the Lithuanians, the last European nation to remain pagan in the thirteenth century.

3. THE RISE OF LITHUANIA

Double resistance to the Mongolian onslaught from the East and to the German *Drang nach Osten* from the West transformed scattered Lithuanian tribes into a powerful unified and multicultural nation, whose grand-princes eventually provided shelter and protection to Russian lands, liberated from the Tatar yoke.

From the very beginning of the German penetration in the Baltic region, the Lithuanians appeared as the most dangerous

---

[20] The otherwise very well-informed study by A. M. Ammann, *Kirchen-politische Wandlungen im Ostbaltikum bis zum Tode Alexander Newskis. Studien zum Werden der Russischen Orthodoxie* (Orientalia Christiana Analecta 105), Rome, 1936, shows total insensibility to that aspect of the problem in its criticism of the options taken by Alexander.

[21] The difference of attitude, in this respect, between Alexander Nevsky and Daniel of Galicia is well shown by Vernadsky, *Mongols*, pp. 148–50. We have discussed this in the preceding chapter.

enemy. It is a resounding defeat of the Livonian Knights by the Lithuanians (1236) which prompted, in 1237, the merger of the Livonian and the Teutonic orders. On the other hand, the struggle against the Knights and their Polish allies often brought about an alliance between pagan Lithuanians and Orthodox Russians.[22] The unification of Lithuania was primarily the work of the Grand-prince Mindovg (early 1230s–1263). During the first decades of his reign, Western Crusaders seemed to have the upper hand in the region. The pressure of the Order, initial military defeats and rebellions of his own tribal leaders forced Mindovg into searching for accommodation with the Germans. In 1250, he concluded an agreement with the Grand Master of the Order, sending him 'many gifts' and accepting 'to send envoys to the Pope and be baptized'.[23] The baptism actually took place, presumably in 1251. Mindovg also received a kingly crown from the pope, and reversed his previous alliances, accompanying the Knights in a campaign against Galicia. In 1253, as we have seen earlier, Daniel of Galicia himself received a king's crown from Rome. The alliance between Mindovg and Daniel – apparently in the framework of a general acceptance of papal suzerainty – was sealed by a marriage between Daniel's and Mindovg's children. Under the new situation, Mindovg was in a position to exercise supremacy over the Russian principalities of Polotsk and Smolensk and even attempt a march on Kiev.

In 1258–9, however, his policies changed as Lithuania encountered the Mongols face to face. The fact that Batu's armies had plundered territories to the east and south of Lithuania, but not Lithuania itself, was probably due to pure chance. But the new ambitions of Grand-prince Mindovg and his deliberate intention to annex Russian principalities provoked the wrath of the Golden Horde. Khan Berke sent his general Burunday against Lithuania, formally ordering Daniel of Galicia and other West-Russian princes to fight with them. The Novgorodian Chronicle may not be correct in stating that the Tatars 'took the entire Lithuanian land and killed the people':[24] Mindovg seems to have avoided a decisive defeat and Burunday's raid resulted mainly in an even greater subjugation of Galicia and Volhynia to Mongol control. The Lithuanian Grand-prince even profited from the new situa-

---

[22] See in particular their reaction vs. the expedition of the Knights and Poles into Volhynia in 1337–8 (*Hyp.*, col. 776; tr., p. 44).

[23] *Hyp.*, col. 816–17 (tr., p. 63).

[24] *Novg.*, p. 310; tr., p. 96.

tion in assuming control of more Russian lands.[25] But he was forced to reverse his alliances again and decisively break with the Order. In 1260, he inflicted upon the Knights a smashing defeat in Durba and concluded an anti-German alliance with Grand-prince Alexander Nevsky of Vladimir. He also formally renounced Roman Catholic Christianity. The West-Russian Chronicle is certainly right in characterizing his conversion of 1251 as politically motivated and hypocritical.[26]

Grand-prince Mindovg was assassinated in 1263 by Lithuanian nobles opposed to his policy of unification, but his achievements were of lasting significance. Throughout the remainder of the thirteenth century and most of the fourteenth, the unified Lithuanian Grand-principality remained strong enough to resist both the German conquest and Mongol control. Its ruling dynasty remained pagan, but its contacts with the West and its ever-expanding control over Russian principalities with an Orthodox Christian population increasingly showed Lithuanian paganism as historically anachronistic. Conversion to Christianity was more and more felt as inevitable, but it presented the Lithuanian princes with an inevitable choice between East and West. This religious dilemma facing Lithuania was also a cultural and political one. And since the Lithuanian Grand-principality played a crucial role in Russian history throughout the fourteenth century, the religious policies of its Grand-princes also influenced Byzantino-Russian relations.

Already in the thirteenth century, some Lithuanian nobles were baptized in the Orthodox Church: in 1265-6, Prince Dovmont 'with 300 Lithuanians, and women and children'[27] arrived in Pskov, was baptized an Orthodox Christian, and, soon, assumed princely power in that Russian city-republic, leading Pskov's armies against the neighbouring German Knights and, also, his fellow-Lithuanians.[28] Throughout the fourteenth century, other Lithuanian leaders seemed quite open to the idea of entering the 'Byzantine Commonwealth', through the mediation of the Orthodox Church. However, the adoption of the Orthodox faith by the

---

[25] See Pashuto, *Obrazovanie*, pp. 381–2.
[26] 'His baptism was fake, for he secretly continued to offer sacrifice to his gods', *Hyp.*, *ibid.*
[27] *Novg.*, p. 85; tr., p. 99–100.
[28] Dovmont was canonized by the Orthodox Church; cf. his fourteenth-century *Life* in N. I. Serebryansky, *Drevne-russkiya Knyazheskiya zhitiya* (Chteniya v obshchestve Istorii i Drevnostei Rossiiskikh pri Moskovskom Universitete, III), Moscow 1915, pp. 138–56.

entire Lithuanian nation would, in practical terms, have meant entering the orbit of the Mongol empire through the agency of Moscow, which had become the residence of the Metropolitan of Kiev and all the Rus'. Hence the preoccupation of the Lithuanian Grand-princes with obtaining from Byzantium a separate metropolitan for Lithuania – a major issue of the fourteenth century, which will be discussed below.

The alternative of the Western option was even more unattractive since it meant domination by the German Knights, the most immediate enemies of the Lithuanians. As we have seen earlier, Mindovg was forced to accept the Western Latin option for a brief period, under the direct pressure of the Knights. His successors, however, extensively utilized the political opportunity offered by the open conflict between the Order, on the one hand, and the Archbishop of Riga and Riga's municipal government on the other. For the brutality of the Knights' rule was resented not only by their Orthodox Russian and pagan Lithuanian neighbours, but by their fellow Latins as well. On the other hand, the respective powers and economic rights of the Order and the prince-bishop of Riga – each directly dependent upon Rome and the German empire – were not clearly defined. The Lithuanians actively supported the Archbishop and the city and, in 1298, the ambassadors of Lithuanian Grand-prince Viten, arriving in Riga, offered their own conversion to the Roman Catholic faith and political alliance against the Knights, clearly hoping for papal support.[29] These plans were crushed for a time by a military victory of the Order, but, around 1309, another document draws light upon political and religious opportunities which were connected with the permanent conflict between Riga and the Order: a letter of John, the Orthodox bishop (and suffragan of the Greek metropolitan of Kiev) of the Lithuanian-held Russian city of Polotsk, addresses the city-council of Riga as his 'children' and mentions Grand-prince Viten as his 'son'; he salutes and bestows his blessing upon the inhabitants of Riga and asks for their friendship.[30] This letter, together with other later witnesses, illustrates the atmosphere of religious tolerance in Lithuania, in contrast with the iron rule of the Order. Pope Clement V himself briefly supported the plea of Riga against the Knights, who were even for

---

[29] On these negotiations see particularly V. G. Vasilievsky, 'Obrashchenie Gedimina v katolichestvo' in *Zh. M. N. P.*, 159, St Petersburg, 1872, p. 148.
[30] *Ibid.*, p. 151.

a short period (1312–13) placed under papal interdict, but no ultimate solution was given to the conflict and the Order kept its power on the Baltic.

Viten's successor Gedymin (1316–41) was an authentic empire-builder. Not only did he reinforce the Grand-principality inherited from Mindovg, but he greatly extended his dominion upon Russian territories previously controlled by the khanate of Kypchak: the principalities of Minsk, Pinsk, Turov, Brest and Vitebsk – the whole of contemporary Byelorussia, or 'White Russia' – accepted his suzerainty, whereas Polotsk and 'Black Russia' had been conquered already by Mindovg. Gedymin also actively supported Pskov against the Knights and succeeded in imposing his son, Narimunt, as prince of Novgorod. In 1340, his other son Lubart became prince of Volhynia. Several of his daughters married Russian princes, the most important of these marriages being that of his daughter Maria with Dimitri Aleksandrovich of Tver. In his correspondence, he assumed the title of 'King of Lithuanians and Russians' (*Lethowinorum Ruthenorumque rex*). Religiously, Eastern Orthodoxy was gradually becoming the dominant confession of his domain: his children were adopting it, as they were marrying Russian princesses and assuming princely positions in Russian lands, and his pagan subjects became subjected to the gradual influence of the Orthodox Christian majority.

Nevertheless, there is no record showing that Gedymin himself seriously envisaged joining the Orthodox Church, whereas in 1323–4 a conversion to Roman Catholicism seemed clearly in the making. The Lithuanian ruler must have felt personal attraction to Latin Christendom and Western Europe and, as was the case with Mindovg and Viten, he considered that a conversion to Roman Catholicism was the surest means for diverting the constant menace of the Teutonic Knights. His predicament was actually the same as that of Byzantine Emperor Michael Palaeologus, who also sought in Rome protection against the Crusading zeal of Charles of Anjou.

In 1322, Gedymin addressed himself to Pope John XXII in Avignon, voicing virulent complaints against the Order, expressing his friendship and solidarity with the city of Riga, as another victim of the Knights, reporting his benevolence towards Roman Catholicism, informing the pope that he had built two churches in his new capital of Vilna and, finally, requesting that papal legates be sent to Lithuania. Similar letters were sent to German cities and the two religious orders of the Dominicans and the

Franciscans, whose missionaries were active in Lithuania.[31] The result of Gedymin's initiative was a temporary peace with the Germans, but the Lithuanian Grand-prince stopped short of embracing Roman Catholicism himself: the legates, who arrived in Vilna in 1324, were informed that Gedymin had changed his mind. According to the report of the legation, he even avoided a second meeting with them under the pretext that 'he was busy with the Tatars'.[32]

This interesting reference to the Mongols unveils the extent of Gedymin's political dilemma. It is clear that an eventual integration of Lithuania into the Western European family of states would have been opposed not only by the Russian Orthodox subjects of the Lithuanian Grand-prince, but more importantly by the khanate of Kypchak. Lithuania's interests in Mongol-controlled Russia were too important to be neglected by Gedymin for the sake of a Western religious commitment: the opportunity for maintaining and expanding political, economic and cultural ties which Lithuania possessed in Pskov, in Novgorod and, particularly, in Tver, depended upon some diplomatic contacts with the Horde, the alternative being a direct military confrontation with the Mongols. Meanwhile, the khan was jealously preventing his Russian subjects from friendly contacts with the West. Among the accusations levelled against the Grand-prince Michael I of Tver, as he was first officially tried, then executed by Khan Uzbek (1319) was that 'he planned to escape to the Germans with his treasure, and had sent money to the pope in Rome'.[33] This bloody affirmation of Tatar rule over Tver, with its anti-Western implications, was, however, followed, in 1320, by a marriage between Michael's son and successor Dimitri with Gedymin's daughter Maria.[34] In 1321, Dimitri travelled to the Horde and was appointed Grand-prince of Vladimir by Uzbek, superseding his Muscovite competitor: the Russian Chronicle emphasizes that Uzbek at that time 'respected' Dimitri, who

---

[31] On these events, see V. Vasilievsky, *op. cit.*, 152–61; also Pashuto, *Obrazovanie*, pp. 42–21; H. Spliet, *Die Briefe Gedimins. Ein Beitrag zur Geschichte der Stadt Riga*, Sinsheim, 1953.

[32] *Nam cum tartaris erat impeditus*, Report of the legates in *Russko-Litovskie Akty*, ed. K. E. Napiersky, St Petersburg, 1868 (quoted in V. G. Vasilievsky, *op. cit.*, p. 192).

[33] *Nik.*, p. 183. The 'Peter's Pence', sent to Rome by medieval rulers was a sign of their subjection to the pope. No other source confirms that Michael of Tver did indeed accomplish this gesture. The accusation brought against him may have been false.

[34] *Rog.*, col. 41.

repeatedly travelled to Sarai.[35] On the other hand, one also learns that precisely during (or immediately following) Gedymin's contacts with the papacy and his negotiations with the Order, 'Khan Uzbek sent [Russian] princes against the Lithuanians; they hurt Lithuania very much and returned to the Horde with many prisoners.'[36] One can therefore understand why the Lithuanian Grand-prince broke off his negotiations with the papal legates, being 'busy with the Tatars' and concerned with maintaining his son-in-law on the crucially important Grand-principality of Vladimir: contacts with the pope and diplomatic relations with the Horde were mutually exclusive.

Throughout the fourteenth century, Lithuania faced the dilemma which confronted Gedymin. Expansion in Russian lands, which gradually developed into the ambition of uniting the entire Kievan domain under the Lithuanian realm, would have implied a pro-Byzantine religious and ideological stand and required some military or diplomatic handling of the Tatar domination. Meanwhile, the Western solution for Lithuanian identity was continuously made unattractive by its inevitable implication of German imperialism. Another alternative however emerged with the rise of Poland, a Slavic land which embraced Latin Christianity and with a tradition of feudal decentralization, similar to the one which prevailed in Lithuania and in Kievan Russia.

4. POLAND TURNS TO THE EAST

Divided between princes of the Piast dynasty, Poland, throughout the thirteenth century, saw the rise of the powerful, and sometimes threatening neighbours: Hungary, the Russian Grand-principality of Galicia, the pagan Prussians and Lithuanians. German colonization of western and north-western Polish lands was mightily supported by the arrival of the Teutonic Knights, called by the Polish prince Conrad of Mazovia to fight the Prussians.

In 1241, at Lignica in Silesia, one of Batu's generals, Subudey, defeated an army of Polish princes, led by Henry the Pious (who was killed in battle), but the Mongols did not occupy Poland permanently. In the long run, the Mongol invasion was propitious to Poland in the sense that it eliminated Russian principalities, as Poland's competitors, and gave the Poles a feeling of becoming the last frontier of European civilization, opposed to the barbarians

[35] *Nik.*, pp. 188, 189. Dimitri, however, was eventually executed by the Tatars, as was his father (1325).
[36] *Nik.*, p. 189.

of the East. In 1320, the long period of national disunity ended, when, with the active support of the pope, to whom he expressed full loyalty, Ladislas (Władisław) Łokietek was crowned king in Cracow. Pope John XXII, who had supported the Archbishop of Riga and the Lithuanian Grand-prince Gedymin, against the encroachment of the Teutonic Order, gave similar support to Ladislas by recognizing him ruler of Pomerania. In 1325, Casimir, son of Ladislas, married Gedymin's daughter Aldona, and a formal alliance was concluded between Poland and Lithuania.[37] From 1328 to 1331, the German Knights and their ally, the king of Bohemia, conducted a successful war against Poland, which lost valuable territories. The common interests of Poland and Lithuania in defending their lands against the German *Drang nach Osten* contributed to a long-lasting rapprochement between the two countries. Later history will show that the cause of Western Christendom was certainly better served by this alliance, than by the Crusading spirit of the Knights. 'The main obstacle to any peaceful conversion of Lithuania [to Roman Catholicism] came . . . from the Teutonic Order, who wished to combine such a conversion with a political submission of the country to German control, while the Lithuanian rulers hoped that when accepting the Christian faith they would be rewarded by the return of the territories formerly conquered by the Teutonic Knights.'[38] The return of Pomerania, lost to the Knights, was similarly hoped for by Poland.

The reign of Casimir the Great (1333–70) established Poland as a major power in Europe and as a largely centralized monarchy. The western borders of the *regnum Poloniae* were fixed, on the one hand, by Casimir's forced acceptance of the Knights' rule in Pomerania (Treaty of Kalisz, 1343), and by a series of dynastic arrangements with his Hungarian, Bohemian and German neighbours. The Hungarian king, Louis the Great, was his nephew, a son of his strong-willed sister Elizabeth, who, through her son, continued to exercise influence in Hungary. Charles IV, king of Bohemia and, eventually (1346), Holy Roman Emperor, married Casimir's granddaughter (1363). These family ties allowed Poland to solve conflicts of interests with its Western neighbours and avoid their competition in its Eastern policy, but it forced Casimir to abandon traditionally Polish areas to German rule. This loss of

---

[37] On this alliance, see Knoll, *Polish Monarchy*, pp. 46–7.
[38] O. Halecki, 'Casimir the Great', in *The Cambridge History of Poland*, Cambridge, 1950, p. 181.

territory in the West found compensation in an eastward expansion which was made possible by the gradual weakening and internal divisions of the Mongol empire. It also originated the age-long feud between Poland and Russia.

The western Russian principalities of Galicia and Volhynia, which had known a page of historical glory under Grand-princes Roman and Daniel in the thirteenth century, were still tributary to the Mongols, but both Hungary and Lithuania became interested in them. In the fourteenth century they also became a field of confrontation between expanding Roman Catholic Poland and the Byzantine Orthodox heritage to which they historically belonged.

The extinction of Roman's and Daniel's dynasty in what was still called the *regnum Russiae*, encompassing the principalities of Halich and Vladimir, led to the enthronement of Bolesłav, the son of the Polish prince of Mazovia and of a granddaughter of Yuri I of Galicia. In 1331, Bolesłav married Euphemia, a daughter of Gedymin of Lithuania. Dynastic connections were, however, insufficient to assure his rule: the power of local Russian boyars and popular opinion demanded that the Polish prince embrace the Orthodox faith and adopt the Russian-sounding name of Yuri (Slavic for George). Of course, he also had to secure the confirmation of Khan Uzbek, to whom he paid tribute.

Yuri II's reign ended in a tragedy connected with the renewed offensive of the Tatars under Khan Uzbek, which deprived his dominion of the role of buffer-state. Crossing Yuri's territory, the Tatars not only made repeated attacks on Hungary, but also, in 1337, entered Poland and besieged Lublin: Yuri was required by Uzbek to send his own troops as allies of the Tatars against the Poles.[39] Summoned by the pope to initiate a Crusade against the Mongol danger, Casimir of Poland and his Hungarian allies began to plan an invasion of Tatar-dominated west Russia. Bolesłav-Yuri was, most probably, soliciting their help, but, in so doing, he antagonized the Galician boyars, who had him poisoned (1340). This sad conclusion was undoubtedly caused by a combination of factors, including pro-Tatar, 'realistic' leanings of Galician boyars and their fears that their formerly Roman Catholic, Polish-born prince would renounce his conversion to Orthodoxy in order to secure Western help against the Mongols: several Latin Christians – presumably Poles – were killed in Lvov, following the death of the prince.

[39] Cf. Knoll, *op. cit.*, p. 123.

With the additional justification of having to avenge Yuri's death, Casimir entered Galicia, but had to face fierce resistance, led by the local boyar Dimitri-Detko, who called for Tatar help against the Poles. The campaign – which included a powerful intervention of Uzbek against the Poles – ended in a compromise: Gedymin's son Lubart was recognized as prince of both Volhynia and Galicia, and Detko effectively continued to rule Lvov, as *starosta*, or *capitaneus terre Russie*, as he is called in papal letters. His government acknowledged some dependence upon Casimir, and some responsibility to Lubart.[40] From 1340 and until his death (before 1386), Lubart opposed Casimir's ambitions in Russia. He was baptized in the Orthodox faith with the name of Dimitri and actively promoted the cause of Russo-Lithuanian commonwealth, ready to assume the inheritance of Kievan Russia in the framework of the Byzantine concept of the *oikouméne*. He was in correspondence with Byzantium, and, for a brief period, succeeded in restoring a metropolitanate of Galicia, which existed under Yuri I. In 1347, Emperor John Cantacuzenos addressed him as his 'nephew'.[41] Eventually, his rule became limited to parts of Volhynia, since Casimir in 1349 in a powerful campaign against the Lithuanians, occupied most of the old realm of Daniel of Halich, assuming the title of *Dominus terrae Russiae*.[42] Casimir's nephew, Louis of Hungary, who also had claims on Galicia, recognized the *fait accompli* in exchange for promises of succession to the Polish crown.

It appears that these events also implied a formal recognition of Casimir's rule in Russia by the Tatars. This recognition in turn demanded that the Polish king pay tribute to the khan: a letter of Pope Innocent VI (1357) expresses the pontiff's disapproval of this situation of dependence on the infidels, created for the sake of political advantage.[43]

The direct implications of the Polish thrust into Russia in the

---

[40] The title of Detko in Theiner, *Pol. Lit.*, No. 566, p. 434. Lubart, through his wife, claimed some personal dynastic qualifications for the rule of the principalities, but historians disagree as to whether he was married to a daughter of Bolesłav-Yuri (Hrushevsky, *Istoriya*, pp. 139–40; Vernadsky, *The Mongols*, p. 203), or to a grand-daughter of Yuri I of Galicia (I. P. Filevich, 'Bor'ba Pol'shy i Litvy-Rusi za Galitsko-Vladimirskoe nasledie', *Zh. M. N. P.*, Nov. 1889, p. 176; Knoll, *op. cit.*, p. 128). But the greatest support for his rule undoubtedly came from his father, Gedymin and his brother Olgerd, who became Grand-prince of Lithuania after Gedymin's death (1341).

[41] MM, I, 265–6.

[42] Filevich *op. cit.*, Jan. 1890, p. 104; Knoll, *op. cit.*, p. 141.

[43] Theiner, *Pol. Lit.*, No. 776, p. 581.

framework of the cultural and ecclesiastical relations between Byzantium and Russia will be further discussed in the forthcoming chapters. A question which must find answer here, however, is whether the antagonism of the Galician population to Polish rule and the resistance of the Lithuanian princes to Polish expansion could be justified in terms of their national or religious interests. We have seen earlier that Lithuania has been drawn to Poland by the common interests of both countries in repulsing the German threat. However, the constant wars opposing Casimir and the sons of Gedymin between 1349 and 1366 show that these common anti-German interests, which were so strong at the time of Wałdisław Łokietek, have ceased to prevail under Casimir. Casimir's ambitions in Russia have made him a powerful competitor to the descendents of Gedymin, who already occupied vast territories which used to belong to Kievan Russia. There is no doubt, on the other hand, that Russian princes, boyars, clergy and a majority of the population showed a distinct preference for Lithuanian rule over the Polish. An important element explaining this distrust of Poland lies in the fact that the unified and strengthened Polish monarchy of Casimir – as well as the Hungarian kingdom of Louis the Great – had acquired largely the same aggressive Crusading spirit as the one which once was the privilege of the Teutonic Knights, and from which the Poles themselves had much to suffer in the past. For Orthodox Russians, as well as for pagan Lithuanians, Polish rule implied acceptance of Latin Christianity and, eventually, Polish culture.[44] In Casimir's correspondence with Rome, his desire to act as a champion of Latin Christendom – strengthened by his interest in depriving the Knights of their monopoly in this field – is most prominent, and in this he received active papal support.

In 1340, Pope Benedict XII, on the one hand, used his diplomatic ties with the Golden Horde to urge Khan Uzbek to recognize the legitimacy of Polish and Hungarian intervention in Galicia to avenge the death of Bolesłav-Yuri.[45] On the other hand, he blessed Casimir's Crusade against the 'schismatic nation of the Russians' (*gens scismatica Ruthenorum*) and after the Polish occupation of Galicia, authorized the Archbishop of Cracow to annul the

---

[44] Documents and facts hardly substantiate the picture of Casimir as an enlightened humanist painted by Oscar Halecki: 'The King's care for all his subjects, without any discrimination of class or race, as well as his broadminded tolerance, are also illustrated by his attitude towards the inhabitants of his Ruthenian provinces', *op. cit.*, p. 177.

[45] Theiner, *Hung.* I, No. 960.

promises made by Casimir to Detko and the Russian boyars.[46] In 1343, Clement VI granted a substantial part of the ecclesiastical revenues to Casimir in support of his policy of fighting 'Tatars, Russians and Lithuanians', who are called indiscriminately, 'pagans and infidels'.[47] In 1349, however, the pope, with Casimir's cooperation, laid plans for a voluntary and peaceful conversion of Gedymin's son Keistut of Lithuania,[48] but the Polish invasion of Galicia and Volhynia – an act directed against Keistut's brother Lubart – put an end to these hopes. In 1357 again, when a purely military approach failed, another round of negotiations on the possibility of a peaceful conversion of the Lithuanian dynasty to Roman Catholicism took place, but, significantly, Casimir demanded that the newly converted lands be subjected to the Polish archbishop of Gniezno.[49] Eventually, the negotiations failed again because the Knights refused to give back conquered territories, even to a Christianized Lithuania. On the eve of his final conquest of most of Volhynia in 1366, Casimir received from Urban V a plenary indulgence to those who would contribute to his campaign against 'Lithuanians, Tatars and other infidels and schismatics'.[50]

The grouping of the Russian 'schismatics' together with the 'infidels' is a characteristic feature of both the papal and Polish mentality of this period and it was reflected in the well-documented practice, in areas controlled by either Hungary or Poland, of rebaptizing Orthodox Christians converting to the Latin Church. Such a demand was imposed – unsuccessfully, of course – upon the Byzantine Emperor John V Palaeologus, by King Louis and his mother, Elizabeth of Poland (sister of Casimir), during John's visit to Buda in 1366, and the Hungarians actually rebaptized Prince Stracimir of Bulgaria and many of his subjects.[51] Similarly,

---

[46] Theiner, *Pol. Lit.*, 566, p. 434.
[47] *Ibid.*, No. 604, 605, 468; cf. similar grants by Innocent VI in 1355–7, *ibid.*, No. 742, 769, 776 (pp. 558, 577–8, 581).
[48] Cf. documentary evidence and discussion in Knoll, *op. cit.*, p. 139.
[49] W. Abraham, *Powstanie organizacyi kościoła łacińskiego na Rusi*, I, Lwow, 1904, p. 368.
[50] Theiner, *Pol. Lit.*, No. 833.
[51] These facts are reported by the ex-emperor John Cantacuzenos in his Dialogue with the papal legate Paul in 1367; cf. Meyendorff, 'Projets', p. 173. Joseph Gill (*Byzantium and the Papacy, 1198–1400*, Rutgers University Press, New Brunswick, N.J., 1978, p. 216), expresses doubt as to the accuracy of this information given by Cantacuzenos, but he ignores abundant evidence which indicates that rebaptism of Orthodox Christians was performed routinely in Hungarian- and Polish-dominated areas (see below, Ch. 10, pp. 243–4). Also, the letter of the Franciscan Vicar of Bosnia, written in 1379 and quoted by Gill (op. cit., p. 302, n. 53), since it forbids re-baptisms, implies that re-baptisms were in fact taking place.

in 1370, Casimir threatened to 'baptize' the Russians in Galicia, unless his conditions for the administrative independence of the local Orthodox Church were met.[52] This practice was not officially condoned in Rome, and the popes of the fourteenth and fifteenth centuries always accepted Orthodox converts to the Roman communion through a simple confession of faith, recognizing the 'validity' of their Orthodox baptism; but the papacy generally encouraged the Crusading spirit of the Hungarians and the Poles, who had replaced the Teutonic Knights as effective promoters of Latin Christianity in Eastern Europe, and constantly used, in its documents, a terminology which practically identified 'infidels' and 'schismatics' as enemies of the Church. One should not wonder, then, that East European Catholic rulers forgot (or were unaware of) canonical sophistication and enforced their political and religious interest with drastic rigour.

Historians frequently associate with the reign of Casimir the Great the emergence of a new Polish messianism, which interprets the Polish role in European history as that of a bulwark against a barbarian 'East'. One can wonder whether King Casimir himself was fully conscious of playing such a role, or whether he was simply pursuing an immediate opportunity for the expansion of his power.[53] In any case, his struggle against the 'East' was less a defence of his country against the Mongols (during the latter part of Casimir's reign the khanate of Kypchak was torn apart by internal feuds and ceased to be a real threat for Europe), than a policy of political and religious expansion in Lithuania and Russia, and therefore the beginning of the age-long struggle between the Polish and the Russian nationalities in Eastern Europe. For Casimir, the 'East' began at the borders of Latin Christendom, and therefore included not only the Mongols, but also the Byzantine inheritance in Russia.

5. THE MONGOLS AND THEIR RUSSIAN SUBJECTS

Whatever the paradoxes of political schemes and temporary alliances which involved Western principalities of the old Kievan Russia in the thirteenth and fourteenth centuries, the Mongol domination of Russia as a whole not only brought initial ruin to the country, but also, as long as it lasted, was felt by the Russians as a continuous calamity. The contemporary sources – mostly

[52] MM, I, 577; cf. infra, Appedix, 4.
[53] Cf. a good discussion of this point in Knoll, *Polish Monarchy*, pp. 172–7.

chronicles and hagiographic documents – are unanimous in describing the Tatar yoke as a divine punishment for human sins and for the weaknesses and struggles of Russian princes.[54]

The internal feuds within the empire of Kypchak occasionally provided Russian princes with some latitude for political manoeuvre, but – at least in the thirteenth century – such temporary political intrigues brought only further disaster. Grand-prince Dimitri of Vladimir chose to support the cause of Nogay, the semi-independent Mongol general, against the legitimate Khan Tokhta, who had appointed Michael of Tver as Grand-prince. A thorough devastation of the Grand-principality of Vladimir by Tokhta's armies (1293) was the result, which was also followed by the ultimate defeat and death of Nogay (1300).

The reigns of Khans Tokhta (1291–1312) and Uzbek (1313–41) marked the apogee of Mongol rule in Russia. From the Russian princes, the Golden Horde required tribute, obedience and, whenever necessary, military help against its enemies. The khan's will was imposed either directly upon each prince, or, occasionally, at special princely conferences attended by the khan's representatives. Under Tokhta, two such meetings were held: in Vladimir in 1296, attended by the khan's delegate Oleksa Nevrui, and, in 1304, at Pereyaslavl'.[55] The adoption of Islam by Khan Uzbek is, sometimes, connected with an end of the policy of religious toleration, which characterized the early Mongol rule in Russia: in fact, there is no evidence that the privileged position of the Church was modified during his reign. We have seen, however (avove, p. 60–1), that Uzbek energetically discouraged any connection between Russians and the West, and that he reaffirmed Tatar power in Volhynia-Galicia, helping local resistance to Polish ambitions.

The direct dependence of the northern Russian principalities upon the Horde expressed itself in repeated trips to Sarai by all the princes and in the deadly struggles among them to secure the Khan's favour. Servility, bribery and internecine wars were among the means constantly used to achieve the desired goal. It is during that period that the shrewd, persistent and unscrupulous policy of the princes of the young principality of Moscow – especially against their competitors in Tver – secured the rise of that city to its position of leadership in Russia.

---

[54] We have no possibility of discussing here in detail the political and economic regime which prevailed in Russia during the period of Mongol occupation, and refer to the several excellent monographs on the subject, e.g. Nasonov, *Mongoly i Rus'*; Vernadsky, *The Mongols*; Spuler, *Die Goldene Horde*.

[55] *Troits.*, pp. 347, 351.

From the conquest onwards, the khan of the Tatars is unfailingly given the title of *tsar* in Russian chronicles and official
documents. When, during the reign of Dimitri and Basil I, the
Muscovite Russians resumed minting money (which had stopped
in 1240), their coins showed, on the obverse, the name of the
reigning grand-prince, and on the reverse, in Arabic script, the
name of the reigning khan.[56] These, and other signs, show that the
Russians considered their conquerors as having taken the place of
the Christian emperor ('tsar') of Constantinople, by virtue of a
decree of divine Providence. This acceptance of the khan's power
was basically a Christian idea, but it did not exclude obvious
hatred of Tatar rule. It did require, however, that the Scriptural
passages on obedience to the emperor be applied to the khans, i.e.,
the precept 'Honour the King' (I Peter, 2.17) and other similar
texts. In 1246, Prince Michael of Chernigov, before refusing to
participate in a pagan fire-ritual and accepting a martyr's death,
addressed the khan with a full recognition of his legitimacy as
ruler. 'I bow to you, O tsar, for God has given you the tsardom and
the glory of this world . . .'[57]

Sarai, from where the khans governed Russia, gradually
acquired the aspect of an empire's capital. As described by the
Arab traveller Ibn Battuta, who visited it during the reign of
Uzbek, it was 'one of the finest of cities, of boundless size, situated
in a plain, choked with the throng of its inhabitants, and possessing
good bazaars and broad streets'. Among the inhabitants, in addition to Mongols, Ibn Battuta mentions 'the Alans, who are Muslims, the Comans [Kypchaks], the Circassians, the Russians, and
the Greeks [*Rum*] – [all of] these are Christians. Each group lives
in a separate quarter with its own bazaars.'[58] The Russian princes
would sojourn for months at the khan's court and settle their
affairs with the Mongol rulers, and, also, use the numerous international contacts which were available in Sarai. Not infrequently,
the settlements led to bloody conclusions: the executions of several
successive princes of Tver by Uzbek are proof that the exercise of
political power in Russia was risky and that the khan's arbitrary
power was the only ultimate criterion of legitimacy.

The relations between the Golden Horde and Byzantium were

---

[56] Cf. Cherniavsky, '*Khan or basileus*'.
[57] *Mosk.*, p. 138.
[58] H. A. R. Gibb, tr., *The Travels of Ibn Battuta, A.D. 1325–1354*, II, Cambridge, 1962
pp. 515–16 (transcription of the proper names adapted to Byzantine and Slavic
usage).

constant and generally friendly. No significant military confrontation ever took place between the Eastern Empire and the Mongols: quite to the contrary, it is the Mongol onslaught which
destroyed the Seljuq power in Asia Minor. On the other hand, the
Tatar attacks on Byzantium's neighbours in the Balkans – the
Bulgarians and the Serbs – were rather advantageous to the
immediate Byzantine political concerns. Finally, the Genoese
presence in the Black Sea depended upon the benevolence of both
Greeks and Mongols, and the Italian merchants constituted a
permanent and interested link between Constantinople and Sarai,
a link carefully maintained and cultivated by the Byzantines.
Significantly, each of the first three Palaeologan emperors arranged for their illegitimate daughters to marry a Mongolian khan:
thus Euphrosyne, daughter of Michael VIII, became the wife of
Khan Nogay;[59] Maria, daughter of Andronicus II married
Tokhta,[60] and Ibn Battuta recounts that, around 1332, the third
wife in Uzbek's harem was a daughter of the emperor of Constantinople (possibly an illegitimate offspring of Andronicus), that
she was surrounded in Sarai with a staff of Greek servants and
travelled to Constantinople to give birth to her first child.[61]

The ties between Constantinople and the Golden Horde had
direct consequences in Russia, which was under the political and
military control of the khans and under the ecclesiastical administration of the Byzantine patriarchate. The two administrations
frequently acted in coordination. We have spoken earlier of the
diplomatic role played by the Greek metropolitan of Russia and
by his suffragan, the bishop of Sarai, in the earlier period of the
Mongol occupation of Russia (see above, p. 46). The sources
clearly allude to the continuation of this active diplomacy pursued
by Byzantine ecclesiastics in the later period. The conferences at
which the khan's policy was imposed upon Russian princes were
attended by the representatives of the Church, as well as the envoys
of the khan: the bishop of Sarai, Ismael, attended the conference
in Vladimir (1296),[62] and the Greek metropolitan Maximus was
with the princes in Pereyaslavl' in 1304.[63] Furthermore, official
documents such as Russian recommendations to Constantinople

---

[59] Pachymeres, Bonn, I, 344.
[60] *Ibid.*, II, 268.
[61] *Tr. cit.*, pp. 488, 498–9; cf. S. Runciman, 'The Ladies of the Mongols', Εἰς μνήμην
Κωνσταντίνου Ι. Ἀμάντου, Athens, 1960, pp. 46–53.
[62] *Lvov.*, p. 174.
[63] *Troits.*, p. 351.

for the election of candidates to the metropolitan's see also went through Sarai.[64] Byzantine officials travelling to Russia were closely aware of the local political problems, involving Russian princes and the Tatars, as we can see, for example, in the correspondence of Manuel Gabalas, who later became Metropolitan of Ephesus under the name of Matthew. Being on a diplomatic mission in Russia in 1331–2, he may be alluding, in a letter addressed to a Constantinopolitan 'philosopher' (perhaps Nicephorus Gregoras, who was an acquaintance of the Metropolitan of Kiev, Theognostos), to the bloody feud between Ivan I of Moscow (ὁ τῶν Ῥῶς ἡγεμῶν) and Alexander (Ὀλέκης) of Tver – a matter which is apparently familiar to his correspondent as well.[65]

The links between Byzantium and the Golden Horde make one understand better why, throughout the fourteenth century, the patriarchate of Constantinople attempted to preserve the unity of its ecclesiastical administration in Russia under a single metropolitan, residing in Mongol-occupied territories, rather than, for example, in Lithuania. This does not imply, however, that either Byzantium or the Church were not aware of the miseries of the Mongol occupation: precisely because the metropolitan, as an emissary of the empire, enjoyed a privileged position in the eyes of the khan, he was able to intercede for the interests of the Church, act as a mediator in princely feuds and exercise a power of intercession with considerable authority. Never was the Greek metropolitan, appointed in Constantinople, seen by the Russians as an ally of the hated Tatars but rather as an advocate and a possible recourse against the arbitrary rule of the invaders. Culturally, by providing a permanent link with Byzantium, the Church kept open for Russian society, isolated from the rest of Europe, a connection with Christian civilization. While recognizing the khan as their *de facto* emperor, the Russians were also reminded, through the Church, of the survival of a Christian empire. The Church provided them with a 'heavenly citizenship', which helped them to forget the miseries of the day, but it also preserved them as members of a historical commonwealth, centred in Constantinople, which was to serve as a basis for the revival of the fourteenth century. As long as there was no open conflict between the Golden

---

[64] Letter of Patriarch Philotheos to the Archbishop of Novgorod (1354), MM, I, 347; on the diplomatic role of the bishop of Sarai, see also Nasonov, *Mongoly i Rus'*, pp. 44–7.

[65] Kourouses, Γαβαλᾶς, pp. 248–52. The very obscurity of the passage containing the allusion is an indication of the writer's and the correspondent's familiarity with Russian affairs.

Horde and Byzantium, the *status quo* could be maintained and the future secured. Under those circumstances, one understands that the Byzantines lacked confidence in the attempts of the Lithuanian Grand-princes to destroy the *status quo* and to pull Russia into greater dependence upon Western European interests and concerns.

4

The Metropolitanate of Kiev and all Russia

The ecclesiastical title of 'metropolitan' was formally defined in the canonical legislation of the fourth century. It was used to designate the bishop of the main city (μητρόπολις) in each province (*provincia*, ἐπαρχία) of the Roman empire. The Council of Nicaea, gathered by Emperor Constantine not only to settle disputes, but also to sanction the new and official alliance between the empire and the universal Church (325), codified a system, in which any action requiring a *collective* participation of several bishops – particularly the consecration of a new candidate to the episcopate – would be performed by all the bishops of each 'province' and confirmed by the 'metropolitan'.[1] Provincial bishops would also gather twice a year as a synod and act as a court presided over by the metropolitan, settling all pending disputes.[2] One of the basic characteristics of that system is the parallelism between the structures of the Empire and of the Church: the 'province' was a concept of civil administration, which provided the framework for the jurisdiction of the episcopal synod, headed by a 'metropolitan'.

This parallelism between civil and ecclesiastical administration was confirmed and generalized in later centuries. The Council of Chalcedon (451), in its famous Canon 28, grants to the archbishop of Constantinople, now elevated to the status of 'New Rome', the right to effect consecrations of metropolitans in the civil 'dioceses' of Pontus, Asia and Thrace, each 'diocese' grouping a large number of 'provinces'.[3] This was the formal basis of larger administrative units or 'patriarchates'. The trend towards centralization was not general, however: Emperor Justinian still mentions metropolitans 'consecrated either by their own synods, or by the most-blessed patriarchs',[4] a text which shows that in his time, there was not yet full uniformity as to the patriarchal control over the

[1] Canon 4, Rhalles-Potles, I, p. 122.
[2] Canon 5, *ibid.*, p. 124–5.   [3] *Ibid.*, pp. 280–1.
[4] *Novella* 123, 3, *Corpus juris civilis.* III., *Novellae*, ed. R. Schoell, Berlin, 1928, p. 597.

consecration of metropolitans. This flexibility will be maintained, at least in some areas, throughout the Middle Ages, and will be discussed later in connection with the history of the Church in Russia.

The parallelism between civil and ecclesiastical administrations, having been accepted as a pattern inside the borders of the Empire, was clearly inapplicable in 'barbarian lands', where there were no 'provinces', and therefore no place for 'metropolitans'. Thus Canon 28 of Chalcedon, quoted above, mentions 'metropolitans' residing in imperial dioceses, but only 'bishops' located in 'barbarian lands': these bishops, if they previously depended upon the dioceses of Pontus, Thrace or Asia, are to be consecrated by the patriarch of Constantinople. In this context, the famous Byzantine canonists Zonaras and Balsamon, writing in the twelfth century, directly apply Canon 28 to Russia: 'the Russians,' they write, are 'barbarians' depending upon the diocese of Thrace; therefore, their 'bishops' are to be consecrated by the patriarch of Constantinople.[5] The obscurity, which surrounds the beginnings of the Church in Russia, where the presence of a 'metropolitan' is not apparent before 1037, may be due to the fact that the original Byzantine hierarchy in Kiev was made up of missionary bishops, and that the appointment of a 'metropolitan' had to wait for what the Byzantines saw as a more permanent incorporation of Russia in the Byzantine οἰκουμένη under the reign of Yaroslav.[6] But even after that period Balsamon considers Russians as living in 'barbarian' lands.

There is another canonical text which must have influenced the status of the Church in Slavic lands in general and in Russia particularly, because it describes the office of metropolitan in terms more easily applicable to 'barbarian' lands. Canon 34 'of the Holy Apostles' – which in fact reflects the ecclesiastical practices in the diocese of the 'Orient' (Syria) in the fourth century – reads: 'Let the bishops of every nation [ἑκάστου ἔθνους] recognize one who would be the first among them, and let them consider him as their head and do nothing without seeking his opinion, but let each of them administer the affairs of their own community [παροικία] and the villages [χώραις] which depend on it. But

---

[5] Rhalles-Potles, II, pp. 283, 285.
[6] The literature on this subject is immense; for up-to-date summaries, which, however, do not solve the issue in a final way, see L. Müller, *Zum Problem des hierarchischen Status und der jurisdiktionellen Abhängigkeit der russischen Kirche vor 1039*, Köln-Braunsfeld, 1959; and Poppe, *Państwo i Kościół*.

neither he should do anything without asking the opinion of all. For thus there will be concord [ὁμόνοια], and God shall be glorified, through the Lord, in the Holy Spirit: the Father, the Son and the Holy Spirit.'[7] The Byzantine commentators of the twelfth century – Aristenos, Zonaras and Balsamon – interpret this text as referring to the canonical structure of the 'province'. On the other hand, even modern canonists have wondered about the use of the term 'nation' [ἔθνος] in this text, and some have used it to justify the existence of national churches, as they have emerged in the nineteenth century.[8]

In any case, whatever the original meaning of the term ἔθνος, Canon 34 'of the Holy Apostles' found natural application in areas outside the Empire, where the Roman provincial administration did not exist. In those areas, the titles of bishops frequently used national appellations (ὁ Βουλγαρίας, ὁ 'Αλανίας, ὁ Ζηκχίας, etc.), rather than names of cities, as in traditional imperial territories. This was also the case with the Greek metropolitan appointed to Russia: in Byzantine sources, he is more often referred to as metropolitan 'of Russia' [ὁ 'Ρωσίας], than by his more precise title of metropolitan 'of Kiev'.[9] The Byzantine historian Nicephorus Gregoras, writing in the second half of the fourteenth century, in his well-known passage about the 'very numerous nation' [ἔθνος πολυανθρωπότατον] of Russia, specifies that that nation 'is placed under a single high-priest [ἀρχιερεύς]', who is himself dependent upon the patriarchate in Constantinople.[10] Similarly, and more officially, Patriarch Anthony and his Synod, writing in 1389, describe the rationale and the functions of the metropolitanate of Russia in social and political terms.

From the beginning, since the Russians became Christians and sub-

[7] Rhalles-Potles, *op. cit.*, I, p. 45.

[8] Cf. V. I. Beneshevich, *Syntagma XIV. Titulorum*, St Petersburg, 1906, p. 68. For a clear use of ἔθνος in the sense of 'population of a province', and not of 'nation', see Sozomen, *Hist. VII*, 6, PG, 67, col. 1436 BC. On this issue, see Peter, Bp. 'Problemy svyazannye s avtokefaliei', in *Vestnik Russkogo Zapadnoevropeiskogo Patriarshego Ekzarkhata*, No. 97–100, Paris, 1978, p. 78.

[9] See for example, Gelzer, 'Beiträge', p. 247 (ὁ Κυέβου), as compared with p. 255 ([μητρόπολις] τῆς Μεγάλης 'Ρωσίας). In the fourteenth century, as it appears in letters of Emperor John Cantacuzenos in 1347, the official title of the Russian metropolitan was fully identical with that of metropolitans of the empire itself with 'Russia' practically identified with an imperial 'province', (ἱερώτατος μητροπολίτης Κυγέβου, ὑπέρτιμος καὶ ἔξαρχος πάσης 'Ρωσίας, MM, I, p. 261). The title of ὑπέρτιμος καὶ ἔξαρχος does not appear in later documents and may have been given as a personal privilege to Metropolitan Theognostos only. The shorter title ὁ 'Ρωσιας also remains in use (Gelzer, *Notitiae*, p. 599).

[10] Greg, *Hist.*, 36, 21–3, Bonn, III, 512–13.

mitted themselves to our great, catholic and apostolic Church of Christ, the entire province of Russia [ἡ 'Ρωσίας ἐπαρχία[11]] has been placed under the pastorship and administration of a single metropolitan. This did not occur simply, or, as one says, by chance. The divine Fathers of old have determined that the great population of that nation, which numbers thousands, or rather is innumerable [τὸ πολυάνθρωπον ἔθνος ἐκεῖνο καὶ μυριάριθμον], should have one single leader and catholic teacher.[12] The reason for that determination was that the territory of Russia being vast, was divided between so many different civil powers and so many states [πολιτείας], that it possessed many authorities, and even more local rulers. Furthermore, between the latter there are differences in views, as well as in interests and territory: they struggle and fight against each other, engaging in wars, and battles and fratricidal killings. Thus, the divine fathers, foreseeing those things through the Divine Spirit . . . considered that it was neither good, nor useful that the spiritual leadership [of Russia] be dispersed, but that the one metropolitan should bind and connect the people both to himself and to each other. Since it was impossible to bring together a single civil rule, [they established] one spiritual authority, considering rightly that, once placed under one single leader and guide, [the Russians] would find peace with themselves and with each other, honoring the one head,[13] which is an image of the perfect, primordial and unique Head, Christ, 'on whom', according to the divine Apostle, 'the whole body fitly joined together and compacted' depends (Eph. 4, 15–16), 'and is brought to the unity of faith'.[14]

These texts of Gregoras and of the Patriarchal Synod reflect a Byzantine vision of Russia, which inspired a very consistent policy of the Byzantine authorities towards that country, as a single 'nation' (ἔθνος), ecclesiastically united under a single head. The 34th 'Apostolic' Canon was certainly seen as a canonical authority matching exactly the situation and providing the terminology necessary to describe the ecclesiastical administration in Russia. It is true that separate metropolitanates may have appeared briefly

[11] The use of the technical term ἐπαρχία ('province') is significant: canonically, a 'metropolitan' necessarily heads a 'province'. The meaning of this text is to justify the discrepancy between the notion of 'province' (a small administrative unit of the Roman empire) and the reality of 'Russia' in 1389.

[12] Διδάσκαλον καθολικόν; cf. the title of *katholikos* traditionally used to designate primates of Christian nations beyond the borders of the empire (i.e., *katholikos* of Georgia). The title seems to have been first used in the fourth century by the metropolitan of Seleucia-Ktesiphon, cf. H. Leclercq, 'Katholikos', DATL, 8, 1 (1928), cols. 686–9.

[13] The terminology used in this synodal decree is closely connected with that of Canon 34 'of the Holy Apostles'. Note particularly the term 'head' (κεφαλή) used in describing the office of the metropolitan of the Russian 'nation' (ἔθνος).

[14] MM, II, p. 116–17; cf. also App. 10, pp. 307–10.

in Pereyaslavl' and Chernigov in the eleventh century,[15] but these may only have been ephemeral results of still tentative Byzantine policies towards Russia. Similar attempts initiated in Russia itself in the twelfth and fourteenth centuries will face strong opposition on the part of the patriarchate. In the long run, Byzantium was directly responsible for having established in Russia a unified ecclesiastical structure, which was limited only by the ethnic boundaries of the Russian nation and not, as was the case with the other metropolitans of the patriarchate, by the administrative limits of a Roman 'province'. The 'national' character of the Russian metropolitanate was originally aimed at facilitating administrative control and diplomatic effectiveness, but it also created in Russia a tradition of ecclesiastical centralization, which persisted long after the fall of Byzantium, in the independent Russian Church of later centuries.

I. STATUS AND POWER OF THE METROPOLITAN

Byzantine sources contain a number of official lists of metropolitanates, with their suffragan dioceses (*Notitiae episcopatuum*). In considering any of those lists, particularly those belonging to the fourteenth century, one is struck by the unusual status of the metropolitanate of Russia. With its enormous size and geographical expansion, it is listed among the traditional sees of Asia Minor and the Balkans, which constituted the traditional territory of the patriarchate and which still were supposed to coincide with the ancient Roman provinces. At the beginning of the fourteenth century, the jurisdiction of the patriarch included 112 metropolitans. Under emperors Andronicus II (1282–1328), Andronicus III (1328–41) and the first years of John V (1341–7), twenty-six 'autocephalous archbishops'[16] and eight bishops were also promoted to metropolitans. With the shrinking of the empire and the establishment of independent churches in Bulgaria and Serbia, the actual authority of many of these prelates was minimal: they were 'metropolitans' only in title. Nevertheless, the metropolitan of Russia, whose authority was immense, occupied the sixtieth place in the order of seniority. Moreover, during the reshuffle of metropolitan sees which occurred under Andronicus II, the see of Russia

---

[15] Cf. Poppe, *Państwo i kościół*, pp. 164–70.
[16] Normally an 'autocephalous archbishop', had no suffragan bishops and was directly dependent upon the patriarch (see below, note 36).

was demoted from the sixtieth to the seventy-second position.[17] The demotion does not seem to have been a deliberate humiliation of the metropolitan of Russia, since similar changes in order of priority concerned other sees also, but it clearly illustrates the peculiarly Byzantine ability to reaffirm again and again a theoretical immutability of the *oikoumène*, ideally headed by the emperor and the patriarch, and to ignore, for the sake of this theory, the most obvious historical realities. At the same time, this formal ideological conservatism was itself used, with great skill and realism, to maintain the prestige of the 'imperial city' and to perpetuate its influence and administrative control in areas, which – like Russia – would otherwise long ago have totally escaped its reach. Only occasionally, the personal pride of the metropolitan and the national self-consciousness of the Russians were enhanced by favours accorded to them in the Byzantine protocol, such as the sealing of patriarchal letters sent to Russia with lead, whereas other metropolitans were receiving sealings of wax.[18]

In Russia itself, the number of dioceses headed by suffragan bishops varied greatly, following historical and political changes. The Greek episcopal lists of the fourteenth century always carefully distinguish the dioceses situated in territories controlled by the Grand-prince of Vladimir-Moscow. These areas of north-eastern Russia are generally designated as 'Great Russia', (ἡ Μεγάλη Ῥωσία), whereas the term 'Little Russia' (ἡ Μικρὰ Ῥωσία) referred to the former Grand-principality of Galicia-Volhynia in the south-west.[19] The six dioceses of Halich, Vladimir-in-Volhynia, Peremyshl', Lutsk, Turov and Kholm are the permanent 'Little Russian' group, whereas Chernigov (sometimes shifting to Bryansk), Polotsk and Smolensk shift from the north-eastern to the south-western group with the expansion of the Lithuanian Grand-principality. The dioceses of Pereyaslavl' and Belgorod ('Ασπρόκαστρον τὸ μέγα) exist intermittently, whereas that of Yuryev (ὁ ῞Αγιος Γεώργιος εἰς τὸν Ῥῶσιν ποταμόν) disappears in the fourteenth century. The permanent northern 'Great Russian' group includes the dioceses of Vladimir-on-the-Klyazma, Novgorod, Rostov, Suzdal, Sarai, Ryazan, Tver, Kolomna and Perm (the last two were set up in the late fourteenth century).[20]

Although he had not resided in Kiev since the Mongol con-

---

[17] Cf. Gelzer, *Notitiae*, pp. 597–601.
[18] For a late fourteenth-century evidence to this effect, see Rhalles-Potles, v, p. 509.
[19] Cf. particularly Gelzer, 'Beiträge', pp. 246–53.
[20] Cf. Makary, *Istoriya*, IV, 1, pp. 107–9, 337.

quest, the primate of the Russian Church kept his traditional title and continued as the diocesan bishop in the city of Kiev. However, the actual limits of his particular jurisdiction were determined by the political events of the thirteenth and fourteenth centuries. In 1299, the Greek Metropolitan Maximus established his permanent seat in Vladimir-on-the-Klyazma, the capital of the northern Grand-princes, adding that city to his own original diocese of Kiev.[21] His successor Peter resided in the new capital of Moscow, where he built a cathedral, without relinquishing jurisdiction over either Kiev or Vladimir. As a result, the Metropolitan considered as his own three cathedrals in Russia: St Sophia in Kiev, the Dormition cathedral in Vladimir, and the newly built Dormition Church in the Moscow Kremlin. In addition, when visiting his flock in the Grand-duchy of Lithuania, he occupied an official residence in Novgorodok (Nowogródek) and personally controlled the Orthodox ecclesiastical establishments in Lithuania's capital, Vilna, as well as in the city of Grodno.[22] In fact, the Metropolitan was the diocesan bishop of two dioceses – Kiev and Vladimir – and in addition exercised canonical control over churches in the political capitals of the two 'Russias': Moscow and Vilna. The geographical dispersion of his jurisdictional rights and their symbolic importance added to his unique power and prestige, as the one ecclesiastical leader of a 'very numerous nation' (ἔθνος πολυάνθρωπον). Since the Metropolitan was clearly not in a position to administer personally all these establishments, situated in different and often conflicting countries and at great distances, his permanent vicars resided in Kiev, Vilna and Moscow. During the time of his absence, they acted on the metropolitan's behalf, exercising extensive powers over the clergy and even the bishops, although they had no episcopal rank themselves.[23]

It goes without saying that, as diocesan bishop of both Vladimir and Kiev, the metropolitan received a large income from properties acquired by these dioceses throughout the centuries.[24] He was also the beneficiary of several forms of ecclesiastical taxation, including revenues from ecclesiastical courts. A long dispute

---

[21] *Troits.*, pp. 348–9.
[22] In 1451, Metropolitan Jonas entrusted to his vicar the ecclesiastical establishments of these three cities, which 'belong to the metropolitan from of old', RIB, vi, col. 571.
[23] Numerous references to official documents and chronicles quoted in Makary, *Istoriya*, v, 2, pp. 89–92.
[24] Cf. M. I. Gorchakov, *O zemel'nykh vladeniyakh vserossiiskikh mitropolitov, patriarkhov i svyateishego Sinoda*, St Petersburg, 1871.

between the metropolitan and the city of Novgorod concerning
the metropolitan's judiciary rights in dioceses other than his own
will be discussed below. The primate of the Russian Church also
received a regular income from the other bishops, who, at their
consecration, had to promise 'the accurate remittance of all taxes
due to the throne of the metropolitan' by their diocese.[25] Since the
see of the metropolitan of Kiev and all Russia was occupied by a
prelate appointed from Constantinople and, especially, since he
was himself frequently a Greek, the rich revenues of the metropolitanate were of substantial interest to the impoverished Byzantine authorities. The metropolitan could also be of great help in
influencing the Russian princes to send additional gifts to Constantinople. Substantial donations were in order at the appointment of each new metropolitan (we will discuss historical cases
below), and it can be surmised – although concrete evidence is
lacking – that the metropolitanate was sending regular contributions to the patriarch, similar to those which he received from his
own bishops. Finally, there are several examples of Russian donations which met extraordinary requests coming from Constantinople: following the collapse of the apse of St Sophia in
1346, a substantial monetary contribution for its restoration was
sent from Russia, undoubtedly through the mediation of the
influential and powerful Greek metropolitan, Theognostos, a
friend of Nicephorus Gregoras, who reports the facts.[26] In 1398, a
large sum of money was again sent to Constantinople, besieged by
the Turks.[27] In 1400, Patriarch Matthew applied directly to
Metropolitan Cyprian, requesting more funds for the defence of
Constantinople.[28] Finally at the time of the preparations for the
Council of Florence, the metropolitan of Russia was expected to
contribute alone the sum of 100 000 *hyperpyra*, whereas other 'rich'
sees, such as Georgia and Serbia, were not counted upon for more
than 20 000 each.[29] These facts alone would be sufficient to
explain the consistent policies of the Byzantine patriarchate, aim-

[25] Promise of Euthymius II, archbishop of Novgorod in AAE, No. 370; also the
Order for the election of bishops (1423) in RIB, vi, col. 439.
[26] *Hist. byz.* xxviii, 34–5; xxxvi, 30–1; ed. Bonn, iii, pp. 198–9, 516. The Russian
Chronicle (*Troits.*, p. 369) confirms the visit to Constantinople, in 1347, of an
embassy of the Muscovite Grand-prince Symeon and of Metropolitan Theognostos.
[27] *Troits.*, p. 448.
[28] MM, ii, pp. 359–61.
[29] S. Syropoulos, *Memoirs*, in V. Laurent, ed., *Les 'Mémoires' du Grand Ecclésiarque de
l'Eglise de Constantinople Sylvestre Syropoulos sur le Concile de Florence (Concilium Floren-
tinum Documenta et Scriptores B, vol.* ix) Rome, 1971, pp. 120–2.

ing at preserving its control over a united metropolitanate of Russia.

2. EPISCOPAL ELECTIONS

The most obvious and traditional function of the metropolitan consisted in securing and controlling episcopal elections. The procedure is known to us from contemporary sources, which indicate that the formal requirements of the ancient canons was followed with surprising faithfulness, although the extraordinary conditions under which the Russian 'province' of the patriarchate had to be administered – distance to the patriarchal centre, tremendous geographic expansion, political divisions – prevented the normal functioning of the most essential and permanent element in the life of an ecclesiastical province: the episcopal synod, which was canonically entitled to perform episcopal elections and required to meet twice a year (Nicaea, Canon 5) to solve pending issues. For the election of a bishop, the presence of *all* the bishops of a province was required (Nicaea, Canon 4). In Russia, however, no general meeting of the bishops ever occurred. Only once, in 1274, did Metropolitan Cyril use the occasion of the consecration of a new bishop in Vladimir, to hold a deliberative assembly of bishops, which settled disciplinary and liturgical matters. But, even then, only four bishops participated, besides the metropolitan himself and the newly consecrated Serapion of Vladimir. In fact, the synod of Vladimir had no better attendance than the other gatherings of Russian bishops convoked by the metropolitan for episcopal consecrations which could not be performed by the primate alone.[30]

Contemporary evidence provides exact information on the procedure followed in episcopal elections under Metropolitan Theognostos (1328–53) for the period 1328–47,[31] which is confirmed in the text of an *Order for the election of a bishop (ustav kako dostoit izbirat' episkopa)* of 1423.[32] An invitation was sent by the

---

[30] The Orthodox church strictly follows the early Christian practice requiring the participation of *several* bishops (at least two or three, cf. Apostolic Canon 1, Rhalles-Potles, II, 1) in an episcopal consecration. By far the most complete study on the subject is by I. Sokolov, 'Izbranie arkhiereev v Vizantii', VV, XXII, 2, 1915–16, pp. 193–255.

[31] The manuscript *Vaticanus graecus* 840, of the fourteenth century (R. Devreesse, *Codices Vaticani graeci*, III, Vatican, 1950, p. 388) contains 13 Greek Acts of election for that period (Regel, *Analecta*, pp. 52–6; on these texts see also V. Vasilievsky, 'Zapisi o postavlenii russkikh episkopov pri mitropolite Feognoste', *Zh. M. N. P.*, 255, II, Feb 1888, pp. 445–63).

[32] RIB, col. 437–64.

metropolitan to all the bishops to attend the election, but only a few actually came: five for the consecration of John of Bryansk-Chernigov (19 November 1335); four in the case of the consecration of Athanasius of Vladimir (May 1328), Theodore of Halich (May 1328), Paul of Chernigov (April 1332), Athanasius of Sarai (June 1334), Basil of Novgorod (August 1331); three for the consecration of Tryphon of Lutsk (6 December 1331) and Daniel of Suzdal' (2 March 1330); and only two in the case of Anthony of Rostov (October 1329), Isaac of Sarai (30 October 1343), Euthymius of Smolensk (August 1345), Nathanael of Suzdal (7 August 1347) and Theodore of Tver (March 1330). To fulfil the canonical requirement, all the absentees had to pledge in writing that they would accept the election performed in their absence: the acts of election specifically mention each time this written consent given by 'all the bishops of Russia'.[33]

According to the order of election, the bishops present, after a deliberation conducted in the presence of a ranking member of the metropolitan's own clergy (but in the absence of the metropolitan himself), selected three candidates for the vacant see, of whom the metropolitan personally chose one, and presided over his consecration.[34] Under those circumstances, the bishops had actually very little influence on the selection of candidates. In pre-Mongol times, local Russian princes frequently interfered in elections of bishops, but, since the conquest, their dependence upon Mongol overlords and frequent moves from one principality to another to suit the requirements of seniority, or the whims of the Tatars, seem to have limited their power in the selection of bishops. On the other hand, the latter, at their consecration, had to promise not to succumb to any pressure from civil authorities and to obey only 'the metropolitan of Kiev and all Russia'.[35]

From these procedures of election, as well as from other historical evidence, it clearly appears that neither the bishops nor the local Russian princes offered a real challenge to the unique power exercised by a metropolitan, whose appointment depended only on Constantinople and who, especially when he was a Greek,

[33] Συναινούντων καὶ τῶν λοιπῶν ἐπισκόπων ἀπάσης 'Ρωσίας, *ed. cit.*, p. 52; cf. 'Order', *ed. cit.*, col. 438–9.

[34] This procedure is found in Byzantine civil and ecclesiastical legislation, with some variation as to the composition of the electoral college which chooses the three candidates. Justinian (Nov. 123, *Corpus juris civilis*, III, ed. Schoell, Berlin, 1928, p. 594) admits the participation of lay leaders of the city; this practice will be retained in Novgorod (see below).

[35] 'Order', *ed. cit.*, col. 453–4.

enjoyed the status of a foreign diplomat, respected by the Mongols and controlling an immense wealth dispersed in several states. Therefore, it was the form of the *metropolitan's* appointment which really mattered in terms of the power and prestige of the Church.

There was, however, one city and one diocese, which, although a part of the metropolitanate, succeeded in maintaining a privileged status of relative independence: Novgorod. A commercial city, connected with the Hanseatic League of German states and, controlling a vast territory reaching to Finland, the Arctic Ocean and the Urals, Novgorod succeeded in maintaining great political independence. It also enjoyed the enviable privilege of being the only major city of Russia which avoided military occupation by the Mongols. Internally, not unlike the Italian city-states, it maintained a measure of democracy, whose most important expression was the city-assembly, or *veche*. Whereas it would be a mistake to identify its regime with that of modern democracies (voting rights in the *veche* were reserved for landowners and the assembly was controlled by a business aristocracy), Novgorod was governed by the collegial cooperation of several power centres: a prince, whose power was limited to judicial and military affairs, and two elected officials, the *posadnik* and the *tysyatski*, who were in charge of internal government and represented the citizenry. Its spiritual head, the bishop, occupied the fourth prominent position in the city government. Since the twelfth century, he assumed the title of 'archbishop'. In the Byzantine Church, that title was normally reserved for 'autocephalous' prelates, who were not dependent upon a metropolitan, but directly responsible to the patriarch.[36] Although the archbishop of Novgorod was never called 'autocephalous', the procedure of his election was quite different from that of the other bishops: it partially followed the Justinianic legislation which required that an assembly of local clergy and eminent citizens select three candidates for the vacant see; however, whereas, in the case of suffragan bishops, Justinian granted the metropolitan a right to select and consecrate one of the three candidates, the bishop of Novgorod was selected *by lot*, so that the metropolitan had practically no say in the selection, except in the theoretical right to refuse consecration of the chosen candidate.[37] However, the archbishop of Novgorod was never allowed to seek

---

[36] See particularly Chrysostomos, Ὁ τίτλος τοῦ ἀρχιεπισκόπου, *Theologia*, 13, Athens, 1935, pp. 289–95; also Beck, *Kirche*, pp. 67–8.

[37] Cf. N. Nikitsky, *Ocherk vnutrennei istorii tserkvi v Velikom Novgorode*, St Petersburg, 1879; also Sokolov, *Arkhierei*, pp. 318–29; cf. Makary, *Istoriya*, v, 2, pp. 101–16.

consecration directly in Constantinople, and therefore never became really 'autocephalous'.

In the fourteenth century, tension frequently arose between the metropolitan and the archbishop, especially at those times when threats to the unity of the metropolitanate gave Novgorod additional opportunities to assert an independent stand. An example of this latent tension is the discrepancy between the act of consecration of Basil Kalika as archbishop of Novgorod (25 August 1331), as found in the official Greek registry of Metropolitan Theognostos, on the one hand and, on the other hand, the Chronicle of Novgorod. According to the registry, the election and consecration were performed according to procedures accepted in the case of all other bishops, with the bishops present selecting the three candidates.[38] The registry seems to show that there was no formal recognition by the metropolitan of Novgorodian privileges. The Chronicle of Novgorod however relates that, after the voluntary resignation of Archbishop Moses, 'the men of Novgorod, having deliberated much, were without a bishop for about eight months; and all Novgorod and the abbots and priests chose Gregory Kalika, who had been designated by God ... In January [he] was shorn as a monk, received the name of Basil; he was then installed in the Archbishop's palace, until they should send him to the metropolitan.' The text then relates the consecration of Basil by Theognostos, performed in Vladimir-in-Volhynia, where the metropolitan was travelling that year.[39] Obviously, Theognostos went through the motions of a regular election by the bishops, but he had no real alternative to the consecration of Basil, who had already been chosen and installed as acting-archbishop in Novgorod. Moreover, Theognostos confirmed the jurisdictional rights of the archbishop of Novgorod over Pskov and, in a quite unusual move, which shows that the metropolitan of Russia enjoyed quasi-patriarchal rights, granted to Basil the right to wear a *polystavrion* (*rizy krestsaty*) (1346),[40] i.e. a *phelonion*, or 'chasuble', ornamented with four crosses, a privilege bestowed upon distinguished Byzantine prelates only.[41] While playing upon Novgorodian pride,

---

[38] Regel, *Analecta*, p. 56.

[39] *Novg.*, pp. 342–3; Engl. tr. (modified here), p. 126. The selection of Basil by lot is indicated by the conventional expression 'designated by God' ('*Bogom naznamenana*').

[40] *Novg.*, pp. 343–4, 358. Byzantine sources confirm that the initiative of this action came from Theognostos himself, MM, 1, p. 348.

[41] It appears, however, that in the fourteenth century a larger number of Byzantine ecclesiastical officials were granted this distinction and included dignitaries of the patriarchate without episcopal rank.

Theognostos vigorously asserted his own power over the archbishopric, which provoked a Novgorodian reaction in the form of
direct complaints to Constantinople and also a less than loyal
attitude of the archbishop in the struggle for the unity of the
metropolitanate – a debate which will be discussed below.

3. SOURCE OF THE METROPOLITAN'S POWER: HIS APPOINTMENT FROM CONSTANTINOPLE

If the metropolitan of Kiev and all Russia could play, throughout
the stormy periods of the Mongol invasion and the conflicts
between various political centres of Eastern Europe, a role largely
unaffected by local circumstances and pressures, maintaining a
permanent centre of administrative unity between the Russian
principalities and a diplomatic link between Byzantium, the
Golden Horde, the Grand-principalities of Moscow and Lithuania
and the kingdom of Poland, it was largely because, throughout the
thirteenth and the fourteenth centuries, he remained an appointee
of the emperor and patriarch of Constantinople. Thus, because of
the traditional prestige of the Church – which was expanding,
rather than diminishing, in the fourteenth century – Byzantium
could exercise, throughout Eastern Europe, a political, cultural
and religious influence much greater than one would expect from
a weak, impoverished and embattled empire.

The legislation of Justinian was flexible on the question of the
election of metropolitans. It allowed for the consecration of
metropolitans either by their own synods, or by the patriarch (cf.
above, p. 73). In the late Byzantine period, however, the growth
of patriarchal centralization made it accepted practice that metropolitans be elected by the patriarchal synod in Constantinople: the
patriarch would personally choose a candidate among three presented by members of his synod.[42] The practice had been questioned in Russia in the eleventh and twelfth centuries and was
directly challenged in the fifteenth, in favour of the ancient procedure which allowed the election and consecration of metropolitans by the synod of the province. Throughout the thirteenth

---

[42] Balsamon, Commentary on Canon 28 of Chalcedon, Rhalles-Potles, II, p. 284;
cf. Sokolov, *op. cit.*, p. 251; E. Herman, 'Appunti sul diritto metropolitico nella
Chiesa bizantina', OCP, XIII, 1947, pp. 529–33. The synod (σύνοδος ἐνδημοῦσα)
was made up of metropolitans present in Constantinople. The metropolitan of
Russia himself took part in its deliberations during his visits to the capital. Cf. also
Darrouzès, *Recherches*, pp. 472–82 (a discussion of the formal procedure of election);
also *Documents*, pp. 11–36, 117–89.

and fourteenth centuries, however, the patriarchal power in this area remained unquestioned.

Of course, centralization of ecclesiastical power in Constantinople also implied greater influence on the part of the emperor. The very formal canonical prohibitions against the election of clergy by civil authorities[43] were never understood in Byzantium as excluding imperial 'consent', or 'confirmation' of elections performed by the patriarchal synod. The distinction was clearly hypocritical at the time of the empire's great strength, when emperors could exercise decisive influence on all ecclesiastical affairs, including episcopal elections. But this is not necessarily true of the later period. Whereas the emperor's will remained decisive in the appointment of patriarchs (he chose one candidate out of three presented by the synod), his control was far from absolute in general Church affairs. The patriarch and his synod were generally strong enough to withstand imperial pressure, if they really so desired. For example, they resisted successfully the plans for union with the Roman Church. In patriarchal acts of episcopal elections in the fourteenth century, formal imperial approval is sometimes, but not always, mentioned.[44] In the case of the metropolitan of Russia, however, whose political role was immensely greater than that of a regular Byzantine provincial primate, 'symphony' between Church and emperor was indeed a necessity. This appears very clearly in the acts of election of Russian metropolitans of the fourteenth century: in 1354, the Bishop of Vladimir, Alexis, is transferred to the metropolitan see of Kiev by synodal decree approved by the emperor (εὐδοκίᾳ καὶ ἐπικρίσει τοῦ κρατίστου καὶ ἁγίου μου αὐτοκράτορος).[45] A similar formal procedure appears in the election of Pimen (1380).[46] Also, using one of his most traditional rights – based upon the idea

---

[43] II Nicaea, Canon 3: 'Any election of a bishop, a priest, or a deacon by civil powers remains void (ἄκυρον)', Rhalles-Potles, *op. cit.*, p. 564.

[44] Cf. under Patriarch Isidore (1348) the transfer of a metropolitan from Palaiopatras to Monembasia (κοινῇ ... ψήφῳ τοῦ περὶ ἡμᾶς χοροῦ τῶν ἱερωτάτων ἱεραρχῶν ... καὶ γνώμῃ τοῦ κρατίστου καὶ ἁγίου μου αὐτοκράτορος), MM, I, p. 274; however imperial 'opinion' is not mentioned for similar transfers in 1343 and 1345 (*ibid.*, pp. 233–5, 242–3). In 1380, the Synod of Patriarch Neilos formally acknowledged the right of the emperor to confirm the elections and transfers of metropolitans; however, some unilateral imperial acts were challenged by the Church. Cf. V. Laurent, 'Les droits de l'empereur en matière ecclésiastique. L'accord de 1380–1382', REB, XIII, 1955, pp. 5–20.

[45] MM, I, pp. 338, 352.

[46] Χάριτι τοῦ παναγίου Πνεύματος διὰ τῆς ἡμῶν μετριότητος ψηφῷ τῆς περὶ αὐτὴν ἱερᾶς συνόδου ... καὶ εὐδοκίᾳ καὶ ἐπινεύσει τοῦ κρατίστου καὶ ἁγίου μου αὐτοκράτορος, MM, II, p. 17.

accepted in Nicaea (325) that administration of the Church was to conform to that of the state – the emperors normally defined the geographical limits of ecclesiastical jurisdiction of patriarchs and metropolitans.[47] John VI Cantacuzenos exercised this right in a chrysobull suppressing the metropolitanate of Galicia (1347); he also himself informed the metropolitan and the Russian princes of his decision.[48] The imperial chrysobull was confirmed *post factum* by the synod.[49] Similarly, John V presided over a synod which limited the borders of the new metropolitanate of Lithuania (1361).[50] In other similar cases, however, imperial decisions are not mentioned: for example, in the re-establishment of the metropolitanate of Galicia (1371),[51] or the final reinstatement of Cyprian as metropolitan (1389).[52] It is difficult to ascertain whether the omission is due to the absence of the emperor from the city at the time when the decisions were taken, or to a deliberate will of the patriarchate to act independently, or simply to the fact that imperial documents relative to those events are not preserved.

Keeping firm administrative grasp upon the Russian metropolitanate, the Byzantine authorities, since the beginning of Russian Christianity, regularly secured the appointment of a Greek prelate to occupy the position of metropolitan. The two Russians who assumed that position – Hilarion (1051) and Clement (1147–55) – did so through a deliberate break with tradition, which, at least in the case of Clement, was violently opposed not only by Constantinople, but by those Russians who intended to maintain the canonical *status quo*. Only in the thirteenth century, as the weakened Byzantine government, exiled in Nicaea, was forced to adopt a much more flexible policy towards the Orthodox Slavs, were Russian princes allowed to present their own candidates for the metropolitanate, with the patriarchate still preserving its right to accept or reject them. But since, in the thirteenth and fourteenth centuries, several political centres were in violent competition for the control of Russia, each of them became interested in installing its own candidate for the primatial see of Kiev, or, eventually, to split the metropolitanate by creating separate ecclesiastical provinces. The struggle between these various

---

[47] Cf. many references in Bréhier, *Institutions*, pp. 436–7.
[48] Zachariae, *Jus*, III, pp. 700–3; MM, I, pp. 261–3, 263–5, 265–6; cf. below, app. I, pp. 280–2.
[49] MM, I, pp. 267–71.
[50] MM, I, p. 426.
[51] MM, I, pp. 578–80.
[52] MM, II, pp. 116–29.

provincialisms, on the one hand, and the unitarian view generally upheld in Byzantium, on the other, stands at the very centre of East European history during that period.

The new flexibility of Byzantine ecclesiastical policies in Russia did not imply that the idea of appointing Greeks to occupy the distant, but powerful metropolitanate was totally abandoned. The list of metropolitans for the thirteenth and fourteenth centuries shows a remarkable alternation in the ethnic background of incumbents: Joseph (a Greek, 1237–40); Cyril (a Russian, 1242–81); Maximus (a Greek, 1283–1305); Peter (a Russian, 1308–26); Theognostos (a Greek, 1328–53); Alexis (a Russian, 1354–78). The troubles which followed the death of Alexis (to be discussed below) led to a strengthening of Byzantine control under Cyprian (a Southern Slav, 1389–1406), Photius (a Greek, 1408–31) and Isidore (a Greek, 1436–41).

The consistently regular alternation of Greek and Russian metropolitans for over a century (1237–1378) could, perhaps, be considered accidental, if the Byzantine historian, Nicephorus Gregoras, in a book of his *Roman History*, where he presents an admittedly biased, but in some ways well-informed discussion of Russian affairs, did not describe it as a matter of deliberate policy of the Byzantine government. He writes: 'From the time when this nation [of the Russians] embraced true religion and accepted the divine baptism of the Christians, it was decided once for all that it would be placed under one single high-priest [ἀρχιερεῖ] . . . and that this primate would be subject to the throne of Constantinople . . . ; he would be selected alternately from among that nation [of the Russians] and from those who were born and raised here [i.e., in Byzantium], so that, after the death of each incumbent, there would be an alternation in succession for the ecclesiastical primacy in that country; thus, the link between the two nations, being strengthened and confirmed, would forever preserve a unity of faith . . .'[53]

The suggestion made by Gregoras that a formal agreement on the alternation existed since the time of Vladimir is unlikely and it is not confirmed by historical evidence: until the thirteenth century, the see of Kiev was regularly occupied by Greek prelates,

[53] In an important article, D. Obolensky has drawn attention to this text, which appears in a corrupt form in the Bonn edition of Gregoras (*Hist. byz.*, 36, 22–3, III, pp. 512–13). The correct text had been published previously by V. Parisot, *Livre XXXVII de l'histoire romaine de Nicéphore Grégoras. Texte grec complet donné pour la première fois, traduction française, notes philologiques et historiques*, Paris, 1851, p. 68. Cf. D. Obolensky, 'Byzantium, Kiev and Moscow'.

sent from Constantinople.[54] Moreover, a very official text of the fourteenth century – the act of election of Alexis as metropolitan in 1354 issued by Patriarch Philotheos – describes the appointment of a Russian-born metropolitan [ἐκεῖσε γεννηθεὶς καὶ τραφείς] as an *exceptional* act of condescension on the part of the patriarchate. Having mentioned the particular consideration shown by his predecessor, the Greek Theognostos, for Alexis (Theognostos had implicitly designated Alexis as his successor) and the recommendations received from Grand-prince Ivan Kalita of Moscow, the synodal act considers the appointment of a Russian as 'contrary to custom and to the safety of the church' (εἰ καὶ οὐδὲν ἦν σύνηθες διόλου καὶ ἀσφαλὲς τοῦτο τῇ ἐκκλησίᾳ), and condones it specifically 'for Alexis and for him alone' (εἰς αὐτὸν δὴ τοῦτον καὶ μόνον τὸν 'Αλέξιον). Finally, a definite decision is taken for the future: 'We by no means permit or concede that any one be appointed primate in Russia, if he comes from there, but only if [he is a native of] this God-glorified and God-exalted and blessed city of Constantinople, venerable in virtue and behaviour, well-versed and educated in preaching, knowledge and experience with ecclesiastical laws, able to manage canonical issues for the common good and in accordance with ecclesiastical and canonical order and to lead the Christian people of Russia to pastures of salvation, in full independence of mind and without any external interference. And we suggest that patriarchs who will succeed us also act accordingly, since this is better and contributes greatly to the building-up of the Church of God.'[55]

It appears to us that the presence of such a passage in an official act of the patriarchate excludes the possibility that a *formal agreement* concerning an alternation between Greek and Russian metropolitans of Kiev was in existence in the fourteenth century. Gregoras, who was in close personal touch with leading Constantinopolitan circles and, probably, a personal acquaintance of metropolitan Theognostos of Russia,[56] might be speaking of an *accepted policy* practiced by the Byzantines since the thirteenth century, which he would have ascribed – in admittedly very general terms – to the very origins of the establishment of the Church of

---

[54] The interesting discussion by D. Obolensky of the appointments of Kievan metropolitans in the eleventh and twelfth centuries (*ibid.*, pp. 45–75) shows the 'possibility' that some of them might have been Russians, nominated by Russian princes. But there is no hard evidence, except for Hilarion and Clement (whose appointment was challenged) that this was so, and no facts to show a regular alternation between Greeks and Russians.

[55] MM I, pp. 337–8.   [56] Cf. Obolensky, *ibid.*, pp. 30–1.

Russia. Furthermore, one could surmise that the policy of alternation was personally favoured by Gregoras' correspondent and friend, the powerful metropolitan Theognostos, who succeeded the Russian Peter and nominated the Russian Alexis to succeed him. The existence of such unwritten policy-guidelines may also explain the emphasis with which Patriarch Philotheos makes his point about Russian appointments: a staunch defender of patriarchal centralization, Philotheos may have been personally opposed to the views and policies described by Gregoras and supported by Theognostos. The trend towards centralization (to be discussed below) will indeed characterize the administration of 'hesychast' patriarchs, of whom Philotheos was the strongest. The confusing developments which occurred after the death of Alexis (1378) and which included nominations and consecrations of Russian candidates to the metropolitanate, happened very much against the will of Philotheos, whose efforts would eventually lead (after his own death) to a restoration of a Byzantine appointee, Cyprian, as sole metropolitan (1389). One can also observe that the two successors of Cyprian, Photius and Isidore, were both 'born and raised' in Constantinople, in full accordance with the synodal decision of 1354 taken under the presidency of Philotheos, so that the advice given by Philotheos to his successors not to appoint metropolitans nominated by Russian princes was actually followed between 1389 and 1441.

In any case, Byzantine policies in Russia, throughout the fourteenth century, tended to strengthen administrative control over the Church by the patriarchate. In spite of some inconsistencies provoked mainly by the vagaries of the internal situation in Byzantium and by contradictory pressures of foreign powers, the dependence of the Russian metropolitan upon the centre of the Orthodox 'commonwealth' provided him with great additional powers in asserting a policy of unification at a time when centrifugal tensions will greatly increase and a separate political centre will compete for the inheritance of the Kievan realm. Perhaps the greatest obstacle to a consistent leadership by Constantinople was found in the distance separating Byzantium from the residence of the metropolitan in northern Russia (Moscow, since 1308). The voyage took months, so that long periods of time separated the death of a metropolitan and the arrival of a successor. However, at no time did the patriarchate forfeit its right to consecrate a new metropolitan in Constantinople, whether he was a Greek or a Russian. Understandably, the various interests involved in the new appointments came into play during the long vacancies and added to the difficulties of keeping the metropolitanate as a unit.

4. FIRST CHALLENGES TO UNITY

In the preceding chapters, we have described the 'metropolitan of all Russia' as the main representative in Russia of Byzantine universalism. We have also seen how Metropolitan Cyril (1242–81), a nominee of the Grand-prince of Galicia – in the extreme south-west of Russia – spent most of his tenure as metropolitan in the Mongol-dominated north-east, thus inaugurating the trend of the Church policies dominant in the following century. His successor, the Greek Maximus (1283–1305), established himself permanently in the Grand-principality of Vladimir-on-the-Klyazma. We will later discuss more fully the reasons for this option taken by the metropolitans, which undoubtedly and from the beginning was supported by Constantinople. But some of these reasons can be clearly seen on the basis of facts described in the preceding chapters: the generally friendly relations between the government of Byzantium and the Golden Horde, strengthened by Genoese commercial interests; the Crusading movement, led by the Teutonic Knights and soon emulated by Poland, which threatened, from the West, the very survival of the Byzantine Commonwealth and of the Orthodox faith; the relative un-reliability of the princes of 'Little Russia', tempted by Western alliances, and of the Grand-princes of Lithuania, still formally pagan, but also occasionally attracted by Western Christianity. Under those circumstances, the Mongol empire, even if it imposed a heavy burden upon the population of Russia (but not upon the Church and its Greek leaders!), appeared as a more secure framework of the maintenance of the Byzantine heritage.

However, the transfer of the metropolitan's seat away from its traditional residence in Kiev and his policies of solidarity with north-eastern princes, vassals of the Tatars, provoked secessionist moves in the south-west. These moves, which led to the creation of separate metropolitanates in Galicia and Lithuania were not directed against Byzantine Orthodoxy, but were aiming at safe-guarding it in areas, which were now ecclesiastically under-administered and whose princes justifiably felt abandoned after the metropolitan's departure to the north. How could he provide the south-western dioceses with bishops, and exercise a meaningful leadership when he was separated from them not only by distance, but also by severely kept political borders? Was not the Orthodox flock of Galicia-Volhynia ('Little Russia' in Greek sources) and Lithuania left as a defenceless prey to Western proselytistic imperialism? Such were undoubtedly the arguments presented to the patriarchate in Byzantium in favour of the creation of separate metropolitanates in Western regions of Russia.

The Galician Grand-prince Yuri I (1301–8), a grandson of Daniel, had succeeded in briefly restoring a country, devastated by Mongols and under pressure from Poland and Lithuania, to the position of buffer-state between East and West. It appears that he even reassumed the title of 'king' (*rex Russiae*) which belonged to his grandfather.[57] As in the case of Daniel, such an act normally presupposed diplomatic contacts with the papacy, which was the legal source of such titles, and therefore a threat to the traditional belonging of Galicia to the Byzantine *oikouméne*. Although there is no evidence that Yuri I was seriously inclined to change his religious allegiance, he was in a position to challenge the Byzantines in demanding the relatively modest favour of a separate metropolitanate, repeating the diplomatic scenario played by the Bulgarians and the Serbs in the thirteenth century, when they obtained from Byzantium the recognition of their independent Churches. In any case, Greek sources formally testify to the elevation of the bishop of Halich to the status of a metropolitan with the bishops of Vladimir-in-Volhynia, Kholm, Peremyshl', Lutsk and Turov, as his suffragans. The event occurred under Emperor Andronicus II and at the beginning of the second patriarchate of Athanasius I (1303–9).[58] It is remarkable that no mention of this action is to be found either in the Russian chronicles, or in the recently published voluminous correspondence between Emperor Andronicus II and Patriarch Athanasius,[59] but we know that Athanasius promoted a programme of Church reform, based upon strengthening the power of the patriarchate, so that the establish-

---

[57] Hrushevsky, *Istoriya*, p. 113.

[58] The following item appears in the *Notitia episcopatum* of Andronicus II with the metropolitans of Halich receiving the number 81 in the order of precedence of the metropolitanates (the metropolitan 'of Russia' (i.e. 'Kiev and all Russia') being downgraded from No. 60 to No. 71): Πά. Ὁ Γαλίτζης. Αὕτη ἐπισκοπὴ ἐξ ἀρχῆς οὖσα τῆς Μεγάλης ᾽Ρωσίας ἐτιμήθη εἰς μητρόπολιν παρὰ τοῦ ἀοιδίμου βασιλέως κυροῦ ᾽Ανδρονίκου Παλαιολόγου τοῦ γέροντος ἐπὶ τοῦ ἁγιωτάτου πατριάρχου κυρίου ᾽Αθανασίου ἐν ἔτει᾽ δωια τῆς γ᾽ ἐπινεμήσεως, Gelzer, *Notitiae*, p. 599; 'Beiträge', pp. 255, 260–1; cf. Grumel-Laurent, *Régestes*, I, 4, No. 1592, pp. 374–5. The list of the suffragans appears in the synodal act of 1347, suppressing the metropolitanate of Halich (MM, I, p. 269).

[59] A.-M. Talbot, ed., *The Correspondence of Athanasios I* (CFHB, VII), Dumbarton Oaks Texts, III, Washington, D.C., 1975.

ment of numerous new metropolitanates, all responsible directly to Constantinople,[60] may have been in line with his views about Russia as well. So a metropolitan of Halich, presumably Niphon, was appointed in 1303–5.[61] But as far as Galicia is concerned, these views changed rapidly. By a stroke of diplomatic virtuosity, which was to be repeated by Byzantine patriarchs later in the fourteenth century, Athanasius soon restored the unity of the metropolitanate of Russia.

The death of the Greek metropolitan Maximus occurred in 1305 in Vladimir-on-the-Klyazma, where he was also buried. It does not seem that the appointment of a Greek successor was considered, which confirms the hypothesis, discussed above, of an unwritten agreement concerning an alternation of Greek and Russian candidates for the see. However, the situation was complicated – and would remain so throughout the fourteenth century – by the existence of two Russian Grand-principalities. As a result, Patriarch Athanasius and the Byzantine authorities were confronted with two candidates (Niphon, the original appointee to the see of Halich is not mentioned in connection with the events of 1305–8: he either died, or was obliged to resign his see). The candidate proposed by the 'king' of Galicia, Yuri I, Peter, the head of a monastery in Galicia and noted iconographer, was presumably selected to replace Niphon as metropolitan of Galicia. His competitor, Geronty, was sent to Constantinople by the Grand-prince of Vladimir, Michael Yaroslavich of Tver, as candidate for the see of 'all Russia'.

Three years passed before a solution was given to the ecclesiastical situation in Russia. This long delay cannot be explained only by the time required for the admittedly long trips to Constantinople: clearly, negotiations and pressures prolonged the hesitations of the patriarchate before it took action. Finally, in May–June 1308, Peter, the candidate from Galicia, was appointed

---

[60] One of the *Notitia* signals the particular predisposition (φιλοτιμία) of Andronicus II to set up new metropolitanates (Gelzer, 'Beiträge', p. 261). Andronicus was the main supporter of the patriarch's policies (cf. A. M. Talbot, 'The patriarch Athanasius and the Church', DOP, 27, 1973, pp. 13–28). There is no evidence however to support Sokolov's view that Andronicus aimed at a greater control of the emperor over ecclesiastical appointments and was seeking the transfer of ecclesiastical revenues to the State (*Arkhierei*, pp. 206–15). For a thorough discussion on the establishment of the metropolitanate of Galicia, see particularly Pavlov, 'O nachale'; Tikhomirov, *Galitskaya Mitropoliya*; cf. also Golubinsky, *Istoriya*, II, 1, pp. 96–7; Hrushevsky, *Istoriya*, pp. 269–71; Ammann, *Abriss*, pp. 88–9.

[61] The name of Niphon, as the first metropolitan of Halich, occurs in a letter of King Casimir of Poland, written in 1370 (MM, I, 577).

93

as sole metropolitan for the see 'of Kiev and all Russia'[62] by Patriarch Athanasius and his synod. This striking diplomatic compromise, which put a temporary end to Galician separatism, but also gave the Galician candidate authority over the whole of the Russian Church, clearly shows that, in the Byzantine view, the unity of the metropolitanate had priority over the complaints from 'Little Russians' that their area was ecclesiastically under-administered.

Peter arrived in Vladimir-on-the-Klyazma, in northern Russia, in 1309, having visited Kiev, and possibly Galicia-Volhynia, on the way. He eventually chose, as his permanent residence, the still unassuming city of Moscow and became, as we shall see below, one of the initial builders of Moscow's supremacy. Two other names of separate 'metropolitans of Galicia' – Gabriel and Theodore – appear in the sources in the period between 1325 and 1347: both were eventually either deposed or reduced to the rank of simple bishops through the interventions of Peter's successor, the Greek Metropolitan Theognostos.[63] These brief reappearances of

[62] For the date, see Golubinsky, *op. cit.*, p. 105. Since the list of King Casimir (see app. 4, p. 287) names Peter as a successor of Niphon in Galicia, H. Gelzer has supposed the existence of two candidates named Peter ('Beiträge', p. 257). A. S. Pavlov, on the other hand, proposed the hypothesis of an initial appointment of Peter as metropolitan of Galicia (1305–8) and his transfer to the metropolitanate of Kiev after the rejection of Geronty's candidacy (*op. cit.*, p. 221). It would seem more reasonable to suppose that the presence of Peter's name on Casimir's list reflects his nomination to the see by Yuri I: Peter may even have acted in Galicia as metropolitan-elect before going to Constantinople (see the example of Cyril, above, Ch. 2, p. 40).

[63] The presence of a bishop of Lutsk at the funeral of Metropolitan Peter in Moscow (1326) seems to indicate him as suffragan of the metropolitan of Kiev, and not of Halich (*Troits.*, p. 358). If there was no metropolitan of Halich in 1326, one appears – with the title of ὑπέρτιμος – on the presence-list of a synodal act of April 1331 (MM, I, p. 164). One can presume that this was Gabriel, mentioned in Casimir's list as successor of Peter, and that he was struggling in Constantinople for the preservation of his title, for Metropolitan Theognostos was actively asserting his power in Galicia-Volhynia, consecrating a 'bishop' of Halich, Theodore (May 1328; Regel, *Analecta*, p. 52) and a bishop of Lutsk in December 1331 (*ibid.*, p. 53). In 1332, he also visited Constantinople and Sarai, presumably settling the abolition of the metropolitanate of Galicia (*Nik.*, p. 206). However, the Polish interventions in Galicia-Volhynia after the death of Yuri I (1336–7) may have revived trends favouring ecclesiastical independence from the metropolitan residing in Moscow. Theodore, who had been consecrated 'bishop' of Halich by Theognostos, and acted as his faithful suffragan in 1330–5, seems to have assumed, some time between 1341–4, the title of metropolitan, since he is mentioned with that title in the list of Casimir. The acts of John Cantacuzenos suppressing the metropolitanate again mentions that it was 'uncanonically' re-established during the civil war (1341–7) between himself and Ann of Savoy (κατὰ τὸν πρὸ ὀλίγου δὲ γεγονότα καιρὸν τῆς συγχύσεως, Zachariae, *Jus*, III, p. 700), under Patriarch John Calecas (MM, I, p. 262); cf. Tikhomirov, *op. cit.*, pp. 75–89; Pavlov, *op. cit.* 223–8; F. Tinnefeld, 'Kirchenpolitik', p. 365.

the metropolitanate of Galicia were undoubtedly due to the initiative of princes Bołeslav-Yuri and Lubart, but neither of them eventually succeeded in establishing a sufficiently permanent power-base to substantiate their claims (cf. above, Chapter 3). Confused by these erratic events, the drafter of a Byzantine *Notitia* makes the comment that 'the metropolitan of Halich received that honour many times, but was again demoted to the rank of bishop by the power of the metropolitan of Russia'.[64]

During the same period, the sources point also to a separate metropolitan 'of the Lithuanians', whose appearance clearly results from the growing power of Grand-prince Gedymin. It was created by Emperor Andronicus II and Patriarch John Glykys (1315–19).[65] The incumbent, Theophilus, took part in the Synod of Constantinople in 1317, 1327 and 1329.[66] His residence was in the old capital of Lithuania, Novgorodok (Nowogródek, Νοβογραδοπούλιον) and his suffragans were in Polotsk and, possibly, Turov.[67] In 1330, however, Theophilus died, and the powerful Metropolitan Theognostos made sure that he got no replacement.[68]

These first threats to the unity of the metropolitanate, provoked by political circumstances in Eastern Europe, did not modify the basic policies of the Byzantine ecclesiastical administration in Russia. They were handled with flexibility, but the full authority of the patriarchate was preserved and continued to exercise a decisive influence. As we will see later, it will survive much more serious challenges, which will come not only from the various political powers competing for leadership in Russia, but also from internal crisis in Byzantine society itself.

[64] Τὸν μὲν Γαλίτζης πολλάκις τιμηθέντα, εἰς ἐπίσκοπον αὖθις ὑποβιβάζεσθαι τῇ τοῦ ʻΡωσίας δυναστείᾳ, Gelzer, 'Beiträge', p. 261).

[65] ʻΟ Λιτβάδων. Τὰ Λιτβάδα, ἐνόρια ὄντα τῆς Μεγάλης ʻΡωσίας, μητρόπολις γεγόνασι παρὰ τοῦ αὐτοῦ βασιλέως ἐπὶ τοῦ ἁγιωτάτου πατριάρχου κυροῦ ʻΙωάννου τοῦ Γλυκέος, Gelzer, 'Beiträge', p. 266).

[66] MM, I, pp. 72, 143, 147.

[67] Cf. MM, I, p. 425. Turov traditionally belonged to 'Little Russia' and, therefore, to the metropolitan of Halich. But it had been occupied by Gedymin.

[68] A contemporary notebook, preserved in the *Vatic. gr.* 840, contains an inventory of Theophilus' personal belongings performed by the chancery of Metropolitan Theognostos (cf. Priselkov-Fasmer, 'Otryvki', pp. 48–70). Since no 'bishop' of Lithuania was appointed, the see was considered as unoccupied (σχολάσας, cf. Gelzer, 'Beiträge', p. 261). It found a new incumbent in 1355.

5

Victory of the Hesychasts in Byzantium: ideological and political consequences

Long regarded as a hair-splitting debate in a narrow circle of theologians, the religious controversies of the fourteenth century have now been generally recognized as reflecting a crisis of civilization and their conclusion as having had profound consequences for the future of Byzantine society and the post-Byzantine period.[1] Their repercussions in the Slavic countries and in Russia were likewise substantial. Of course, the Slavs were not in a position to contribute in any way to the substance of the theological debates, but they did receive in that period from Byzantium a renewed spiritual leadership and accepted the intellectual cultural and ideological goals of Byzantine 'Hesychasm'.

The term 'Hesychasm' cannot be used in the specific context of Byzantine history without reservations.[2] Its original meaning goes back to the beginnings of Eastern Christian monasticism in the fourth century, when hermits, living in solitude, or 'silence' (ἡσυχία), were already called 'Hesychasts' (ἡσυχασταί), to distinguish them from monks living in community ('cenobites'). The practice of breathing techniques, aimed at achieving concentration upon the 'prayer of the mind', or 'Jesus-prayer' is also, and more specifically, designated as 'Hesychasm', especially in the Byzantine context, where these techniques became increasingly popular in the thirteenth and the fourteenth centuries.

The theological debates of that period did begin precisely by a controversy, involving Byzantine 'Hesychasts', who found a powerful apologist in the person of Gregory Palamas (1296–1359), a monk of Mount Athos who eventually became archbishop of Thessalonica. The debates involved Byzantine society as a whole and ended in the victory of Palamas and his followers. This was

[1] See the helpful bibliographical review by D. Stiernon, 'Bulletin sur le palamisme', *REB*, 30, 1975, pp. 231–41; also see Podskalsky, *Theologie*.
[2] Cf. Meyendorff, 'O vizantiiskom isikhazme'; also *Byzantine Hesychasm* (London, 1974), Introduction.

not simply the victory of a group of hermits who desired to follow a particular spiritual tradition in the wilderness of Mount Athos: the result of the controversy determined the attitudes and policies of the Byzantine Church as a whole. The theology of Palamas, formulated on the occasion of his 'defence' of the hesychast monks,[3] involved a broad discussion on the very nature of the Christian faith itself. It affirmed the possibility of direct ('mystical') knowledge of God and the primacy of incarnational, eschatalogical and sacramental values over secular concerns. This provoked a polarization – not new in Byzantine society – between a monastic-dominated Church and the 'humanists' who promoted the study of Greek antiquity and who were becoming increasingly attracted by the opportunities in the West, particularly in Italy, with the beginning of the Renaissance. The victory of the Hesychasts encouraged trans-national contacts between monastic communities, promoted numerous new translations of Byzantine texts into Slavic, and undoubtedly had a profound impact upon Russian medieval civilization, which will be discussed below. In terms of ecclesiastical policies in Russia, the monks strongly reaffirmed the supremacy of a patriarchate which they now controlled as the instrument of unity and Orthodox integrity. Their essential motivation went certainly beyond 'Hesychasm' as a technique of spirituality, and was rather aiming at maintaining the values and structures of the Orthodox faith in the midst of a rapidly changing political situation in the Middle East and Eastern Europe. The various dimensions of these events, occurring in Byzantium itself, and their impact upon the life of the entire 'commonwealth' deserve serious discussion and evaluation.

I. CRISIS IN THE BYZANTINE RELIGIOUS AND CULTURAL OUTLOOK

The historical circumstances of the theological debates in Byzantium in the fourteenth century are well-known.[4] Around 1330, Barlaam, the 'Calabrian philosopher', came to Constantinople

---

[3] The major work of Palamas – a collection of nine treatises, divided in three groups and popularly referred to as 'Triads' (cf. Philotheos, *Life of Palamas*, PG CLI, col. 91. 588D: ἐννέα μὲν οὖν οἱ πάντες ὁμοῦ τῷ σοφῷ τηνικαῦτα συντάττονται λόγοι ... εἰς τρεῖς διῃρημένοι τριάδας); cf. their ed. with a French transl., J. Meyendorff, ed., *Grégoire Palamas, Défense des saints hésychastes* (Spicilegium Sacrum Lovaniense, 30–1), 2 vols., second revised ed., Louvain, 1973.

[4] Cf. Meyendorff, *Introduction* (Eng. tr. as *A Study*); cf. also above, note 1.

and soon acquired some prestige in intellectual circles, enjoying the support of Emperor Andronicus III and his 'Grand Domesticus', John Cantacuzenos. In 1337-8, however, he entered into a theological debate with Gregory Palamas – then on Mt Athos – on the nature of theological discourse. His position tends to emphasize the unknowability of God and the inadequacy of human theological reasoning: in a fierce attack against the Latin scholastic interpretation of Trinitarian dogma, Barlaam challenges Aquinas' claim to 'prove' divine truths,[5] but unavoidably implicit in his anti-Latin polemics is the question of whether the Greek side can claim to 'prove' the 'rightness' of its own theological position. To that question, Barlaam answers negatively: neither side – at least in the dispute on the procession of the Holy Spirit – can claim 'apodictic' victory, because Aristotelian logic is able to reach either conclusion on the basis of the available revealed premises. In his reactions to Barlaam's position, Gregory Palamas on the one hand denies that Aristotelian logic can serve as a criterion in showing which theological arguments are truly decisive; on the other hand, he develops at length the patristic doctrines of 'deification' (θέωσις), or communion (κοινωνία), with God, which represent, in his opinion, the only acceptable context for a Christian epistemology. In order to maintain the basic antinomy of the Eastern Christian understanding of God–man relationships – 'God is absolutely transcendent in His essence', but 'man, in Christ, shares the life of God' – Palamas also develops the distinction, in God, between 'essence' and 'energy'.

The position of Palamas was endorsed by the Council of 1341, and Barlaam left for Italy. However, the theology of Palamas was, for a time, opposed by Gregory Akindynos, later by the philosopher Nicephorus Gregoras. From 1342 to 1347, Patriarch John Calecas, mainly from political motivations, supported Akindynos, but he was deposed after the end of the civil war, which saw the victory and enthronement of John VI Cantacuzenos (1347). Cantacuzenos was, or had become in 1341, a staunch supporter of Palamas. He presided over two councils (1347, 1351) which again endorsed the theology of the monks. Gregory Palamas himself was elected archbishop of Thessalonica (1347) and his immediate

---

[5] Barlaam's personality and thought has been recently the subject of much debate. For our own interpretation, see 'Un mauvais théologien de l'unité au XIVe siècle: Barlaam le Calabrais' in *1054-1954. L'Eglise et les églises*, II, Chevetogne, 1954, pp. 47-64 (repr. in *Byzantine Hesychasm*, London, 1974, V). For a more recent account of Barlaam's thought and more positive evaluation see G. Podskalsky, *op. cit.*, pp. 126-50.

friends and disciples, Isidore Boukharis, Callistos and Philotheos Kokkinos were successively enthroned as patriarchs.

The main spokesmen of the anti-Palamite opposition included the brilliant Calabrian 'philosopher', Barlaam, the more subdued, but intellectually consistent theologian Akindynos, and the scholarly, but somewhat pathetic historian Nicephorus Gregoras. In the latter part of the century, a significant group of Byzantine Thomists – led by the brothers Demetrios and Prochoros Kydones – also opposed Palamism, but in the context of a deliberate trend towards a rapprochement with Italy and the Latin West.

Since the beginning of the debate between Barlaam and Palamas, the issue of ancient philosophy, of which Palamas invariably spoke as 'the wisdom from outside' (ἡ θύραθεν σοφία), opposing it to the true teaching of the apostles and fathers of Christianity, was an object of controversy. A certain polarization between those who promoted the study of Greek antiquity – frequently designated as 'humanists' – and the monastic traditionalists had been a permanent element in the intellectual life of Byzantium, at least since the ninth century, and its recurrence in the Palaeologan period followed certain patterns of the past. However, the political possibilities and cultural options open to the Byzantines were now quite different. Here are three interconnected aspects of the situation, which gave the victory of the Hesychasts its particular significance.

(a) The conquest of Constantinople by the Crusaders in 1204 and the survival of Latin dominion in various parts of the former empire, even after the recapture of the city in 1261, led the Greeks to a new consciousness of their *Hellenism*. The term *Hellenes* had been used in the New Testament to designate the 'pagans', as distinct from Christians ("Ελληνες σοφίαν ζητοῦσιν, ἡμεῖς δὲ κηρύσσομεν Χριστὸν ἐσταυρωμένον, I Cor. 1.23), and it never ceased to be used throughout the Middle Ages in this religiously pejorative sense. However, the Byzantines were also aware that they were speaking the *language* of the ancient Hellenes: whereas their empire was 'Roman' and, as citizens, they were *Rhōmaioi*, they spoke 'Hellenic',[6] so that their entire civilization was expressed in that language. The Western Crusaders, who conquered Byzantium, belonged to the 'Roman' church and were citizens of the (Western Holy) 'Roman' empire, but they spoke Latin, or Frankish, and, in that sense, they were clearly distinct from those

[6] See for example οἱ Ἑλληνιστὶ φθεγγόμενοι, Chrysostom, *In Acta apost. 21*, PG, LX, col. 164.

who spoke 'Hellenic'. It is this language and this civilization which was now directly threatened, and the words *Hellas* and *Hellenes* became closely associated with the defence, by the Byzantines, of their cultural identity. The Empire of Nicaea, in particular, was seen as the *Hellenikon*, or as *Hellas*, and the emperor began to be compared not only with the biblical images of David and Solomon, but also with Alexander or Achilles.[7] This new discovery of 'Hellenism' implied greater identification with the language, the civilization and the history of ancient Greece. This identification was inevitably romantic, frequently only rhetorical. It was also quite compatible with the provincial nationalisms of Nicaea, or Epirus.[8] It did not represent a sharp break with Byzantium's past, since Byzantine intellectuals had never ceased to preserve and cultivate the ancient Greek heritage, but political weakness and constant struggle for survival, which characterized Byzantine society in the Palaeologan period, led to an attitude of ethnic defensiveness: 'Hellenic' culture, precisely because it was embattled and threatened from all sides, and because it could not any longer enjoy the shelter of a powerful empire, became, for some Byzantine intellectuals, the ultimate value to be maintained at all costs.

Under such circumstances, the victory of the Hesychasts was felt by some of those who are most frequently called the Byzantine 'humanists' as a tragedy of major proportions. And it did, indeed, represent a serious option taken by Byzantine society at a crucial historical moment: the leadership of the Church (with its decisive influence upon the life of state and society as well) now belonged to religious zealots with a different set of priorities.

There is no doubt that the leadership of Byzantine monasticism in the fourteenth century shared the traditional monastic distrust for 'secular studies' (ἡ ἔξω σοφία) and Palamas attacked Barlaam precisely on the grounds that he forgot the only possible Christian meaning of the word *Hellēn* – that of 'pagan' – and accepted the ancient philosophers as guides in defining the criteria of Christian theology.[9] However, it would be mistaken to identify the leaders

[7] On Nicaea as the centre of this new 'Hellenic' self-consciousness, see A. E. Vacalopoulos, *Origins of the Greek Nation. The Byzantine Period, 1204–1461*, New Brunswick, N.J., 1970, pp. 27–45; J. Irmscher, 'Nikäa als Zentrum des griechischen Patriotismus', *Revue des Etudes Sud-Est Européennes*, 8 (1970), pp. 33–47; M. Angold, *A Byzantine Government in Exile. Government and Society under the Lascarids of Nicaea (1204–1261)*, Oxford, 1975, pp. 29–31.

[8] Cf. the pertinent remarks of M. Angold, *op. cit.*, pp. 31–3.

[9] See particularly J. Meyendorff, ed., *Grégoire Palamas. Défense*; also *Introduction à l'étude de Grégoire Palamas*, Paris, 1959, pp. 173–94 (Eng. tr., *A Study*, pp. 116–33).

of Hesychasm as fanatics and obscurantists: Palamas himself studied Aristotle under the humanist Theodore Metochites[10] and did not condemn 'secular learning' as such.[11] Furthermore, John Cantacuzenos, whose support for Palamas and his disciples was unfailing after 1341 and whose attitude, in this respect, cannot be explained by political considerations alone, acted also as mecene and friend of 'humanists' like Demetrios Kydones. Patriarch Philotheos, a major figure of the Byzantine Church in the four-teenth century, wrote an *Encomion* of Palamas where praises for the hesychast leader are frequently intermingled with rhetorical references to Antiquity.[12] Formally what separated the religious zealots from the 'humanists' was only a question of methodological emphasis and theological inspiration. The hesychast churchmen were not aiming at the suppression of 'Hellenism' in Byzantium, but their primary concern was in the preservation of the Church, throughout Eastern Europe and on a supra-national level. In this sense, they became guardians of the older idea of the Byzantine Orthodox Commonwealth and the 'New Rome', which gradually, in the mind of the humanists, was being replaced with the nar-rower, more nationalistic and more secular-romantic idea of Byzantium (or even only Nicaea) as the new 'Athens'.[13] A formal discussion on the role of Aristotelian syllogisms in theology reflec-ted, in fact, a much deeper opposition between the understanding of man and of human society. Before the middle of the fourteenth century, Byzantine civilization lived for centuries with the un-resolved dilemma between 'Athens' and 'Jerusalem', the Academy and the Gospel, the wisdom of Antiquity and the immediacy of Christian mystical knowledge. The hesychast controversies brought this dilemma to the fore.[14] One can argue – as modern historians (and theologians) do – whether the resulting crisis was inevitable, whether the alternatives were rightly defined and whether the

---

[10] *Introduction*, p. 47 (*A Study*, pp. 29–30).

[11] Cf. the well-balanced remarks by G. Schirò, 'Gregorio Palamas e la scienza profana', *Le Millénaire du Mont Athos*, II, Chevetogne, 1964, pp. 81–96.

[12] See, for example, his glorification of secular learning at Constantinople, combined with the standard definition of secular philosophy as 'servant' of 'true wisdom' (PG, CLI, col. 554 AB).

[13] For Nicaea, as 'Athens', see Gregory of Cyprus, *Autobiography*, in W. Lameere, *La tradition manuscrite de la correspondence de Grégoire de Chypre*, Brussels-Rome, 1937, 179; Constantinople is identified with 'Athens' in the famous dialogue *Florentios* by Nicephorus Gregoras, P. L. M. Leone, ed. *Niceforo Gregora. Fiorenzo o intorno alla sapienza*, Naples, 1975.

[14] Cf. Meyendorff, 'Spiritual trends', p. 62 (also in P. Underwood, *The Kariye Djami*, vol. 4, Princeton, N.J., 1975, p. 106); cf. also Medvedev, *Gumanizm*, p. 29.

conflict was beneficial to the survival of Byzantine civilization, but one cannot deny the reality and the importance of the crisis itself.

(b) It has been noted several times, in recent studies on Byzantine 'humanists' and intellectuals that they represented, in Byzantine society, a close-knit elite, small in numbers and closely dependent upon the waning material welfare of the ruling class.[15] It is in that milieu that the sophisticated, romantic and socially conservative revival of 'Hellenism' was taking place, and that the anti-Palamite opposition recruited most of its influential members. If one recalls, on the other hand, that besides Constantinople, Thessalonica and Mistra, there were practically no centres where the 'humanists' could find any popular, material, or political support, one realizes that the ideals they represented no longer stood much chance of succeeding. And, whenever they consented to consider the facts realistically, they became aware of the doom to come.[16]

In contrast, the world of Byzantine monasticism, which was not limited, in its ideals, by the concern for the preservation of antique Hellenism, enjoyed widespread influence in the popular masses not only on territories still controlled by the Empire, but also in Turkish-occupied lands and certainly in Slavic lands. Its major centre, Mount Athos, was a permanent point of encounter with equally strong impact upon Greeks, Slavs, Georgians and, even, Arabs. Furthermore, the patriarchate of Constantinople – as we have already noted – exercised its administrative powers in immense territories, and countries, such as Russia, which would certainly not feel any commitment to the ideals of antique Hellenism, but continued to hold Christian Byzantium, its Church and its imperial tradition, in great esteem. In Constantinople itself, the history of the Church has known numerous confrontations between the more politically-minded episcopate and the monastic rigorists, especially in questions of Church – state relations, but the takeover of the patriarchate by the monks in the middle of the fourteenth century made such conflicts unlikely in the future. It also resulted in greater independence of the Church from imperial policies, an independence which became particularly obvious at

---

[15] See particularly I. Ševčenko, 'Society and intellectual life in the fourteenth century', *XIVe Congrès International des études byzantines*, Bucharest, 1971, Rapports I, pp. 8, 30; I. P. Medvedev, *op. cit.*, pp. 18–19.

[16] Cf. Ševčenko, 'The decline'. Cf. also the brilliant account by Donald M. Nicol, *Church and Society in the Last Centuries of Byzantium*, Cambridge, 1979.

the time of the conversion of Emperor John V to the Roman Church (1369). Could John V even dream of imposing his views and attitudes upon the Church, as Michael VIII had done after 1274? Through the mere size of its administrative apparatus, its international connections, and the support it received from the people, the Church, after the hesychast victory, was, in many ways, a more powerful body than the impoverished Empire. Psychologically and institutionally, this newly gained power made the survival of the Church possible after the empire's fall.

Under these circumstances, it is remarkable to note the stern loyalty to the old imperial system, which was still shown by the Church, whenever no major issues of theology or faith opposed it to the reigning emperor. Emperor John Cantacuzenos, for example, authoritatively exercised the traditional imperial power in choosing patriarchs and in defining borders of the ecclesiastical provinces.[17] The ideal of the universal empire is also expressed in the often-quoted letter of Patriarch Anthony to Grand-prince Basil of Moscow in 1397: 'It is not possible for Christians', he wrote, 'to have the Church and not to have the empire. . . .'[18] A visual expression of the same loyalty to the imperial idea can be seen in the representation of the Byzantine imperial pair together with that of the Russian Grand-prince and his wife on the episcopal vestment, or *sakkos*, of the metropolitan of Kiev, Photios (1408–31).[19]

Similar references can be easily multiplied to show that, after the victory of the Hesychasts, the Byzantine Church continued very actively to maintain and to promote the ideal of a Christian *oikouméne*, centred in Constantinople and headed by the emperor, whose role was defined in traditional terms of *Roman* and Christian universalism, whereas the concern of the 'humanists' for the preservation of *Greek* civilization was *de facto* resulting in an understanding of Byzantium as a Greek *nation* (γένος). 'The consciousness of being "Roman",' writes A. Vacalopoulos, 'gradually faded and was supplanted by a sense of "Greekness", though without any obvious break with historical tradition or the immediate past. The Hellenes merely adopted the political and cultural heritage of both ancient Greece and the Eastern Roman Empire . . . , which

---

[17] Imperial intervention was particularly obvious in the deposition of Callistos and the enthronement of Philotheos in 1353. On Cantacuzenos' letters concerning the ecclesiastical affairs in Russia, see above, p. 87.

[18] MM, II, pp. 188–92.

[19] Bank, *Iskusstvo*, plates 287–8; cf. also below, Chapter 10, p. 257.

over the centuries a Greek tradition eventually encompassed.'[20] This judgement is quite pertinent in its first part, as a description of the 'humanist' élite, but it fails to realize that the heritage of ancient Greece and that of the Christian Empire represented, in fact, the poles of an unresolved tension, which has *never* been 'encompassed' either in the Palaeologan period, or later. The more secular outlook implied by the incipient 'Hellenic' national-ism could certainly be considered as more realistic in terms of the actual situation prevailing in the fourteenth century, but it also presupposed a certain detachment from the values – religious, cultural and political – carried on for centuries by Christian Byzantium and which were still shared by the Orthodox Slavs. By taking over the patriarchate, the Athonite monks did much to maintain the position of Byzantium as the 'Queen of cities' – the Slavic *Tsar'grad* – and made possible the survival of the 'Roman' universalism it represented for several more centuries. But they did so at the price of a long and painful conflict with the 'human-ists', who then began to discover the West as the ultimate refuge of their cultural ideals.

(c) The discovery by some Byzantine intellectuals that the West could become a true heir of Hellenism is the third major aspect of the Byzantine spiritual crisis in the fourteenth century. In the past, the Byzantines – and particularly those among them who prided themselves on secular learning – looked upon Western 'bar-barians' with contempt, and considered Latin as hardly a civilized language. After the eleventh century, the military might of the Western Crusaders won the respect of the Byzantines, but, also, developed in them an attitude of justified defensiveness, hardly favourable to positive cultural encounters. In the Palaeologan period, the activity of numerous Genoese and Venetian merchants throughout 'Romania' made personal contacts easier and more frequent, and even sometimes contributed to their popularity among the Greeks. Some Byzantine intellectuals, in the middle of the fourteenth century, made the exhilarating discovery that Latins were not necessarily brutal soldiers or grasping merchants, and that Latin scholars who knew all about Aristotle and Plato were more numerous and better equipped than their Greek counterparts. Among those who experienced this discovery was Cantacuzenos' own secretary, Demetrios Kydones, who learned Latin at a convent of Dominicans in Genoese Galata, and was

---

[20] A. Vacalopoulos, *op. cit.*, p. 175.

amazed at the intellectual prowess of the Latins.[21] He became an advisor of Emperor John V and was closely involved in the latter's travel to Rome and conversion to the Roman Church.[22] The common trait of those Byzantines who, like Demetrios Kydones, or his brother Prochoros, or Manuel Calecas, or John Kyparissiotes, discovered and assimilated Thomist thought and methodology,[23] or who, like Bessarion in the next century, were willing to integrate themselves culturally in the Italian Renaissance, was that they did so as Greek patriots, convinced that Hellenism was doomed in Byzantium, but that – intellectually and culturally – it could still find shelter in the West.

Understandably, this particular group of intellectuals could hardly find a common language with the Hesychasts and considered the monks' victory in 1347–51 as a national disaster. In fact, the conflict between them lay, as we have seen earlier, in a different concept of the very nature of Byzantine civilization and in a different set of priorities. However, as we also have seen, it would be a mistake to consider the monastic party as totally opposed to the study of Greek antiquity, and it would be equally erroneous to reduce its stand to anti-Latinism. John Cantacuzenos, who consistently supported Palamas and his disciples, became also an articulate spokesman in favour of a union-council between the Churches of Constantinople and Rome. He made the proposal through ambassadors sent to the pope Clement VI at the very beginning of his reign (1347).[24] He reiterated it after his abdication as a spokesman of both church and state (1367)[25] and received full support of the reigning patriarch Philotheos, who informed other Orthodox prelates of the forthcoming council.[26] We will see below that Philotheos' envoy to Russia, Metropolitan Cyprian, will also promote the idea of a union-council in cooperation with the Grand-prince of Lithuania. Furthermore, Palamas himself developed his theology of energies in a way which was similar to the positions of Patriarch Gregory of Cyprus (1283–9), who made an 'overture' to the Latins by accepting to speak of an

---

[21] Demetrios' own description of his discoveries in his *Apologia*, in Mercati, *Notizie*, pp. 365–6; cf. Ševčenko, 'The decline', pp. 176–7; Meyendorff, *Byzantine Theology*, pp. 105–6.

[22] On this voyage, the classical monograph is still that of Halecki, *Empereur*.

[23] Cf. S. G. Papadopoulos, Ἑλληνικαὶ μεταφράσεις θωμιστικῶν ἔργων. Φιλοθωμισταὶ καὶ ἀντιθωμισταὶ ἐν Βυζαντίῳ Athens, 1967.

[24] Cantacuzenos, *Hist.* IV, 9, Bonn, III, III, pp. 53–62; cf. Gay, *Clément VI*, pp. 94–118.

[25] Meyendorff, 'Projets', pp. 149–77.

[26] MM, I, pp. 491–3 (Letter of Philotheos to the archbishop of Ohrid).

'eternal' procession of the Spirit from the Son.[27] He also had repeated contacts with the Genoese of Galata and the Hospitallers on Rhodes,[28] and so did also Patriarch Callistos, after his deposition in 1353.[29] Furthermore, Cantacuzenos sponsored, even after the hesychast victory, translations of Latin theologians into Greek and used them in his own writings. This openness to the West, which we find in Cantacuzenos and his hesychast friends, called for dialogue, not capitulation. Characteristically, the council planned by Cantacuzenos involved the full representation of the Eastern Church, including delegates of the other Eastern patriarchs, of the churches of Georgia, Bulgaria and Serbia, as well as particular representatives of 'distant' metropolitanates of the patriarchate of Constantinople: Russia (with some of his bishops), Trebizond, Alania and Zechia.[30] According to the vision implied in the plan, the true spokesmen for the East are those who speak on behalf of the entire Byzantine *oikouméne* – the 'Commonwealth' which includes the entire Orthodox world, in its multinationality – and not only a few Greek patriots, concerned with the preservation, at all costs, of Greek intellectual sophistication.

On all three levels which we have just described – the importance of 'secular' culture, universalism vs. nationalism, relations with the West – the parties which took part in the controversy of the fourteenth century clearly differed in priorities, although in formally defining their ideological positions, both sides remained faithful to accepted norms. For example, the theologians of Hesychasm never forbade the reading of ancient authors and, between 1351 and 1453, until the fall of Constantinople, Byzantine humanists could freely pursue Hellenic learning,[31] provided they accepted – at least formally – the Orthodox faith: without this freedom, the emergence of personalities like Bessarion and Gemisthos Pletho would have been impossible. On the other hand, the humanists at no time challenged the universal imperial claims

---

[27] Cf. Meyendorff, *Introduction*, pp. 25–30.
[28] This information is given by Akindynos, *Letters to Gregoras*, Marc. gr., 155, fol. 79.
[29] Cant., *Hist.*, IV, 38, Bonn, III, p. 275.
[30] Cf. Meyendorff, 'Projets', pp. 158, 166, 173. According to the project of Cantacuzenos, the metropolitan of Russia is the only one, among the 'distant' prelates, who would be called to the forthcoming council together with several of his suffragans. This detail shows Cantacuzenos' awareness of the situation in Russia; the Greek prelate who presided over the immense country, as 'catholic metropolitan' (καθολικὸς μητροπολίτης), enjoyed a prestige comparable to that of patriarchs or foreign καθολικοί.
[31] Cf. D. M. Nicol, 'The Byzantine Church and Hellenic learning in the fourteenth century', *Studies in Church History*, v, ed. G. J. Cumming, Leiden, 1969, pp. 23–56.

of the Palaeologans, or the idea of the Orthodox *oikouméne*, but they clearly did not put their hopes and their trust in such ideas, and preferred either to bemoan the weakness of their *nation*, or to console themselves with new opportunities available in the West.[32] In a sense, therefore, the coexistence of a monastic theology and of a more secular-oriented 'humanism', which characterized Byzantine society at all times, continued after the hesychast victory of 1347–51. The new factors of the situation were the formal commitment of the Church to the *theological position* of Gregory Palamas, which affirmed the doctrine of 'deification' (θέωσις) as the basis for an understanding of man's destiny, and practically implied a priority of transcending religious concerns, over all others. Recognizing the differences in historical, cultural and doctrinal contexts, one can compare the hesychast victory in Byzantium with the takeover of ruling positions in the Western Church by the Cluniac monks in the eleventh century: religious zealotism, increased 'barbarian' (Germanic vs. Italian in the West, Slavic vs. Greek in the East) influence upon political and ecclesiastical priorities, greater centralization of the Church (around the papacy in the West and around the patriarchate in the East) were the elements which can justify a comparison of the two situations.

In terms of Byzantino-Russian relations, the practical results of the internal crisis in Byzantium led to a more active administration by the patriarchate of its Russian metropolitanate and to a strong spiritual and intellectual renewal of Byzantine influences, especially in monastic circles, frequently through the mediation of Southern Slavs. The consistency of Byzantine policies in Russia was, sometimes, interrupted by inner troubles in Constantinople and by external pressures. The political vagaries and internal upheavals during the reign of John V Palaeologus (1353–91), the extreme financial weakness of the imperial treasury, which made it susceptible to bribes by powerful Italian merchants, and East European rulers, the constant Turkish menace upon Constantinople and, finally, direct pressures of Western powers, especially Hungary and Poland, caused some dramatic reversals and inconsistencies. But, ideologically, the leadership given by hesychast patriarchs – particularly Philotheos Kokkinos – remained basically the same and exercised a decisive impact upon Russia in the fourteenth century.

---

[32] Numerous texts quoted in I. Ševčenko, 'The decline'.

2. THE PATRIARCHATE OF CONSTANTINOPLE:
CLAIMS TO UNIVERSALITY

Throughout its history, Eastern Christian monasticism offers numerous examples of opposition to episcopal and patriarchal institutions, traditionally more inclined than the monks towards political 'realism' and doctrinal compromise. The controversy of the monks of Studios against Patriarch Tarasios, Nicephorus and Methodius during the iconoclastic period, the role of the monastic zealotism in the 'Ignatian' opposition against Patriarch Photius in the ninth century, the stand taken by Byzantine monks against several patriarchs at the end of the thirteenth century, all show that monastic loyalty to the patriarch and the bishops was never unconditional. Monks always suspected possible betrayals, by the bishops, of their doctrinal or moral integrity. Furthermore, ever-recurring trends in Eastern monasticism produced spiritualized interpretations of ecclesiastical hierarchy: in the neo-platonic tradition going back to Origen and reinterpreted in the peculiar system of Pseudo-Dionysius, the hierarchy is described in terms of a personal *state*, not ecclesiastical function, and the bishop is seen as 'a deified and divine man', with the implication that the loss of personal holiness involves also the loss of his hierarchical position.[33]

Another spiritualistic trend in monasticism, associated with the writing of Pseudo-Macarios and sometimes labelled as 'Messalian' (although neither the author of the Macarian writing, nor his more eminent disciples can be reproached with heretical Messalianism),[34] also struggled against formal, automatic, or magic interpretation of hierarchical power. Some authors representing this trend, including the great Symeon the New Theologian – whose popularity among Byzantine Hesychasts was very great – could also speak, as Pseudo-Dionysius, of 'true' priests and bishops, meaning charismatic leaders, and condemn those who desire priesthood for material reasons, and episcopacy as a source of wealth.[35] In the fourteenth century, the Hesychasts stood in the same tradition and it is certainly in the same spirit that Palamas

---

[33] See for example, Ps.-Dionysius, *On the ecclesiastical hierarchy*, i, 3, PG iii, col. 373C; cf. R. Roques, *L'univers dionysien: Structure hiérarchique du monde selon le pseudo-Denys*, Paris, 1954, pp. 98ff.
[34] See the brief outline of these trends in Meyendorff, *Byzantine Theology*, pp. 66–75.
[35] Cf. for example *Hymn XIX*, ed. J. Koder, Syméon le Nouveau Théologien, *Hymnes*, ii (Sources Chrétiennes, 174), Paris, 1971, p. 96.

himself, in 1340, wrote the 'Haghioretic Tome', signed by the leaders of Athonite monasticism, as a theological manifesto, quite independent of any statement of the hierarchy.[36] Similarly, during the civil war (1341–7), Palamas and his disciples opposed the reigning patriarch, John Calecas.

And nevertheless, it is the renewed monastic influence in the fourteenth century that led to an administrative and ideological reassertion of the ecumenical patriarchate in its leadership of the Byzantine Orthodox world. The reassertion began before the actual victory of the Palamites in 1347–51. Certainly, the Hesychasts shared the basic principles of Eastern Christian ecclesiology, which were incompatible with any tendency towards absolutizing the power of the patriarch and the bishops and considering them as infallible. But the Palamites of the fourteenth century also held a strongly Christocentric and sacramental view of the Church,[37] in at least some contrast with more spiritualistic views, which had been apparent in the hesychast tradition of earlier centuries. Furthermore, their concern for moral and social issues (in some contrast with the eremitic monastic trends of the past, and parallel to the ideology of the Western Cluniac movement) made them look at the patriarchate and its administrative apparatus as a legitimate tool for the preservation of permanent values, which included both Christian Orthodoxy and Byzantine Christian civilization, as they understood it. In this sense, as we noted before, the religious zealots who occupied positions of leadership in the Byzantine Church and who enjoyed widespread popular support and strong backing from political leaders like John Cantacuzenos in Byzantium, and John Alexander in Bulgaria, can be designated

---

[36] PG, CL, cols. 1225–36; cf. Meyendorff, *Introduction*, pp. 350–1; this 'independence' of the *Haghioretic Tome* is underlined, but also overemphasized by L. M. Clucas, 'Eschatological Theory in Byzantine Hesychasm: a parallel to Joachim da Fiore', BZ, 70, Oct. 1977, 2, pp. 324–46. Rightly pointing at the 'prophetic' claims of the Athonite monks, Clucas sees its origins in evagrianism, messalianism, and Western mysticism (Joachim da Fiore). Whereas parallelisms between all these movements are unquestionable, one should evaluate each of them in the light of the 'prophetic and 'spiritual' content of New Testament eschatology. Eastern Christianity has, at all times, kept very much in evidence the polarity – inherent to the Christian faith itself – between personal experience and ecclesiastical institutions, as much of monastic history clearly shows. The problem of the heretical, or sectarian movements were not in that they affirmed the polarity, but in that they rejected it, by excluding the sacramental structures of the Church and recognizing only 'spiritual' and 'prophetic' leadership in an exclusive way. The Byzantine Hesychasts of the fourteenth century – whose affinity with earlier 'spiritual' movements is obvious – stopped short of those exaggerations. Their victory led to internal reform and strengthening of the institutions, not their disappearance.

[37] See particularly my *Introduction*, pp. 249–56 (*A Study*, pp. 179–84).

as 'Hesychasts' only with reservations (although many of them were Athonite monks): they were promoting a new religious maximalism and, on the basis of fundamental theological options, fought for basic cultural and political priorities, not simply for a particular tradition of spirituality.

The canonical texts which establish the authority of the Church of Constantinople are very specific in motivating that authority: 'The bishop of Constantinople shall enjoy privileges of honour [τὰ πρεσβεῖα τῆς τιμῆς] after the bishop of Rome, because Constantinople is a New Rome.'[38] The same motivation is even more explicitly stated in the canonical text which can be considered as the real foundation charter of the patriarchate, the 28th Canon of the Council of Chalcedon: . . . '[The Fathers] justly judging that the city, which is honoured with the presence of the emperor and the senate and enjoys equal privileges with the old imperial Rome, should, in ecclesiastical matters also, be magnified as she is and rank next after her.'[39] Clearly, the privileges of the Church of Constantinople were based upon the principle of parallelism between the political and the ecclesiastical organization of the Christian *oikoumène*, and the authority of the patriarch came from his being the bishop of the imperial capital.[40] The Council of Chalcedon (Canons 9 and 17) also gave him the right to hear appeals of bishops against their metropolitans.[41] There is every reason to believe that this right of appeal was originally limited to the imperial dioceses of Asia, Thrace and Pontus, i.e. the territorial limits of the patriarchate of Constantinople.[42] However, several Byzantine authors, including Aristenos,[43] consider that the right of appeal has no geographic limitations and that the

---

[38] Council (Second Ecumenical) of Constantinople, A.D. 381, *Canon 3* (Rhalles-Potles, II, p. 173).

[39] *Ibid.*, p. 281.

[40] Cf. Maxime de Sardes, *Le patriarcat oecuménique dans l'église orthodoxe*, Paris, 1975, pp. 97–153. Some anti-Latin polemicists made use of the legend according to which the apostle Andrew the 'first-called' preached in Byzantium. This tradition would entitle Constantinople to be considered as an 'apostolic' see, equal (or even superior to) Rome, Antioch, Jerusalem, etc. (F. Dvornik, *The Idea of Apostolicity in Byzantium and the Legend of the Apostle Andrew*, Cambridge, Mass., 1958, pp. 138–299). One does not find this view expressed by the major 'hesychast' authors of our period.

[41] Rhalles-Potles, II, pp. 237, 258–9.

[42] This is the opinion of the twelfth-century commentator Zonaras: Οὐ πάντων δὲ τῶν μητροπολιτῶν πάντως ὁ Κωνσταντινουπόλεως καθιεῖται δικαστής, ἀλλὰ τῶν ὑποκειμένων αὐτῷ, ibid., p. 260; cf. A. Pavlov, 'Teoriya vostochnogo papizma v noveishei russkoy literature kanonicheskogo prava', *Pravoslavnoe Obozrenie*, 1879, nov., dec.; also Πηδάλιον, Athens, 1841, p. 105.

[43] Rhalles-Potles, II, p. 240.

patriarch of Constantinople can issue sentences on conflicts in other patriarchates than his own.

It is also in this last sense that Byzantine authors frequently interpret the title of 'ecumenical patriarch', which the archbishop of Constantinople assumed, as a regular title, in the sixth century.[44] According to Nicetas of Ancyra, an author of the eleventh century, the title refers to the patriarch as the 'common judge' (κοινὸς δικαστής), because Canon 9 of Chalcedon has given him right to issue judgements of appeal 'from all the provinces' (πασῶν τῶν ἐπαρχιῶν).[45] Along the same line, the patriarch of Constantinople is commonly called 'common father and teacher of the entire universe' (κοινὸς πάσης τῆς οἰκουμένης πατὴρ καὶ διδάσκαλος).[46]

However, the very authors using such titles to designate the patriarch, admit that the titles have mostly rhetorical character. The same Nicetas of Ancyra, having established the above-mentioned rights of the patriarch, immediately warns his reader: 'But do not exaggerate the importance of the title of patriarch, which is given to him. For every bishop is also called "patriarch" . . . [Here follows a reference to St Gregory of Nazianzus, *Or.* 43, 37, PG 36, col. 545C, where Gregory's father, a bishop, is mentioned as "patriarch"], and the titles of precedence are common to all of us [bishops], since all the bishops are fathers, shepherds and teachers; and it is clear that there are no special canons for metropolitans, distinct from those which apply to archbishops, or bishops. For the laying-on of hands is the same for all, and our participation in the divine liturgy is identical and all pronounce the same prayers.'[47] This sacramental and eucharistic understanding of the episcopacy, implying the identity of all the bishops, also served as the central argument of Byzantine polemicists against Roman primacy: all bishops possess the same apostolic succession and are all 'successors of Peter', as of other apostles as well, whereas the special privileges of some – the pope, or the patriarch of Constantinople – were determined and limited by the conciliar canons. They possess no divine origin and can be modified by new canonical provisions.[48]

---

[44] Cf. bibliography in Bréhier, *Institutions*, p. 487.
[45] Ed. Darrouzès, *Documents*, pp. 222–4.
[46] John Chilas, metropolitan of Ephesus (XIVth c.), *ibid.*, p. 396; cf. also p. 389.
[47] *Ed. cit.*, p. 224.
[48] Cf. J. Meyendorff, 'St. Peter in Byzantine Theology' in Meyendorff, J., et al., *The Primacy of Peter in the Orthodox Church*, London, Faith Press, 1963, pp. 1–20; cf. also J. Darrouzès, 'Les documents byzantins du XIIe siècle sur la Primauté romaine', REB, 23, 1965, pp. 42–88.

It is quite obvious, therefore, that between the real power of the Byzantine patriarch, as described by the canons and sanctioned by practice – a power frequently defined in most superlative rhetorical terms – and the real ecclesiological convictions of the Byzantine theologians about the nature of episcopal power, there exists a gap which requires an historical explanation.

3. THE PATRIARCHATE OF CONSTANTINOPLE: CLAIMS TO UNIVERSALITY

In the case of the patriarchate of Constantinople, it is obvious that the power of its incumbent is always defined in reference to his position in the Christian *oikoumène*, the universal empire and the universal church indivisibly united. The title of 'ecumenical patriarch' has no other meaning. Of course, the empire of Justinian, of Basil II and of John V Palaeologus hardly represented the same political reality, and the relationships between the patriarch and the powerful emperors of the past were different from those which prevailed during the Palaeologan period. However, the principles and ideals of the *oikoumène* had remained the same, with the patriarchate now carrying a much heavier responsibility for their preservation than it ever had in the past, precisely because the emperors were now politically much too weak to play their former role in the Christian world. Of course, the patriarch, in the fourteenth century, was not invested with the external signs of imperial power (which the Roman popes had assumed already in the early Middle Ages and which were also to be adopted by the patriarchs of Constantinople after the capture of the city by the Turks), but was gradually and *de facto* taking up the position of main spokesman for the Orthodox 'family of nations'.

The fact that the patriarchate – at this very crucial moment of its history – was in the hands of the monastic party led to important consequences, in terms of political and ideological priorities. The monastic takeover did not occur with the hesychast victory of 1347: it was rather connected with a reaction of public opinion against the arbitrary policies of Emperor Michael VIII (1259–82), who imposed the 'Uniate' John Beccos as patriarch and, indirectly, contributed to the moral prestige of the monks who opposed him.[49] However, it is certainly the personality of Patriarch Athanasius I (1289–93, 1303–9) which, on the one hand,

---

[49] On the recruitment of patriarchs in Byzantium, see Bréhier, *Institutions*, pp. 482–6. Noting the predominance of monks among candidates to the patriarchate during

reflects the new influence of the monastic milieu in Byzantine
society and also serves as model to the hesychast patriarchs of the
later part of the century.[50] A rigid ascetic, Athanasius assumed the
patriarchal throne with a programme of reforms, which made him
unpopular in some circles, but which showed his personal commitment to the defence of the poor, the order of the Church and moral
principles in social behaviour. Fully endorsing monastic ideals of
spirituality, he enforced discipline and poverty in monasteries. He
was also greatly concerned with the order of the Church, and
forced bishops, who under various pretexts, sojourned in the
capital instead of residing in their dioceses, to return to their sees.[51]
Unfortunately, we do not know much about his policies in the
Balkans and Russia, since the register of acts for his patriarchate is
not preserved, but we know that, under his rule, the order of
metropolitan sees was modified and new sees were created, including a see in Galicia, separate from that of 'Kiev and all
Russia',[52] but the exact motivation and circumstances of this
action are unknown.

Furthermore, whereas he accepted the Byzantine political
ideology of the empire and expressed the greatest respect for the
'divine majesty' of Andronicus II, acknowledging his traditional
power in the field of Church administration, Athanasius also
demanded from the emperor a strict adherence to the faith and
ethics of Orthodoxy, and obedience to the Church. Upon returning to the patriarchate in September 1303, he had Andronicus
sign a promise 'not only to keep the Church fully independent and
free [ἀκαταδούλωτον πάντη παὶ ἐλευθέραν], but also to practise
towards Her a servant's obedience, and to submit to Her every
just and God-pleasing demand'.[53] Stern and inflexible in many

the Palaeologan period, Bréhier considers the election of the monk Athanasius I
(1289) as a turning point in this respect. One could argue, however, that Arsenius
(1255-9, 1260-5) – also a monastic – by his opposition to Michael did even more
to accredit the prestige of the monks. After 1289, only two patriarchs were not of
monastic background: John Glykys (1315-19) and John Calecas (1334-47).

[50] Palamas himself mentions Athanasius as a saint and a model of the Hesychasts
(Tr. 1, 2, 12, ed. J. Meyendorff, *Grégoire Palamas, Défense des saints hésychastes*, second
edition, Louvain, 1973, p. 99; cf. also Meyendorff, *Introduction*, p. 34, note 34).

[51] For Athanasius' personality and activities, see A.-M. Talbot, *The Correspondence of
Athanasius I, Patriarch of Constantinople, Letters to the Emperor Andronicus II, members of
the Imperial family and officials. An Edition, Translation and Commentary*, Washington,
D.C., 1975; cf. also J. C. Boojamra, *The Ecclesiastical Reforms of Patriarch Athanasius
of Constantinople*, unpublished dissertation, Fordham University, New York, 1976.

[52] See above, p. 93.

[53] V. Laurent, 'Le serment de l'empereur Andronic II Paléologue au patriarche
Athanase Ier, lors de sa seconde accession au trône oecuménique', REB, 23, 1965,
p. 136.

ways, Athanasius was not an extremist: a fierce adversary of the so-called 'Arsenites' – the 'zealot' monks who did not accept the deposition of Patriarch Arsenius and also rejected all of his successors, whom they considered as illegitimately elected – he expressed sympathy not only for Arsenius himself, but also for Gregory of Cyprus (1283–9), whose 'humanist' interests were well-known.[54]

Quite naturally, the ideals of Patriarch Athanasius would serve as inspiration to the monks who, after 1347, came, like him, to occupy the patriarchate. Although none of them possessed a temperament really similar to that of Athanasius or were as zealous as he in trying to reform society as a whole, the spiritual continuity between them is obvious. Gregory Palamas himself (as also Nicholas Cabasilas) preached against usury[55] and explained the existing political miseries as inevitable because of the injustices inflicted upon the poor.[56] Patriarch Callistos (1350–3, 1354–63) in his still unpublished homilies, follows Athanasius' example in castigating the deficiencies of the clergy.[57] Also, Philotheos (1353–4, 1364–76) attacked the frivolity with which things divine were treated in Constantinople,[58] and undertook a major reordering of liturgical rubrics. Also, and most significantly, the power and authority of the ecumenical patriarchate was re-emphasized anew, especially in terms of its concern for the 'universal' Church. It would have been interesting, of course, to know more about the relationships which prevailed, in the second part of the fourteenth century, between the patriarchate and the imperial court. Unfortunately, no evidence comparable with the correspondence between Emperor Andronicus II and Patriarch Athanasius is preserved for that period, but there is enough evidence (which will be discussed below at greater length) to show that the patriarchate, especially under the second tenure of Philotheos (1364–76) could

---

[54] *Letter 2 to the Emperor*, ed. Talbot, p. 6.
[55] *Hom.* 45, ed. S. Oikonomos, Athens, 1861, pp. 45–9; Cabasilas, PG 150, cols. 728–94.
[56] Cf. *Hom.* 1, PG, CLI, col. 12D; 16B; *Hom.* 22, col. 292.
[57] *Cod. Athon.* 229 (Chilend. 8), s. XV, pp. 126–30 (Διδασκαλία περὶ εὐταξίας κλήρου).
[58] PG, CLI, col. 585A. The significance of this passage was noticed by L. M. Clucas (*op. cit.*, p. 343), although it does not reflect as this author suggests any particular study of the 'three ages', but simple concern for religious integrity. It also paraphrases a very famous passage of St Gregory of Nazianzus (τὰ θεῖα παίζειν, *Or.* 22, 8, PG XXXV, col. 1140C), on the frivolity with which the inhabitants of the capital deal with theological issues. The passage does not concern liturgical practices, as Clucas suggests.

pursue a foreign policy in Eastern Europe quite independent of the pro-Western initiatives of Emperor John V.

As basis and motivation of this patriarchal policy, official documents described the role of the Church of Constantinople in terms of a 'universal solicitude'. A document issued in 1355 by Patriarch Callistos is particularly revealing. It is addressed to the group of hesychast monks in Bulgaria – including St Theodosius of Trnovo – who apparently were advocates of Constantinopolitan centralism. They were, together with Callistos himself, fellow disciples of St Gregory of Sinai, on Mount Athos.[59] In this document, Callistos sternly criticizes the Bulgarian patriarch of Trnovo for failing to mention the ecumenical patriarch, as his superior. The patriarch of Constantinople, according to Callistos, 'judges in appeal, straightens out, confirms and authenticates' (καὶ ἐπανακρίνει καὶ διευθετεῖ καὶ ἐπιψηφίζεται καὶ τὸ κῦρος δίδωσιν) the judgements of the other three ancient patriarchs: Alexandria, Antioch and Jerusalem. How much more, he asks, he must also be recognized as the 'lord' (κύριος) of the Church of Bulgaria, whose primate, according to Callistos, has received the title of 'patriarch' in only an honorific sense, but is not essentially different from one of the metropolitans, subjected to Constantinople.[60] We will see below that this restrictive view was hardly shared by the patriarch of Trnovo himself who, in 1352, had even consecrated a metropolitan of Kiev without referring to Constantinople.

This trend towards reaffirmation of Constantinople's primacy is also apparent in patriarchal documents relative to Russia. In 1354, the synodal act of Patriarch Philotheos appointing bishop Alexis as Metropolitan of Kiev and all Russia proclaimed: 'The holy Catholic and Apostolic Church of God [i.e. of Constantinople], which administers always all things for the better, according to the unfailing privilege and power granted to it from on high, by the grace of Christ, manifests its concern and solicitude over all the most holy Churches wherever they are found [εἰς πάσας μὲν τὰς ἑκασταχοῦ εὑρισκομένας ἁγιωτάτας ἐκκλησίας], so that they may be governed and directed for the good and in accordance with the Lord's law.'[61] In 1370, addressing Grand-prince Dimitri

---

[59] See Meyendorff, *Introduction*, p. 63; cf. also Obolensky, 'Late Byzantine culture', pp. 13–15.

[60] MM, I, pp. 436–9: cf. a Russian translation of the document with reference to an ancient Slavic text of the same in *Trudy Kievskoy dukhovnoy akademii*, Kiev, 1871, II, pp. 555–72.

[61] MM, I, p. 336; cf. the literal coincidence of these formulas with the preamble of the *Act* of Callistos, which sets the limits between the metropolitanate of Kiev and the newly-recognized metropolitanate of Lithuania (MM, I, p. 425).

of Moscow, Philotheos calls himself bluntly the 'common father, established by the most high God, of all the Christians found everywhere on earth'.[62] In another letter, written in the same year to the princes of Russia, urging them to submit themselves to their metropolitan Alexis, Philotheos expresses the theory of 'universal solicitude' in a way, practically undistinguishable from the most authoritarian pronouncements by Roman popes:

Since God has appointed Our Humility as leader [προστάτην] of all Christians found anywhere in the inhabited earth, as solicitor and guardian of their souls, all of them depend on me [πάντες εἰς ἐμὲ ἀνάκεινται] the father and teacher of them all. If that were possible, therefore, it would have been my duty to walk everywhere on earth by the cities and countries and to teach there the Word of God. I would have had to do so unfailingly, since this is my duty. However, since it is beyond the possibility of one weak and mightless man to walk around the entire inhabited earth, Our Humility chooses the best among men, the most eminent in virtue, establishes and ordains them as pastors, teachers and high-priests, and sends them to the ends of the universe. One of them goes to your great country, to the multitudes which inhabit it, another reaches other areas of the earth, and still another goes elsewhere, so that each one, in the country and place which was appointed for him, enjoys territorial rights, an episcopal chair and all the rights of Our Humility.[63]

In 1393, Patriarch Anthony (1389–90, 1391–7) not only re-affirms, in a letter to Novgorod, his leadership of 'all the Christians of the universe',[64] but also, in his letter to the Muscovite Grand-prince Basil I, indignantly reproaches Basil for having forgotten that 'the patriarch is a vicar of Christ [τὸν τόπον ἔχει Χριστοῦ] and sits on the very throne of the Master'.[65]

There is no doubt that the definition of the patriarch as 'vicar' of Christ is directly inspired by the *Epanagoge*, the well-known legal compendium of the Macedonian period, describing the functions of the Byzantine *oikouméne* and defining the role of the 'ecumenical patriarch' not in terms of his sacramental functions, but rather in his political and social responsibilities: the author (possibly Photius) wants to affirm the role of the patriarch as 'a living image of Christ' (εἰκὼν ζῶσα Χριστοῦ)[66] in society, without according

---

[62] Ἐγὼ γοῦν κατὰ τὸ χρέος ὅπερ ὀφείλω ὡς κοινὸς πατὴρ ἄνωθεν ἀπὸ Θεοῦ καταστὰς εἰς τοὺς ἀπανταχοῦ τῆς γῆς εὑρισκομένους χριστιανούς, MM, I, p. 516.
[63] MM, I, p. 521; cf. below, App. 2, pp. 283–4.
[64] MM, II, p. 182.   [65] MM, II, p. 189.
[66] *Epanagoge aucta*, II, 1, Ed. Zachariae, *Jus*, IV, p. 182.

that particular religious function to the emperor. Verbal dependence upon the *Epanagoge* also appears in the text of Philotheos quoted above as it appears in the definition of the functions of the patriarch in the *Epanagoge*:

> The throne of Constantinople, receiving its honour from the empire, was given primacy through synodal decrees . . .
> The responsibility and care for all the metropolitanates and dioceses, the monasteries and churches, and also judgement and sanction, depend upon the patriarch of the area [τῷ οἰκείῳ πατριάρχῃ ἀνάκεινται].[67] But the incumbent of the see of Constantinople can . . . rule on issues arising in other thrones and pass final judgement on those.[68]

We have seen above that the canonical tradition and ecclesiology of the Byzantine Church are incompatible with the formal literal meaning of the letter of Philotheos, which represents the patriarch as a 'universal' bishop with the local metropolitans acting only as his representatives. The language used by the patriarchal chancery in drafting documents addressed to Russia must have been chosen for *ad hoc* reasons with the aim of impressing the still relatively unsophisticated Slavs with the importance of Byzantium as centre of the Christian world, even at the expense of strict canonical consistency. Hesychast monks, once invested with ecclesiastical power, quickly learned the effectiveness of diplomatic rhetoric! It is important to note, however, that the source of this rhetoric is to be found in *civil law*, representing Byzantine political ideology, and not theological and canonical literature *per se*. In fact, as 'the most stable element in the Byzantine Empire',[69] the Church was becoming the guardian of the *oikouméne* and of the ideology which sustained it. Documents, which were the basis of the ideology, had been translated into Slavic and some were known in Russia.[70] One may presume that both the Byzantine

---

[67] The *Epanagoge* presupposes the existence of the 'pentarchy' of five equal patriarchs: Rome, Constantinople, Alexandria, Antioch and Jerusalem. Philotheos, however, uses expressions in a broader, universal context (Phil.: πάντες εἰς ἐμὲ ἀνάκεινται; Epan. – τῷ οἰκείῳ πατριάρχῃ ἀνάκεινται).

[68] *Epanagoge*, II, 9–10, *ed. cit.*, p. 183.

[69] Ostrogorsky, *History*, p. 487.

[70] Cf. above Chapter I, p. 18; there does not seem to be any direct evidence that the *Epanagoge* was translated before the sixteenth century, when it appears as part of the *Syntagma* of Matthew Blastares (cf. Žužek, *Kormchaya*, p. 201, note 14). The use made of the *Epanagoge* in patriarchal acts of the fourteenth century may indicate a trend towards promoting that document as an official statement of Byzantine political ideology. The *Syntagma* of Blastares is also a fourteenth-century legal collection.

authors of the official patriarchal correspondence and the Russian recipients of it were aware of the difference between strictly ecclesiological concepts on the one hand and the *civil* definitions of the 'ecumenical' patriarch as they appear in the *Epanagoge* on the other. In any case, the Byzantine Hesychasts – as we have seen earlier – were always ready to defy patriarchs whom they considered heretical (e.g. John Calecas, in 1341–7), and the Russians remained their faithful disciples in this respect, when, in the next century, they rejected the union of Florence, signed by the ecclesiastical officialdom of Constantinople. Neither side was ready to accept a form of Eastern 'papacy'. However, the rhetorical re-affirmation of strong patriarchal leadership by the patriarchs of the fourteenth century, using legal texts which reflect imperial ideology rather than canon law, played a substantial role in maintaining the administrative unity of the Church in Russia and in strengthening the religious and cultural influence of Byzantium, particularly in the north-eastern Grand-principality and in Novgorod.

At a time when the power of the Mongol *tsar* over Russia began to weaken, the Byzantine Church promoted the authority of the traditional Christian imperial centre of Constantinople, requiring that the name of the Byzantine 'tsar' be mentioned in the churches again: the Byzantine emperor, it said, is 'the emperor of all Christians' and the patriarch is 'the universal teacher of all Christians' (καθολικὸς διδάσκαλος πάντων τῶν χριστιανῶν).[71] This conception, so emphatically emphasized, was challenged, on the one hand, by centrifugal trends with a potentially pro-Western orientation in Lithuania, and, also, by the local nationalism of the Grand-principality of Moscow, whose leader will himself aspire first to independence and, later, to the inheritance not only of the Byzantine emperors, but also of the Mongol *khan*, whose territories he was eventually to conquer.[72]

The incipient trends leading in these various directions constitute the most interesting and dramatic side of the various ecclesiastical, cultural and political events of the fourteenth century in Eastern Europe.

---

[71] Cf. the famous letter of Patriarch Anthony IV to Grand-prince Basil I, MM, II, 189; cf. below, Chapter 10, pp. 254–6.
[72] Cf. Cherniavsky, '*Khan* or *Basileus*'.

6

Cultural ties: Byzantium, the Southern Slavs and Russia

In the thirteenth and fourteenth centuries, the empire of the Palaeologi, restored after the Latin occupation of Constantinople, was politically and economically a very minor power, but its intellectual and cultural prestige remained remarkably strong. Historians used to insist upon the role played by Byzantium in influencing the beginnings of the Italian Renaissance. More recent publications tend to limit the importance of this Greek impact on Italy. In any case, Byzantine civilization did indeed play a more decisive role in shaping cultural history in its traditional sphere of influence, the Slavic lands.

Indeed, the so-called 'second South-Slavic' (Serbian and Bulgarian) influence upon Russian civilization, which occurred in the fourteenth and fifteenth centuries, and which admittedly had a widespread impact upon cultural, religious, literary and artistic developments in northern Russia, had its initial source in Byzantium. Because of their close ties and neighbourhood with Constantinople, the Southern Slavs were instrumental in the development of a more literary and ornate style (*pletenie sloves* – 'weaving of words'), of more stabilized and hellenized principles of spelling, of a richer and more sophisticated vocabulary. These traits appeared not only in translations from the Greek accomplished by bilingual, mostly Bulgarian and Serbian, monks,[1] but also in original Slavic writings in Bulgaria, Serbia and Russia. The Slavs were not only passive imitators of Byzantine models: in several areas – particularly art, hagiography and preaching – they showed great creativity and, in the field of art, Slavic artists were certainly not inferior to the Greeks. Furthermore, the universalistic ideology promoted by the Byzantine Church presupposed, on the part of the Byzantines, a greater concern and respect for the

---

[1] Cf. particularly Sobolevsky, *Yuzhnoslavyanskoe vliyanie*; also Likhachev, 'Nekotorye zadachi'.

Slavs than was ever shown in the past. The Slavs were grateful for this friendship. For example, a Russian pilgrim, visiting St Sophia, notes the kindness and humility of Patriarch Isidore (1347–50) and remarks that the Patriarch 'loves Russians much' (*vel'mi lyubit Rus'*).[2] Patriarch Callistos, on the other hand, composed a *Life* of a Bulgarian saint, Theodosius of Trnovo, and entertained close personal connections in Bulgaria, where his spiritual master, St Gregory of Sinai, had found refuge.[3] In 1362, the leaders of the Bulgarian Hesychast movement, Theodosius and Euthymius, were warmly welcomed in Constantinople.[4] These examples, along with many others, illustrate a new sense of solidarity between Greeks and Slavs, but they also show that the cultural primacy of Byzantium was always maintained and recognized, particularly in monastic circles. Translation work, transmission of liturgical and disciplinary reforms, travels of pilgrims to Constantinople, and of artists, ecclesiastics and diplomats to and from Byzantium constituted the various channels through which ideas and patterns of Byzantine civilization poured into Russia with greater intensity than during the previous two centuries.

One can also find important examples of Russian literary influence upon Southern Slavs,[5] which show that the Slavic Orthodox world, together with Byzantium, really constituted a multi-national religious and cultural community, conscious of its unity and allowing for great mobility of persons and ideas.

I. NATURE AND LIMITS OF THE BYZANTINO-RUSSIAN
LITERARY TIES: RENAISSANCE, PRE-RENAISSANCE?

If the very fact of closer cultural relations between Russia, the Southern Slavs and Byzantium in the fourteenth century is readily admitted by historians, there exists a great variety of views as to the specific character of these relations. What was, first of all, the

---

[2] *Khozhdeniya Stefana Novgorodtsa*, ed. M. N. Speransky, *Iz starinnoi Novgorodskoi literatury XIV veka*, Leningrad, 1934, pp. 51–2; cf. also I. Ševčenko, 'Notes on Stephen, the Novgorodian pilgrim to Constantinople in the XIV-th century', *Sudost-Forschungen* XII, 1953, pp. 165–75.

[3] The original Greek text of the *Life* is lost, and the contemporary Slavic version may have been interpolated by the translator (ed. V. I. Zlatarski, in *Sbornik za narodni umotvoreniya, nauka i knizhnina*, XX, Sofia, 1904, pp. 1–44; on the *Life*, see V. Kiselkov, *Zhitieto na sv. Teodosii Trnovski kato istoricheski pametnik*, Sofia, 1926); cf. letter of Callistos to Bulgarian monks (including St Theodosius) in 1355, MM, I, 436–42.

[4] Cf. I. Dujčev, 'Tsentry', pp. 112–14; also Obolensky, 'Late Byzantine Culture'.

[5] Cf. Speransky, *Iz istorii*, pp. 13–14, 55–103; also Moshin, 'O periodizatsii', pp. 70–85.

nature of the Byzantine 'Palaeologan Renaissance', and was it passed on to the Slavs with all the implications which it had in Byzantium?

Both in literary pursuits, and in art, the Palaeologan period of Byzantine history saw a resurgence of interest in Greek antiquity: this is the most general and the most widely admitted feature of the 'Palaeologan Renaissance'. However, most specialists would also admit today that 'antique literary and scientific culture was endemic in Byzantium', that 'what we call Byzantine renaissances are just intensifications of the élite's contacts with antiquity – which were never lost – rather than rediscoveries of ancient culture', and that 'the renaissance of the early Palaeologi was one such intensification of an uninterrupted tradition'.[6] Clearly, as we have also seen in the preceding chapters, the ideology represented by the so-called 'humanists' – a narrow and aristocratic élite of littérateurs – was far from possessing that dynamism and inspiration which made possible the Renaissance in Italy. In Byzantium, there was no real ground for a true 'Renaissance', but rather a tradition of peaceful, frequently inconsistent, and sometimes charmingly creative coexistence of cultural features of Greek antiquity with Christian faith and spirituality.[7] In the preceding chapter, we have also seen that, in the thirteenth century, during the Empire's exile in Nicaea, the resurgence of interest in Greek antiquity became associated with a new and more specific national and ethnic consciousness. Threatened by the Crusaders, members of the Byzantine social and intellectual élite gained awareness of their 'Hellenism', expressed primarily in the language which they spoke and in the cultural tradition of antiquity.

If one now considers the general problem of the *transmission* of Byzantine culture to the Slavs, one is immediately faced with two overwhelming facts which determined that transmission: (1) The principle adopted from the beginning in Eastern Christianity to *translate* both Scripture and liturgy into the vernacular, excluded the Church from the role it played in the West and which consisted in giving the 'barbarians' a tool of access to classical antiquity: the Byzantine Church did not teach them Greek, as the Western Church taught them Latin. (2) If the newly emerging 'Greek' consciousness of the Byzantines contributed to the revival of

---

[6] I. Ševčenko, 'Theodore Metochites, the Chora and the Intellectual Trends of His Time', in P. A. Underwood, ed., *The Kariye Djami*, vol. 4, Princeton, N.J., 1975, p. 19.

[7] Cf. Meyendorff, 'Spiritual Trends', p. 95.

secular Hellenic culture, this particular impulse was, by definition, limited to Greeks and could not be transmitted to the Slavs. On the contrary, as with all forms of nationalism, it contained a potential divisiveness, which contributed to the weakening of Byzantine universalism and, in later times, to further antagonism between Greeks and Slavs.

Added to the general élitist character of Byzantine Hellenic 'humanism', these two factors clearly precluded any substantial transmission of secular Greek culture to the Slavs, and to the Russians in particular. We have already seen (cf. above Chapter 1), that the overwhelming majority of Byzantine texts translated into Slavic during the centuries which followed the baptism of the Rus' was religious and ecclesiastical in character. The same can be said about the 'second' Byzantine and South-Slavic influence: the great mass of translated literature reflected the ecclesiastical ties between Byzantium and Russia. However, in the fourteenth century, an even narrower selection was made in favour of two areas: the liturgy and the general area of monastic spirituality, which included hagiography and patristic (particularly hesychastic) literature on personal prayer.

The major factor in the development of the liturgy in Russia in the fourteenth century is the generalized transfer, from Constantinople to Russia, of the *Typikon* of Jerusalem, or, more precisely, the *Typikon* of the monastery of St Sabbas in Palestine. No scholar has, so far, given an exhaustive explanation of the remarkable fact that, already in the twelfth century, the Church of Constantinople, then at the peak of its prestige and influence, acquiesced in the replacement of the existing orders of its liturgy (the *Typikon* of the Great Church, the *Typikon* of St John of Studios) with the Order of the Monastery of St Sabbas in Palestine.[8] Obviously, the Arab occupation of the entire Middle East had not suppressed the prestige of the Holy Land and of ancient Palestinian monasticism, its practices and traditions. The change took place only gradually and was not imposed through any formal decree. It did not involve any spectacular modification of the liturgy, but only the structure of daily and festal services and monastic discipline, whereas the basic features of these services remained the same, as they had resulted from a synthesis between the 'cathedral' and the 'monastic' structures. This synthesis had occurred in the tenth and

---

[8] The best compendium of information concerning these liturgical changes is still to be found in M. Skaballanovich, *Tolkovy Tipikon. Ob 'yasnitel 'noe izlozhenie Tipikona s istoricheskim vvedeniem*, 1, Kiev, 1910, pp. 410–16.

eleventh centuries.[9] It is, nevertheless, quite significant that the *pattern* of the reform was not Constantinople, but Jerusalem: the symbolic, eschatological and spiritual dimension of this influence was strengthened by the fall of Constantinople under Latin rule in 1204 and by the subsequent monastic predominance in the Church. Monastic pilgrimages to the Holy Land were a frequent occurrence during the Palaeologan period and involved important leaders like Patriarch Athanasius I and Sabbas of Vatopedi.[10]

The adoption of the Palestinian *Typikon* among Slavs was in progress at least since the time when St Sava of Serbia introduced it on Mount Athos, whereas his successor, Archbishop Nikodim, translated it into Slavic in 1319.[11] The *Pandectae* and the *Taktikon* of Nikon of the Black Mountain, an author of the eleventh century, whose writings were widely known in Slavic translation, also contributed to the popularization of Palestinian traditions in liturgy and discipline.[12]

Elements of the Jerusalem *Typikon* appear in official pastoral instructions coming to Russia from the patriarchate of Constantinople in the late thirteenth century, for example, in the *Responses* of the Patriarchal Synod to the bishop of Sarai, Theognostos (1276)[13] and in an *Instruction* of the Greek metropolitan of Kiev, Maximus (1283–1305).[14] However the systematic unification of liturgical and disciplinary practices in accordance with the Palestinian pattern will be accomplished during the tenures of Cyprian (1390–1406) and Photius (1408–31), as metropolitans of Russia.[15] One of the characteristics of this liturgical reform, both in Byzantium and in Slavic lands, is that it was aiming at unification and codification of liturgical practices: it is during that period that very detailed sets of rubrics, regulating the performance of the eucharistic liturgy and of the daily office, appeared in Constantinople and were immediately transmitted to the Slavs. These collections are associated in the manuscripts with the name of

---

[9] Cf. A. Schmemann, *Introduction to liturgical theology*, 2nd ed., New York, 1975, pp. 152–70.

[10] *Vita Athanasii* by Theoktistos, ed. A. Papadopoulos-Kerameus, 'Zhitiya dvukh vselenskikh patriarkhov XIVv', in *S. Petersburg, Universitet, Istoriko-filologicheskii fakul'tet, Zapiski*, 76, 1905, p. 7; Philotheos, *Vita Sabae*, ed. A. Papadopoulos-Kerameus, 'Ανάλεκτα 'Ιεροσολυμιτικῆς Βιβλιοθήκης, V, pp. 264, 285–6.

[11] L. Stojanović, *Stari srpski zapisi i natpisi*, I, Belgrade, 1902, No. 52, pp. 22–4.

[12] Cf. I. Mansvetov, *Tserkovny Ustav (Tipik), ego obrazovanie i sud'ba v grecheskoi i russkoi tserkvi*, Moscow, 1885, pp. 187–92, 265–9.

[13] RIB, VI, col. 129–40 (Slavic text); *Prilozhenie*, cols. 5–12 (Greek text); cf. V. Grumel-Laurent, *Régestes*, IV, 1427.

[14] RIB, VI, cols. 139–42. [15] See particularly Mansvetov, *Kiprian*.

Patriarch Philotheos (1353–4, 1364–76), who was certainly instrumental in their widespread distribution, even if the original set of rubrics was completed in Constantinople, as early as the tenure of Patriarch Athanasius I (1289–93, 1303–9).[16] This concern for order and liturgical conformity is another indication which should disprove the conception of the Byzantine monastic revival in the fourteenth century as a phenomenon of mystical esotericism. In their active concern for centralizing the patriarchate and codifying the liturgy, the monks who had come to control the Church saw a necessary framework for their equally active promotion of monastic spirituality.

In the fourteenth century, the vast corpus of Byzantine hymnography, which covers the various liturgical cycles – daily, weekly, yearly and paschal – was preserved in the form it had taken in the ninth and tenth centuries. However, some additions continued to be made. For example, hymns and prayers written by Patriarch Philotheos became particularly popular. Not only did Philotheos write the special office in honour of St Gregory Palamas, whom he canonized in 1368,[17] but he also became the author of several other devotional and liturgical texts. And since Philotheos had permanent contacts with Slavic lands, his hymns and prayers were translated into Slavic during his lifetime, either in Bulgaria, or in Russia.[18]

Together with the reform of the *Typikon* and other liturgical influences, Byzantium, in the fourteenth century, passed on to the Slavs and, particularly, to Russia, an immense body of spiritual, predominantly monastic and hesychastic literature.[19] The oldest monastic library of northern Russia, that of the Lavra of the Trinity, founded by St Sergius (c. 1314–92) contains a number of fourteenth- and fifteenth-century Slavonic versions of such authors as St John Climacus, St Dorotheos, St Isaac of Nineveh, St Symeon the New Theologian and St Gregory of Sinai, who can be considered as the classics of hesychastic spirituality.[20] The same

---

[16] I. Mansvetov, *Tserkovnyi Ustav*, pp. 192–6; the rubrics of the Eucharistic liturgy of St John Chrysostom, ascribed to Philotheos, were translated into Slavic by Metropolitan Cyprian and are found in his own autograph *Sluzhebnik (Euchologion)*, cf. Prokhorov, 'Gimny', p. 148.

[17] This office was included in the *Triodion* (liturgical book containing the hymns of the Lenten period) for the Second Sunday of Lent; cf. Meyendorff, *Introduction*, pp. 168–9 (*A Study*, p. 112).

[18] Syrku, *K istorii ispravleniya*, pp. lxxix–lxxxvi, 172–5; Prokhorov, 'Gimny', pp. 140–9.

[19] Cf. Obolensky, 'Late Byzantine Culture', pp. 8–12.

[20] Prokhorov, 'Keleinaya literatura', pp. 317–24.

authors also appear in the fifteenth-century library of St Cyril of Beloozero.[21] If one compares the content of these major Russian monastic libraries with their contemporary Byzantine counterparts – on Mt Athos, on Patmos, or on Mt Sinai – one is immediately struck by their close parallelism: Russian monks read the same Fathers, the same *Lives* of saints, as their Greek brothers, and the 'second South-Slavic' or 'Byzantine' influence on Russia has provided enough translations to put Russian monasteries practically on a par with those of Greek-speaking lands. It is only in the area of pure theology that Russian libraries clearly differ from their Byzantine counterparts: copies of the theological treatises of the Cappadocian Fathers, of St Cyril of Alexandria, of St Maximus the Confessor, and, indeed, of the polemical treatises published in the fourteenth century by Palamite theologians are almost totally absent in Russian libraries. Among the significant exceptions are the writings of Pseudo-Dionysius the Areopagite, with some *scholia* by Maximus the Confessor, translated by the Serbian monk Isaiah on Mount Athos in 1371:[22] a manuscript of this version came to Russia as soon as it was completed, and was copied personally by Metropolitan Cyprian (before 1406).[23] Other exceptions include short treatises on the debates between Palamas and his adversaries composed by David Dishypatos,[24] and materials related to anti-Jewish[25] and anti-Latin polemics,[26] which were of direct relevance in Russia.

As these examples show, the flow of literature coming from Byzantium to Russia was predominantly following ecclesiastical and monastic channels. These ecclesiastical circles did not generally give a high priority to secular writings for transmission to the

---

[21] N. Nikol'sky, 'Opisanie rukopisei Kirillo-Belozerskogo monastyrya sostavlennoe v kontse XV veka', in *Obshchestvo lyubitelei drevnei pis'mennosti, Izdaniya*, 113, St Petersburg, 1897.

[22] Cf. B. Moshin, 'Zhitie startsa Isaii, igumena Russkogo monastyrya na Afone', *Sbornik Russkogo arkheologicheskogo obshchestva v korolevstve Yugoslavii*, Belgrade, 1940, pp. 125–67.

[23] Cf. G. M. Prokhorov, *Pamyatniki literatury vizantiisko-russkogo obshchestvennogo dvizheniya epokhi Kulikovskoi bitvy*, avtoreferat, Leningrad, 1977, pp. 25–6.

[24] See Meyendorff, *Introduction*, p. 404; on the Slavic transl., see G. Prokhorov, *ibid.*, pp. 13–16; some theological writings of Palamas himself, including a short treatise against Akindynos and his *Confession of faith* were translated in Bulgaria (see M. G. Popruzhenko, 'Iz istorii religioznago dvizheniya v Bolgarii v XIV-m veke', *Slavia*, 7 (1928–9), pp. 536–48 and particularly K. Ivanova-Konstantinova, 'Nyakoi momenti na Bulgaro-Vizantiiskite svyazi', *Starobulgarska Literatura*, 1, Sofia, 1971, pp. 209–42.

[25] Cf. G. Prokhorov, 'Prenie Grigoriya Palamy "s khiony i turki" i problema "zhidovskaya mudrstvuyushchikh" ', TODRL, xxvii, 1972, pp. 329–69.

[26] Cf. Popov, *Obzor;* Pavlov, *Opyty.*

Slavs. Among secular texts reaching Russia, there is an absolute predominance of chronicles and other historical texts, and practically no philosophical or scientific materials.[27]

Under such circumstances, in what sense can one say that the 'Palaeologan Renaissance' influenced the Slavs at all? As we have noted earlier, the term 'Renaissance' is already misleading when applied to fourteenth-century Byzantium. It becomes even more ambiguous in the Slavic context. In Byzantium, the humanists who cultivated the literary and intellectual traditions of Greek antiquity were a narrow élite, increasingly attracted by the West. Their connections with the Slavic world were non-existent, or tenuous. One known exception is the interest of Nicephorus Gregoras in the affairs of the Russian Church and his possibly personal contacts with Metropolitan Theognostos of Kiev and all Russia (1328–53), whom he mentions as a 'wise and God-loving man'.[28] Theognostos, according to Gregoras, having received the Palamite *Tomes*, recognized in them nothing but 'Hellenic polytheism' ('Ελληνικὴν πολυθεΐαν), 'threw them on the ground and refused to hear their content'. Gregoras further asserts that the metropolitan composed long refutations of Palamite theology, sent them to the patriarch (obviously John Calecas) and the Synod, including appropriate anathemas against the Palamites.[29]

If the event described by Gregoras really took place,[30] it would be the only case of a Byzantine Church leader in Slavic lands taking part, on the anti-Palamite side, in the theological controversies of the fourteenth century. One could presume that Gregoras has in mind an act of official support by Theognostos of the anathemas launched against Palamas by Patriarch John Calecas in 1344, and which was presumably required from all the metropolitans of the patriarchate, since the anathemas were proclaimed officially by the patriarch and the synod.[31] Even if Theognostos did support

---

[27] R. P. Dmitrieva, 'Svetskaya literatura v sostave monastyrskikh bibliotek XV i XVI vv. (Kirillo-Belozerskogo, Volokolamskogo monastyrei i Troitse-Sergievoi Lavry)', TODRL, XXIII, 1968, pp. 143–70.

[28] *Hist. Byz.* XXXVI, 24, Bonn, III, p. 513.   [29] *Ibid.*, XXVI, 47, p. 114.

[30] Gregoras was an emotional and partial adversary of the Palamites and 'was apt at times to select and twist the facts to conform with his political aims', Obolensky, 'Byzantium, Kiev and Moscow', p. 29. His information about the anti-Palamite actions of Theognostos finds no confirmation in any other contemporary source: however, the arguments proposed by A. Tachiaos to show that Theognostos was an all-time friend of Cantacuzenos and therefore a supporter of Palamism even in 1341–7 are based on conjectures only (see 'Επιδράσεις, pp. 17–29).

[31] Cf. Meyendorff, *Introduction*, pp. 110–12 (*A Study*, pp. 73–5). In that case, the Palamite 'Tomes' mentioned by Gregoras, as condemned by Theognostos, are the Haghioretic Tome and the Tome of 1341. This, however, may imply a contradiction,

the official policies of the patriarchate in 1344, there is no evidence whatsoever that he had any conflict with the hesychast patriarchs Isidore, Callistos and Philotheos, until his death in 1353, or that he gave any support to the group of anti-Palamite bishops led by Matthew of Ephesus (whom Theognostos must have known, since Matthew had travelled to Russia in 1331–2)[32] who opposed Palamism after 1347.[33]

There is therefore no reason to believe that anybody promoted in Russia those intellectual trends which make up the so-called 'Palaeologan Renaissance' in Byzantium, whereas there is ample evidence of a massive influx of traditional hesychastic literature, which was accepted readily and without any need for theological polemics. If polemics there were, they occurred on a level quite different from the learned disputations between Byzantine theologians. Thus, a Novgorodian Chronicle, under the year 1347, reproduces the text of a letter of Archbishop Basil Kalika of Novgorod to his colleague, Bishop Theodore of Tver, trying to prove the existence of an 'earthly paradise':[34] the text implies that, in Tver, this existence (in a geographically determinable sense) was denied. The arguments used on both sides closely followed the concepts, current in ascetical literature, of a spiritual paradise (παράδεισος νοητός) accessible in the personal experience of the saints. Both sides also believed that God's creation as a whole is, in some sense, incorruptible. Attempts at identifying this very rudimentary controversy between Russian bishops and the theological debates between Palamites and anti-Palamites[35] clearly led nowhere. Neither Basil nor Theodore opposes the reality of a real vision of divine light: their difference lies only in the field of 'mystical geography'. One can only note the increased use of a mystical terminology, the recurrence of references to spiritual experience and to the vision of light by the disciples on the Mount of Transfiguration which appear in the *Letter* of Basil Kalika, and illustrate the atmosphere which existed in Russia under the impact

damaging to Gregoras' credibility: Patriarch John Calecas did not anathematize the Tome of 1341 (which he had signed himself), but attempted to interpret it in an anti-Palamite sense.

[32] Kourouses, Γαβαλᾶς, pp. 248–52.

[33] J. Meyendorff, *op. cit.*, pp. 132–4, 152–3; our present-day knowledge of the history of the events of this period eliminate the arguments of A. D. Sedel'nikov in favour of an anti-Palamite reaction of Theognostos after 1351 (cf. 'Motiv o rae v russkom srednevekovom prenii', *Byzantinoslavica*, VII, 1937–9, pp. 164–6); on this point see also A. Tachiaos, Ἐπιδράσεις, pp. 17–29.

[34] PSRL, III, second edition, St Petersburg, 1879, pp. 224–30.

[35] As in A. D. Sedel'nikov, *ibid.*, pp. 169–72.

of Byzantine Hesychasm. As shown also by other signs, such as the remarkable revival of monasticism, Hesychasm was bringing to Russia a more *personal* form of religion, which was promoting not only monastic spirituality as such, but also ideas on the deification of the body and transfiguration of the entire creation.[36]

If one uses the term 'Renaissance' to designate this greater personalism and creativity – and not in the more widely accepted context of a revival of Greek antiquity – one can indeed understand the term 'pre-Renaissance' used by D. S. Likhachev to designate the cultural developments in Byzantium, in South-Slavic lands, and in Russia in the fourteenth century, a 'pre-Renaissance' which, however, neither in Byzantium nor in Russia (for admittedly different reasons) became a 'Renaissance'.[37]

2. CHANNELS OF COMMUNICATION

Constantine of Kostenets, a Bulgarian monk writing in Serbia around A.D. 1418 and criticizing the incompetence of copyists, proclaims that only those Slavic texts can be relied upon which were copied in Trnovo, or on Mount Athos, and which are properly imitating Greek models in content and in style.[38] There is no doubt that Constantine was pointing to the two major centres of distribution of Slavic manuscripts in the fourteenth century.

Since the pioneering works of K. Th. Radchenko[39] and P. Syrku,[40] the Bulgarian empire of Tsar John Alexander (1331–71), with its capital in Trnovo, has been justly recognized as a major workshop for the penetration of Byzantine ideas, texts and personalities into the Slavic world. Liturgical texts and monastic literature (including hagiography) constitute, as we have already seen, the two major areas of this penetration. The beginning of the hesychastic revival in Bulgaria is generally associated with the

---

[36] Cf. my observations on this point in *Introduction*, pp. 195–256 (*A Study*, pp. 134–84); also in 'O vizantiiskom isikhazme', pp. 295–7.

[37] The concept of a 'pre-Renaissance' repeatedly occurs in recently published works by D. S. Likhachev. For a most comprehensive statement see *Razvitie russkoi literatury X–XIII vv. Epokhi i stili*, Leningrad, 1973, pp. 75–127; cf. also his earlier study 'Predvozrozhdenie na Rusi v kontse XIV-pervoy polovine XV veka', *Literatura epokhi Vozrozhdeniya i problemy vsemirnoi literatury*, Moscow, 1964, pp. 139–82.

[38] On these ideas of Constantine, see D. Obolensky, *ibid.*, p. 17.

[39] *Religioznoe i literaturnoe dvizhenie v Bolgarii v epokhu pered Turetskim zavoevaniem*, Kiev, 1898.

[40] *K istorii ispravleniya*; see also M. Heppel, 'The Hesychast Movement in Bulgaria: the Turnovo School and its relations with Constantinople', *Eastern Churches Review*, 7, 1975, pp. 9–20.

name of St Gregory of Sinai, whose *Life* was written by Patriarch Callistos of Constantinople.[41] Having lived on Mount Athos, Gregory, in 1325–8, moved to Paroria, over the Bulgarian border, where he established a monastic centre. From there, hesychastic spirituality spread throughout the Balkans, including the Romanian lands.[42] Callistos' Bulgarian disciple, Theodosius, established another monastery in Kilifarevo, where he was joined, and eventually succeeded by, Ethymius, later patriarch of Trnovo (1375–93). One of the major concerns of these monastic leaders in Bulgaria was the translation of Greek texts into Slavic. In Russia, the number of Byzantine literary texts available in translation from the Greek, doubled between the years 1350 and 1450: this was largely due to translations imported from Bulgaria.[43] More than anyone, Metropolitan Cyprian – whose career in Russia will be discussed later – contributed to this importation: a Bulgarian by birth, he personally spent much energy in translating Greek texts, copying manuscripts and transmitting Byzantine ideas and usage.[44] In 1379, he made a solemn visit to Trnovo, where he was graciously received by Patriarch Euthymius.[45] During the patriarchate of Euthymius, the Bulgarian capital, Trnovo, had become a major centre of communication between Byzantine traditions and Slavic lands, and one understands why Constantine Kostenets referred to it as one of the two major centres for the production of Slavic manuscripts.

The second centre mentioned by Constantine is more ancient and more traditional. Since the tenth century, Mount Athos has been not only a place of prayer and contemplation, but a point of cultural encounter between Greek, Slavic, Georgian, Syrian and, even, Latin monks. In the fourteenth century, the history of Athos is marked by the revival of Hesychasm, but also by a renewed

---

[41] Ed. I. Pomyalovsky, in *Zapiski ist.-fil fakul'teta Sanktpeterburzhskago Universiteta*, xxxv, 1896, pp. 1–64.

[42] See particularly E. Turdeanu, *La littérature bulgare du XIVe siècle et sa diffusion dans les pays roumains*, Paris, 1947, pp. 5–15.

[43] A. I. Sobolevsky, *Perevodnaya literatura*, pp. 1–14.

[44] Cf. particularly Dmitriev, 'Rol' i znachenie', pp. 215–54; also I. Ivanov, 'Bŭlgarskoto knizhovno vliyanie v Rusiya pri mitropolit Kiprian', *Izvestiya na Institut za bŭlgarska literatura*, VI, Sophia, 1958. For an older, and also more critical view see N. N. Glubokovsky, 'Sv. Kiprian, mitropolit vseya Rossii (1374–1406), kak pisatel'', *Chteniya v Obshchestve istorii i drevnostei rossiiskikh*, 1892, I, January, pp. 358–424.

[45] This visit to 'the church which nourished and instructed us' and to its 'father' (Patriarch Euthymius) is mentioned by another Bulgarian, Gregory Tsamblak, who also became metropolitan of Kiev, in his *Encomion* of Cyprian (ed. Angelov in *Iz starata*, p. 183).

Slavic presence, connected primarily with Serbian predominance in the Balkan peninsula. Connections between Mount Athos and Serbia were very tight since the time of St Sava, the founder of the Serbian Church, whose early career was spent on Mount Athos: both in terms of Byzantino-Slavic relations and in terms of production of Slavic manuscripts, the Serbian Athonite monastery of Khilandari supersedes Zographou, its Bulgarian counterpart.[46] One should remember, however, that ethnic distinctions between Slavic monks, especially on Mount Athos, were rarely emphasized, that close personal contacts existed between the various local branches of the hesychast revival and that the Serbian empire of Stefan Dušan, which exercised its sovereignty over Athos,[47] was deliberately multiethnic. In any case, either in its Serbian, or in its Bulgarian version, the Slavic monastic presence on Mount Athos had a decisive influence in the Balkans: 'The entire history of the South-Slavic literatures is, in effect, a history of greater or lesser impacts by Athonite ideals upon the spiritual culture of Orthodox Slavdom in the Balkan peninsula.'[48] In fact, all the leaders of the Bulgarian literary renaissance – including Theodosius, Euthymius and Cyprian of Kiev – were Athonite monks, and their activities in Slavic lands were pursued in close contact with other Athonite Hesychasts – Callistos and Philotheos – who had become patriarchs of Constantinople.

Contacts between Mount Athos and Russia were also numerous, both through the presence of Russian monks on the 'Holy Mountain' and through the mediation of Southern Slavs. However, Russians did also have direct connections in Constantinople itself, which appear, in the fourteenth century, to be even better established than those of the Southern Slavs. Permanent quarters were reserved in the city for the Russians, who occasionally shared them with Serbians and Bulgarians. No evidence exists on the possible direct continuity with earlier Russian settlements in the capital city – commercial, diplomatic or military – which are well documented for the Kievan period, but the needs created by the administrative dependence of the metropolitanate of Russia upon

---

[46] Moshin, 'O periodizatsii', p. 94.

[47] For a list of the various *largesses* bestowed by Dushan upon the monasteries, see I. Dujčev, 'Le Mont-Athos et les Slavs du Moyen Age', *Le Millénaire du Mont-Athos, 963–1963*, II, Chevetogne, 1964, pp. 138–9.

[48] G. A. Il'insky, 'Znachenie Athona v istorii slavyanskoi pis'mennosti' ZhMNP, 1908, No. 11, p. 38; cf. the more recent and very complete survey of the Slavic presence on Mount Athos in the fourteenth century by Dujčev, 'Tsentry', pp. 121–9.

the patriarchate and the constant travelling of diplomats and pilgrims between Constantinople and its huge ecclesiastical dependence in the north are quite sufficient to explain the existence of 'Russian quarters' in the city during the Palaeologan period.

When, on 28 June 1389, Ignatius of Smolensk, who was accompanying Metropolitan Pimen on his voyage to Byzantium, reached Constantinople, he was greeted by 'the Russians who lived there' (*Rus' zhivushchaya tamo*).[49] The same author informs us that Russians (presumably, but not necessarily monks) living at the monastery of St John the Baptist of Studios entertained the visitors.[50] Other sources signal the presence at the Studios of Euthymius (later patriarch of Trnovo) and of Cyprian of Kiev. Another Russian monk, St Athanasius of Vysotsk lived in Studios after 1401. Occasionally, one finds mention of the presence of the same monks at the monasteries of the Virgin Perivleptos and of St Mamas, which was made famous in the eleventh century by the mystic St Symeon the New Theologian.[51] We also have material evidence of the presence of Russian scribes at the Studios – where Metropolitan Cyprian in 1387 personally copied the *Ladder of Paradise* by St John Climacus – and at the Perivleptos. Of ten manuscripts found in Russia and known to have been copied in Constantinople at the end of the fourteenth and at the beginning of the fifteenth century, two were executed at the Studios, five at the Perivleptos.[52] One understands, therefore, that the monastery of Studios is associated by another Russian pilgrim, Stephen of Novgorod, with books coming to Russia.[53] It appears, therefore, that the area where all three monasteries of Studios, St Mamas and the Perivleptos were located – i.e., the south-western corner of the walled city of Constantinople – was the Russian (and Slavic) quarter, a home for Russian monks and pilgrims, a place for literary contacts and personal friendships, which did play an

---

[49] *Nik.*, p. 99; the account of Ignatius, together with those of other Russian pilgrims to Constantinople – a very important source for the history of the period – will be the subject of a forthcoming publication by George P. Majeska, *Russian Travellers to Constantinople in the 14th and the 15th centuries*, in the collection of *Dumbarton Oaks Studies*.

[50] *Ibid.* (*tamo zhivushchaya Rus'*).

[51] The sources concerning the presence of Slavic monks in the three monasteries are conveniently referred to in I. Dujčev, *ibid.*, pp. 114–15.

[52] Vzdornov, 'Rol' masterskikh', pp. 189–94. See also G. I. Vzdornov's excellent and very full review of literary contacts between Byzantium and Russia in *Issledovanie o kievskoy Psaltiri*, Moscow, 1978, pp. 80–91.

[53] Stephen attributes the sending of these books to St Theodore of Studios himself, an obvious anachronism (Speransky, *Iz istorii*, p. 56).

important role in Byzantino-Russian relations in the fourteenth century.

Finally, as we have seen earlier, numerous travellers journeyed back and forth between Constantinople and northern Russia. These included Russian metropolitans seeking confirmation and consecration by the patriarch, Greek prelates appointed to the metropolitanate of Kiev and, occasionally, returning home for official or personal business, bishops – particularly the bishop of Sarai – invested with diplomatic assignments, Russian monks seeking to witness monastic life in the Middle East, Greek artists (including the great Theophanes) hired to decorate Russian churches. Five Russian pilgrims, who visited Constantinople in the late fourteenth and early fifteenth centuries, have left accounts of their visits.[54] In Moscow there seems to have existed a Greek monastery, St Nicholas, and direct ties with Constantinople existed at the monasteries Bogoyavlensky and Simonovsky,[55] so that at least some Russian churchmen were able to learn Greek.

3. RUSSIAN MONASTICISM: ST SERGIUS, ST STEPHEN OF PERM

The extraordinary revival of monasticism in northern Russia in the fourteenth and the fifteenth centuries cannot be fully understood, except in the context of the renewed contacts with Byzantium and the Southern Slavs. In the absence of much positive information about monastic life after its forced interruption in Kiev by the Tatar onslaught in 1240, one must suppose that a serious decline took place in the thirteenth century, to be followed by a spectacular revival connected with the name of St Sergius of Radonezh (c. 1314–92) and those of his practically innumerable disciples: during the second half of the fourteenth century and the first decades of the fifteenth over 150 new monasteries were founded in the forests of northern Russia.[56]

---

[54] These are Stephen of Novgorod (ed. M. N. Speransky, *ed. cit.*, pp. 50–9), an Anonymous of the early fourteenth century (ed. M. N. Speransky, *ibid.*, pp. 128–37), Ignatius of Smolensk (ed. S. V. Arsen'ev, in *PPS*, IR, 3, St Petersburg, 1887, pp. 1–33), Alexander the *diak* (PSRL, 4, St Petersburg, 1848, pp. 357–8) and the monk, Zosima (ed. Kh. Loparev in PPS, VIII, 3, St Petersburg, 1889, pp. 1–26).

[55] Cf. Tikhomirov, *Svyazi*, pp. 18–19, 24.

[56] Ikonnikov, *O kul'turnom znachenii*, p. 119; for a general survey of monastic history in Russia during that period, see I. Smolitsch, *Russisches Mönchtum. Enstehung, Entwicklung und Wesen, 988–1917*, Würzburg, 1953, pp. 79–100; also Fedotov, *Religious Mind*, II, pp. 195–264.

The personality of St Sergius is known to us primarily through his *Life*, written originally by his disciple and contemporary, Epiphanius the 'Wise' in 1418 and later re-edited by an immigrant from the Balkans, Pachomius the Serb in 1440–59. Both of these authors are themselves representative witnesses of Byzantine and South Slavic ideas and literary forms adopted in Russia: Epiphanius by his ornamented style (*pletenie sloves*) and Pachomius by his deliberate emphasis on such character traits of hesychast literature as the vision of divine light.[57] The respective contributions of Epiphanius and of Pachomius to the very many manuscript versions of the *Life* are not fully deciphered yet,[58] but the figure of St Sergius himself emerges with sufficient clarity.[59]

Following the ideals of early Christian monasticism, Sergius lives for years in complete 'solitude' (the *Life* uses the term *bezmolvie*, the Slavic equivalent of the Greek ἡσυχία) in the 'desert' – which, in Russia, was in fact a forest – north of Moscow, where he established friendship with a bear. Endowed with great physical strength, he excelled in manual work, particularly carpentry. Against his will, he was eventually forced by circumstances to accept the company of other monks. He was then ordained a priest and became abbot of a big monastery, Holy Trinity. However, even in this new position of authority, he continued to work with his hands, to wear rags and to enforce, more by his own personal example than by acts of authority, the ideals of monastic poverty and detachment among his brothers, the monks. In 1378 he refused the offer to succeed Alexis as 'Metropolitan of Kiev and all Rus''.

The *Life* of Sergius always emphasizes his simplicity, humility and brotherly love, and presents only a few examples of mystical, or miraculous events. According to his biographers, his disciples Isaac and Simon saw Sergius surrounded with divine light, while he celebrated the eucharistic liturgy. Another disciple, Micah, witnessed a visit to Sergius by the Virgin Mary and the apostles Peter and John. These accounts could easily have been considered

---

[57] On Pachomius, see particularly V. Yablonsky, *Pakhomy Serb i ego agiograficheskie pisaniya*, St Petersburg, 1908.

[58] Cf. the latest study on the subject by V. P. Zubov, 'Epifany Premudry i Pakhomy Serb (K voprosu o redaktsiyakh Zhitiya Sergiya Radonezhskogo)', TODRL, ix, 1953, pp. 145–58.

[59] Cf. a shortened English version of the *Life* in G. P. Fedotov, *A Treasury of Russian Spirituality*, New York, 1950 (Harper Torchbook, New York, 1965), pp. 54–83; cf. also, by the same author, an excellent chapter on St Sergius in *Religious Mind*, ii, pp. 195–229.

as hagiographic clichés, if they did not fit with other facts connecting Sergius with the general atmosphere created in Russia by the hesychast influence.

While certainly not an intellectual, Sergius belongs to a milieu concerned with books and theology: as a boy, he miraculously learns how to read and later dedicates his Church to the 'Holy Trinity'.[60] Moreover, he belongs to a group of Russian monks, who – like their Bulgarian counterparts, Theodosius and Euthymius – maintain direct contacts with Constantinople. In the case of Sergius, these contacts illustrate the fact, which we have noted above, that the term 'Hesychasm', applied to the religious 'zealotism' in Eastern Europe in the fourteenth century, can be used only in its broadest sense. While practising eremitism and solitude, Sergius does not consider it as the only desirable form of monasticism. After a direct correspondence with Patriarch Philotheos himself, he introduced community discipline at Holy Trinity.

It is unlikely that the text of the letter by Patriarch Philotheos to Sergius, found in the *Life*, is the actual text sent from Constantinople[61] but the very detailed account of the episode by Epiphanius – Sergius' contemporary – is certain proof that the monastery of the Holy Trinity cherished its connections with Byzantium, particularly with the hesychast Patriarch Philotheos, and respected the disciplinary and liturgical reforms introduced by him. Another patriarchal letter, undoubtedly authentic, and whose addressee was most probably Sergius, called the community to obedience after it had resisted the introduction of cenobitism.[62]

---

[60] On this see S. Bulgakov, 'Bladodatnye zavety prep. Sergiya russkomu bogoslovstvovaniyu', *Put'*, 5, Paris, 1926, pp. 3–19.

[61] Slavic text in the *Life*, ed. N. S. Tikhonravov, *Drevniya Zhitiya prepodobnago Sergiya Radonezhskogo*, Moscow, 1892 (repr. with a useful introduction by L. Müller, Munich, 1967), pp. 44–5; Engl. tr. in G. P. Fedotov, *A Treasury*, p. 73; tentative rerendering into Greek in A. Tachiaos, 'Επιδράσεις, p. 48. E. E. Golubinsky is certainly right in supposing that the introduction of community life at Holy Trinity did not come about through the surprise arrival of a short patriarchal letter (as the *Life* recounts it), but followed some debate and correspondence involving the patriarch, Metropolitan Alexis (whom Sergius, according to the *Life*, asks to translate the letter from the Greek) and St Sergius himself (E. E. Golubinsky, *Prep. Sergy Radonezhsky i sozdannaya im Troitskaya Lavra*, Moscow, 1892, pp. 22–3).

[62] RIB, VI, 21, cols. 187–90. The editor, A. Pavlov, identifies the author of the letter as Patriarch Neilos (1379–88). However the mention of the patriarchal deacon Georges Perdikes, whose trip to Russia in 1361 is firmly documented, points rather at Patriarch Callistos (second patriarchate, 1354–63) as the author (cf. A. Tachiaos, 'Επιδράσεις, pp. 52–5). Perdikes had been to Russia also in 1354 (MM, I, p. 349) and may have been the patriarchal envoy who brought to Sergius the letter of Philotheos as well. A small golden cross which, according to tradition,

We will see below that St Sergius belonged to the group of monks who kept in close touch with Metropolitan Cyprian, whom Philotheos had appointed to succeed Alexis. Before coming to Moscow in 1378, Cyprian notified St Sergius and his nephew, the abbot of Simonovsky monastery, Theodore, of his arrival[63] and, after his expulsion from Moscow, complained again to the same monks of his misadventure.[64]

This particular episode involves the problems of Sergius' political commitments and activities, which cannot be fully understood without a discussion of the extremely complex situation which prevailed in the relationships between the Grand-princes of Moscow and Lithuania, the various Russian principalities, which gravitated in their orbit, and the khans of the Golden Horde. There is no doubt that, especially after the support he received both from the patriarchate and from Metropolitan Alexis in building up a disciplined community at Holy Trinity (1363), Sergius remained in close touch with the Muscovite court, became the God-father of two of Grand-prince Dimitri's sons and accomplished for him several diplomatic missions, including the conclusion of an 'eternal peace' between Moscow and Ryazan in 1385.[65] Much more questionable was his mission of 1363 to Nizhni-Novgorod, where Prince Boris, with Tatar help, was challenging Moscow's authorities. On the orders from Metropolitan Alexis, who headed the Muscovite government, he became part of a delegation which closed all the churches in the city, applying a sanction frequently used in the Latin West, but unknown in Eastern tradition.[66] This controversial episode, which took place at the very beginning of Sergius' friendship with Moscow, is not reported in the *Life* of Epiphanius, and most chronicles omit Sergius' name when they list the members of the delegation. Clearly, the authors did not consider that the visit to Nizhni-Novgorod contributed to St Sergius' holiness or historical merits. These omissions and other indications point to the fact that the loyalties of Sergius and his circle to Moscow were not unconditional. Pachomios recalls the

was brought as a gift of patriarch Philotheos to St Sergius and was venerated as such at the Trinity monastery, seems to be a piece of Russian, fifteenth-century craft (cf. however, a plea for its possible authenticity in O. A. Belobrova, 'Posol'stvo Konstantinopol'skogo patriarkha Filofeya k Sergiyu Radonezhskomu', *Soobsch-cheniya Zagorskogo gosudarstvennogo istoriko-khudozhstvennogo muzeya-zapovednika*, Zagorsk, 1958, pp. 12–18).

[63] Text in PS, 1860, No. 2, pp. 84; cf. below, app. 7, pp. 292.
[64] Text in RIB, VI, cols. 173–86; cf. below, app. 8, pp. 293–9.
[65] *Rog.*, col. 151.
[66] On this episode, see Fedotov, *Religious Mind*, II, 225–6.

'great oppression' suffered by the city of Rostov under Moscow's rule, which obliged Sergius' family to leave for Radonezh. On the other hand, we have seen the ties of the monastic group, headed by Sergius, with Metropolitan Cyprian who opposed the creation, in Moscow, of a separate metropolitanate without jurisdiction over the entire territory of 'Russia'. And one wonders whether it is pure coincidence that the most famous of all patriotic acts of St Sergius – the blessing bestowed upon Grand-prince Dimitri before his battle against the Tatars in 1380 – was followed by the return of Cyprian to Moscow and his acceptance by Dimitri. There are many reasons to believe, therefore, that Sergius' political position corresponded to that of Cyprian: while approving Moscow's claim of leadership in Russia, he did not approve either Muscovite or Lithuanian separation from the broader unity inherited from Kievan times and strengthened by the Byzantine connection.

The great spiritual potentials which were emerging in the framework of the religious revival of the fourteenth century are seen not only in the unparalleled significance of St Sergius, as the patriarch of Russian monastic revival, with his human traits and gifts for leadership, but also in the case of his contemporary, St Stephen of Perm, scholar and missionary (1340–96). His biography, as that of his friend Sergius, was written by the same Epiphanius the Wise, monk at Holy Trinity.[67] In the case of St Stephen, we discover that Greek manuscripts and their Slavic translations, which were reaching Russia in great numbers, could have a remarkable effect on some gifted and curious Russian minds. Epiphanius informs us that Stephen, the son of a cleric of Ustyug – a city in the remote north-east, located on the Dvina river, the 'land of midnight', according to the biographer – could learn at home 'all the literary art and the power of books' (*vsei gramotichnei khytrosti i knizhnei sile*).[68] Eventually, Stephen received monastic tonsure in Rostov, under the sponsorship of the bishop of Rostov, Parthenios, presumably a Greek.[69] In his monastery there were many books, which he perused with diligence, and acquired the reputation of a good copyist (*svyatyya knigi pisashe khytre i gorazde i borzo*). He also learned Greek and always kept Greek books in his cell.[70] This newly acquired knowledge allowed him to become an apostle to the Zyrians, a Finnish people living

---

[67] Ed. E. V. Druzhinin, Moscow, 1897; repr. D. Čiževskij, *Zhitie sv. Stefana episkopa Permskogo* (Apophoreta Slavica II), 's-Gravenhage, 1959.
[68] *Ed. cit.*, p. 5.   [69] Cf. Golubinsky, *Istoriya*, II, 1, p. 267.
[70] *Ed. cit.*, p. 8.

in the region of Perm, for whom he translated Scripture and liturgical books, as Saints Cyril and Methodius did for the benefit of the Slavs. His mission began in 1378–9, the year of the death of Metropolitan Alexis, when he was ordained a priest. The Zyrian alphabet, which he invented, was a totally original creation, quite unlike either the Greek or the Slavic script. In 1383, he was consecrated bishop by Metropolitan Pimen. Before his death in 1396, he wrote a refutation of the Strigolniks, a heretical, anti-institutional sect possibly connected with the Bogomils, or Cathars.[71] Comparing Stephen's missionary activity to that of the early apostles of Christianity, Epiphanius gives examples of his own learning, quoting Byzantine sources to illustrate the universality of Christendom. At the end of the *Life*, he paraphrases the famous sermon of Hilarion of Kiev addressed to Vladimir and applies it to Stephen: 'The Roman land praises the two apostles Peter and Paul; the land of Asia honours and blesses John the Theologian; Egypt, Mark the Evangelist; Antioch, Luke, writer of the Gospel; Greece, the apostle Andrew; the land of the Rus', the great prince Vladimir who baptised it; Moscow venerates and honours Peter, its metropolitan, as its new wonderworker; the land of Rostov, its bishop Leonty; but you, O bishop Stephen, you receive the praises of the land of Perm, for through you we were shown the light.'[72]

Also, recounting his death, Epiphanius makes a significant re-affirmation of his world-view. St Stephen's demise occurred:

During the reign of the Orthodox Greek Emperor [Tsar] Manuel, reigning in the Queen of cities, under Patriarch Anthony, Archbishop of Constantinople, under Patriarchs Dorotheos of Jerusalem, Mark of Alexandria, Neilos of Antioch, under the Orthodox Grand-prince Basil Dmitrievich of all Russia, in the seventh year of his tenure, under Archbishop Cyprian, Metropolitan of all Russia, who was in Kiev in those days [of Stephen's death], under the other pious and Christ-loving princes [list of names, which include Vitovt, 'grand-prince' of Lithuania who is not designated as 'Christ loving', and the Grand-prince Michael of Tver], in the sixteenth year of the rule of *tsar* Tokhtamysh, who also controlled the horde of Mamaï, whereas a second *tsar*, Temir Qutlug, ruled the empire beyond the Volga.[73]

[71] Ed. in RIB, vi, cols. 211–28.   [72] *Ed. cit.*, pp. 89–90.
[73] *Ed. cit.*, p. 85. On the use of the title *tsar* for both the Byzantine emperors and the Tatar khans, Cherniavsky, '*Khan* or *Basileus*'. One should note, however, the clearly 'Byzantine' conception of Epiphanius which emphasizes the orthodoxy, universality and uniqueness of the emperor of Constantinople, and the distinctiveness of his reign (*tsarstvo*), from the *de facto* rule (*vladychestvo*) of the several Tatar khans.

Clearly, there was a unity of ideology and inspiration between the concerns and activities of Greek and Russian monks in the fourteenth century, which included ideological faithfulness to the Byzantine 'Commonwealth', renewed interest in Byzantine literary traditions and books, a sense of legitimate cultural pluralism, religious revival and missionary expansion.

4. HESYCHASM AND ART

No written document explicitly bears witness to the connections which may, or may not have existed between the intellectual and religious movements in Byzantium during the Palaeologan period, and the development of pictorial arts. Nevertheless, the issue is often raised by art historians. What is the cultural and religious background of the so-called 'Palaeologan Renaissance', which led Byzantine and Slavic artists to a more innovative style, to greater closeness to life, to imitation of antique models? In reference to Byzantine painters of the late thirteenth and early fourteenth centuries, André Grabar writes: 'We see them foreshadowing the discoveries of Cavallini and Giotto, and at the same time those of the Italian painters of the fifteenth century who will revive the great style of classical painting.'[74]

Most specialists tend to associate this artistic development with the revival, in late Byzantine society, of interest in classical Antiquity. This view may find confirmation in the fact that, during that period, most religious foundations 'were instituted by representatives of the most illustrious and powerful of the noble families . . . , repositories of wealth and power', and as we have seen earlier, it is in the same rather narrow and sophisticated milieu that the study of antiquity was also promoted. The example of Theodore Metochites, a noted and wealthy scholar-humanist, renovating the monastery of the Chora in Constantinople, comes immediately to mind. Scholars who endorse this view also generally believe that the victory of the Hesychasts at the councils of 1341, 1347 and 1351 was detrimental to the development of the artistic 'Renaissance'. Indeed, art historians detect, precisely in the middle of the fourteenth century, a change in the artistic patterns and style. 'The modest innovations of the preceding period are not relinquished, but no new ones are made', and this is explained by the triumph of 'monastic rigorism', the belief, sup-

[74] 'The artistic climate in Byzantium during the Palaeologan period', in P. A. Underwood, ed., *The Kariye Djami*, vol. 4, Princeton, N.J., 1975, pp. 7–8.

ported by Palamite theology, that God could be known 'directly', through a life of piety in the bosom of the Church and through the sacraments that lead every believer to a mystic communion with Christ. . . .' 'A program of this kind, which would conform to the Byzantine traditions of the early Middle Ages, obviously cut religious art off from real life and prevented it from renewing itself by means of individual initiative.'[75]

This view of Hesychasm as having had a stifling effect on artistic style can find further support in the fact that monks preached and practised poverty, and could not, therefore, sympathize with the extraordinary expenses required for mosaic decorations, or other works of art: some of them, including Patriarch Athanasius I and Gregory Palamas himself, were even accused of iconoclasm.[76]

However, this simplified scheme involves the very nature of the so-called Palaeologan 'Renaissance', discussed in the preceding chapter. It can be easily countered with other facts. Monastic rigorism was influential much before the triumph of Palamism in 1341–51 and its greatest promoters, Patriarchs Arsenius and Athanasius, dominated the Byzantine church precisely during the very flourishing of the 'Renaissance', i.e., during the early Palaeologan period. On the other hand, one can note that quite a number of Byzantine humanists not only continued, after 1351, their activities and writing in Constantinople, but also enjoyed the support of the imperial court, establishing numerous contacts with Italy, where their artistic tastes could only be strengthened: as late as the first half of the fifteenth century, George Gemisthos Pletho (*c.* 1360–1452) and his disciple and friend, Bessarion of Nicaea (1402–72) were, among several other humanists, powerful personalities indeed, and certainly enjoyed the possibility of influencing artists. Moreover, members of the officially Palamite hierarchy, like Patriarch Philotheos himself, referred to secular learning with respect,[77] or, like Neilos Cabasilas, archbishop of Thessalonica, were 'passionately enthusiastic about the books of Thomas [Aquinas]',[78] because of the latter's use of Aristotle.

If the Palamite victory of 1347–51 did not put an end to such

---

[75] *Ibid.*, pp. 89; cf. also V. N. Lazarev, *Istoriya vizantiiskoy zhivopisi*, 1, Moscow, 1947, p. 225. References to recent art-historical publications, expressing the same view, could easily be multiplied.

[76] Cf. Meyendorff, 'Spiritual trends', *ibid.*, p. 105.

[77] Cf. his reference to Theodore Metochites, the restorer of Chora, *Encomion of Palamas*, PG, CLI, cols. 559 D-560 A.

[78] Demetrius Kydones, *Apologia*, III, in Mercati, *Notizie*, p. 391.

intellectual pursuits, is it really legitimate to attribute to it alone the interruption of the admittedly only incipient 'pre-Renaissance' in art? No really hard fact can be presented in support of this view.[79] One wonders whether this interruption – which art historians must still define and date with greater precision than they were able to do so far – should not rather be associated with more general factors, political, cultural and economic, which prevailed in decaying Byzantium during the decades which preceded its fall.

More significant still is the fact that the artistic trends which characterize the Palaeologan period greatly flourished in Slavic lands, where the purely Greek interests in antiquity could not be exported. Furthermore, as we have already shown, the monastic movement, inspired by hesychastic ideals and literature, was largely instrumental in all the contacts which existed between Byzantium and the Slavic lands, including particularly Russia. It would be difficult to imagine that an art to which the monastic milieu was supposedly hostile in a systematic way could have acquired such great popularity and official civic and ecclesiastical sponsorship in Slavic lands.

It would be impossible to discuss here the well-known development of Palaeologan art throughout the predominantly monastic churches in the Balkans in the fourteenth century. In Russia, the chronicles signal many artistic contacts with Constantinople: in 1344, for example, Greek artists brought to Russia by Metropolitan Theognostos decorated the church of the Dormition in the Moscow Kremlin.[80] But by far the most famous Byzantine master working in Russia is undoubtedly Theophanes 'the Greek'. His career is known to us from the chronicles, but also, quite interestingly, from a letter written around 1415 by Epiphanius the Wise, author of the *Lives* of St Sergius and St Stephen of Perm, to the abbot Cyril of Tver.[81] Having first worked in Constantinople,

---

[79] V. N. Lazarev (*Feofan Grek i ego shkola*, Moscow, 1961, p. 27) refers to a passage by Joseph Bryennios, supposedly criticizing 'movement' in iconography. The reference is based on a mistranslation: Bryennios complains that some people 'throw the holy icons casually, and attempt to predict the future from the trajectory they follow' (κινοῦντες ἀτάκτως τὰς ἁγίας εἰκόνας, τὰ μέλλοντα δῆθεν διὰ τῶν κινημάτων αὐτῶν τεκμαιρόμεθα, ed. E. Voulgaris, III, Leipzig, 1784; repr. in L. Oeconomos, 'L'état intellectuel et moral des Byzantins vers le milieu du XIVe siècle d'après une page de Joseph Bryennios', *Mélanges Ch. Diehl*, I, Paris, 1930, p. 227). Bryennios clearly refers to an irreverent form of fortune-telling, not to iconographic style. [80] *Troits.*, p. 366.

[81] The letter was first published in PS, 1863, III, pp. 324-8, and repr. by Archim. Leonid in PPS, v, 3, pp. 3-6. For the addressee of the letter, see A. Sedel'nikov, 'Iz oblasti literaturnogo obshcheniya v nachale XV veka (Kirill Tverskoi i Epifany "Moskovsky")', AN, *Otd. russkogo yazyka i slov., Izvestiya*, xxxi, 1926, pp. 159-76.

Chalcedon, Galata and Caffa, Theophanes came to Novgorod and decorated, in 1378, the Church of the Transfiguration, and other monuments. He also worked in Nizhni-Novgorod and, finally, in Moscow, particularly in the churches of the Annunciation and of the Archangel Michael in the Kremlin. His works at the church of the Transfiguration in Novgorod and his iconostasis in the church of the Annunciation are still preserved, and have accredited his fame as one of the greatest painters of all times. Always personal, dynamic and colourful, using slightly impressionistic methods and original compositions, reflecting a very suggestive sense of human psychology, Theophanes succeeds in showing man's quest for God and God's gift of 'deification' to man, in an unequalled way. In his creations, personal genius is combined with the best achievements of Palaeologan art.

But where does Theophanes stand in relation to the spiritual and cultural crisis, exemplified in the 'hesychast controversies'? If one were to agree with those who interpret Byzantine Hesychasm as conservative reaction, as a rejection of the *humanum* for the sake of the *divinum*, as a monastic refusal of intellectual criticism and cultural creativity, one has no other choice than to associate Theophanes with the 'humanists' and even to interpret his departure for Russia as an exile from his monastic-dominated motherland, similar to the flight of several Greek humanists to Italy.[82] One would also have to consider that the contemporary and quite remarkable artistic flourishing in northern Russia also reflected the same humanism and was therefore in spiritual contradiction with the monastic literature and ideology brought from Constantinople: indeed, in 1405, the great Andrei Rublev worked under Theophanes' direction in decorating the church of the Annunciation in Moscow.[83]

However, such a violent contrast between the hesychast movement and the most creative aspects of Palaeologan art can be upheld only if one accepts a much too narrow definition of what the religious movement in the fourteenth century really was: we have insisted earlier on the fact that it was a movement promoting not the cause of exclusive asceticism ('Hesychasm', as eremitic monasticism), but wide religious, cultural and social principles. It is quite possible that, in many concrete instances, monastic rigorism was detrimental to artistic creativity in the fourteenth century, as at other times,[84] but the principles and the theology of

[82] Cf. V. N. Lazarev, *ibid.*, pp. 14–34.   [83] *Troits.*, p. 459.
[84] Cf. my own observations on this point in 'Spiritual trends', p. 106.

Palamite Hesychasm cannot be accused of *deliberately* stifling artistic creativity.

The issue of the relationship between Byzantine Hesychasm and art inevitably involves the debate on the very nature of the Byzantine theological trends in the fourteenth century, which had been continuing during the past two decades and which cannot be analysed here. Whereas some consider Palamism as stifling conservatism, others, on the contrary, see it as an innovation, contrary to the traditions of Greek patristic, best upheld by Barlaam and his disciples.[85] Also, the view has been recently expressed that the Hesychast and Palamite insistence on the possibility of a direct vision of the uncreated divine light by man eliminates, as unnecessary, the christological and other arguments in favour of the veneration of icons, brought out by Byzantine Orthodox theologians since the eighth and ninth centuries.[86]

The author of the present book has given his own view on the matter[87] and considers these oppositions as based on misunderstandings. Chalcedonian and post-Chalcedonian christology, based on the notion of a 'hypostatic union' in Christ of divinity and humanity served as the conceptual framework for both iconodulic theology and Palamite Hesychasm: without reference to this common christological ground, neither one of these two developments is understandable. 'Hypostatic union' and the patristic doctrine of 'deification' (θέωσις), implies that divine life becomes accessible through the *human flesh* of Christ and of the saints. The innumerable references of Palamas to such texts as the homily on the Transfiguration by St John of Damascus[88] – the great defender of 'matter', as a legitimate channel of grace during the iconoclastic controversy or to the christology of St Maximus the Confessor, clearly indicate a basic unity of theological inspiration. One may certainly argue the point that monastic asceticism did not encourage the promotion of expensive decorations of churches, or that the use of mental prayer could – on the level of piety – make such decorations unnecessary, but it remains obvious that nothing

---

[85] Cf. for example Podskalsky, *Theologie*, pp. 126–60; for a very full bibliographical review covering the current discussion on the nature of Palamism, see D. Stiernon, 'Bulletin sur le palamisme', REB, 30, 1972, pp. 231–341.

[86] H.-G. Beck, 'Von der Fragwürdigkeit der Ikone', *Bayerische Akademie der Wissenschaften. Phil.-Hist. Klasse. Sitzungsberichte*, 1975, Heft 7, Munich, 1975, pp. 40–4.

[87] See particularly *Christ in Eastern Christian Thought*, Washington, D.C., 1969 (2nd ed., New York, 1975).

[88] PG, xcvi, cols. 557C–596B; cf. particularly Palamas, *Triads*, iii, 1, 22, ed. J. Meyendorff, *Grégoire Palamas. Défense des saints hésychastes*, 2nd ed., Louvain, 1973, ii, pp. 596–9.

in Palamite theology challenged the legitimacy of Christian art, whose reality, in all epochs, was grounded on the 'incarnational' message of Christianity.

Whether or not the triumph of Palamism in Byzantium led to stifling conservatism in art, it is obvious that the monastic movement in Slavic lands, and particularly in Russia, produced quite the opposite results. Theophanes the Greek was a close friend of Epiphanius the Wise, the author of the *Life* of St Sergius. Epiphanius praises him for his original style: when Theophanes was painting, he 'never looked on existing models', but 'in his spirit, encompassed distant and intellectual realities, while his spiritual eyes contemplated spiritual beauty'.[89] When he was decorating the churches of the Annunciation and of St Michael in Moscow, he enjoyed the patronage of Metropolitan Cyprian, and his brilliant apprentice, Andrei Rublev, was a monk of the monastery of the Holy Trinity.

In Russia, the monastic revival was based less on the technical and conceptual side of Hesychasm, than upon the general spiritual and religious revival which accompanied it. And art was part of this revival. Not only is there no incompatibility between the art of Theophanes and Rublev, on the one side, and Hesychasm on the other, but, clearly, artists and monks belonged to the same milieu.[90] This does not mean, however, that all the manifestations of individual genius, which appear in the art of Theophanes, are to be explained by references to hesychast theology,[91] or that, among the Hesychasts, one has to draw a sharp distinction between promoters of authentic spirituality (like Nicholas Cabasilas), and the 'scholastic polemicists' (like Palamas).[92] The Byzantine monastic revival came to Russia both as a consistent world-view, and as a renewal of personal religiosity, individual prayer and a more conscious understanding of culture and of Christianity. It must have also created an atmosphere favourable to artistic creativity. No Barlaam arose to challenge it, so there was

---

[89] *Letter to Cyril*, ed. Leonid, p. 4; repr. in V. Lazarev, *op. cit.*, p. 113.

[90] Cf. M. V. Alpatov, 'Iskusstvo Feofana Greka i uchenie isikhastov', VV, 33, 1972, pp. 190–202. One should add here that the official formulations of Palamite theology were brought to Russia by metropolitan Cyprian, friend of St Sergius, together with the *Synodikon of Orthodoxy* as it was used in Constantinople (RIB, VI, cols. 239, 241).

[91] This is the tendency adopted by N. K. Goleizovsky, 'Zametki o Feofane greke', VV, 24, 1964, pp. 139–49; 'Isikhazm i russkaya zhivopis XIV–XVvv.', VV, 29, 1968, pp. 196–210.

[92] The distinction is drawn by Beck, *Kirche*, p. 780 and others. It also appears in M. V. Alpatov, *ibid.*, pp. 196–7.

no need to import and to translate the polemical writings of contemporary Byzantine theologians. But the young and relatively rich Grand-principality of Moscow was able to supply, better than impoverished Byzantium, opportunities for the development of art. The building of new churches, the establishment of monasteries, the persistent admiration expressed by Russians for the Byzantine cultural inheritance created the right conditions for the work of Theophanes, of Andrei Rublev and for their numerous disciples. Their message to their contemporaries pointed to communion with God, as the most essential content of human destiny: their art, just as the spirituality and the theology of the Hesychasts, intended to show that such communion was *possible*, that it depended both on divine grace and upon human desire to achieve it, and that it concerned not only a disincarnated human spirit, but the totality of human existence, body and soul, assumed by God in Jesus Christ. The identification of this trend with 'stifling conservatism' can only proceed from the unconscious belief, shared by many historians, that 'progress' implies a 'secular' understanding of man. But if one adopts such a prejudicial view, basically inherited from the Enlightenment, there remains no possibility for any positive understanding of medieval civilization, and particularly the Byzantine inheritance, and for seeing it as anything but the 'dark ages' of mankind's history.

7

Byzantium and Moscow

The story of the rise of Moscow in the fourteenth century, its struggle for leadership against other northern principalities – particularly Tver – its eventual victory, largely due to a ruthless and shrewd political use of Tatar power, its confrontation with the Grand-principality of Lithuania and, finally, its becoming the unquestionable capital of a Russian empire, has been often and skilfully told by numerous historians. Our own purpose will consist in presenting these events as they were viewed from Byzantium and, also, in defining the role played by Byzantine diplomacy in the development of Russian history. As we pointed out earlier, this diplomacy was exercised primarily through the one administrative structure which Byzantium directly controlled, i.e., the Church, which supported the new political development. It is therefore fully legitimate to ask the question: in what sense and to what degree is Byzantium responsible for the rise of Moscow?

Grand-prince Olgerd, or Algirdas of Lithuania (1345–77) was a faithful follower of the policies of his father Gedymin. While belonging as his father to the traditionally pagan Lithuanian princely dynasty, he was successively married to two Russian Orthodox princesses: Maria Yaroslavna of Vitebsk, and after 1349, Ul'yana Aleksandrovna of Tver. During his entire reign, he opposed the expansion of the Teutonic Knights in the Baltic region, competed with Poland for the possession of Galicia and succeeded in controlling Volhynia (1352). His influence over the policies of Novgorod and Pskov was very strong, but ephemeral, whereas the extension of his rule over Central Russia was quite spectacular: he successively occupied Bryansk and Smolensk (1357), Kiev (1362), Podolia (1363–4), Chernigov (c. 1370), and, eventually his domain reached the Black Sea. Much of this expansion occurred at the expense of the Mongol rule in Russia, although the khans gave him occasional support against Moscow. Profiting from internal dissensions in the Horde, he was able to inflict a serious defeat on the Tatars in 1363. However, his repeated attempts at capturing Moscow did not succeed.

More explicitly than his father Gedymin – who had leanings towards Roman Catholicism – Olgerd accepted as a fact that he was ruling a state with an overwhelmingly Russian and Orthodox population. Since Lithuanians had not yet developed a written language, all official documents of state were drafted in Russian (or 'Slavonic'). It is sometimes believed that Olgerd, on the occasion of one of his two marriages with a Russian princess, embraced the Orthodox faith, which would be a condition for the celebration of the marriage in church.[1] However, if such a conversion really took place, it was accomplished in secret, for Byzantine official documents always refer to Olgerd as 'impious' (ἀσεβής)[2] and 'fire-worshipper' (πυρσολάτρης),[3] and the Russian chronicles as 'pagan, enemy of God and impious'.[4] The actual attitude of Olgerd in religious matters is most probably the one which is reported by the Byzantine historian Nicephorus Gregoras. In his description of the political rulers of Russia, Gregoras mentions Olgerd's military predominance over the other princes and describes him as a 'worshipper of the sun', but he also informs us that the Lithuanian Grand-prince had expressed willingness to embrace the Orthodox faith, if only the Orthodox metropolitan of Russia, successor to Theognostos (d. 1353), were to reside in his domain and not in Moscow.[5] We will see below that Olgerd's plan of action consisted in unifying Russia under his own rule, and presupposed his conversion, which he was ready to accomplish in exchange for support by Byzantium. This plan met with sympathy in some circles of the Church and the imperial court of the Palaeologi, and was connected with major conflicts both in Constantinople and in Russia. But ultimately, it did not succeed.

While Lithuanian expansion was occurring inevitably at the expense of Mongol rule in Russia, the Golden Horde kept northeastern Russia firmly under its control. Respectful of the existing political and religious institutions of the land, the khans used those institutions as tools of their own government and taxation system in Russia. Since political leadership traditionally belonged to the 'grand-prince of Vladimir', the Tatars made sure that this position

---

[1] Cf. P. M. Batyushkov, *Belorussia i Litva*, St Petersburg, 1890, p. 70.
[2] MM, I, p. 523 (in 1370).
[3] MM, II, p. 12 (in 1380), i.e. already after his death.
[4] 'Zloverny i bezbozhny i nechestivy', *Troits.*; p. 402.
[5] *Hist.*, XXXVI, 34, Bonn, III, pp. 517–18.

was held by a prince sufficiently subservient, or weak enough to need Mongol support against his competitors. Whereas, in principle, the right of succession to the Grand-principality belonged, as in the Kievan period, to the oldest representative of the family of princes, who reigned in the various appanages (*udely*), the khans made this right conditional on receiving their formal investiture (*yarlyk*) and, in practice, designated the holder of the title arbitrarily. The chosen incumbent kept his own principality, while receiving the city of Vladimir in addition. During the reigns of the powerful khans Tokhta (1290–1312) and Uzbek (1312–42), the Golden Horde skilfully played upon the rivalry between the two strongest contenders for the Grand-principality: the princes of Tver and of Moscow.

Enjoying clear family seniority, Prince Michael of Tver was granted the Grand-principality by Tokhta in 1304–5, but in 1318 Khan Uzbek became fearful of Michael's influence and power (the Tverian prince succeeding in controlling the rich republic of Novgorod) and yielded to the intrigues of his younger cousin, Yuri of Moscow. Michael was put to death in Sarai and, for the first time, the Grand-principality was granted to the prince of Moscow. The latter, very appropriately, had married the khan's sister, who became a Christian.

A very minor city, first mentioned in the chronicles under the year 1147, Moscow had been given in appanage to the youngest son of Alexander Nevsky, Daniel. The assumption of the title of 'Grand-prince of all Russia' by Daniel's son Yuri was something of a revolution, which could not have happened without an adroit manipulation of Tatar politics by Yuri. But other factors also favoured Moscow: the geographic centre of Russia, located at the crossing of trade routes linking the Volga, the Don and the Dnieper with the region of Novgorod and the Baltic Sea, heavily colonized, rich in population and resources, the little principality provided its shrewd princes with ample means to achieve their ambitions. Actually, the growth of Moscow's power was so rapid, especially since Grand-prince Yuri established his control over Novgorod as Michael of Tver did before him, that Uzbek again shifted his support and appointed Dimitri of Tver, the son of the murdered Michael, as Grand-prince (1322). Dimitri soon took revenge for the murder of his father by killing Yuri in Sarai (1325). This act brought Uzbek's anger (Yuri was his brother-in-law!) and was followed by the execution of Dimitri (1326). The remaining representative of the house of Tver, Alexander, also appointed

Grand-prince, resorted to an heroic, but politically unwise act: he openly rebelled against Tatar rule. The khan's envoys were massacred in Tver (1327). The result was predictable: in 1328, a punitive force of Mongol and Muscovite troops sacked the city of Tver, while Alexander fled to Pskov, which was in the Lithuanian sphere of influence. Ivan I Kalita, prince of Moscow and brother of Yuri, was appointed Grand-prince of Vladimir by Uzbek.[6]

Within the limits of the Grand-principality of Vladimir, the struggle for leadership opposed Moscow and Tver, and, on a larger scale, Moscow and Lithuania. This struggle involved the fate of the crucially important, rich and influential city-republic of Novgorod, which had never been militarily conquered by the Mongols, but remained a part of the political and economic system of the Grand-principality of Vladimir. While very zealously keeping its independence, Novgorod never aspired to dominate Russia as a whole, and limited itself to an economically profitable exploitation of its vast domains in the north, which produced timber, wax and furs, for export to Western Europe. By tradition and national solidarity, however, it always accepted a prince from the ruling family, whose functions were strictly limited in the framework of a minute balance of power in the city government. The archbishop of Novgorod (see above, Chapter 4) was also a powerful figure of that government. Elected locally, he enjoyed a much greater freedom from the metropolitan than other Russian bishops, and occasionally was in direct touch with the patriarch in Constantinople. However, Novgorod, with its relatively 'democratic' regime, was weakened by internal disputes and centrifugal trends in its vast empire. It was also crucially dependent upon food supplies coming from areas with more autocratic princely regimes, especially the principality of Moscow. In the fourteenth century, Moscow, Tver and Lithuania struggled for influence in Novgorod. Only occasionally could the Novgorodians play one principality against another. Eventually, the Moscow prince won the upper hand.

I. BYZANTIUM AND MOSCOW

We have seen earlier how the Galician abbot Peter, originally a candidate for the see of Galicia, was appointed head of the entire Church of Russia, after the rejection by Constantinople of a com-

---

[6] The best account of these events in English is to be found in Fennell, *Emergence*, pp. 60–110.

peting candidate Geronty, nominated by Michael of Tver, Grand-prince of Vladimir. The new metropolitan arrived in northern Russia in 1309, only to be immediately faced with the struggle between Tver and Moscow.

Contemporary documents report that Michael, aided by the bishop of Tver, Andrew, made repeated attempts at unseating Metropolitan Peter. One may note that Bishop Andrew was of Lithuanian princely descent,[7] which represents one of several examples of the ties which united the principality of Tver with Lithuania in the fourteenth century. A formal complaint against Peter was filed before Patriarch Athanasius I (second patriarchate: 1303–9) by the bishop of Tver. A special patriarchal envoy came to Russia for investigation and a council was held at Pereyaslavl', at which Peter was formally cleared of accusations against him.[8] But Tver's campaign against the metropolitan continued for some time, after the second resignation of Patriarch Athanasius. The authors of the *Lives* of Peter, who report these events, do not indicate the nature of the formal accusations against him. However, these can be found explicitly stated in a correspondence between Michael of Tver and Patriarch Niphon (1310–14): according to Michael, Peter had been too lenient in matrimonial discipline (he was allowing marriages in the sixth degree of relation) and had been practising simony.[9] Bishop Andrew, on the other hand, sent an envoy, the monk Akindynos, to Constantinople, in whose presence the patriarchal synod issued appropriate condemnations of simony,[10] whereas Niphon formally, in his letter to Michael, censured Metropolitan Peter for his alleged misdeeds. This censure, however, had no practical effects.

It is difficult to establish the truth about those accusations: the reproach of simony was used rather frequently in disputes involving ecclesiastics[11] and during the reign of Andronicus II, debates took place in Byzantium itself, as to the exact meaning of the term. E. Golubinsky suggests, for example, that Metropolitan

---

[7] Cf. *Troits.*, pp. 344–5.

[8] Cf. the *Life* of Peter by a contemporary witness, Prochoros of Rostov (1327) in Makary, *Istoriya*, IV, I, p. 310; also another *Life* by Metropolitan Cyprian, in Angelov, *Iz starata*, pp. 170–1.

[9] The reply of Patriarch Niphon to Michael's letter is preserved in a Slavic translation (RIB, VI, pp. 148–50).

[10] Cf. the report on the subject by Akindynos to Grand-prince Michael in RIB, VI, pp. 150–8.

[11] Patriarch Niphon, who censured Peter, was himself formally accused of simony, cf. Nicéphoros Choumnos, in J. F. Boissonade, *Anecdota graeca*, v, Paris, 1833 (repr. Hildesheim, 1962), pp. 255–83.

Peter may have limited himself to a standard and accepted practice of minimal taxation, in cases of ordination to the priesthood, a taxation which was seen as an uncanonical abuse by some.[12] In any case, except for the prince and the bishop of Tver, nobody took up the accusations against Peter, who is traditionally remembered as a saintly prelate. One can therefore be sure that, justified or not, the accusation of simony was directly connected with political factors: Peter's presence on the metropolitan's throne was undesirable to the prince of Tver, who was also, until his death in Sarai (1318), the Grand-prince of Vladimir.

There can be little doubt that if Peter succeeded in maintaining his position against the will of the Grand-prince, he must have received some local help, and the source of this help is not difficult to find. The council which acquitted him from Andrew's accusations was held in Pereyaslavl', a town belonging to the appanage of Moscow. The text of the *Life* of Peter by Metropolitan Cyprian seems to imply that the location was chosen by the unnamed envoy of Patriarch Athanasius, who also presided over the assembly.[13] One may, therefore, assume that Athanasius stood by his appointee to the metropolitanate of Russia, and gave him every opportunity to clear his name. Some understanding between the patriarchal envoy and the prince of Moscow was also likely, since the council was held under their joint sponsorship.[14] One should not be astonished, therefore, to learn that, in 1311, the metropolitan took a firm stand for Moscow and against Tver, in a military confrontation between the principalities. Furthermore, he established connections at the Golden Horde: in 1312, and for unknown reasons, he deposed the bishop of Sarai, Ismael, and consecrated his own candidate Barsanuphius (Varsonofy).[15] In the next year, he personally travelled to the Horde, accompanying Grand-prince Michael himself, and met with the new khan Uzbek, where 'he was treated with great honour by the *tsar* (Uzbek)'.[16] In his confrontation with Tver, Peter was clearly the winner.

---

[12] *Istoriya*, II, 1, pp. 108–10.

[13] 'Poslannyi patriarkhom klirik priide na Rus', sobor sobiraet v grade Pereyaslavli', ed. Angelov, *Iz Starata*, p. 171.

[14] This understanding seems to have been abandoned by the successor of Athanasius, Patriarch Niphon, who wrote to Michael of Tver in a manner quite unfavourable to Peter (cf. above note 11), but Niphon's short tenure (1310–14) had little impact over the affairs of Russia, where the alliance between Moscow and the metropolitan had become an accomplished fact.

[15] *Troits.*, p. 354.

[16] *Nik.*, p. 178. Already in 1308, Peter had also received a *yarlyk* from Khan Tokhta, confirming privileges to the Church. The text is not preserved, but it is quoted in

But Michael's hostility towards Peter provoked a reaction which had been neither foreseen, nor desired by the prince of Tver. The metropolitan allied himself with the prince of Moscow, Tver's enemy. In northern Russia, the head of the Russian Church – who continued to bear the title of metropolitan *of Kiev* – had no formally defined episcopal see: Vladimir, the capital of the Grand-principality, had been the normal residence of metropolitans Cyril and Maximus, and the latter was buried there. But Michael's control of the city must have made Peter's stay in the capital rather uncomfortable. According to his biographer Cyprian, the metropolitan travelled much 'visiting cities and villages'; among the cities, however, he singled out Moscow, in spite of the fact that it was 'small and had a small population', and 'began to sojourn in that city in preference to others'. The biographer does not mention any personal connection between Peter and Yuri Danilovich – perhaps because the latter's reputation as a murderer of Michael of Tver (1318) did not particularly recommend him for mention in the saint's *Life* – but there is no doubt, as the Council of Pereyaslavl' shows, that Michael's hostility made Peter's connection with Moscow inevitable at an early date of his tenure as metropolitan.[17] Thus, it is not Yuri Danilovich of Moscow who is seen by Peter's biographers as the metropolitan's main friend and supporter, but Yuri's brother and successor Ivan I Danilovich, surnamed 'Kalita' (the money-bag). 'That city [of Moscow]', writes Cyprian, 'was ruled by the pious Grand-prince Ivan [Cyprian uses the Hellenized form of *Ioann*], son of Daniel, grandson of the blessed Alexander [Nevsky], whom the blessed Peter saw resplending in Orthodoxy, merciful to the poor, honouring the holy churches of God and the clergy, loving divine Scriptures, well instructed in the teachings of the books. So the holy hierarch of God [Peter] loved him very much.'[18]

This information of Cyprian about the friendship between Peter and Ivan reproduced almost literally the text of the earlier *Life* of Peter,[19] but the fact that the merits of Moscow and of its prince

later similar documents (cf. Priselkov, *Yarlyki*, pp. 68–9). However, there is no reason to believe that Peter was made a conscious instrument of the Golden Horde, as asserted by Grekov (*Vostochnaya Evropa*, pp. 42–3); the policy of the khan consisted in playing Tver and Moscow against each other, not to favour Moscow unilaterally.

[17] Cf. E. Golubinsky, *op. cit.*, pp. 136–8.   [18] *Ed. cit.*, p. 172.

[19] Cf. in Makary, *op. cit.*, pp. 310–11. The traditional attribution of this earlier *Life* to Prochoros, bishop of Rostov, is questioned by V. A. Kuchkin, 'Skazanie o smerti mitropolita Petra', TODRL, xviii, 1962, pp. 59–79.

are exalted in this way by Metropolitan Cyprian, a great 'Helleno-phile', a friend of Patriarch Philotheos and an articulate promoter of Byzantine policies in Russia in the second half of the fourteenth century, is highly symptomatic. Cyprian rightly sees the settlement of the metropolitan's see in Moscow as prefiguring the entire course of political and ecclesiastical developments in his own time,[20] and, in this, he reflects the view prevailing in the circles close to Patriarch Philotheos.

But was there a deliberate policy of the Byzantine authorities *at the time of Metropolitan Peter*, which dictated his choice? Un-doubtedly, as we have seen earlier, the patriarchate and imperial administrations decided the issue of having the head of a unified metropolitanate reside in Vladimir, and not in Kiev, or Galician or Lithuanian territories. There does not seem to be any reason to suppose, however, that the Byzantines gave initial preference to Moscow over Tver: it is the Tverian opposition to Peter, which must have pushed both himself, and his Byzantine superiors in Constantinople towards supporting Moscow.

The support was apparently not entirely consistent on the part of the weaker and ephemeral successors of Athanasius I on the patriarchal throne. We have already seen that Niphon (1310–14), although himself accused of simony and eventually compelled to resign, gave credence to the accusations of simony against Peter by the bishop and prince of Tver. The short patriarchate of John Glykys (1315–19), which also ended with a resignation, was marked by the establishment in Lithuania of a separate metro-politanate which deprived Peter of his jurisdiction over vast terri-tories controlled by Gedymin I of Lithuania.[21] Gedymin could only look with disfavour upon a metropolitan entertaining perma-nent connections with the Golden Horde and politically identified with a vassal of the khan. Under the circumstances, he was financially and diplomatically able to sway the Byzantine authori-ties to appoint a separate metropolitan of Lithuania. But it is reasonable to assume that if the metropolitan had remained in the good graces of the prince of Tver – a city whose bishop Andrew was himself of princely Lithuanian stock and whose leaders were (and will remain throughout the fourteenth century) in close political touch with Lithuania – the division of the metropolitanate

[20] On the relevance of the *Life of Peter* by Cyprian, as an historical and ideological document indicative of Cyprian's own convictions, see L. A. Dmitriev, 'Rol' i znachenie', pp. 236–54. This issue will be further discussed below.

[21] Cf. above, Ch. 4.

would not have occurred. Clearly Peter's identification with the interests of Moscow, however justified in his eyes, involved a political price to pay, by facing the hostility of other leaders of Russia.

Ivan I Kalita replaced his brother Yuri as prince of Moscow at the end of 1325. A year later, on 20 December 1326, Metropolitan Peter died in Moscow, where he was also buried. The friendship between them, which is mentioned in Peter's *Lives*, and the decision to establish the metropolitan's permanent residence in Moscow did therefore occur during the year which preceded Peter's death. As we have seen earlier, Peter had been certainly in close touch with Moscow since he arrived in northern Russia (1309), but decisive steps were taken precisely during the last year of his life: on 4 August 1326, Ivan laid the foundation for a stone church of the Virgin's Dormition in Moscow and Peter – 'with his own hands', to use the chronicler's expression – built his own tomb in its walls.[22] The 'Metropolitan of Kiev and all Russia' clearly intended that Moscow, and not Vladimir, become his burial place and henceforth be seen as the religious centre of the country.

If the role of the Byzantine authorities in Metropolitan Peter's decision-making cannot be defined with great precision (one can only assume that his initial move to northern Russia was approved by Patriarch Athanasius), the interrelation between developments in Constantinople and in Russia becomes more obvious during the period of Metropolitan Theognostos.

The appointment of Metropolitan Theognostos, a Greek from Constantinople, where he entertained friendships with representatives of the intellectual élite (including Nicephoros Gregoras), coincided with the end of the civil war between Andronicus II and Andronicus III (1328). A 'new generation' had come to power in Byzantium, with a leading role played by John Cantacuzenos, the 'Grand Domesticus' (chief executive official) of Andronicus III and unquestionably a great statesman.[23] Whereas internal and external circumstances prevented him from always carrying out his views in practice, Cantacuzenos was a consistent promoter of the imperial idea based on religious and cultural ties which linked Byzantium with the Orthodox nations of Eastern Europe. We do not know whether he was personally responsible for the appointment of the new metropolitan of Russia, but Theognostos, during his entire tenure (1328–53), acted with great authority in maintaining the administrative scheme which expressed the traditional

[22] *Troits.*, p. 358.   [23] Cf. Ostrogorsky, *History*, p. 448.

Byzantine policies in Russia and reflected the views of Canta-cuzenos: one metropolitanate uniting all the dioceses and trans-cending the political feuds between the princes of Moscow, Tver, Lithuania and Galicia. Immediately and unfailingly, Theognostos followed the pattern established by his predecessor Peter in choosing Moscow as the metropolitan's residence and in giving the Muscovite rulers support against their competitors.

These facts are remarkable because Theognostos was not, initially, a candidate favoured by Moscow. Peter, before his death, had designated the abbot Theodore as his successor[24] and diplo-matic efforts must have been undertaken by Ivan I after Peter's death to obtain Theodore's confirmation by Constantinople. These efforts were another example of Moscow's uphill struggle for power: in 1326 Ivan did not possess yet the title of Grand-prince of Vladimir, which belonged to his enemy, Alexander of Tver. It is the latter who normally was entitled to nominate candi-dates but the nomination of Theodore came from Moscow.

In any case, the divisions between Russian princes favoured the candidacy of an outsider, named directly from Constantinople, and the new Greek metropolitan Theognostos met no opposition in northern Russia upon his arrival there in 1328. On his way, he visited the south-western principalities, and affirmed his power in the area, particularly in Galicia. For Halich, he consecrated a *bishop* Theodore, clearly excluding the existence at that time of a separate Galician metropolitanate.[25] However, the princes Bolesław-Yuri and Lubart-Dimitri – both closely allied with the Lithuanian princely family – were soon able to obtain the title of metropolitan for the bishop of Halich. Already in 1331, a 'metro-politan' of Galicia is mentioned in a somewhat dubious presence-list of the Synod of Constantinople.[26] If this reference reflects a

---

[24] *Life*, in Makary, *op. cit.*, p. 311. Characteristically, Metropolitan Cyprian, who himself had to struggle for the metropolitanate against a candidate nominated in Moscow, omits this detail in his own version of Peter's life.

[25] Regel, *Analecta*, pp. 52–3.

[26] MM, I, 164; τοῦ Γαλίτζης καὶ ὑπερτίμου. This mention and the act where it appears would require critical study, since the manuscript has suffered changes and the text may thus be giving misleading information (see Darrouzès, *Régistre*, p. 99). Another source – a letter of King Casimir of Poland – mentions the name of a metropolitan of Galicia, Gabriel, who held that position after Peter and before Theodore (MM, I, 577). If the mention in MM, I, 164 is spurious, one would have to presume that Gabriel held the metropolitanate of Galicia some time during the tenure of Metropolitan Peter. In any case, it does not seem possible that Theodore was the metropolitan of Galicia in 1331 as supposed by P. Sokolov (*Arkhierei*, p. 53) and J. L. I. Fennell (*Emergence*, p. 128) since acts of unimpeach-

historical fact, one must presume that the 'metropolitan' of Galicia was consecrated in Constantinople without possibility of rejoining his see and that Theognostos was in conflict with the policies of Patriarch Isaiah (1323–32). Indeed, Theodore continues to appear as *bishop* of Halich in well-attested lists of Russian bishops of that period.[27] Theognostos presumably did not recognize any competing primate in Halich. One fact is sure, however: some time during the civil war which opposed in Byzantium the government of Ann of Savoy to John Cantacuzenos (1341–7), Patriarch John Calecas, an ardent enemy of Cantacuzenos, issued a synodal act appointing Theodore as metropolitan of Galicia,[28] certainly against the will of Theognostos. Theodore, bishop of Halich, had come personally to Constantinople, although accusations had been levelled against him and he was responsible to his metropolitan, and not directly to the patriarchate. Against the objections of Theognostos, Calecas re-established a separate metropolitanate, making Theodore independent of Kiev.[29] Soon after his victory and assumption of the imperial throne, Cantacuzenos proceeded with the formal abolition of the metropolitanate of Galicia. The solemn manner in which this act was performed must reflect the fact that the ecclesiastical unity of Russia was seen, by the government of Cantacuzenos, as a matter of great importance. An imperial chrysobull was issued in August 1347[30] and imperial letters announcing the abolition were addressed to Metropolitan Theognostos, to the Grand-prince 'of all Russia', Symeon of Moscow, and to Dimitri-Lubart of Volhynia. The synod formally confirmed the imperial decree and Patriarch Isidore called the metropolitan of Galicia to judgement in Constantinople.[31]

Since the metropolitan of Lithuania Theophilos had died in 1330 and had not been replaced,[32] Theognostos remained, for the

---

able authenticity (Regel, *Analecta*, pp. 52–5) mention Bishop Theodore as a faithful suffragan of Theognostos in 1328–32 (see also above, Ch. 4, n. 63).

27 In 1329, 1331 and 1332, Regel, *Analecta*, pp. 53–4.

28 The synodal act of John Calecas is formally mentioned by Patriarch Isidore and his synod (MM, I, 270). The fact that the appointee was the former bishop Theodore is attested by King Casimir (MM, I, 577).

29 In 1347, Cantacuzenos writes to Lubart-Dimitri: 'Ἐλθὼν δὲ πρὸ ὀλίγου ἐνταῦθα ὁ ἀρχιερεὺς Γαλλίτζης, καίτοι γε λαλουμένων κατ'αὐτοῦ αἰτιαμάτων, δι' ἅπερ ὤφειλεν ἀποδοῦναι λόγον εἰς τὸν ἱερώτατον μητροπολίτην Κυγέβου . . ., ὅμως σύνδρομον εὑρὼν τὸν γεγονότα ἐνταῦθα καιρὸν τῆς συγχύσεως καὶ ὑπελθὼν τὸν χρηματίσαντα πατριάρχην Κωνσταντινουπόλεως ... προεβιβάσθη ἀπὸ ἐπισκόπου εἰς μητροπολίτην (MM, I, 265); cf. also letter to Theognostos (MM, I, 262).

30 Zachariae, *Jus*, III, pp. 700–3 (also in MM, I, 268–70, as part of the synodal decree on the same matter); cf. below, app. I, pp. 280–2.

31 All these documents are in MM, I, 261–71.   32 See above, Ch. 4, n. 68.

rest of his tenure (1347–53), the sole metropolitan 'of all Russia' and received the title of Exarch – μητροπολίτης Κυγέβου, ὑπέρτιμος καὶ ἔξαρχος πάσης 'Ρωσίας[33] – which belonged only to senior Byzantine metropolitans and would not be renewed for his successors.[34]

Travelling throughout the domains of Muscovy, Novgorod and Lithuania, visiting the Golden Horde twice, Metropolitan Theognostos actively pursued the policies of his Russian predecessor Peter in supporting the rise of the Muscovite principality. During the first four years of his tenure (1329–33), the stone church of the Dormition was completed in Moscow and four more stone churches were built.[35] Moscow was rapidly acquiring the prestige of a metropolis and could rival the more ancient capital of Vladimir. In 1339, Theognostos proceeded with another action of great significance for Moscow's prestige: the canonization of Metropolitan Peter, at whose tomb miracles had been testified since the day of his burial. In times past, several Russian saints had been canonized either by the metropolitan, or locally: in the case of Peter, however, Theognostos – wishing to emphasize his loyalty and allegiance to Byzantium and to enhance the significance of his act – requested an official document from the patriarch John Calecas, who, while expressing some astonishment at being asked to act on a matter of local concern, recommends that a liturgical veneration of Peter be started.[36]

From the very beginning of his tenure, Theognostos did not limit his activity to purely ecclesiastical affairs, but committed his personal prestige to Moscow's political interests. In 1328, almost immediately upon his arrival in northern Russia, during a visit to Novgorod, he excommunicated Prince Alexander of Tver, who – as we have seen – had rebelled against the Tatars, lost his title of Grand-prince, seen his city sacked by a combined Mongolo-Muscovite army and found refuge in Pskov, and later in Lithuania, challenging Moscow, and the metropolitan. Alexander, eventually returned to Pskov, where he reigned as prince until 1339, when he was executed in the Golden Horde by Khan Uzbek.[37] A recently

[33] Address of the letter of Cantacuzenos, MM, 1, 261.
[34] Theognostos is addressed as μητροπολίτης 'Ρωσίας καὶ ὑπέρτιμος in 1339 by Patriarch John Calecas (MM, 1, 191); the title of his successor Alexis will be μητροπολίτης Κυέβου καὶ πάσης 'Ρωσίας καὶ ὑπέρτιμος (MM, 1, 350). Cf. V. Grumel, 'Titulature des métropolites byzantins. II. Métropolites hypertimes', *Mémorial Louis Petit. Archives de l'Orient chrétien*, 1, Paris, 1948, pp. 152–84.
[35] Cf. E. Golubinsky, *op. cit.*, 1, 2, pp. 148–50.   [36] MM, 1, p. 191.
[37] A. Nasonov, ed., *Pskovskie Letopisi*, Moscow–Leningrad, 1941, pp. 17–18; cf. Fennell, *Emergence*, pp. 117–18.

published letter of the Byzantine diplomat Manuel Gabalas, who in 1331–2 found himself in Russia in the entourage of Metropolitan Theognostos, indicates how remarkably well-informed Byzantine officials were on these events and how closely connected they were with Moscow and its interests.[38] Fearful and distrustful of Lithuania, most Byzantine ecclesiastics and diplomats – much before the triumph of Hesychasm – considered that Moscow's policy of appeasing the Mongols and winning the khan's support by being loyal to him, coincided much better with the interests of the Church and the Byzantine Commonwealth than the rebellions of Alexander of Tver, or the pro-Western leanings of Gedymin. They also sympathized with the view expressed in the Russian Chronicle: '[When] grand-prince Ivan Danilovich [Kalita of Moscow] obtained the grand-principality of all Russia, there came a great peace for forty years; the infidels ceased to fight against the land of the Rus' and kill Christians; the Christians found relief and appeasement away from the great troubles, the many oppressions and from Tatar violence, and there was great peace in all the land.'[39] Byzantine diplomats did not mind the fact that this 'peace' was, sometimes, attained through servility to the Horde and unhesitating violence against less subservient principalities, like Tver or Rostov.

This pro-Muscovite attitude was undoubtedly favoured by Cantacuzenos, but it was not consistently applied by his political adversaries. There was a connection between Byzantium's internal struggles and its foreign policy. This connection is formally acknowledged in several official sources, published in 1347, and is even better attested for ecclesiastical events later in the century. According to the documents issued by Cantacuzenos and the patriarchal synod in 1347, the re-establishment of the separate metropolitanate of Galicia – an act directed against Moscow and, consequently, against the wishes of the Golden Horde, and most probably connected with the invasion of Galicia-Volhynia by Casimir I of Poland[40] – was enacted by Cantacuzenos' political enemies during the civil war: Patriarch John Calecas and the government of Ann of Savoy in Constantinople. Cantacuzenos does not specify the political motivations of his enemies: he only

---

[38] The excommunicated (κακῶς ἀπολωλώς) Alexander is mentioned under the nickname of 'Ολέκης, and Ivan of Moscow is identified as ὁ τῶν 'Ρῶς ἄρχων (cf. Κουρούσης, Γαβαλᾶς, pp. 248–52).

[39] *Troits.*, p. 359.

[40] Cf. Knoll, *Polish Monarchy*, pp. 132–5; cf. above, Ch. 3.

reproaches Calecas with acting 'against the divine and holy canons', and mentions 'those who wrongly administered the empire and the affairs of society' (τοὺς τὴν βασιλείαν καὶ τὰ κοινὰ πράγματα κακῶς καὶ ἐπισφαλῶς διοικοῦντας) and who, instead of 'seeking the common good, only fulfilled their own desires', clearly meaning the regent Ann and her government.[41]

Establishing a direct connection between the civil strife in Constantinople and the ecclesiastical developments in distant Galicia, Cantacuzenos says nothing about the concrete motivations, which led the Byzantine authorities, sometime between 1341 and 1346, to support the claims of Bishop Theodore against the wishes of Metropolitan Theognostos. However, these motivations can be – at least hypothetically – understood, if one considers the developments in the Mongol empire and its relationships with its neighbours.

As we have seen earlier, the political and economic system in the eastern Mediterranean and the Black Sea was based on the absolute predominance of the Italian republics of Genoa and Venice, which controlled the commercial routes leading to Sarai and the East. Their well-being was dependent upon their economic grip on Constantinople and the prosperity of their colonies on the northern shores of the Black Sea which implied an alliance with the Golden Horde. The embattled regency of Ann of Savoy, faced with the rebellion of Cantacuzenos – a consistent enemy of the Genoese and supported by the Turks – was dependent upon the Italians more than any other Byzantine regime.

This political and economic system was brutally shattered by a change in Mongol attitudes. In the year which preceded his death (1341), Khan Uzbek threatened to invade the Byzantine empire itself (or, at least the Byzantine and Italian possessions in the Crimea) and an imperial embassy, headed by the father of Demetrios Kydones, went to Sarai to appease his wrath.[42] Demetrios praises his father for having achieved success in his embassy and even convinced Uzbek to conclude a new treaty with Byzantium.[43] The effects must have been rather short lived, because

[41] Letter to Lubart, MM, I, 265; similar expressions in the chrysobull (*ed. cit.*, p. 700; cf. MM, I, 268), in the Letters to Theognostos (MM, I, 262), to Symeon of Moscow (MM, I, 264), and in the synodal act suppressing the metropolitanate of Galicia (MM, I, 267).

[42] R. J. Loenertz, 'Notes d'histoire et de chronologie byzantines', REB, 17(1959), pp. 162–6; V. Laurent, 'L'assaut avorté de la Horde d'Or contre l'empire byzantin', REB, 18 (1960), pp. 145–62.

[43] *Ad Ioannem Cantacuzenum oratio prima*, 17, ed. R. J. Loenertz, *Demetrius Cydones, Correspondance*, I (Studi e testi, 186), Vatican, 1956, p. 9.

Uzbek's son Djanibek again put a violent end to the political and economic system which controlled the Black Sea: he took the Venetian colony of Tana (1343) and in 1346, began a prolonged and murderous siege of Genoese Caffa.[44] Faced with a common danger, the Venetians and the Genoese were forced to momentarily forget their competition and conclude a defensive alliance. Pope Clement VI appealed for a Crusade to save Caffa.[45] Under such circumstances, one may suppose that the Byzantines, whose interests were inseparable from those of the Italians in the Black Sea, could not refuse a minor concession to a united Latin diplomatic front: the establishment of a new ecclesiastical province in Galicia-Volhynia, which would serve the local interests of another anti-Tatar Crusader, King Casimir of Poland. Protests coming from Moscow could not have a major effect at this juncture.

Having begun his expansion towards the East in 1340–1, King Casimir was faced with three obstacles: (a) the nominal dependence of Galicia-Volhynia (Μιχρὰ 'Ρωσία, 'Little Russia', in the contemporary Byzantine documents) upon the Horde; (b) the fears of the local Orthodox populations, led by the *boyarin* Detko, of a Roman Catholic takeover, with readiness to ask for Tatar help against the Poles, following Moscow's example; and (c) the competition of Lithuania, which also coveted the region.[46] In 1343, Casimir obtained financial and moral support from Pope Clement VI in his holy campaign 'against Tatars, Russians and Lithuanians'.[47] However, he was able to occupy only the region of Sanok in Western Galicia, whereas the major part of 'Little Russia' – following Detko's death (1344) – fell into the hands of Lubart, son of Gedymin, and brother of the new and powerful Grand-prince of Lithuania, Olgerd. Lubart was baptized an Orthodox Christian under the name Dimitri. Casimir was obliged to accept – temporarily – a modus-vivendi with Lubart,[48] making sure that all connections with Tatar-dominated north-eastern Russia were severed. Under such circumstances, the appointment of Bishop

---

[44] Apparently Djanibek was up to tightening the finances of the Horde. In addition to his attack on the privileged Italian colonies on the Black Sea, he also reduced the privileges of the Russian Church against which some Russians were complaining to the Mongol authorities. Metropolitan Theognostos, however, was able to visit Sarai personally in 1342 and obtain some advantages by bribing the khan himself, Uzbek's widow, Taidula, and several Mongol officials (*Nik.*, p. 215). He obtained a formal reinstatement of tax-exemptions for the clergy, but not for the whole of Church properties (cf. Priselkov, *Yarlyki*, pp. 69–77).

[45] On these events, see Heyd, *Commerce*, pp. 192–7.

[46] Cf. above, Ch. 3.   [47] Theiner, *Pol. Lit.*, I, 604–5.

[48] Knoll, *op. cit.*, p. 137.

Theodore of Halich as metropolitan – which must have happened precisely when the arrangement between Casimir and Lubart was concluded, i.e., in 1345–6[49] – is fully understandable. It certainly served the plans of Casimir, and also must have pleased Lubart. Gedymin himself, and all his children, had been finding their way out of their ancestral paganism by expressing readiness to convert to Christianity in exchange for political advantages. In the case of Lubart-Dimitri, the advantages included the rule over an ancient Russian principality, enhanced by the prestige of a separate metropolitan.

In 1347, however, Cantacuzenos won the civil war, while Venice and Genoa made peace with Djanibek. The new Byzantine emperor was now able to re-establish normal diplomatic contacts in eastern Europe and, while making attempts at loosing the Genoese control of the Byzantine economy, actively embarked, with the help of newly appointed hesychast patriarchs, on restoring the prestige of the empire in Russia. He soon received a letter from Symeon of Moscow – undoubtedly written with the advice of Metropolitan Theognostos – which called 'the empire of the Romans and the most holy Great Church of God, as the source of every piety, the teacher of lawfulness and sanctification', and requested the reunification of the metropolitanate.[50] Symeon also sent a large monetary contribution for repairing the church of St Sophia; according to Nicephoros Gregoras, however, the money was used to repay Cantacuzenos' debts to the Turkish Emir Orkhan.[51] The ideological loyalty of Symeon, as well as his generosity, had immediate effect: In letters addressed to his 'nephews' (ἀνεψιοί): Symeon of Moscow, 'grand prince of all Russia' (μέγας ῥὴξ πάσης 'Ρωσίας) and Dimitri-Lubart, 'prince of Vladimir [in-Volhynia]' (ῥὴξ Βολοδιμήρου), Cantacuzenos announced the suppression of the metropolitanate of Galicia. The treatment of the two princes differed not only in the titles used in the letters but also in the fact that Symeon received an imperial *encolpion* with relics of the True Cross and of four martyrs,[52]

---

[49] Cantacuzenos, writing in 1347, is very precise in saying that Theodore came to Constantinople 'recently' (πρὸ ὀλίγου) in order to arrange his appointment (MM, I, 265).

[50] MM, I, 263.   [51] *Hist. Byz.*, XXVIII, 35–6, ed. Bonn, III, pp. 199–200.

[52] MM, I, 264–5. Symeon also obtained from Constantinople a dispensation for divorcing his second wife and his third marriage, to Mary, daughter of the fiercest of Moscow's former enemies, Alexander of Tver. Metropolitan Theognostos had initially objected to the marriage for obvious canonical reasons (*Rog.*, col. 57), but also because the marriage did not coincide with his own policies in Tver (Fennell, *Emergence*, p. 230).

whereas Lubart got a lesson in history and canon law: 'You know', writes Cantacuzenos to the prince of Volhynia, 'that since the time when the nation of the Russians received the knowledge of God and was illumined through holy baptism, it has been a self-evident custom and law, that there be, in the whole of Russia – Great Russia and Little Russia as well – a single metropolitan: the one of Kiev; he consecrated bishops in all the most-holy episcopates, so that whenever anyone tried to change this situation . . . , the previous order and custom were soon restored again, as you yourself know well.'[53] The victory of Theognostos was total: not only was he again the sole metropolitan in Russia, but he was able to obtain from Djanibek a new decree (*yarlyk*) giving new guarantees to ecclesiastical courts, which received protection against the infringements by the princes.[54]

During the following two years, the joint policy of Cantacuzenos and Moscow produced spectacular results. Not only was Metropolitan Theognostos able to visit Volhynia in 1348 and assert his jurisdiction in the area,[55] but Symeon of Moscow – with the co-operation of both the metropolitan and the khan – succeeded in concluding matrimonial alliances between his own family and the courts of Lithuania and Tver.[56] Increasingly, the Grand-prince of Moscow acquired the stature of leader 'of all Russia'.

2. OLGERD AND MOSCOW

The last years of Theognostos' tenure as metropolitan of all Russia (1349–53) were however marked with significant setbacks for the policies defined by Cantacuzenos in his documents of 1347. In Constantinople itself, the efforts of the new emperor to untie the Genoese economic control of Byzantium ended in failure (1349) and his attempts at finding support with the Venetians resulted in a war between Genoa and Venice, fought mostly in Byzantine territorial waters. In 1352, after the famous battle of the Bosphorus, the Genoese remained in control of Pera and Galata and

---

[53] MM, I, 265.
[54] Priselkov, 'Yarlyki', pp. 79–81.
[55] *Nik.*, p. 221. The fate of Metropolitan Theodore is unknown. One may doubt that he complied with the formal canonical indictment received from Patriarch Isidore (MM, I, 271).
[56] Two daughters of Alexander of Tver – Maria and Ul'yana – married respectively Symeon of Moscow (1347) and Olgerd of Lithuania (1349); cf. Fennell, *Emergence*, pp. 225–40.

maintained their economic domination of the Black Sea.[57] Since Genoese power in that area was dependent entirely upon an alliance with the Golden Horde – which Genoa succeeded in restoring – and since Moscow's power also depended upon the khan's goodwill, this Genoese triumph did not hurt Muscovite power immediately. However, Tatar policies in Russia were based on maintaining a balance among the various princes. Similarly, the Genoese influence both in Constantinople and in Sarai, fully determined by crude commercial interests, also tended to support division and competition among the rulers of Russia and, as such, contradict the ideal of a unified Orthodox Commonwealth, promoted by Cantacuzenos and his friend Patriarch Philotheos Kokkinos.

The year 1349, which saw the defeat of Cantacuzenos by the Genoese in Constantinople, witnessed the conquest of Galicia and Volhynia by Casimir of Poland. Lubart was able to hold on to the city of Lutsk only, while Casimir assumed the title of *dominus terrae Russiae*.[58] The Chronicle of Novgorod gives a characteristic account of the conquest. 'The King of Cracow [i.e., Poland] with a large force seized the country of Volhynia by deceit, and did much injury to the Christians, and he converted the sacred churches to the Latin service hated of God.'[59] The latter information is confirmed by Polish sources; a Latin hierarchy and a number of Latin churches were erected in the newly occupied territories. As Casimir faced a Lithuanian counter-offensive, he solicited and received both moral and financial support from Rome in his new crusade against 'pagans' and 'schismatics'.[60] Between 1349 and 1364, Poland had to face Lithuania in a long struggle for the possession of Galicia and Volhynia. Led by the three sons of Gedymin – Olgerd, Keistut and Lubart – Lithuania appeared as a bulwark against both the Teutonic Order and Poland, and as a defender of Orthodox Christianity: actually, Lubart was already an Orthodox prince and Olgerd was expressing his readiness to follow his example, provided that he – and not the Grand-prince

[57] Cf. M. Balard, 'A propos de la bataille du Bosphore. L'expédition génoise de Paganino Doria', *Travaux et Mémoires*, 4, Paris, 1970, pp. 431–69; C. P. Kyrris, 'John Cantacuzenus, the Genoese, the Venetians and the Catalans (1348–54)', *Byzantina*, 4, 1972, pp. 331–59. Both of these articles refer to abundant earlier bibliography.

[58] Cf. above, Ch. 3, pp. 63–4.

[59] *Novg.*, p. 361, Engl. tr., p. 143.

[60] Cf. Knoll, *op. cit.*, pp. 143–77. The author tends to look favourably at this Polish expansion; however, he signals enough facts which – if seen by a Byzantine or a Russian – fully justify the distress of the Novgorodian chronicler.

of Moscow – was recognized as the unifier of Russia in the framework of the Byzantine Commonwealth. In his struggle with Casimir, he occasionally received Tatar help as well and his diplomacy relentlessly (and sometimes successfully) tried to drive a wedge between Sarai and Moscow.

The now inevitable confrontation between the Grand-principality of Lithuania and the Grand-principality of Vladimir-Moscow was to constitute the greatest challenge to the traditional scheme of Byzantine policies in Russia. In order to understand fully the meaning of this confrontation, it is important to remember that both sides claimed to represent a 'Russian' state and, on the other hand, recognized the symbolic supremacy and leadership of the Byzantine empire: the double challenge of Poland and the Teutonic Knights strengthened Olgerd's commitment to the Eastern Christian *oikouméne*, whereas the princes of Moscow were loyal to Byzantium by the very fact that they had welcomed the Metropolitan of Kiev in their domain. Thus, Byzantium was challenged to act as an arbiter between them.

Around 1350, besides the relatively small territory inhabited by pagan Lithuanians (Zhemaytia), Olgerd's domains were mostly composed of traditional Orthodox and Russian lands: the so-called 'Black Russia' (Grodno, Slonim, Novgorodok), the principalities of Polotsk and Vitebsk (later known as 'White Russia', or Byelorussia) and in the south, the greater part of Volhynia and Galicia. The official language of the state was Russian. In 1352, the Lithuanian Grand-prince received decisive support from Khan Djanibek,[61] and this allowed him again to conclude a temporary but advantageous truce with Casimir. Characteristically, this shift of Tatar politics in favour of Olgerd implied immediate weakening of Moscow's power: the authorities of Novgorod challenged at the Horde the position of Grand-prince held by Moscow, and Archbishop Moses complained in Constantinople against 'improper matters' committed by Metropolitan Theognostos.[62] Anti-Muscovite moves also occurred in Tver and Nizhni-Novgorod.[63] A more confident Olgerd decided to restore the separate metropolitanate of Lithuania, whose throne had remained vacant after the death of Metropolitan Theophilos[64] around 1330, for he knew

---

[61] Spuler, *Goldene Horde*, pp. 107–9.
[62] *Novg.*, p. 363, Eng. tr. p. 145.
[63] Cf. Grekov, *Vostochnaya Evropa*, p. 57.
[64] A Byzantine source describes the metropolitanate of Lithuania as 'vacant' (σχολάσας), rather than 'suppressed' at the time of Theognostos (Gelzer, 'Beiträge', p. 261); cf. also Sokolov, *Arkhierei*, p. 271.

very well that, as long as Moscow remained the residence of the metropolitan 'of all Russia', who controlled the only unified administrative structure extending to all the Russian lands, the Lithuanian dynasty lacked credibility as a rallying point for Russian principalities. For Olgerd, therefore, there were only two alternatives: to obtain the transfer of the metropolitan's see back to the south-west, or to divide the metropolitanate.

In 1352, Olgerd sends his candidate, Theodoret, to Constantinople with the request that he be consecrated 'Metropolitan of Russia' (μητροπολίτης 'Ρωσίας).[65] Such a consecration could obviously not be performed before the reigning metropolitan's death, but Theognostos had been sick since 1350[66] and his demise was expected soon: Olgerd wanted to have his candidate ready or, perhaps envisaged him to be appointed metropolitan 'of Lithuania'. But in Constantinople, Cantacuzenos was still in charge and resisted the pressure, although Olgerd may have obtained the support of the Tatars (and their Genoese allies). In any case, the candidacy of Theodoret was rejected.

However, in 1352, an anti-Cantacuzenist coalition was gaining momentum in the Balkans: fighting for power against his father-in-law, John V Palaeologus obtained the alliance of the Serbs and the Bulgarians, while Cantacuzenos, supported by Turkish forces, was barely able to hold his ground.[67] This conflict between Cantacuzenos and the two Slavic kingdoms in the Balkans had also ecclesiastical repercussions. In 1346 already, Stefan Dušan of Serbia had presided in Skoplje over the establishment of a Serbian patriarchate: this was done with the acquiescence of the Bulgarian patriarch of Trnovo and the autocephalous archbishop of Ohrid, but in defiance of Byzantium, which was then torn apart by civil and religious strife. Only in 1352, did the ecumenical patriarch react by excommunicating the Serbian Church. One can presume that Dušan's hostility against Cantacuzenos in that year contributed much to the general atmosphere in which this canonical sanction (obviously ignored by the Serbs) was taken by Patriarch Callistos and his synod.[68] There is no evidence in 1352

---

[65] Patriarch Philotheos, writing in July 1354, speaks of the arrival of Theodoret in Constantinople in 1352 (πρὸ δύο χρόνων ἦλθεν ἐνταῦθα, MM, I, 350). On the episodes of 1352–4, see my article 'Alexis and Roman'.

[66] *Troits.*, p. 371.

[67] A clear picture of the situation in Ostrogorsky, *History*, pp. 529–30.

[68] Cf. V. Moshin, 'Sv. patrijarkh Kalist i Srpska tsrkva', *Glasnik Srpske pravoslavne tsrkve*, Belgrade, 1946, No. 9, pp. 198–202; cf. by the same author, *O periodizatsii*, p. 99.

of a formal canonical break between Constantinople and Trnovo, but, three years later, in 1355, Callistos will complain against the spirit of independence in the Bulgarian Church, whose patriarch had discontinued the liturgical mention of his colleague of Constantinople.[69] This spirit obviously prevailed as early as 1352 and was another aspect of Bulgarian hostility towards Cantacuzenos. It is illustrated by the case of Theodoret, Olgerd's candidate to the metropolitanate of Kiev: after being rebuked in Byzantium, he received his consecration and appointment as metropolitan of Russia from the Bulgarian patriarch of Trnovo.[70]

The consequences of this action, which implied an agreement between Lithuania, Bulgaria and, probably, Serbia, could have been extremely serious: the metropolitanate of Russia was to be detached from the patriarchate of Constantinople. One imagines that Olgerd's plan was to establish an autocephalous church, for it is unlikely that either the Russians or the Bulgarians envisaged a permanent canonical dependence of the Russian Church upon the patriarchate of Trnovo. In any case, both in terms of resources and prestige, the blow would have been very severe for an impoverished and divided Byzantium.

Having returned to Russia, Theodoret, for a period of at least two years, assumed ecclesiastical power in territories controlled by Olgerd.[71] Furthermore, he was in control of the historic and prestigious see of Kiev,[72] and the rich and influential Moses, Archbishop of Novgorod, was wavering in his allegiance to the ageing Metropolitan Theognostos.[73] Our sources do not formally specify the episcopal title of Theodoret: was he consecrated at Trnovo as metropolitan 'of Lithuania' only, or 'of Kiev and all Russia'? In the former case, the action of the Bulgarian patriarchate

---

[69] Cf. MM, I, 436–42; cf. above, Ch. 5, p. 115.

[70] According to a letter of Patriarch Philotheos, written in July 1354, the arrival of Theodoret to Constantinople and his 'flight' to Trnovo occurred 'two years ago' (πρὸ δύο χρόνων), i.e. in 1352 (MM, I, 350).

[71] One should note, however, that Athanasius, bishop of Vladimir-in-Volhynia, who had been consecrated by Theognostos in 1328 (Regel, *Analecta*, p. 52), was present at the funeral of Theognostos in Moscow in 1353 (*Troits.*, p. 373). This suggests that the dioceses of Galicia-Volhynia remained, at least in part, loyal to the canonical metropolitan of Kiev.

[72] According to a patriarchal act of 1354, Theodoret resided in Kiev (ἀντιποιεῖται τοῦ Κυέβου καὶ εὑρίσκεται ἐν αὐτῷ, MM, I, 352). Since the reign of Gedymin, Kiev – although formally subject to the Horde – found itself increasingly under the aegis of Lithuania (cf. Fennell, *Emergence*, p. 122).

[73] Cf. the complaints of Moses against Theognostos in 1352 (cf. above, n. 62), and the warning issued by Patriarch Philotheos to Novgorod in 1354 against Theodoret (MM, I, 350–1).

would be nothing more than a filling of a vacant see and was not to be interpreted as a formal challenge to Theognostos, as 'metropolitan of Kiev'. However, the activities of Theodoret in Kiev and Novgorod clearly suggest the real scope of his ambitions: sponsored and supported by Olgerd, he was in the process of building up an all-Russian Church independent of Constantinople and based in the historic see of Kiev. Thus the very basis upon which the Byzantine Commonwealth in Eastern Europe had been established since the tenth century was in danger of being replaced by a more polycentric system, open to influences from the West, as the various separate dealings of both the Balkan Slavs and the Galician princes have shown in the recent past.

The reaction of the Byzantine patriarchate was predictable: Theodoret was deposed and excommunicated.[74] However, the authorities of Constantinople had enough experience in diplomacy to realize that anathemas would not suffice in facing the threat by Olgerd and Theodoret. They moved towards strengthening the unifying authority of the legitimate metropolitan of Kiev and all Russia, residing in Moscow, by establishing additional ties between his see, the Grand-principality of Vladimir and the Golden Horde. These measures were taken by Metropolitan Theognostos himself and by the new patriarch, Philotheos Kokkinos, a close friend of Cantacuzenos, who replaced Callistos in the see of Constantinople in September 1353.

On 6 December 1352, Metropolitan Theognostos consecrated Alexis, a Russian abbot and the metropolitan's vicar in Moscow since 1350, as bishop of Vladimir. Since Vladimir, the official capital of the Grand-prince, was also the residence of the metropolitan and had not had a separate bishop since the beginning of the century, the appointment of Alexis implied his candidacy to the ailing metropolitan's succession. This implication is recognized by Byzantine and Russian sources: after the consecration ambassadors from the Grand-prince Symeon of Moscow and of the metropolitan (including a Greek, named Michael and surnamed *Scherbaty*) went to Constantinople to secure in advance the designation of Alexis as the successor of Theognostos.[75] The mission met with obvious success. It returned to Moscow when Theognostos was already dead (11 March 1353),[76] so that Alexis travelled immediately to Constantinople in order to receive the investiture as metropolitan. He was made to wait an entire year in Byzan-

---

[74] MM, I, 350.   [75] *Troits.*, p. 373.   [76] *Troits.*, pp. 373-4.

tium, before, finally, in July 1354, the act of his transfer from the bishopric of Vladimir to the metropolitanate of Kiev was issued by Patriarch Philotheos and his Synod.[77] The delay was certainly due not only to the need for submitting the Russian candidate to a full year of examinations and tests, as the patriarchal *act* affirms,[78] but also to the almost certain fact that Olgerd was exercising his own diplomatic pressure upon the Greeks, opposing the consecration of Alexis. Other diplomatic contests of the same kind suggest that impoverished Byzantium used such opportunities to obtain substantial contributions from Russian princes. Either because it was the highest bidder, or – still more likely – because Cantacuzenos and Philotheos had greater confidence in Moscow than in Vilna, as potential ecclesiastical centre of Russia, Moscow ended up as the winner. Not only was Alexis appointed Metropolitan of Kiev and all Russia, but Philotheos specifically obtained through the intermediary of the bishop of Sarai the support of the Golden Horde for his nomination.[79] In formal letters, the patriarch required from the archbishop of Novgorod the acknowledgement of Alexis as metropolitan, and threatened him with excommunication if he recognized Theodoret.[80] Furthermore, in an action which, in 1354, appears rather anachronistic, he formally transferred the residence of the metropolitanate from Kiev to Vladimir.[81] The act of transfer shows full awareness of the fact that the two predecessors of Alexis – metropolitans Peter and Theognostos – already resided in Vladimir (in fact, in Moscow!) because ancient Kiev, destroyed and impoverished, could not provide them with prestige or subsistence. The immediate significance of the act was to emphasize that the presence of Theodoret in Kiev added nothing to his legitimacy since Kiev was not any more the metropolitan's residence. The issuance of such an *act* as late as 1354 can be fully understood only in the light of the struggle between Olgerd and Moscow.

It is certainly in the same light that one has to interpret the appointment of the *Russian* Alexis, as metropolitan. The challenge

---

[77] MM, I, 336–40.
[78] "Ὃν δὴ καὶ ἡμεῖς κατὰ τὸ εἰκὸς ἐξετάσει δεδωκότες ἀκριβεστάτῃ ἐπὶ ὁλόκληρον ἤδη ἐνιαυτόν, MM, I, 337.
[79] He writes to Moses of Novgorod: ἐδεξάμεθα καὶ διὰ τοῦ θεοφιλεστάτου ἐπισκόπου Σαραίου καὶ τὰς συστατικὰς ὑπὲρ αὐτοῦ ἐγγράφους γνώμας τῶν αὐτόθι λοιπῶν θεοφιλεστάτων ἐπισκόπων (MM, I, 347). If one remembers the role played by the Bishop of Sarai, as a liaison between Constantinople and both the Horde and the Russian Church (cf. above, Ch. 3, p. 46), this text should be understood as implying the approval not only of the bishops, but also of the khan.
[80] MM, I, 347–50, 350–1.   [81] MM, I, 351–3.

coming from Olgerd and Theodoret forced the Byzantine patriarchate to make a concession, which would enhance the popularity and authority of the new appointee at the expense of his competitor.[82] The nomination of a Russian candidate was rejected at the time of Metropolitan Peter's death, but had become a necessity in 1354. Interestingly, Alexis – just as Peter – was of southern Russian origin: his father, a boyar from Chernigov, had emigrated to Moscow in 1293–8. This aristocratic and southern origin of the new metropolitan, who also possessed, at the time of his appointment, long experience in civil and ecclesiastical government, made him a particularly suitable candidate.[83] Most probably, he also knew Greek.[84]

The appointment of Metropolitan Alexis and the patriarchal documents which supported it constituted a remarkable boost to Moscow's prestige: having become officially the permanent residence of the metropolitan 'of all Russia' and having succeeded, for the first time, in having its own candidate appointed as head of the Church, the Great-principality of Vladimir, practically monopolized by the Muscovite dynasty, was in a better position than anyone to claim the inheritance of Kievan Russia and of 'Russian unity'.

Unfortunately for Moscow, its triumph was short-lived. Four months later, in December 1354, Cantacuzenos abdicated the imperial throne, and his son-in-law and heir to the legitimate Paleologan dynasty, John V, regained full power with the active help of the Genoese.[85] Patriarch Philotheos had to give his throne back to Callistos (1355–63). As we have seen above, the Genoese shared with the Golden Horde a strong interest in keeping a balance between the various rulers of Russia. Thus, a reconcilia-

---

[82] See above our discussion of the view, reflected by Nicephorus Gregoras, who interprets the alternation of Greeks and Russians on the metropolitanate of Kiev as a matter of deliberate Byzantine policy (Ch. 4, pp. 88–9). Even if such policy was promoted in Byzantium by some government officials, the *Act* of appointment of 1354 presents the case of Alexis as an exception, not as a rule.

[83] On his biography and background, see Golubinsky, *Istoriya*, 172–6.

[84] This is suggested by his long cooperation with the Greek Metropolitan Theognostos and his repeated sojourns in Constantinople. Tradition attributes to Alexis a new Slavic translation of the New Testament, accomplished in Constantinople and preserved in his own autograph; this attribution cannot be considered as proved, cf. the description of the manuscript and bibliography in G. I. Vzdornov, 'Rol' masterskikh', pp. 186–8.

[85] On this, see C. P. Kyrris, *ibid.*, pp. 353–4, also D. M. Nicol, 'The abdication of John VI Cantacuzenus', *Polychordia* (Festschrift F. Dölger), Amsterdam, 1967, pp. 269–83; A. Failler, 'Nouvelle note sur la chronologie du règne de Jean VI Cantacuzène', REB, 34 (1976), pp. 119–24.

tion took place between the new Genoese-controlled regime in Constantinople on the one side, and Olgerd on the other; the reconciliation also included Bulgaria. Olgerd eagerly abandoned Theodoret, whose ultimate fate is unknown, but he obtained a much more substantial prize: the official appointment by Constantinople of his own candidate to the see of metropolitan. The exact date and conditions of that appointment are not indicated in the available sources, but it certainly followed the events of November 1354 and was, more than likely, performed by the new Patriarch Callistos.[86]

The new metropolitan, named Roman, was consecrated 'metropolitan of the Lithuanians' (μητροπολίτης Λιτβῶν),[87] but, as an official Byzantine act recognizes, Olgerd 'had him consecrated..., under the pretext that the lord Alexis was not acceptable as metropolitan in the nation which was under Olgerd's rule, but his real goal was to find a means with Roman's help, of ruling Great Russia'.[88] The new appointment signalled improved relationships between Constantinople and Bulgaria – on 17 August 1355, Roman appears as signatory and witness at an agreement between Emperor John V and Tsar John Alexander of Bulgaria, sealed by a marriage between their children[89] – but it created a great turmoil in Russia.

Whereas, as we have seen, Alexis was of southern Russian extraction, Roman, on the contrary, was a northerner, but also a relative of Olgerd's wife, a Tverite princess.[90] Clearly, the struggle between Olgerd and Moscow, Roman and Alexis, was a struggle for control of Russia as a whole, and not an ethnic competition.

---

[86] Cf. the evidence in my article, 'Alexis and Roman', p. 284, n. 22; Gregoras alone (*Hist.*, xxxvi, 36, *ed. cit.*, p. 519) places the ordination of Roman *before* that of Alexis, i.e., still under Philotheos, but such a chronology is contradicted by the available patriarchal acts; in July 1354, when Alexis was consecrated, Theodoret (and not Roman) was controlling the Church in Olgerd's territories and Philotheos specifically warns Moses of Novgorod against the usurper (MM, I, 350).

[87] Cf. the *Act* of Callistos of 1361, MM, I, 426.

[88] Τὸν 'Ρωμανὸν ἐκεῖνον χειροτονηθῆναι παρασκευάζει ..., προφάσει μὲν τῷ μὴ καταδέχεσθαι ἐν τῷ ὑπ' αὐτὸν ἔθνει τὸν κῦρ 'Αλέξιον ἔχειν μητροπολίτην, τῇ δ' ἀληθείᾳ ἵνα διὰ τοῦ 'Ρωμανοῦ ... σχοίη τινὰ πάροδον ἐν τῇ τῆς μεγάλης 'Ρωσίας ἀρχῇ, Act of Patriarch Neilos (1380), MM, II, 12–13.

[89] Roman signs as ὁ Λιτβῶν μητροπολίτης καὶ ὑπέρτιμος 'Ρωμανός, MM, I, 432–3. It is also in 1355, that Callistos writes to his friends, the Bulgarian hesychast monks headed by Theodosius of Trnovo, reaffirming the patriarchate's claims of supremacy over the Bulgarian Church (see above, Ch. 5, pp. 115–116).

[90] This is confirmed by a Russian chronicle ('Roman chernets syn boyarina Tverskago', *Rog.*, col. 61) and by Nicephorus Gregoras (ἐκ γυναικὸς συγγενὴς τοῦ κηδεστοῦ ῥηγός, i.e. Olgerd, who was married to a Tverite princess, *Hist.* xxxvi, 34, Bonn, III, 518).

According to Gregoras, Olgerd expressed his readiness to be baptized an Orthodox Christian, if only Byzantium would support his claims.[91]

Both metropolitans returned to Constantinople in 1355–6 to defend their respective rights. The Byzantine historian Gregoras and the Russian Chronicles agree in describing the situation as scandalous, with Roman controlling whatever part of Russia came under Olgerd's rule, including Kiev, Bryansk and Tver, and both sides taxing their flock in order to provide the necessary bribes for Byzantine officials.[92] Callistos and his synod formally defined the limits of the metropolitanate 'of Lithuania': it included not only the dioceses which belonged to it at the time of Grand-prince Gedymin (Polotsk, Turov, the metropolitan's residence in Novgorodok), but also 'Little Russia', i.e. the dioceses of Galicia and Volhynia (Vladimir-in-Volhynia, Lutsk, Kholm, Halich and Peremyshl').[93] This settlement reached in 1355–6 maintained Alexis in his title of 'Metropolitan of Kiev and all Russia' but gave to Roman much more territory and power than to any metropolitan of either Lithuania or Galicia before him. But the arrangement was satisfactory neither to him, nor to Olgerd, whose aim was to unify the whole of Russia. Deliberately overstepping his rights, Roman assumed the title of 'Metropolitan of Kiev and all Russia' and took up residence in Kiev.[94]

By 1361, however, Olgerd's fortunes began to turn. The Golden Horde became wary of his growing power[95] and the Genoese, who controlled the Byzantine government, followed suit. On the other hand, Metropolitan Alexis travelled to the Horde and gained great prestige in Sarai by healing the elderly and influential widow of Khan Uzbek, Taidula, of her sickness.[96] Patriarch Callistos scolded Roman for his infringements of Alexis' rights and sent to Russia, as his personal envoy, an important official, the Deacon Georges Perdikes to investigate the 'scandals' between the two metropolitans.[97] Perdikes, an ecclesiastical diplomat and specialist in Russian affairs, had been, already in 1354, entrusted

---

[91] Ibid., 35, p. 518, lines 22–4.
[92] Nicephorus Gregoras sympathized with Roman, but his account is chronologically inaccurate (*ibid.*, xxxvi, 37–40, pp. 519–20); for other references, see my article, 'Alexis and Roman', pp. 284–5.
[93] MM, I, 426: cf. above, Ch. 4, p. 95. [94] MM, I, 427–8.
[95] Cf. I. B. Grekov, *op. cit.*, p. 58. [96] *Troits.*, p. 375.
[97] MM, I, 425–30; for other missions performed by Georges Perdikes, see MM, I, 285 (1348), 566 (1371), and Cantacuzenos, *Hist.* IV, 37, Bonn, III, 270 (1353). Cantacuzenos considers Perdikes as a leading member of the Byzantine clergy (τῶν ἐπιφανεστέρων τοῦ κλήρου τῆς Βυζαντίων ἐκκλησίας).

170

with the mission of supporting the authority of Alexis.[98] In territories controlled by Roman, Alexis was recognized by some as the legitimate metropolitan.[99] Furthermore, in Constantinople, ex-Emperor Cantacuzenos, now a monk, but still enjoying much political and intellectual influence,[100] was able to promote his ideological positions, which, in Russia, required the unity of the metropolitanate. This ideology was, basically, shared by Callistos. In conflict with Cantacuzenos on political grounds, and supported as candidate to the patriarchate in 1354 by the old emperor's political enemies, he joined temporarily the Genoese party, but one may presume that he willingly modified his position on Russian affairs. Thus, after the death of Roman, which occurred in 1362, a patriarchal act of Callistos reunited the metropolitanate again under Alexis.[101]

If anything can be learned from the confused events connected with the Russian metropolitanate, it is the close interconnection between the internal events in Byzantium, the policy of the Italian republics, the Golden Horde and the major struggle for leadership in Russia between Olgerd and Moscow. The role played by the Southern Slavic kingdoms of Serbia and Bulgaria was also not negligible. Eastern Europe, where the Byzantine Orthodox Commonwealth was fighting for its survival, must be seen as a single whole, if the actions and the reactions of its individual member-states are to be understood in their proper context.

The khans of Sarai were obviously primarily interested in keeping their control over Russia and were supporting feuds among Russian princes, avoiding anyone's excessive prominence: thus they skilfully switched their support between Tver and Moscow, between Moscow and Lithuania. However, their respect for the Church and their diplomatic ties with Constantinople, which were recognized and used by the Byzantine ecclesiastical leaders,

---

[98] MM, I, 349.

[99] In 1358–60, Alexis was even able to travel in the territories of Olgerd (*Troits.*, pp. 376–7). The Chronicle *Rogozhskaya* mentions an opposition to Roman in Kiev ('ne priyasha ego Kiyane', col. 61), where Alexis also made a visit, but was himself temporarily arrested by Olgerd (*Act* of 1380, MM, II, 12). The synodal act of 1389, referring to events happening in 1374, affirms that, at that date, Alexis had failed to visit Kiev for nineteen years, i.e. since 1355 (MM, II, 118), but the reference in the Russian Chronicle about a visit of Alexis to Kiev in 1358–60 is too explicit to be put in doubt.

[100] Cf. my article, 'Projets', pp. 149–52; also Maksimović, 'Politička uloga', pp. 155–6.

[101] The text of the Act is not preserved, but it is mentioned in a (cancelled) sigillion of Philotheos of 1370 (MM, I, 526–7); for the date of the sigillion, see Darrouzès, *Régistre*, p. 114.

contributed to settle the metropolitan's see in that Russian principality which was most loyal to the Horde. It is only when Khan Djanibek turned against Genoese and Venetian colonies on the Black Sea, that a Genoese-dominated Byzantium gave support to a more pro-Western Lithuania (1341–6). In the following two decades, as Olgerd of Lithuania succeeded in reaching agreements with the Horde, he also gained occasional help from the pro-Genoese circles in Constantinople for his claims to supremacy over Russia: the case of Metropolitan Roman illustrates this development.

Meanwhile, Cantacuzenos and his friends, the hesychast monks, were committed to a different set of priorities. Always attempting to liberate Byzantium from Genoese exploitation and backed by Turkish allies, Cantacuzenos had no clear stakes in either of the Russian principalities, which were receiving in turn Tatar (and Genoese) support. However, the loyalty to Byzantine ideology shown by Grand-prince Symeon of Moscow and his close co-operation with Metropolitan Theognostos, made Moscow appear as a more reliable and more potent tool for the preservation of Byzantine inheritance in Russia than Olgerd of Lithuania who, being himself still a pagan, was capable of challenging the patriarchate of Constantinople, to the point of having his candidate for the metropolitanate consecrated in Trnovo! Since, for Cantacuzenos, the integrity and at least relative political independence of the Byzantine world was the first priority, he and his friend, Patriarch Philotheos, became consistent promoters of unifying policies, which opposed the claims of Olgerd in 1347–70, but was also to oppose Moscow's exclusivism in the years that followed. The problem was, however, that Byzantium's chronic weakness and governmental instability did not allow these consistent views to be shaped in fully consistent policies.

8

Patriarch Philotheos and Russia
(1364–1376)

The unstable conditions under which the Byzantine empire survived for still another century after the Genoese takeover in 1352, until its final collapse in 1453, have been often described, even if all the concrete details, the attitudes adopted by the various protagonists of the drama and the complicated manoeuvres by the powers involved in the events are not always well known. In any case, it is clear that the Byzantine diplomatic and administrative activities in Russia were influenced by events and changes occurring in the capital. As we have seen earlier, the connection is clearly affirmed by Emperor John Cantacuzenos in documents concerning Russia and issued in 1347: the government of Ann of Savoy and Patriarch John Calecas (1341–6) is blamed for accepting a division of the Russian metropolitanate. Similarly, the consecration of Roman in 1354–5 can be explained only in the framework of the events connected with the abdication of John Cantacuzenos and the retirement of Patriarch Philotheos (November 1354). The confused developments in the history of Byzantino-Russian relations during the second half of the fourteenth century are to be understood in a similar context.

Encouraged by civil wars of Byzantium and competition between Western powers, the Turks were actively expanding their control of the remaining Byzantine territories in Asia Minor. In March 1354, Callipolis (Gallipoli), on the European side of the Dardanelles, was taken, starting the settlement of the Ottomans in Europe. The powerful Serbian empire of Stefan Dušan would have been able to resist their advance, but Dushan died in 1355 and his weak and divided successors were not able to keep together the heterogeneous elements of the Serbian empire. The Turks maintained their advance at the expense of Greek, Serbian and Bulgarian territories, occupying Didymotichus (1361) and

Adrianople (1362), where Sultan Murad I (1362–89) established his residence.

Practically surrounded, Byzantium was, on the other hand, at the mercy of the Genoese and Venetians, who were interested in protecting Constantinople, not for its own sake, but only as a lucrative and necessary trading-post, essential to their commercial interests in the Black Sea. In practice, the imperial government could only resort to stratagems which eventually weakened it even more: to use the fierce competition between Venice and Genoa, or to pay tribute to the sultan, thus becoming a de facto vassal of the Turks, or else to hope for military help from the West, which, however, was always conditioned by a formal acceptance of the pope's ecclesiastical supremacy.[1] Only the patriarchate of Constantinople was able to maintain and even strengthen its prestige and administrative authority in vast areas of the Middle East and Eastern Europe, in spite of the strains provoked by internal events in the capital, which were influencing the selection of patriarchs and their policies.

The reigning Emperor, John V Palaeologus (1341–91), was a weak and wavering personality. Brought to power with the active help of the Genoese in 1354, he eventually became their victim and, at no time, succeeded in either developing, or consistently following an effective policy of government. One aspect of his long reign which recent historical research has demonstrated, is the role of elder statesman played by John Cantacuzenos after his voluntary retirement and acceptance of the monastic habit in 1354 under the name of Joasaph.[2] Throughout the second half of the fourteenth century, the imperial government was, in fact, run by members of the Palaeologi and Cantacuzeni families, who either shared power in Constantinople itself, or divided between themselves the remaining Byzantine cities and territories. If John V was technically the emperor, his father-in-law, John-Joasaph Cantacuzenos remained active and even quite visible, as a policy maker. Whereas John V was more inclined to a policy of expediency, Cantacuzenos insisted on being the guardian of imperial ideology and religious integrity. Serious conflicts between them did not arise, however, because John V never explicitly denied the traditional Byzantine ideological stands, whereas Cantacuzenos

---

[1] Cf. the short survey of these alternatives in Ostrogorsky, *History*, pp. 533–52; a more detailed and updated account in Nicol, *The Last Centuries*, pp. 265–333.

[2] On this see particularly Meyendorff, 'Projets', pp. 149–77; and Maksimović, 'Politička uloga', pp. 119–93.

tolerantly waited for his son-in-law's stratagems to show their ineffectiveness. Even the formal conversion of John V to Roman Catholicism in 1369 was not taken too seriously by the old emperor-monk, who was absent from Constantinople while John V travelled to Rome, but, later, helped John V against the Genoese-sponsored usurpation of Andronicus IV in 1376. John V had no power, and probably no desire, to impose union with Rome upon the Church and his personal conversion provoked in Constantinople neither rebellions nor anathemas, but indifference: what a contrast with the events of the reign of Michael VIII! One may presume that the personal authority of Cantacuzenos – a friend of both John V and of the staunchly Orthodox Patriarch Philotheos – contributed to throwing the episode into oblivion.

The personal relationships between John V and Philotheos are something of a mystery and required delicate balance. The patriarch did not oppose Church-union negotiations – and, therefore, attempts at getting Western help – provided that union was achieved through a formal Council with freedom for both sides to argue their case.[3] On the other hand, John V never formally opposed the theological positions of the Byzantine Church. He remained loyal to the decisions of the Palamite councils of 1341, 1347 and 1351, even if he also used the diplomatic services of Demetrios Kydones who – since 1348 – had been a convinced anti-Palamite devoted to Thomist theology and the Roman Church. These Orthodox convictions of John V – however inconsistent with his conversion in Rome in 1369 – are witnessed by Gregory Akindynos, Palamas himself and Patriarch Philotheos.[4]

[3] Philotheos shared the views of Cantacuzenos on this issue. See particularly Cantacuzenos' correspondence with Popes Clement VI and Innocent VI in 1347-58 (*Cant., Hist.*, IV, 9, Bonn, III, 53-62; cf. R. J. Loenertz, 'Ambassadeurs grecs auprès du pape Clément VI (1348)', OCP 19 (1953), pp. 178-96), and his dialogue with the legate Paul in 1367 (ed. Meyendorff, 'Projets', pp. 172-3); cf. also D. M. Nicol, 'Byzantine requests for an ecumenical council in the fourteenth century', *Annuarium Historiae Conciliorum*, I, 1969, pp. 69-95.

[4] Writing in 1346, at the time when John Palaeologus was only fourteen, Akindynos regretfully mentions that the young emperor (whose legitimate rule he recognizes refusing that of Cantacuzenos) 'shares in the stubbornness and obscurantism' of the Palamites (μέτειστι τῆς ἀπειθείας ταύτης αὐτοὺς καὶ σκαιότητος, Letter to John Calecas, *Marc. gr.* 155, fol. 50; cf. Meyendorff, *Introduction*, p. 120, note 119); a complete critical edition of the *Letters* of Akindynos – an important historical and theological source for the period – by Angela Hero is forthcoming in the series of *Dumbarton Oaks Texts*. The texts of Palamas, witnessing to the Palamite convictions of John V, are found in his treatises against Gregoras, written in 1356-8 (cf. J. Meyendorff, *op. cit.*, pp. 379-82). Refuting the informations, spread by Gregoras, that John V signed the *Tomos* of 1351 under duress by Cantacuzenos, Palamas, on the one hand reaffirms the legitimacy of the Palaeologan emperor

The personal relations which existed between John V and Cantacuzenos may also explain why the affairs of the patriarchate – and, in particular, the affairs of the Russian Church – remained fully under the control of Patriarch Philotheos throughout his second tenure (1364–76). Philotheos himself, writing during that period, emphasizes the role of the old emperor-monk in Byzantine society. 'In addition to the true and first glory which comes from God, [the ex-emperor John-Joasaph Cantacuzenos] also abundantly receives that human glory which comes from below: those who were his adversaries in the past are now benevolent towards him, and those who hated him unjustly do now love him justly, having liberated themselves from their hatred and the lies of which he was the victim, so that truth triumphed by itself. In the past, his subjects bowed before him in obeisance, as their master – although not all did so sincerely for the reasons shown above – but now almost everyone salutes him sincerely with proper good will and love, particularly the emperors and empresses,[5] the entire family vested in gold, loving him, as children love their father . . . This is also the case of the one, who today is the reigning emperor [John V] . . . He considers [the ex-emperor Cantacuzenos] as a pillar of his rule, as a divine counsellor, as the soul of his policies, and of his very life, as a supporter and promoter of his own rule and of that of his children, as leader, father and guardian.'[6] Furthermore, speaking of John V, Philotheos affirms that, besides having had a virtuous mother, the emperor 'recognized the Church of Christ as his mother, so that, following the doctors of the Church with piety and zeal, and having bowed before them his head and soul, he openly and in practice proclaims the admirable confession . . .'[7]

(ᾧ . . . ἡ τοῦ κράτους σφραγὶς ἐκ μητρικῆς νηδύος), and, on the other, recalls his devotion to Orthodoxy ([ᾧ] καὶ τὸ εὐσεβὲς ἔμφυτον τῇ τοῦ βασιλεύσαντος αὐτὸν Χριστοῦ χάριτι) and his opposition to the Akindynists in 1346, which was recognized by Akindynos himself (cf. text above). According to Palamas, John Palaeologus, being still a child, snubbed Barlaam (τῷ Βαρλαὰμ εὐμενῶς ποτε προσιδεῖν οὐκ ἠνέσχετο) and ordered the Akindynists out of the palace (τοῖς περιεστῶσιν ἀνδράσι, παῖς ἔτι ὤν, προσέταττεν . . . τοὺς ἀκινδυνιανοὺς ἐξελαύνειν τῶν βασιλείων, *Coisl.* 100, fol. 233–233 v.) Palamas also recalls the presence of John V at liturgies celebrated by himself as archbishop of Thessalonica and his following the religious convictions of his father, Andronicus III, of his mother, the Empress Ann and of his father-in-law, John Cantacuzenos (*Coisl.* 100, fol. 235v: Greek original quoted in J. Meyendorff, *op. cit.*, p. 163, note 37).

5 The title of 'emperor' (βασιλεύς) did not belong only to John V, but also to his sons Andronicus and Manuel, and to Matthew and Manuel Cantacuzenos, sons of John VI.
6 *Contra Greg.* XII, PG, CLI, cols. 1128D–1129C.   7 *Ibid.*, col. 1130B.

Apart from obvious rhetorical overstatements, such affirmations by a reigning patriarch must reflect some reality, at least in terms of the official attitude of John V towards the patriarchate, now continuously occupied by hesychast patriarchs, and towards Cantacuzenos, a close friend of Philotheos. One may of course suppose that the praises for John were written before his trip to the West and his conversion (1369), but one has also to admit that Philotheos seems to have enjoyed a free hand in ecclesiastical affairs both before the trip, i.e. in 1368 when he anathematized Prochoros Kydones and canonized Gregory Palamas,[8] and after the emperor's return from Italy. In fact, Philotheos took no official note of the fact that his sovereign had renounced Orthodoxy.

At the same time, however, some monastic circles were highly critical of the personality of John V. In an *Encomion* of St Euthymios of Trnovo, Gregory Tsamblak, relating events happening in 1364–5 – the visit of Euthymios in Constantinople – speaks of John as 'loving money, rather than Christ' (*zlatolyubiya pache nezhe khristolyubiya zryashe*): the emperor is idolatrous, crazed and unchaste, but, eventually, under the impact of a miraculous event, he repents and asks forgiveness.[9]

These and many other aspects of the life of the Byzantine court in the last years of the Empire give its activities an air of unreality. With the exception of a narrow circle of friends and attendants, most Byzantines ignored John Palaeologus and his schemes, whereas the patriarchate with its influence extending far beyond the limits of the Empire, was still quite a powerful and largely independent body, which continued to promote its own policies, particularly in the Balkans and Russia.

I. PATRIARCH PHILOTHEOS

Russian sources, not only of the fourteenth century, but also of the later periods attribute to Patriarch Philotheos an extraordinary – almost a legendary – role in the destinies of Muscovite Russia. A

---

[8] Demetrios Kydones, in a letter to Philotheos, expresses his indignation against the condemnation of his brother, which, according to him, was a breach of the promises given to John V by Philotheos (Letter 129, ed. R. J. Loenertz, Vatican, 1956, pp. 164–8; cf. his 'invective' against Philotheos, written in the name of Prochoros, in Mercati, *Notizie*, pp. 296–313). But there is no evidence that the emperor took any action against the patriarch.

[9] Ed. Pen'o, Rusev *et al.*, Sofia, 1971, pp. 152, 156. Tsamblak's views on the corruption of the Byzantine court are to be seen in the light of the conditions under which he would himself be appointed metropolitan of Kiev; see below, pp. 265–6.

full study of his personality, as a leader, as a theologian and as a writer would be important for understanding the events which characterize the history of Eastern Europe during his lifetime. Such a study would have to be based on both Greek and Slavic sources, of which many are still unpublished.

The surname *Kokkinos* (Κόκκινος), the 'red-haired', which belonged to Philotheos, is attributed by Nicephorus Gregoras to 'his fire-like and wild appearance' (διὰ τὸ πυρῶδες καὶ ἄγριον τῆς ὄψεως).[10] In reality, one may rather presume that 'Kokkinos' was his family name.[11] He was born in Thessalonica around the year 1300 in a family of Jewish background, a fact which his ideological enemies – Demetrios and Prochoros Kydones, but also Nicephorus Gregoras – relish with obvious bad taste.[12] During a monastic career on Mount Athos, where he was, for a time, the abbot of the Great Lavra, Philotheos supported Gregory Palamas in his theological struggle during the civil war (1341–7). After the victory of Cantacuzenos, he was elected metropolitan of Heraclea in Thrace.

The political and ecclesiastical events of 1351–4 seem to have left a significant mark upon his subsequent career. In 1351, the Genoese, led by Paganino Doria, sacked his episcopal see of Heraclea. While the metropolitan was not in the city during the catastrophe, he dispensed much energy in helping his flock and preserved a firm personal antagonism against the Genoese for the rest of his life.[13] As metropolitan of Heraclea, he presided, on 10 June 1350, over the consecration of Callistos to the patriarchate,[14] but differences over internal and external policies soon placed the two men in opposition to each other. This conflict between two former Athonite monks and leaders of Hesychasm had, as we have seen earlier, some unfortunate repercussions in Russia. Having refused to crown Matthew Cantacuzenos as

---

[10] *Hist.* xxvi, 14, Bonn, iii, p. 80.

[11] Cf. Stephen *Kokkinos*, official of the patriarchate in 1285 (V. Laurent, 'Les signataires du second synode des Blakhernes', *EO*, xxvi, 1927, p. 148).

[12] On the passage by the Kydones brothers, see Mercati, *Notizie*, pp. 248–9 ('Ἰουδαῖος ὢν καὶ τῆς ἐναγοῦς ἐκείνης γενεᾶς κληρονόμος, μνησικακῶν δὲ καὶ σὺ τῷ Χριστῷ, ὃν ᾔδεις ὑπὸ τῶν σῶν προγόνων ἀνῃρημένον); Gregoras regrets that John V did not use against Philotheos the repressive measures taken against the Jews by Constantine I (*Hist.* XXVI, 15, Bonn, iii, p. 81).

[13] Cf. M. Balard, 'A propos de la bataille du Bosphore. L'expédition génoise de Paganino Doria à Constantinople (1351–1352)', *Travaux et Mémoires*, 4, 1970, pp. 441–3. The writings of Philotheos, concerned with the sack of Heraclea are published in C. Triantafillis, Συλλογὴ ἑλληνικῶν ἀνεκδότων, i, Venice, 1874, pp. 1–46.

[14] Philotheos, *On the Sack of Heraclea*, ed. cit., p. 7.

emperor, Callistos had to abandon the patriarchal throne in August 1353 and find refuge, first, with the Genoese in Galata and later in Tenedos, where John V lived in semi-retirement under the protection of the same Genoese. Philotheos was elected patriarch in November 1353 and crowned Matthew. However, exactly a year later, he had to follow Cantacuzenos into retirement and see the return of Callistos to the patriarchate, in spite of the fact that the Synod expressed its support for Philotheos and stood by its previous decision of deposition against Callistos.[15] One may imagine that, under such circumstances, the latter's position during his second patriarchate (1355–63) was not a comfortable one, especially since the exiled Philotheos did not recognize his legitimacy.[16]

Between Callistos and Philotheos there were no theological differences of any kind,[17] but it is not impossible that personal or temperamental oppositions, going back to their Athonite past, existed between them: Callistos was a disciple of St Gregory of Sinai in the *skete* of Magoula and wrote his *Life*, as well as the *Life* of Theodosius of Trnovo – another of the Sinaite's followers in Bulgaria – whereas Philotheos (and Palamas himself) were rather connected with the Great Lavra. There is no evidence of any personal contact between Gregory of Sinai and Gregory Palamas on Mount Athos,[18] and the hagiographic writings of Philotheos and Callistos differ both in style and orientation. A further study of these texts may lead to interesting clues as to the origins and background of the feud between the two patriarchs. In terms of policies, it is clear that Callistos was not only a stricter legitimist than Philotheos and opposed the elimination of John V in 1352, but that he was favouring ties with the Balkan Slavs and Lithuania, as distinct from the sympathies which Philotheos established in Moscow.

Having come back to the patriarchate in 1363 after the death of Callistos, which occurred during a diplomatic trip to Serres, the residence of Serbian rulers, Philotheos, during his second tenure, left a very significant impact upon the internal and external affairs

---

[15] A. Failler, 'La déposition du patriarche Calliste Ier (1353)', REB, 31 (1973), pp. 5–163.

[16] Cf. references to texts in Meyendorff, 'Alexis and Roman', p. 284, note 22.

[17] During the last years of his life, Gregory Palamas himself, now archbishop of Thessalonica, entertained friendly relations with both competitors for the patriarchate (cf. Meyendorff, *Introduction*, p. 167, note 64); cf. also the praises of Philotheos for Callistos in *On the Sack of Heraclea, ibid.*

[18] Cf. Meyendorff, *Introduction*, p. 64 (*A Study*, p. 41).

of Byzantium. Very close to Cantacuzenos, who appreciated not only his personal loyalty, but also his secular education,[19] which distinguished him from the other 'hesychast' patriarchs of the period, Isidore and Callistos, and which he combined with unquestionable theological skill, Philotheos gave a final seal to the triumph of Palamism by condemning the Thomist version of anti-Palamism in the person of Prochoros Kydones, by publishing several treatises in favour of Palamite theology, by canonizing Palamas in 1368 and by composing in his honour a liturgical service, to be included in liturgical books for the office of the Second Sunday of Lent. He also became the author of numerous other liturgical texts, of which a great part was translated into Slavic, and the codifier of liturgical practices, which also were soon introduced in Slavic lands.[20] His role in supposedly organizing an Orthodox crusade against the Turks, in opposition to the Western projects of John V in 1369–70, has been, in my opinion, exaggerated by O. Halecki.[21] The documents witness only to a routine correspondence with the patriarchs of Antioch and Alexandria and to the official acceptance into the jurisdiction of the ecumenical patriarchate by Philotheos of several dioceses in Northern Greece which had been attached at the time of Stefan Dušan to the patriarchate of Peč.[22] This action was made possible by the local Serbian ruler, John Uglješa, who had offered his alliance to Byzantium. In military terms, the initiative was his and not the patriarch's, and it soon ended with a smashing defeat of the Serbs by Sultan Murad I on the river Maritsa (September 1371). There is no evidence that Patriarch Philotheos was personally instrumental in shaping practical alternatives to the Western schemes of John V, which included the emperor's personal conversion in Rome. Together with his friend Cantacuzenos, he rather chose to ignore them and even to 'cover them up' since no evidence of protests, or breaches of loyalty towards the reigning emperor have reached us.

[19] Cant., *Hist.* iv, 29, Bonn, iii, p. 217. The *Lives* of St Sabbas of Vatopedi, St Germanos and Patriarch Isidore, written by Philotheos, but particularly his *Encomion* of Palamas do indeed show the skill of a rhetorician and abound in references to authors of antiquity.

[20] Cf. Prokhorov, 'Gimny', pp. 120–49. For a comprehensive list of the writings of Philotheos, see also Beck, *Kirche*, pp. 723–6.

[21] *Un empereur*, pp. 235–60; cf. also V. Laurent, 'Philothée Kokkinos', *DTC* xii, 2, Paris, 1935, cols. 1501–2. The idea of an alliance between Byzantines and Serbs appears only in rhetorical discourses by Demetrios Kydones, disappointed by the failure of the pro-Western diplomacy which he himself had engineered.

[22] MM, i, pp. 553–5 (synodal act of May 1371).

Certainly, Philotheos nourished a strong commitment to the unity of the Orthodox world, but his priorities also included a concern for true union negotiations with Rome. Thus, in 1367, he actively cooperated with John Cantacuzenos in trying to secure a wide ecclesiastical representation at the ecumenical council which was planned for 1369 and wrote to the primates of the various churches to secure their participation.[23] Since one of the obstacles to a united Orthodox front was the schism which separated, since 1346, the patriarchates of Constantinople and of Peč, Philotheos, in 1375, recognized the latter and restored unity.[24]

A similar concern for unity will dominate the very active and imaginative policies of Philotheos in Russia. There can be little doubt that he basically shared the principles expressed in the documents of Cantacuzenos restoring the unity of the metropolitanate of Kiev in 1347.[25] Upon his return to the patriarchate after the death of Callistos (1363), he energetically upheld these principles again. However, since the political situation in Russia was changing rapidly, Philotheos undertook necessary diplomatic readjustments, showing that even the support of Moscow, which constituted the backbone of the policy of Cantacuzenos, was not an end in itself, but rather a tool for the preservation of the unity of the metropolitanate under the control of Byzantium, and that Muscovite interests were to be curbed, if they contradicted the higher concerns of the Byzantine Commonwealth. It is precisely these activities of Philotheos during his second patriarchate that became a real legend in Russia, and were remembered in a variety of historical, political and hagiographic documents.

2. DYNASTIC STRIFE IN THE GOLDEN HORDE AND THE RISE OF MOSCOW

During the twenty-four years which followed the death of Khan Djanibek, murdered by his son and immediate successor Berdibek (1357), the khanate of Kypchak found itself in the midst of bloody internal struggles involving members of the ruling dynasty. Instability lasted until the assumption of power by Khan Tokhtamysh (1381). These events themselves reflected dramatic

[23] Cf. his letter to the Archbishop of Ohrid, MM, I, pp. 491–3; cf. Meyendorff, 'Projets', p. 159.
[24] Cf. V. Laurent, 'L'archevêque de Peč et le titre de patriarche après l'union de 1375', *Balcania*, VII, 2, Bucharest, 1944, pp. 303–10 (earlier bibliography quoted).
[25] Cf. above Ch. 7.

changes occurring in the huge domain of the former Eurasian empire of Chingis Khan, such as the end of the Mongol domination of China, the installation of the native Ming dynasty (1368), and the rise of a new Mongolian empire-builder, Timur, or Tamerlane, who was eventually to back the installation of Tokhtamysh as Khan in Sarai.[26]

The dynastic dissension in the Horde, which saw the rapid succession of twenty-five khans during a period of twenty-four years, weakened the Tatar control of Russia. Profiting from the confusion (*zamyatnya*) in the Horde, which is often mentioned in chronicles, various Russian principalities began to enjoy greater leverage in asserting their respective ambitions. Lithuania and Moscow engaged in the bitterest stage of their struggle for supremacy in the whole of Russia. After 1362, however, a Mongol general named Mamai assumed power in the Horde. Since he was not himself a member of the ruling dynasty, he could not formally become khan, but he was able to assure that the changing holders of the office be dependent upon his will. He personally controlled the areas lying to the west of the Volga river – as did Nogay in the late thirteenth century – and his policies dominated the affairs of Russia. Directed by Mamai, the policy of the Mongols still followed the earlier pattern: it tried to secure a continuing competition between the Russian rulers by preserving a balance of power between them and by preventing anyone from gaining ultimate victory. However the Mongol grip on Russia was weakening, so that Lithuania and Moscow gradually gained such strength that the Mongols began to lose control of events.

Having supported the expansion of Lithuania beginning in 1352, and until around 1362, the Horde allowed Olgerd's power to dominate not only Kiev, but also Novgorod itself. Even the Grand-principality of Vladimir was given to Prince Dimitri of Nizhni-Novgorod, a relative of Olgerd. It is also during that period that Roman, Olgerd's candidate to the metropolitanate, was allowed not only to control the ecclesiastical administration in Olgerd's domain, but also to challenge Alexis as metropolitan 'of all Russia'. By 1362, however (after the death of Roman), Olgerd began to face the Mongols' hostility; Prince Dimitri of Moscow was given the *yarlyk* for the Grand-principality and Novgorod fell again in the realm of Muscovite influence.

---

[26] On the internal events in the Horde and its impact on Russian affairs, see particularly Vernadsky, *The Mongols*, pp. 245–63; cf. also Grekov, *Vostochnaya Evropa*, pp. 49–55; Spuler, *Goldene Horde*, pp. 109–21.

This growing power of Moscow and the fierce competition between Olgerd and Dimitri for the control of Tver, provoked another shift of Tatar sympathies. But Moscow was now able to challenge not only Lithuania, but the Horde itself: Prince Michael of Tver, summoned to Moscow by the metropolitan, fell under arrest (1368) and was freed only through direct pressure from Sarai. Assured of Tatar sympathies, Olgerd decided to undertake a final campaign against Moscow: his huge army reached the city and besieged it for three days (November 1368), ravaging towns and countryside in the vicinity. However, the powerful and rich Muscovite prince was able to repel the assault and resumed his attack on Tver as early as 1369, in spite of the fact that Prince Michael of Tver was again given the title to the Grand-principality by the Horde.

After a new and unsuccessful attempt at storming Moscow by Lithuanian troops, Olgerd and Dimitri came to the conclusion that a peaceful coexistence between their two realms was in their mutual interest. In the summer of 1371, a marriage was even concluded between a daughter of Olgerd and a cousin of Dimitri, Prince Vladimir Andreevich.[27] This reconciliation was strongly patronized by Patriarch Philotheos. The Horde saw the extreme danger such an alliance would present for Mongol rule in Russia: in order to provoke Olgerd's jealousy, Dimitri of Moscow was invited to visit Mamai and received the khan's *yarlyk* for the Grand-principality. War broke out again with Lithuania and Tver, but, through the probable intermediary of the patriarchal envoy Cyprian, peace was concluded again in 1373. Meanwhile the Mongols were gradually losing control over the power struggle in Russia. In 1374, in Nizhni-Novgorod – then a principality allied with Moscow – an ambassador of Mamai, Saraika, was arrested and his retinue, numbering 1000, was massacred by the Russians[28] without provoking immediate reprisals. In 1375, the Muscovite prince a: d his allies held a meeting in Pereyaslavl', which resulted in the decision to capture Tver by force. The operation succeeded and Prince Michael and his allies formally capitulated. In 1375–8, Mamai, clearly and understandably upset by Moscow's might, made several incursions in Russia, but these were of little consequence for Moscow. Olgerd, on the other hand, until his death in 1377, limited himself to minor operations, such as his campaign against Smolensk in 1376. Clearly, Moscow's enemies felt, at least temporarily, unable to check its initiatives and expanding power.

[27] *Troits.*, p. 392. [28] *Ibid.*, p. 396.

All these developments modified the elements of the Byzantine diplomatic and administrative activity in Russia. The task of Patriarch Philotheos, who, as we have seen earlier, enjoyed a free hand in the field of ecclesiastical affairs during the reign of the weak and inconsistent Emperor John V, was not an easy one. The pro-Muscovite attitude followed by the Byzantines since the beginning of the century and pursued by Cantacuzenos and his advisors presupposed a solid and unified Mongol rule over Russia, as it existed under Khans Tokhta and Uzbek. However tyrannical and unpopular, this rule provided a stability which could be adroitly used by the Muscovite princes and the leaders of the Church to their own advantage. On the other hand, it served as a foundation for the economic prosperity of the Italian colonies on the Black Sea, on which Byzantium's own economy depended entirely. However, the beginning of dynastic instability in the Horde (1357), which gave both Moscow and Lithuania much more leverage in pursuing their respective interests, led to a situation of direct and almost permanent confrontation between the 'two Russias'. The administrative unity of the metropolitanate could not be preserved simply by settling difficulties in Sarai, through the intermediary of the local bishop. The *pax mongolica* did not impress the parties any more. The former vassals of the khans had become increasingly independent and new means were to be found to preserve the Byzantine Orthodox Commonwealth. On the other hand, both Cantacuzenos and Philotheos nourished a violent antipathy towards the Genoese and were not likely, therefore, to contribute in any way to the interests of these allies of the Golden Horde.

Under such circumstances, the policies of the metropolitans 'of all Russia' remained of crucial importance and Byzantium continued to plan and direct them very closely.

The crisis in the metropolitanate which followed the double consecration of Alexis (1354) and of Roman (1355), shattered the prestige of Byzantium in Russia. However, it resolved itself by the death of Roman (1362), who was given no successor. Unity was restored under Alexis again. The personality and activities of Metropolitan Alexis (1354–78) dominated the problems faced by the Byzantine patriarchate in Russia throughout the second term of Philotheos, as patriarch (1364–76).

The son of a nobleman (*boyarin*), who emigrated from Chernigov to Moscow, Alexis became metropolitan at the age of 56, after having served fifteen years in the ecclesiastical administration of

Theognostos.[29] His personality and experience allowed him to dominate the political life of the Muscovite principality throughout a tenure of twenty-four years. In 1359, Prince Ivan II Ivanovich died, leaving his nine-year-old son Dimitri as prince, and appointing the metropolitan as regent of the state. Greek synodal documents question the legitimacy of the political functions, which Alexis assumed in Moscow. 'Ivan, the Grand-prince of Moscow, before his death, entrusted to [Alexis] the education and upbringing of his son Dimitri, so that [the metropolitan] became fully and immediately absorbed by his concern for the prince.'[30] In fact, by assuming such responsibilities, Alexis was following a well-established Byzantine tradition, which made the head of the Church almost automatically responsible for the fate of the state in cases when imperial power could not be exercised normally. Examples of Byzantine patriarchs acting as regents of the empire are numerous (Patriarch Sergius under Heraclius, Patriarch Nicholas Mystikos in the tenth century and Patriarch John Calecas in the fourteenth). In the case of Alexis, however, the problem was that Dimitri was not a ruler of the whole of Russia, whereas the ecclesiastical jurisdiction of Alexis extended to Polish, Tverian and Lithuanian territories, whose rulers were engaged in a struggle (which from their standpoint was fully legitimate) against the principality of Moscow.

At the beginning of his tenure, during the reign of Ivan I and Khan Djanibek (1342–57), as the power of the Horde appeared still quite formidable, Alexis followed a policy of loyalty and appeasement towards the Tatars, as his predecessors did before him. He saw no other way of placating his competitor, Metropolitan Roman. He visited the Horde twice as he travelled to Constantinople (1354–6), bringing letters of recommendation obtained through the bishop of Sarai.[31] After saying special prayers at the tomb of the saintly Metropolitan Peter in Moscow, he went again to the khan's court in 1357 in order to perform the healing of the influential *Khatun* Taidula, widow of Uzbek.[32] During his stay in Sarai, the metropolitan had a theological debate with Muslims, but he also witnessed the murder of Djanibek and the beginning of the dynastic trouble in the Horde. His diplomatic contacts with the Tatars led to the granting of *yarlyks* of privileges to the Church by both Taidula and Khan Berdibek.[33]

---

[29] The most exhaustive information on his biography is found in Golubinsky, *Istoriya*, pp. 171–225.　　[30] MM, II, p. 117; cf. also MM, II, p. 12.
[31] MM, I, p. 347.　　[32] *Troits.*, p. 375–6.　　[33] Cf. Golubinsky, *ibid.*, pp. 196–8.

Having secured his position at the Horde, Alexis travelled in territories controlled by Olgerd, a fact which indicates that the power of Roman was not uncontested in these areas. He left Moscow for Kiev in January 1358 and remained in territories controlled by Olgerd until 1360.[34] The fact that he did not return immediately to Moscow after the death of Ivan II of Moscow (13 November 1359) would indicate that, conscious of the ambiguities involved, he was not in a hurry to assume the regency in Moscow, which had been granted to him by the deceased prince, and preferred to continue his pastoral responsibilities beyond Muscovite territories. Significantly, immediately after the return of Alexis to Vladimir in 1360, Metropolitan Roman invaded the see of Kiev and even – in the footsteps of Olgerd's armies – extended his power over Bryansk.[35] These offensive actions, which may have been provoked by the new political responsibilities of Alexis in Moscow, had the effect of pushing Metropolitan Alexis even further towards identifying the interests of the Church with those of the Muscovite government.

Thus, in the years that followed, as a regent of the Moscow principality, he contributed to shaping the policies which obtained for Moscow a greater independence from the Tatars, but also bitterly opposed it to other principalities, particularly Tver and Lithuania.

The participation of Metropolitan Alexis in attracting Prince Michael of Tver to Moscow (1368) in order to secure his arrest, is an example of his ambiguous political role.[36] As Michael fled to the court of Olgerd and provoked the first major invasion of Moscow's territory by the armies of the Lithuanian Grand-prince, the Metropolitan, following the example of his predecessor Theognostos, formally excommunicated Orthodox princes, allied to Olgerd, including particularly Michael Aleksandrovich of Tver and Svyatoslav Ivanovich of Smolensk.[37]

There is no doubt that the general policies of Alexis stood in line with that of his predecessors, who also favoured Moscow over its competitors, and with the stated orientation of the Byzantine patriarchate as well. But, later in his tenure, he began to realize

---

[34] Cf. *Troits.*, pp. 376–7.   [35] MM, I, p. 428.
[36] *Troits.*, p. 386; cf. the complaints of the victim: 'He was very angry and complained particularly against the metropolitan for whom he used to nourish much love and confidence as for a true bishop' (*Rog.*, p. 87); cf. the equally sour reproaches of Patriarch Philotheos addressed to Alexis on the occasion of that episode (below, pp. 196–7).
[37] Cf. MM, I, pp. 523–5.

the ambiguities of his situation. He was closely connected with the monastic circles – Greek, South Slavic and Russian – and particularly with St Sergius. Whereas Metropolitans Peter and Theognostos were primarily concerned with building stone churches, enhancing the prestige of Moscow, as a capital, Alexis laid the foundation of four monasteries, including the monastery 'of the Saviour' – built to commemorate his miraculous salvation in a storm on the Black Sea (1355), during his second trip to Constantinople, and whose first abbot was Andronicus, a disciple of St Sergius, and the monastery 'Simonovsky', governed by Theodore, a nephew of St Sergius and an eminent promoter of Byzantino-Russian relations. St Sergius personally was close to the court of the Grand-prince (he performed the baptism of Dimitri's son in 1375)[38] and to the Metropolitan Alexis who attempted to name him as his successor. These facts indicate that Alexis, in his pro-Muscovite attitudes, could not avoid taking into account the instructions he was receiving after 1370 from Patriarch Philotheos, whose envoy, Cyprian, the future metropolitan, was also present at the baptism of 1375 in Pereyaslavl'.[39] These instructions, as we will see below, were quite critical of the indiscriminate support given by Alexis to the Muscovite position in 1368 and advised the metropolitan to consider the legitimate complaints coming from the numerous Orthodox population of south-western Russia.

When Philotheos Kokkinos came back for a second tenure as patriarch on 8 October 1364,[40] Alexis, his appointee as Metropolitan of Kiev and all Russia, was alone in control of the metropolitanate, since Roman had died in 1362. Between 1364 and 1370, with no hesitation, Philotheos backed the prerogatives of Metropolitan Alexis and committed the prestige of the patriarchate behind all his actions, religious and political. Perhaps the most characteristic gesture, expressing hostility and distrust towards Olgerd of Lithuania, was the case of the solemn canonization of three Lithuanian martyrs, Anthony, John and Eustathius, who were baptized by a priest Nestor in Vilna, and martyred by order of Olgerd in 1347.[41] The new saints were probably canonized by Metropolitan Alexis and their cult was aimed at publicly discrediting Olgerd as a potential leader of Orthodox Russia. In 1374, portions of their relics would even be carried to Constantinople, venerated in the 'Great Church' of St Sophia by order of

[38] *Troits.*, p. 397.   [39] *Rog.*, col. 105: cf. Sokolov, *Arkhierei*, pp. 438–9.
[40] MM, I, p. 448.   [41] *Voskr.*, p. 214; cf. Sokolov, *Arkhierei*, p. 355, note 1.

patriarch Philotheos, and even praised in an official Greek *Encomion* composed by the *rhetor* Michael Balsamon.[42] This unusual gesture of Philotheos[43] was not only aimed at supporting the Muscovite cause, but also expressed the reorientation of patriarchal policies towards greater concern for the faithful in Lithuania.

The register of patriarchal documents for that period contains several texts which allow us not only to witness this full support given to the policies of Moscow by Philotheos, but also to determine the exact date when a distinct switch of orientation came into being. The register includes six documents, all exactly dated to June 1370, which were a response of the patriarch to urgent requests, coming from Dimitri of Moscow through his ambassador Daniel, and from Metropolitan Alexis, who had sent to Constantinople an envoy named Avvakum, at the time of the two attempts of Olgerd and his allies of Tver and Smolensk, to capture Moscow.[44] The series includes:

(a) A letter to Dimitri 'grand prince of all Russia' (μέγας ῥὴξ πάσης 'Ρωσίας), which commends the young prince, 'son' of the patriarch, for his love and devotion towards the Church and his 'submission' (ὑποταγήν) to metropolitan Alexis: 'The metropolitan appointed by me', writes Philotheos, 'is an image of God, and is my representative, so that anyone who is submissive to him and is concerned with loving, honouring and obeying him, is actually submissive to God and to Our Humility.'[45]

(b) A letter to Metropolitan Alexis, which clearly indicates that the metropolitan, and not the young price, is in real control in Moscow. Alexis is commended for sending a written report to Constantinople and is encouraged to either visit the capital him-

---

[42] Τοῦ Φιλοθέου φημὶ τοῦ πάνυ ὅς . . . πρῶτος τὸ μαρτυρικὸν αὐτοῖς παρέσχε σέβας καὶ τὴν τιμήν, εἰκόσι καὶ προσκυνήμασι καὶ τελεταῖς ἐτησίοις (ed. M. Gedeon, Νέα Βιβλιοθήκη ἐκκλησιαστικῶν συγγραφέων, Constantinople, 1903, pp. 100–1; cf. also by the same editor, 'Αρχεῖον ἐκκλησιαστικῆς ἱστορίας, I, Constantinople 1911, p. 173). On the canonization of the martyrs in Russia, see N. Elagin, 'Pervye khristianskie mucheniki v Litve', *Zh. M. N. P.*, xxxviii, 1843, pp. 113–29; cf. also Makary, *Istoriya*, IV, pp. 130–1, and E. Golubinsky, *Istoriya kanonizatsii svyatykh v russkoi tserkvi*, Moscow, 1903, pp. 68–71, 542–3. Golubinsky dates the canonization with a later date (fifteenth century), but he ignores the existence of the Greek *Encomion*. On this problem, see J. Meyendorff, 'Byzantium, Moscow and Lithuania in the fourteenth century: the three Lithuanian martyrs in literature and iconography', *Eikon and Logos* (Festschrift Onash), Halle, 1981.

[43] Cf. I. Dujčev, 'Slawische Heilige in der Byzantinischen Hagiographie', *Medioevo Bizantino-Slavo*, II, Rome, 1968, pp. 207–23. Only isolated *Lives* of Slavic saints were translated into Greek, or written by Greeks.

[44] Nos. 264, 265, 266, 267, 268, 269, in MM, I, pp. 516–25.

[45] MM, I, p. 517.

self, or write frequently. The subject of the correspondence includes 'affairs of the Church, of society, and of the empire'.[46] Alexis is further assured of the love and confidence of the patriarch (ἔχω σε φίλον γνήσιον) and is promised support in any of his endeavours (εἴ τι χρήζεις, γράφε τοῦτο μετὰ πληροφορίας, νὰ τὸ πληρῶ). The colloquial style of the letter seems to recall a personal acquaintance between Philotheos and Alexis, established during the stays of Alexis in Constantinople (1354–6). Since Alexis had reported the disobedience of some Russian princes, the patriarch informs him of the content of his letters to them (see below), and solemnly reaffirms the principle of a single metropolitanate of Russia. 'The nation [of the Russians] is very big and numerous; it requires great care, and they all depend on you (καὶ πάντες ἀνάκεινται εἰς σέ).'

(c) A circular letter to the princes of Russia (ῥῆγες πάσης Ῥωσίας), calling them to nourish 'fear, honour, submission and obedience' towards the 'most holy Metropolitan of Kiev and all Russia, *hypertimos*, brother and concelebrant of Our Humility in the Holy Spirit', as if he were God himself, and as a representative of the patriarch.[47] The addressees are not named, but they certainly represent the group of princes still allied with Moscow, which are encouraged, as 'beloved sons', to maintain their loyalty both to the metropolitan and to the patriarchate.

(d) A letter to the bishop Alexis of Novgorod, which is nothing but a stern threat of deposition, on two grounds: the bishop has appropriated the privilege of wearing a *polystavrion* – a distinction which had been bestowed upon his predecessor Basil only as a personal favour[48] – and he disobeys both his metropolitan and his Grand-prince Dimitri of Moscow. In the letter, the patriarch addresses Alexis of Novgorod as a 'bishop', and not an 'archbishop', implying that he has no superiority over the other suffragans of the Metropolitan of Kiev. The letter must reflect an attempt by the Novgorodians – who were in the midst of a bitter struggle with the Livonian Order[49] – to seek alliance and support from Olgerd, rather than from Moscow, which was itself embattled by Lithuanian armies.

(e) A solemn act of excommunication against those princes –

---

[46] Τὰ πράγματα τὰ ἐκκλησιαστικά, τὰ πολιτικὰ καὶ τὰ τῆς βασιλείας, *ibid.*, p. 519.
[47] It is in this letter and this context that Philotheos defines the universal power of the patriarch in terms which could have been used by a Roman pope of the eleventh century (see app. 2, pp. 283–4).
[48] Cf. above, p. 84.   [49] Cf. *Novg.*, pp. 370–1; Engl. tr., p. 152.

headed by Michael Aleksandrovich of Tver – who 'allied themselves with the impious Olgerd' (προσετέθησαν . . . τῷ ἀσεβεῖ Οὐργέλδῳ). The princes are called to repent before the metropolitan and will then be automatically forgiven by the patriarch also.

(f) A particular act of excommunication against Prince Svyatoslav of Smolensk, whom Metropolitan Alexis had already excommunicated 'justly' (καλῶς καὶ δικαίως ποιήσας).

The unconditional support of Muscovite policies contained in these letters stands in contrast with another document contained in the patriarchal register, which reveals, in the same year 1370, and probably in the same month of June, a very sudden reversal of Philotheos: a patriarchal act, prepared by the chancery for the patriarch's signature, with a copy placed in the register, formally suppresses the metropolitanate of Lithuania, submitting the 'bishop' of Lithuania to the metropolitan of Kiev.[50] However, the patriarch, at the last moment, refused to sign the original: the archivist was obliged to cross the document out in the register and add an explicative note on the appropriate page.[51] The sudden arrival of additional information, at a time when the letters to Alexis and the princes had already been signed and dispatched, would provide the only conceivable explanation for this cancellation, which also inaugurated a more even-handed attitude of Philotheos in the conflict between Moscow and Lithuania. The primary goal of the patriarchate remained the preservation of unity, but Philotheos made the sudden discovery that this goal could not be maintained by simple and indiscriminate support of Moscow. The principality of Tver, the Grand-principality of Lithuania and the kingdom of Poland controlled a sizeable Orthodox population, which needed constant pastoral supervision and the appointment of new bishops. A metropolitan who, like Alexis,

[50] We will remember (cf. above p. 95), that throughout the fourteenth century, the metropolitanate 'of Lithuania' was considered as 'vacant', during periods when no incumbent was appointed. This was the case since the death of Roman (1362), which explains that the metropolitanate could still be (but was not) formally suppressed in 1370.

[51] MM, I, 525–7. Since the document carries no signature, it is not dated either, which led some historians to ascribe it to 1364 (A. Pavlov, RIB, VI, Suppl. 91–8); however, the study of the manuscript by J. Darrouzès shows that the text of the decree was copied into the register by the very hand which also copied the entire series of letters of June 1370, evidently at the same time. However, the other letters received the patriarchal signature, whereas the act suppressing the metropolitanate of Lithuania did not. J. Darrouzès' probable conjecture is that sudden news coming from Russia provoked the cancellation of this particular act (Darrouzès, *Régistre*, pp. 53, 351, 370, and pl. 35).

also held political power in Moscow, could no longer fulfil these responsibilities in a normal way. We do not know which concrete circumstances provoked the cancellation of the act, drafted in June 1370. It is possible that the letter of Olgerd, which we will discuss below, arrived precisely at that time.[52] In any case, written documents, issued in the following months, bring clearly to light the reasons why the Byzantine patriarchate changed its attitude in 1370.

3. THE CHALLENGE OF POLAND AND LITHUANIA

We have seen earlier that, after a protracted competition with the sons of Gedymin for the control of Galicia and Volhynia, King Casimir of Poland in 1366 finally succeeded in annexing the whole of 'Little Russia' to his realm.[53] In 1370, not long before his death (5 November 1370), he wrote directly to Patriarch Philotheos requesting that a certain bishop Anthony be appointed as Metropolitan of Galicia. The letter of Casimir which – as we have seen earlier – gives the list of four previous metropolitans, as an illustration of its otherwise unsubstantiated affirmation that the metropolitanate of Galicia has existed 'from all times' (ἐξ αἰῶνος αἰώνων) is preserved in a very rough Greek text, composed by a clerk, whose native tongue was clearly Slavic.[54] Politely, Casimir, 'King of Poland and Little Russia' (κράλης τῆς γῆς τῆς Λαχίας καὶ τῆς Μικρᾶς 'Ρωσίας) calls himself 'son' of the patriarch, informs him that he has 'acquired' the land of Russia and that he is concerned that 'the law of the Russians' (i.e. Orthodox Christianity) may disappear (ἵνα μὴ ὁ νόμος χαωθῇ τῶν 'Ρώσων), unless a metropolitan is appointed in Galicia. If such an appointment is not made, he will proceed with 'baptizing the Russians into the faith of the Latins'.[55]

This last threat – which occurred at the very time when Philotheos was being faced with the conversion of his own sovereign, John V, in Rome – produced the needed effect: Anthony, who made the voyage to Constantinople and remained

---

[52] Olgerd's letter is not dated in the patriarchal register, but it is mentioned in the correspondence between Philotheos and Alexis in May–August 1371 (MM, I, 320; on the date of this last text and its attribution to Philotheos, see A. Pavlov, RIB, VI, Suppl., pp. 155–6, and J. Darrouzès, *op. cit.*, p. 54).

[53] Cf. above, Ch. 3, pp. 64–7.

[54] MM, I, pp. 577–8; cf. a translation of the letter below, App. 4, p. 287.

[55] On the practice of rebaptizing Orthodox converts to Roman Catholicism, see above, Ch. 3, p. 66.

there several months, was appointed Metropolitan of Galicia in May 1371.[56] The synodal decree of his appointment confirms the danger – mentioned by Casimir himself – of total ecclesiastical disintegration in the region: Anthony is the only Orthodox bishop left in territories controlled by the Poles, so that he would need the help of the neighbouring 'metropolitan of Ouggrovlachia' to perform episcopal consecrations and fill the empty dioceses.[57] The limits of the actual jurisdiction of Anthony are not spelled out very clearly in the patriarchal documents of 1370: his authority over the dioceses of Volhynia (Kholm, Turov and Vladimir) and, even, in the Galician diocese of Peremyshl', are described as temporary, 'until the end of the struggles happening there',[58] i.e. until the achievement of a stable political situation in the area. Writing to Alexis in order to explain his actions both in Galicia and – as we see below – in Lithuanian-controlled territories, Patriarch Philotheos is apologetic and candid. He reiterates his confidence in the metropolitan 'of all Russia', but also regrets that Alexis 'has abandoned all the Christians found there [in Galicia]', that 'he sits in one part [Moscow], and leaves another without pastoral care, without instruction and spiritual supervision'. Since he 'did not visit and did not supervise Little Russia for so many years', King Casimir 'who also rules over Little Russia', has protested, threatening to 'baptize the Russians into the Latin faith'. The establishment of the metropolitanate of Galicia is, therefore, motivated by the obvious interests of the Orthodox Church. 'If the ruler of the place had been Orthodox and belonged to our faith, we could perhaps have temporized and postponed this affair: we would have done so for your sake, even if this would not have

---

[56] MM, I, 578–80.

[57] Orthodox canon law contains the strict requirement that 'two or three' bishops take part in every episcopal consecration (cf. Apostolic Canon 1, Rhalles-Potles, II, p. 4). The 'metropolitanate of Ouggrovlachia', with centre in Argeš, in Vallachia, had been established in 1359 and was undoubtedly of much easier access from Galicia than Moscow (cf. MM, I, 383–5).

[58] MM, I, 579. Curiously, when he writes to Metropolitan Alexis about the restoration of the metropolitanate of Galicia, Philotheos omits Turov in the list of dioceses submitted to Anthony; he also explicitly maintains Lutsk – which is outside of Casimir's conquests – in the jurisdiction of Kiev (cf. MM, I, 583; on this problem, see Tikhomirov, *Galitskaya mitropoliya*, pp. 114–17; an up-to-date map of the conquests of Casimir in 1370, in P. W. Knoll, *op. cit.*, pp. 198–9). It appears, therefore, that the limits of the metropolitanate of Galicia were not stable. For instance one has the firm information that in 1376–7, a bishop of Vladimir-in-Volhynia is consecrated by Metropolitan Cyprian of Kiev, and not by Anthony (RIB, VI, col. 181). However, by that date, the latter may already have been dead (cf. below, Chap. 9, n. 11, p. 202).

been advisable. But since he is not one of ours, but a Latin, how could we refuse his request? He would have immediately appointed a Latin metropolitan, as he said, and baptized the Russians into the faith of the Latins . . . I thank God that he did not act in this way, but wrote to us and requested a metropolitan . . . For this reason we were forced to consecrate his candidate, since we could not act otherwise.'[59] Further developments will prove that the relative confidence and gratitude, expressed by Philotheos towards the Polish king were not justified: the Polish conquest was soon followed with further development of the established Latin hierarchy in 'Little Russia' and with violent measures of discrimination against the Orthodox.[60] However, Philotheos may well have been right in appointing Anthony, who, in spite of adverse circumstances, succeeded in maintaining the Orthodox faith in the region, and also in ordaining Orthodox bishops in neighbouring Moldavia, where Polish and Roman Catholic pressure was also strong and where a separate metropolitanate was established only in 1401.[61]

The change in the Russian policies of Patriarch Philotheos in 1371 were motivated not only by Polish pressure in 'Little Russia' – in fact, a local problem – but also and primarily by the more explicit and more powerful assertion of Olgerd's power and his claim to rule over the whole of Russia. The support given by Philotheos to Muscovite policies before June 1370, which was also expressed in letters addressed to Olgerd himself,[62] provoked a sharp reply by the Grand-prince of Lithuania.[63] Drafted, as was

---

[59] MM, I, 583.

[60] In 1372, Pope Gregory XI ordered the archbishop of Cracow to assign a Latin bishop to Halich, Peremyshl, Vladimir and Kholm and to 'remove' the 'schismatic bishops' who were 'said to be there' (cf. G. Mollat, *Lettres secrètes et curiales du pape Grégoire XI (1370–1378) intéressant les pays autres que la France*, Paris, 1962, Nos. 878, 884). In 1375, the papal order was carried out. Metropolitan Anthony was forced to leave Halich and reside outside of the city (cf. Tikhomirov, *op. cit.*, pp. 118–20; I. Nazarko, 'Galits'ka Mitropoliya', in *Analecta Ordinis S. Basilii Magni*, ser. II, sect. II, vol. III (1–2), Rome, 1958, p. 177).

[61] Cf. MM, II, 528–30; cf. also below, p. 250.

[62] These letters are not preserved, but they are mentioned in Olgerd's reply (MM, I, 580), and in the letter of Philotheos to Alexis (MM, I, 583: ἔγραψα πρὸς ἐκεῖνον περὶ τούτου).

[63] For the probable date see Darrouzès, *Régistre*, p. 117, note 135. The letters of Casimir and Olgerd have manifestly reached Constantinople at the same approximate time, since Philotheos reports their content to Alexis in the same letter of August 1371 (MM, I, 582–5). In the patriarchal register Olgerd is addressed as βασιλεύς τῶν Λητβῶν, but the title is corrected to ῥήξ, which was applied in Byzantine documents to all Russian princes (MM, I, 580–1); cf. Eng. transl. below, App. 5, pp. 288–9.

also the letter of Casimir, by a Slavic-speaking member of his staff, the *pittakion* of Olgerd lists the hostile actions of the Muscovite government, headed by Alexis, especially those concerned with Olgerd's relatives – Michael of Tver and Boris of Nizhni-Novgorod – and launches personal attacks on both the patriarch and the metropolitan. 'With your blessing', he writes to Philotheos, 'their metropolitan, even now, blesses bloodshed. Never, even at the times of our fathers, were there metropolitans like this metropolitan: he blesses the Muscovites (τοὺς Μοσχοβιώτας) to bloodshed, but he never comes to our parts and does not visit Kiev. And whoever pledges allegiance ['kisses the cross'] to me and then defects to them, he frees him from his pledge . . .'

In addition to these well motivated complaints, Olgerd also mentioned the possibility of a common front against the Latin danger: 'The metropolitan', he wrote, 'should have blessed the Muscovites to help us fight the Germans (μετὰ τῶν 'Αλαμάνων) [i.e. the Teutonic Knights], for we fight in their interests'. This was certainly a point which could not be lightly overlooked by Philotheos, who was faced by the crusading spirit of the Latin West in various other regions, particularly Galicia and Bulgaria.[64] The long record of hostility by Lithuania to the Teutonic Order was certainly the greatest credit of Olgerd in the eyes of the Byzantines, so that a reconciliation between the 'two Russias' on the basis of their common interests vis-à-vis the Order on the one hand, and the Tatars on the other, was to become, precisely around 1370, one of the highest diplomatic priorities for Philotheos and his followers.

However, in the conclusion of his letter, Olgerd was asking the patriarch for an impossible favour: the establishment of a second metropolitanate, whose jurisdiction would cover not only the traditional territory of the old 'metropolitanate of Lithuania', which existed in the first half of the century, but all the principalities allied with Olgerd. 'Give us another metropolitan', the Lithuanian prince wrote, 'for Kiev, Smolensk, Tver, Little Russia, Novosil', Nizhni-Novgorod.'[65] Clearly what Olgerd was demanding, was a new metropolitan who would be much more a primate 'of all Russia' than Alexis: he would control not only the tradi-

---

[64] In 1365–6, Stracimir, son of King John-Alexander of Bulgaria, was rebaptized by Franciscan monks, together with thousands of Bulgarians, in the city of Vidin, which had been captured by Louis of Hungary (Document issued by the General of the Franciscans, in L. Wadding, ed., *Annales minorum*, VIII, Rome, 1783, pp. 196–7; cf. J. Meyendorff, 'Projets', pp. 153–5).

[65] MM, I, 581.

tional primatial see of Kiev, and not only such dioceses as Tver and Smolensk, which were never connected with the metropolitanate of Lithuania, but even Nizhni-Novgorod and Novosil', which were situated far to the East and South of Moscow. And since, in 1370, the intentions of Olgerd included the capture of Moscow itself, his plan for the Russian Church was clearly to control it entirely.

Possibly, the Lithuanian Grand-prince was also planning his own personal conversion to Orthodox Christianity, since, according to Nicephorus Gregoras, such was his intention already in 1354[66] and since most of the members of his dynasty had converted already, but no Byzantine or Russian document of that period mentions this possibility explicitly. In any case, Philotheos who, in the period immediately following his second assumption of the patriarchate (1364) had solemnly canonized the Lithuanian martyrs, whom Olgerd had executed,[67] was probably not yet in the mood to trust him to the point of giving Lithuania full control of the Church and, therefore, of all Byzantine interests in Russia. But never before was Vilna so close to superseding Moscow, as capital of a future unified Russia: the diplomacy of Patriarch Philotheos may have been the decisive factor which prevented this from happening.

The rapid sequence of the events happening in 1370–2 is difficult to describe in detail. What is certain, however, is that Philotheos did not succumb to Olgerd's pressure and authoritatively pushed towards peaceful solutions, which alone could restore the somewhat shattered prestige of his appointee, Metropolitan Alexis, in areas hostile to Moscow. To Olgerd, the patriarch wrote, exhorting him 'to love and respect [metropolitan Alexis] according to the ancient custom, as the other princes of Russia do, and to show respect, attention and great love [for the metropolitan], when the latter visits his territories, so that [the metropolitan] may travel throughout these territories without difficulty'.[68] Such instructions were indeed needed since Alexis had been molested in Kiev in 1359. But the patriarch also gave stern instructions to Alexis about Olgerd, whom he now seemed to recognize not as an 'impious fire-worshipper', but as a respectable Russian prince: 'You also', he wrote to Alexis, 'as far as this is possible, make sure to show him love and good disposition; relate to him, as you do to

---

[66] Cf. above, Ch. 7, p. 146.   [67] Cf. above, pp. 187–8.
[68] The actual answer of Philotheos to Olgerd is unfortunately not preserved, but it is quoted in a letter to Alexis (MM, I, 321; on this document, its date and attribution, see above, n. 52).

the other princes, because the Christian people, the people of the Lord, which is presently under his rule, needs your supervision and your instruction; therefore, it is quite imperative that there be love between you and him, so that you may meet him and his people, in order to teach them. Do this with every zeal and without any objection.'[69] John Dokianos, an envoy of the patriarch, departed for Moscow with additional oral instructions.

Did these exhortations have any effect? It seems so. For the Russian chronicles signal that, after the unsuccessful Lithuanian campaign against Moscow, Olgerd's ambassadors were in Moscow in 1371 and arranged for a marriage between two junior members of the Muscovite and Lithuanian dynasties.[70] No major Lithuanian operations took place before Olgerd's death (1377), and the eventual appointment of another metropolitan in 1375 for Lithuanian-controlled parts of Russia was not, as we will see below, to be the drastic kind of move envisaged by Olgerd in 1370, but, rather an ad hoc diplomatic manoeuvre aimed at preserving the unity of the metropolitanate.

While this correspondence between Olgerd, Alexis and Philotheos was taking place, the patriarch became involved also in the struggle between Moscow and Tver. It may well be that patriarchal diplomacy, exercising its soothing effect upon relations between Moscow and Lithuania, had actually deprived Prince Michael Aleksandrovich of Tver of unconditional support by Olgerd. In any case, the unfortunate prince, deceived by the Muscovites and excommunicated by Alexis, formally appealed to Constantinople. Supported by his bishop Basil – who also had been sanctioned by the metropolitan – Michael sent Archimandrite Theodosius to the Byzantine capital asking for justice. He may have been encouraged by the fact that the Golden Horde, disturbed by Moscow's power, had just bestowed upon him the Grand-principality.[71] Having received the formal appeal, Philotheos, in September 1371, accepted the role of supreme judge and invited both parties to send proxies to Constantinople for a judgement to be rendered by September 1372.[72] However, he also – as he did in the case of Lithuania – exhorted Alexis to act as an impartial shepherd of his flock and not as a political leader. 'I see nothing good', writes Philotheos, 'in that you indulge in scandalous conflicts with Michael, Prince of Tver, and that you both go to

[69] MM, I, 321–3; cf. below, App. 6, pp. 290–1.
[70] *Troits.*, p. 392 (cf. above, p. 183).   [71] *Rog.*, col. 95.
[72] Letter to Alexis (MM, I, 585–6), to Michael (*ibid.*, 586).

[ecclesiastical] court. Try to make peace with him, as his father and teacher, and if he is wrong somewhat, you, as a father, forgive him and accept him as your son . . . But he also must repent and seek forgiveness, as I demand from him in writing . . . Your Holiness knows perfectly well that, when we consecrated you, we made you Metropolitan of Kiev and all Russia: not of a part only, but of all Russia. But now I hear that you visit neither Kiev, nor Lithuania, but stay in one place . . . This is contrary to the tradition of the holy canons. It is your obligation to oversee the whole land of Russia, to nourish love and a fatherly disposition towards all princes, and to love them equally . . .'[73]

If the metropolitan is thus exhorted to solve the conflict peacefully, the patriarch sends the same appeal to Grand-prince Michael. 'Abandon the scandals and judicial procedures; go and make peace with your father, the metropolitan, and seek his forgiveness . . . And if you both make peace, according to my instructions, then let both yourself and the metropolitan send me your envoys to inform me. I will then love you, pray for you, bless you, forgive you and have you as my true son.'[74]

It does not seem that the parties accepted the patriarchal summons. No sources indicate that their proxies ever went to Constantinople. However, in the midst of a series of spectacular reversals in the struggle between Tver and Moscow, described earlier, the policies of Philotheos in Russia were very actively and skilfully pursued by a special patriarchal envoy, the Bulgarian monk Cyprian, one of the most brilliant personalities of Eastern Orthodoxy in the fourteenth century.[75]

He arrived in Lithuanian-controlled territories at the end of 1373 and reached a quick understanding with Olgerd. Quite remarkably, at the end of the same year, Michael of Tver and Dimitri of Moscow also reached a peace agreement. Michael resigned the prerogatives of a Grand-prince and, presumably, the canonical sanctions issued by Metropolitan Alexis were lifted. The agreement implied a major setback for the divisive diplomacy of the Horde. It is greeted by a Tverian chronicler as 'a relief for Christians who rejoiced with a great joy, whereas their [Mongol] enemies were put to shame'.[76] In the same year, the menace of a military confrontation between Muscovites and Lithuanians near

[73] MM, I, 321. [74] MM, I, 591.
[75] On Cyprian, see particularly Obolensky, *Philorhomaios*, also Tachiaos, Κυπριανὸς. On his mission to Russia in 1372–5, see particularly, Prokhorov, *Povest'*, pp. 25–31.
[76] *Rog.*, col. 105; cf. also the praises for the success of the mission of Cyprian in the patriarchal *act* of 1389, MM, II, pp. 118–19.

Lyubutsk ended in a peace agreement.[77] We do not know whether Cyprian participated directly in this peace-making, which resulted briefly in what a historian recently called an anti-Tatar alliance grouping Moscow, Tver and Olgerd, but one may presume that he did, for on 9 March 1374, he is present in Tver, together with Metropolitan Alexis himself, who visited the rebellious city and consecrated a new bishop, Euthymius. On the same year, Cyprian's friend Dionysius was consecrated bishop of Suzdal.[78] Cyprian further accompanied the metropolitan to Pereyaslavl', for the important princely meeting of 1375, whereas Bishop Dionysius witnessed the execution of the Tatar ambassador, Saraika, in Nizhni-Novgorod.[79]

Following the departure of the metropolitan and of the patriarchal envoy, Prince Michael Aleksandrovich of Tver became again involved in an anti-Muscovite plot, which was organized by a mysterious personage named Nekomat of Surozh, a representative of Genoese interests,[80] and which included the Tatars and Lithuania. Facing this last attempt at Tverian separatism, Dimitri and his allies marched upon Tver and forced Michael to capitulate in late August 1375. The distinctive Genoese and Tatar involvement in these events on the side of Tver were certainly enough to compromise Michael in the eyes of the patriarchal envoy Cyprian, whose superior in Constantinople, Patriarch Philotheos, as well as his friend Cantacuzenos, were the leaders of the anti-Genoese party in Byzantium. Again, Moscow appeared as a more reliable ally than other princes of Russia. The short-lived attempt of Philotheos to be even-handed in dealing with the conflict between Tver and Moscow, was betrayed by Tver, so that Moscow's ultimate victory became inevitable.

In the light of all these facts, it becomes apparent that the change in the attitude of the Byzantine patriarchate in 1370 was tactical, and not ideological. The principle of the unity of Byzantine ecclesiastical administration was not abandoned, but only adjusted to new realities. The restoration of a metropolitanate in Galicia was a condition for the Church's survival in Poland, and was presented as a temporary measure. In the rest of Russia, the conquests of Olgerd expanded so rapidly in the sixties, that a metropolitan residing in Moscow and, in addition, heading the Muscovite government itself, could no longer be expected to

---

[77] *Troits.*, p. 395.   [78] *Ibid.*   [79] *Troits.*, p. 398.
[80] Prokhorov, *Etnicheskaya integratsiya*, pp. 102–3 and *Povest*, pp. 31–8. On Nekomat and the Genoese, see below, Ch. 9, p. 223; cf. *Rog.*, cols. 109–10.

administer the territories under Lithuanian control. The pressure to divide the metropolitanate, as Callistos had done in 1355, became very strong. However, Philotheos did not succumb to these pressures. He only instructed Alexis to adopt a more even-handed and a less political attitude towards the enemies of Moscow, and he obtained some results on this account. War with Lithuania subsided and the Tverian problem was solved. However, since Alexis was almost an octogenerian, the urgent problem of his succession was the real key to the future, and Philotheos decided to handle it in a way which would avoid the division of the metropolitanate. The architect of the elaborate diplomatic game needed to attain that goal will be the Bulgarian monk Cyprian, envoy of Philotheos to Russia in 1372–3, and a close friend of monastic circles in northern Russia. His remarkable personality dominates the ecclesiastical, cultural and political situation in Russia after 1370. Byzantino-Russian relations, relations with the Latin West, historiography, hagiography and liturgical practice have all been marked by his personality and ideas, which – just as those of Philotheos Kokkinos and John Cantacuzenos – implied the unity of the Byzantine Orthodox Commonwealth and envisaged Russia, from the Carpathians to the Volga, as an inseparable part of it. The major obstacles which stood in the way of this programme were, on the one hand, the rivalry between Moscow and Lithuania, and, on the other, the Golden Horde, whose oppressive rule in Russia was perpetuated precisely by the struggles between various Russian rulers.

The new political situation clearly required peace and, possibly, alliance, between Moscow and Lithuania. Obviously, this went against some traditional patterns, which were taken for granted in Moscow. The Muscovites were expecting all-out support from the Church for their immediate interests, as it existed in the times of metropolitans Peter and Theognostos, culminating in the assumption of the regency by Alexis. A form of provincial nationalism, nourished by hatred for the Lithuanian dynasty and traditional servility towards the Horde, was promoted by powerful circles in Moscow. They provoked resistance, and even violent opposition to Cyprian and also found allies in the pro-Genoese party in Constantinople.

The appointment of Cyprian as metropolitan turned out to be the last major action of Patriarch Philotheos, relating to Russia, but it also signalled the beginning of a new crisis to be discussed in the next chapter.

9

Metropolitan Cyprian and Moscow's separatism (1376–1381)

On 2 December 1375, in Constantinople, Philotheos consecrated his former envoy to Russia, the Bulgarian monk Cyprian, as 'Metropolitan of Kiev, Russia and Lithuania'.[1] The title was unusual, as well as the timing: Metropolitan Alexis was still alive and his title was 'metropolitan of Kiev and all Russia'. It is understandable, therefore, that those who were politically, or ideologically opposed to both Philotheos and Cyprian, considered his appointment as uncanonical.[2] However, the more candid account, found in the *Act* of Patriarch Anthony (1389)[3] reflects the motivations of Philotheos, which were notably different from the deliberate desire to divide the metropolitanate, as was the case with the consecration of Roman by Callistos in 1355. While recognizing that the appointment of another metropolitan during the lifetime of the incumbent required the exercise of 'extreme *oikonomia*' (οἰκονομίᾳ μεγίστῃ χρησάμενος),[4] Philotheos was concerned that,

---

[1] The date is given by Cyprian himself in his *Last Will*, reproduced in the chronicle (*Nik.* p. 196); cf. Golubinsky, *Istoriya*, p. 214. The original title of the new metropolitan is found in the synodal act of 1389, MM, II, 120. Tinnefeld ('Kirchenpolitik', p. 375), on the basis of the Act of 1380 (MM, II, 14), considers that the official title of Cyprian was Κυέβου καὶ Λιτβῶν. However, the Act of 1380 is notoriously inaccurate in quoting titles (it also refers to the title as Λιτβῶν καὶ Μικρᾶς 'Ρωσίας, MM, II, 13). In fact, Cyprian always claimed that he was originally consecrated as Metropolitan 'of Russia'.

[2] This is the case, in particular, with the synodal act of Patriarch Neilos of 1380, of which we will speak later (MM, II, 12–18).

[3] The consecration of Cyprian and the subsequent events received different interpretations in 1380 (II, 12–18) and in 1389 (II, 116–29) for reasons which will soon become clear. The account of 1389, however, appears to be in general more objective and more accurate (cf. Obolensky, *Philorhomaios*, pp. 87–8), cf. large excerpts of both documents translated below, App. 10, pp. 304–8.

[4] The Byzantine canonical concept of *oikonomia* is frequently and inaccurately interpreted as implying an arbitrary use of canons to suit political expediency. In fact, however, the theory of *oikonomia* presupposes a concern for the salvation of 'the multitude', which sometimes cannot be assured, if one adheres to a strict and formal application of canonical rules, and is based on the biblical use of the term

in territories controlled by Olgerd, 'such a numerous nation was abandoned without episcopal supervision, and was in danger of utter catastrophe and spiritual perdition, by being united to another church'. He did not however want 'to divide Russia into two metropolitanates', and, therefore, appointed Cyprian, as metropolitan 'of those parts, which for many years had been left by Metropolitan Alexis outside of his pastoral care'. The policy of the patriarchate was still that 'the ancient state of affairs should be returned again in the future under one metropolitan'. So the act of election of December 1375 (συνοδικὴ πρᾶξις) stipulated that 'Cyprian, after the death of Alexis, should assume jurisdiction over the whole of Russia and be metropolitan "of all Russia"'.[5]

Philotheos was thus consistent with the attitude which he adopted in 1370: a metropolitan, as politically committed as Alexis was, on the side of Moscow, was not in a position to sustain the unity of the metropolitanate and the interests of the Byzantine Commonwealth.[6] On the other hand, the situation was so urgent, that it was impossible to wait for the death of Alexis, whose friendship and loyalty Philotheos also appreciated. Thus, the shrewd patriarch resolved the dilemma by adopting a temporary *oikonomia*, with the help of a trusted diplomat, whose expertise in peacemaking between Russian princes was proven effective in 1373–5 and whose close personal ties, not only with Alexis, but also with the leaders of Russian monasticism – particularly St Sergius – were considered sufficient to make him eventually acceptable as metropolitan 'of all Russia'.

We know relatively little about Cyprian's background before

(cf. Meyendorff, *Byzantine Theology*, pp. 88–90). In the case of the appointment of Cyprian, *oikonomia* involved concern for the Orthodox population of Olgerd's domains.

[5] MM, II, 120. The synodal act of 1375 is, unfortunately, not preserved, except for a brief fragment (Act of 1389, MM, II, p. 120), but its content is discussed and criticized in the act of 1380 (MM, II, 12–18). This latter text confirms the information that Olgerd was threatening to appoint a metropolitan of the Latin faith in Lithuania (*ibid.*, p. 16). Most Russian historians, including particularly E. E. Golubinsky, following the views expressed in the act of 1380, consider the appointment of Cyprian as a gesture of hostility to Alexis and detrimental to the unity of the metropolitanate. For the contrary view with which I concur, see A. E. Presnyakov, *Obrazovanie Velikorusskago Gosudarstva*, Petrograd, 1918, pp. 314–17; and I. N. Shabatin, 'Iz istorii russkoi tserkvi', *Vestnik russkogo-zapadnoevropeiskogo patriarshego Ekzarkhata*, 49, 1965, pp. 43–5.

[6] In all the documents issued by the patriarchate after 1370 and also in the letter of Cyprian to St Sergius, the only reproach addressed to the otherwise highly respected figure of Alexis is his inability – or unwillingness – to visit Kiev, 'Little Russia' and Lithuania.

his arrival in Russia.[7] It does not seem that he really belonged to the Bulgarian family of the Tsamblaks, as has been widely assumed, because the meaning of the one text upon which this assumption is based is not fully clear.[8] But he was certainly a Bulgarian, who had been a monk on Mount Athos[9] before entering the service of Patriarch Philotheos, becoming a member of his immediate entourage (οἰκεῖος καλόγηρος),[10] while also preserving his personal connections in Bulgaria. A diplomat, a translator of numerous Byzantine texts into Slavic, a promoter of hesychast spirituality and ideas and a loyal supporter of the patriarchate of Constantinople, Cyprian, after years of struggle, eventually succeeded in his difficult mission and occupied the metropolitan's throne in Moscow. But this will occur, on a permanent basis, only in 1390.

But there is no doubt that this was his goal from the moment of his consecration. He never intended – neither was this the intention of Patriarch Philotheos – to remain a metropolitan of Lithuania only, but his activities were directed at restoring the affairs of the one Metropolitanate of Kiev. Arriving in Kiev from Byzantium on 9 June 1376,[11] he succeeded in making full use both on Lithuanian and Polish territories of the political and ecclesiastical independence which belonged to him as a patriarchal and imperial envoy. He consecrated a bishop to the long vacant see of Vladimir-in-Volhynia and restored the properties of the metropolitan's residence in Novgorodok and of St Sophia cathedral in Kiev. He undoubtedly gained the confidence of Olgerd, and later of his son Jagiello, who probably was an Orthodox Christian. But he

[7] Among the recent studies on Cyprian, see particularly Tachiaos, Κυπριανός, pp. 163–241; Dmitriev, 'Rol' i znachenie', pp. 215–64; Obolensky, *Philorhomaios*.

[8] The text is by the Metropolitan of Kiev, Gregory Tsamblak (1415–19), who speaks of Cyprian as 'the brother of our father' (ed. Angelov, *Iz starata*, p. 185), which has been generally interpreted as meaning that Cyprian was Gregory's uncle, and therefore a Tsamblak. But the text may also be an allusion to the spiritual ties between Cyprian and Patriarch Euthymius of Trnovo, the common 'father' of Bulgarian monks (cf. J. Holthusen, 'Neues zur Erklärung des Nadgrobnoe Slovo von Grigorij Camblak auf den Moskauer Metropoliten Kiprian', *Slavistische Studien zum VI. Internationalen Slavistenkongress in Prag 1968*, Munich, 1968, pp. 372–82).

[9] He testifies himself to his sojourn on the Holy Mountain in his *Answers* to St Athanasius Vysotsky (RIB, vi, col. 263). [10] MM, ii, 118.

[11] He indicates the date himself in his extremely interesting personal letter to St. Sergius and other monks, written on 23 June, 1378, RIB, VI, col. 181–2. (tr. below, App. 8, p. 296). The letter also contains information about his activities in 1376–8. The consecration of a bishop for the diocese of Vladimir-in-Volhynia, which belonged to the Metropolitan of Halich, seems to indicate that Anthony of Galicia was already dead and that 'Little Russia' was placed by Philotheos under the jurisdiction of Cyprian. This seems to be confirmed by the appointment, in 1381, of a new Metropolitan of Galicia (his name is unknown) by Patriarch Neilos (Rhalles-Potles, v, p. 305; cf. Sokolov, *Arkhierei*, p. 536).

also remained faithful in principle to the official Byzantine position on the hierarchical distinctions between Russian princes. As Canta-cuzenos had done in 1347, he reaffirmed the primacy of the Grand-prince of Vladimir-Moscow: 'I prayed God for him', he writes to St Sergius, 'for his princess and his children; I love him from my whole heart and wished well to him and his domain . . . And wherever I celebrated a solemn liturgy, I ordered that the ceremonial acclamation of "many years" be sung to him first, and then to others.'[12] Having probed the situation in Novgorod by announcing to the local archbishop his appointment by Patriarch Philotheos, he respected the loyalty to Moscow expressed by the Novgorodians.[13]

In his letter to St Sergius, Cyprian also claims that he interceded with Olgerd for pro-Muscovite prisoners (particularly from Kashin).

But these expressions of loyalty by Cyprian towards Grand-prince Dimitri remained insufficient as a means of reconciling the Muscovite government with the fact of his appointment to Kiev. Muscovite circles, which exercised a prevailing influence on the Grand-prince – the 'boyar-party'[14] – considered that since, after the fall of Tver (1375), the menacing anti-Muscovite axis, includ-ing Olgerd, Tver and the Horde was no more in existence, the interests of the Grand-principality would be best served by a return to the old pattern of loyalty to the Tatars and friendship with their allies, the Genoese merchants. This party had little con-cern for the wider unity of the 'Russian land' which included the entire south-western domain of the former Kiev realm. It was rather moved by immediate and local concerns and intended to use the metropolitanate as an instrument of provincial, Muscovite interests within the framework of the Mongol empire. It saw no use in an alliance with Lithuania, in the name of liberation from the Tatar yoke, because such an alliance would have deprived Moscow of its newly acquired sense of self-sufficiency and local nationalism.

Such provincial views were not shared by all in Moscow, how-ever. The monastic and ecclesiastical circles, nourished by the universalist ideology of the Byzantine tradition, considered that a 'metropolitanate of all Russia' was unthinkable, unless it included Kiev and the entire south-west, and favoured a coalition of all

---

[12] *Ibid.* He must also have been behind the project of marriage between Jagiello and a daughter of Dimitri, which was negociated after the death of Olgerd (L. Cherepnin, 'Dogovornye i dukhovnye gramoty Dimitriya Donskogo', *Istoricheskie Zapiski*, 24 (1947), pp. 247–50). [13] *Novg.*, p. 374 (Engl. tr., p. 155).
[14] See particularly Prokhorov, 'Etnicheskaya integratsiya', pp. 104–5.

Russian princes against the Tatars. Cyprian, when he visited Lithuania, Tver and Muscovy in 1373–4, promoted such a coalition and was able to gather a substantial following, which included St Sergius and Theodore, Abbot of Simonovsky. The correspondence between these leaders of Russian monasticism with Cyprian in 1378 proves that they also supported his candidacy as metropolitan. Furthermore it appears that the aged Metropolitan Alexis himself who, in the fifties and sixties, as regent of the Muscovite state, had perforce become the very symbol of Muscovite nationalism, had, in his later days, understood the dimensions of the political dilemma, faced by the Church, and had become a supporter of Cyprian's views. Since Cyprian is seen both by his own enemies and by many contemporaries as a challenger to Alexis, the basic concurrence in the views of these two major figures of Russian ecclesiastical history is of crucial importance. It can be deduced from the following facts: (1) the close contacts between Cyprian and Alexis, during Cyprian's first trip to Russia (1373–5) are well attested in the chronicles,[15] and in 1378, confirmed by Cyprian himself, who indignantly protests against attempts at counting Alexis among his enemies;[16] furthermore, the synodal act of 1380 – virulently hostile to Cyprian and attempting to interpret negatively every one of his actions – recognizes that the mission of Cyprian in 1373 was one of peace between princes (εἰρηνεύσοντα αὐτοὺς μετ' ἀλλήλων), that Metropolitan Alexis, in 1375, was fully convinced of Cyprian's good intentions and was favourably disposed towards him (τὴν ὑπὲρ αὐτοῦ πᾶσαν ἀναδεξαμένου φροντίδα), being his 'friend' (φίλος).[17] (2) That, in 1374, Metropolitan Alexis consecrated Archimandrite Dionysius, a proven supporter of the monastic party and of loyalty towards Byzantium as bishop of Suzdal[18] and, before his death, recommended St Sergius of Radonezh as his successor to the metropolitanate.[19] (3) That, upon the arrival of Cyprian to Kiev in 1376, whereas Grand-prince Dimitri expressed formal opposition, Alexis – even according to the act of 1380 – made every effort to appease the minds through encyclicals and personal advice.[20]

[15] Cf. above, Ch. 8, pp. 197–8.
[16] 'They utter calumnies against our brother, the metropolitan', *Letter to Sergius*, RIB, VI, 180.
[17] MM, II, 13–14.   [18] *Troits.*, p. 395.
[19] Epiphanius, *Life of Sergius*, ed. N. S. Tikhonravov (repr. L. Müller), pp. 55–6.
[20] Θροῦς δ' ἐπιγείρεται μὲν πλεῖστος ..., καταστέλλεται δ' ὅμως ταῖς τοῦ μητροπολίτου Ἀλεξίου καὶ κοινῇ πρὸς ἅπαντας καὶ ἰδίᾳ πρὸς ἕκαστον συχναῖς ὑποθήκαις καὶ συμβουλαῖς, MM, II, 14; cf. also P. Sokolov, *Arkhierei*, p. 462.

If Alexis had expressed a formal canonical protest against Cyprian's appointment, the *Act* would certainly have mentioned it. One should rather think that Patriarch Philotheos took pains to explain the appointment of Cyprian as a means of maintaining the unity of the metropolitanate after the death of Alexis, that these explanations were brought to Alexis in the winter of 1375–6 by two special patriarchal envoys, the Greek protodeacons Georges and John,[21] and were considered as satisfactory by the old metropolitan.

These facts also confirm Cyprian's understanding of the last will of Alexis, a problem which we will discuss below: it is highly unlikely that the metropolitan succumbed to the pressure of the 'boyar' party and suggested the appointment of Michael-Mityai, sanctioning the division of the metropolitanate.

In the years which followed the consecration of Cyprian as Metropolitan of Kiev, three major protagonists of the great Russian drama left the scene of history. In 1376, Philotheos was deposed from the patriarchate by the pro-Genoese Emperor Andronicus IV. In 1377, Olgerd of Lithuania died, leaving the Grand-principality to his son Jagiello, an Orthodox Christian with whom Cyprian entertained close connections. Finally, Alexis, already an octogenarian, died on 12 February 1378 and his death opened a new and prolonged crisis in the relations between Byzantium and Russia.

I. BYZANTIUM, THE GENOESE AND THE GOLDEN HORDE

We have spoken earlier of the importance of the Genoese and Venetian settlements on the northern shores of the Black Sea for the understanding of East European history in the fourteenth century. With the Genoese in control of Galata, in Constantinople itself, and the Venetians holding solid positions in the Aegean and the Crimea, the Byzantine Empire could make no substantial foreign policy decision involving Italian interests without the acquiescence of either Venice, or Genoa. However, the fierce competition which opposed the two Italian republics to each other sometimes allowed for, at least, some leverage. John VI Cantacuzenos (1347–54) tried to liberate Byzantium from the Genoese grip with the help of the Venetians, but failed. The Genoese,

---

[21] *Troits.*, p. 401. One is tempted to identify the two protodeacons with the seasoned Byzantine experts in Russian affairs, George Perdikes and John Dokianos, cf. Prokhorov, *Povest'*, pp. 48–9.

helped by the advancing Ottoman Turks – to whom they had offered economic advantages – contributed to the restoration of John V and the retirement of Cantacuzenos in 1354.

The unsuccessful voyage of John V to Rome (1369–70), which showed that the Papacy – even after the formal conversion of the emperor to the Roman faith – was not in a position to provide help, or even to put an end to the debilitating rivalries between Venice and Genoa, was followed by the stunning victory of Sultan Murad on the Maritsa over the Serbs (1371), which secured Turkish control over much of the Balkans. In 1372–3, John V concluded a treaty with Murad, which made him practically a vassal of the Turks.

This new situation did not put an end to the struggle between the Italian republics. The only difference was that both Venice and Genoa were now treating with Murad, rather than with the Byzantines, seating or unseating Greek emperors with Turkish co-operation. Thus, in 1376, John V, who had ceded the island of Tenedos to Venice, was deposed – with Turkish help – by the Genoese, in favour of his son Andronicus IV, who had promised the said island to Genoa.

We have seen earlier that the obvious commercial interests of the Genoese required cooperation with the Golden Horde. It is therefore quite natural that Genoese diplomats and merchants were also ready to give the Tatars a helping hand in maintaining their control of Russia. Information about Genoese activities in Moscow is scarce,[22] but the Russian chronicles mention the role of the *Surozhane* (inhabitants of Surozh, or Sougdaia), whose nationality is not always clear,[23] but whose political activities are fairly obvious. After 1370, they are seen actively opposing the plans for a reconciliation between Moscow, Tver and Lithuania, which were promoted by Patriarch Philotheos and his envoy Cyprian and which implied a threat to the control of Russia by Mamai. In 1374, when the reconciliation seemed to have been achieved, the

---

[22] One of the reasons for the scarcity is the absence, in the patriarchal registry, of all the acts pertaining to the tenure of Patriarch Macarios (1376–9), whose appointment by the pro-Genoese Emperor Andronicus IV, was considered as illegitimate.

[23] Among Russian historians, there has been a debate on the question whether the *Surozhane* were Armenians, Greeks, Italians, or Russian merchants connected with Surozh (V. E. Syroechkovsky, *Gosti-Surozhane*, Moscow, 1935; cf. M. V. Levchenko, *Ocherki po istorii russko-vizantiiskikh otnoshenii*, Moscow, 1956, pp. 525–6; M. N. Tikhomirov, 'Puti', p. 22; etc.). The question of the *Surozhane*'s nationality appears rather immaterial to us. Their political role, however, appears clearly in the chronicles as one of Genoese diplomatic agents, supportive of the Tatars. On their role at Kulikovo, see below.

Surozhanin Nekomat, accompanied by a Tatar ambassador, shuttled between Moscow, Tver and Lithuania and, eventually, brought from the Horde a decree appointing Michael of Tver as Grand-prince. Michael then broke his oath of allegiance to Dimitri of Moscow.[24]

The occupation of Tver by the Muscovites in 1375 – a clear challenge to Mamai – was followed by years of hesitation on the part of Dimitri. The boyar party in Moscow favoured the traditional policy of loyalty to the Horde, a policy which in the past was also supported by Byzantium and the Church, but which was now opposed by Philotheos, Cyprian, and their monastic friends in Moscow, who urged peace with Lithuania and the shaking off of the Tatar yoke. Dimitri was pressed to appoint, as successor to Alexis, a metropolitan who would pursue a pro-Tatar policy, even if that meant neglect of the Orthodox population of Lithuania and the end of the unity of the metropolitanate. But such an appointment presupposed the rejection of Cyprian. The several mentions of Genoese money, used for the promotion of a 'Muscovite' metropolitan, show that the Genoese merchants were actively involved in Byzantine and Russian ecclesiastical policy.

The years between 1375 and 1380 represent a period of intense diplomatic manoeuvring. Mamai and his Genoese allies attempted to use diplomacy and money in re-establishing the old Mongol rule upon increasingly restless Russians. A direct military confrontation was envisaged – and dreaded – on both sides. Military skirmishes occurred with mixed results.[25] Finally, in 1380, Mamai decided to settle matters, as his predecessors did so often in the past, by crushing the Russians in a massive military onslaught.

Clearly, these events also involved the future of the Byzantine religious, cultural and political presence in Russia. Until 1376, the strong hand of Patriarch Philotheos had remained remarkably successful in securing this presence. In spite of the humiliations incurred by Emperor John V, the patriarch was in a position to pursue a fully independent policy in Russia, particularly through the intermediary of his friend and envoy Cyprian. This policy consisted in keeping the metropolitanate united, but, since 1370, it also implied promoting reconciliation between Moscow and

---

[24] *Rog.*, pp. 109–10; *Erm.*, p. 110.
[25] In 1376, Dimitri briefly occupied Velikie Bolgary on the upper Volga. In 1377, the Tatars defeated a small Russian army on the river Piyana, but, in 1378, an important punitive expedition, led by one of Mamai's lieutenants, was stopped by the Russians on the river Vozha, south-west of Moscow.

Lithuania in an alliance against the Horde. The internal dissensions in Sarai and the growth of Moscow's power convinced Philotheos that unconditional loyalty to the Tatars was no longer needed, especially since such a loyalty on the part of the Church would imply an ecclesiastical secession of the south-western dioceses and a threat of Latin domination over the Orthodox in Lithuania and 'Little Russia'. Loyalty to the weakening Horde was only in the interest of the Genoese, whom Philotheos – and his friend John Cantacuzenos – had always hated and whose control of Galata and of all the Byzantine economy was the very symbol of the Empire's humiliation. These lofty and far-sighted views of Philotheos, Cyprian and the monastic party in Moscow appeared unrealistic to many members of the Muscovite political élite, who were accustomed to have the Church identify itself with the immediate concerns of the Grand-principality and for whom the Lithuanians appeared as even greater enemies than the Tatars themselves. Until his death in 1389, Dimitri was torn apart between the views of the two groups and, while acquiring the reputation of a national hero, seemed to have tragically lacked consistency and sense of purpose: his hesitation and reversals partially explain the crisis of Byzantino-Russian relations between 1378 and 1390.

But the crisis was also made inevitable by events in Byzantium. In August 1376, Andronicus IV, a passive agent of the Genoese, overthrew his father, John V, and forcibly appointed his own candidate, Macarios, to the patriarchate: Philotheos was deposed, locked in a monastery and died a year later.[26] The patriarchate lost the political independence which the strong personality of Philotheos was able to maintain. According to Cyprian, the new Patriarch Macarios was appointed 'through the evil will' of Andronicus IV: he was 'crazed' (*bezumny*), and 'deprived of reason', enthroned 'in violation of ecclesiastical tradition and

---

[26] This information about the end of the patriarchate of Philotheos is given in Cyprian's *Encomion (Pokhval'no Slovo)* of Metropolitan Peter (VMC, Dec. 21, col. 1643); cf. below, App. 9, pp. 300–1. The autobiographical and historical importance of the writings of Cyprian on his predecessor Peter, has been emphasized by Dmitriev, 'Rol' i znachenie', pp. 236–54, and Tachiaos, Κυπριανός, pp. 213–15. They exist in at least two redactions: the shorter one, recently published by G. M. Prokhorov (*Povest'*, pp. 204–15) may have been written in 1381–2, during the brief tenure of Cyprian in Moscow after the battle of Kulikovo (*op. cit.*, p. 114). The longer version, published in VMC, contains an explicit reference to the death of Emperor Andronicus IV (*ed. cit.*, col. 1644) which occurred in 1385, ans is therefore obviously later. It may have been published by Cyprian himself after 1390. Cf. a translation of the *Encomion* (longer version), below, App. 9, pp. 300–2.

rules'.[27] The anger of Cyprian is understandable: sent to Russia with instructions by Philotheos, he was now left without support of his mother-Church. Indeed, Constantinople was now to back his adversaries in Moscow, as he was not long in finding out.

Diplomatically isolated, Cyprian showed uncommon courage and sense of purpose. Soon after the death of Alexis, which occurred on 12 February 1378, he travelled to Moscow and claimed the late prelate's succession as 'metropolitan of all Russia', in accordance with the terms of his appointment by Philotheos in December 1375. This visit is witnessed by two personal letters of Cyprian. On Thursday, 3 June 1378, he found himself in Lyubutsk, close to the border of the Muscovite territory (approximately 150 km. south-west of Moscow). From there, he wrote a note to his Muscovite friends, St Sergius of Radonezh and Theodore, the abbot of Simonovsky, announcing his arrival and, implicitly, asking for support: 'I am coming to my son, the Grand-prince, in Moscow; I am coming, bringing peace and blessing, as once Joseph was sent by his father to his brothers. Whatever some say about me, I am a bishop, and not a military man. I bring a blessing, as the Lord who sent his disciples to preach, teaching them saying: "He that receiveth you receiveth me" (Mat. 10.40; John 13.20). So, be ready to see me, wherever you see fit. I am looking forward to seeing you and being consoled with spiritual consolation.'[28]

Twenty days later, Cyprian wrote again to the same monks, Sergius and Theodore, *after* an obviously brief and dramatic sojourn in Moscow, on his way back to Kiev. The letter[29] – a very emotional and personal document – contains the only preserved description of the visit. It implies that the metropolitan was not even allowed to meet with his supporters in Moscow, and that his correspondents are still not fully aware of his misfortunes. Cyprian bitterly criticizes them for remaining silent, but also asks them to write to him about their interpretation of the events. The matter of his complaint is the following.

As Cyprian was travelling towards Moscow, Grand-prince Dimitri ordered the roads blocked to prevent the metropolitan from reaching the capital, but Cyprian and his retinue succeeded in avoiding the barriers and in reaching the city. They had

---

[27] *Ibid.*, col. 1643.
[28] Text in *PS*, 1860, May, pp. 84–5. This edition was not reproduced, together with other letters of Cyprian, in RIB, vi; tr. below, App. 7, p. 292.
[29] Text in RIB, vi, cols. 173–86; tr. below, App. 8, pp. 293–9.

nourished the hope that no one would dare to arrest the metropolitan. However, once in Moscow, he was immediately put under the military guard of an official named Nicephoros, in a dark cell, deprived of his clothes, and suffered insults, cold and hunger. Furthermore, the Muscovite authorities deprived his servants of their forty good horses, clothes and other belongings, and expelled them from the city without saddles. Cyprian himself was finally led out of the city by Nicephoros and other officials, who – in order to humiliate the metropolitan – were riding his servants' confiscated horses and were dressed in their clothes. Insults were uttered not only against Cyprian, but also against the patriarch, the emperor and the synod, since Cyprian was showing credentials signed by Patriarch Philotheos, Emperor John V and the Synod of December 1375. The late Philotheos was called 'a Lithuanian'. The Grand-prince, according to the letter, reproached Cyprian himself with 'having been in Lithuania first'. But 'What is wrong in that?' asks Cyprian rhetorically, going to some length in describing his sojourn of 'two years and fourteen days' in Kiev, where he always mentioned the name of Dimitri first at official commemorations, tried to appease political passions, and succeeded in restoring dioceses and church properties, which had been neglected during the tenure of Alexis.

In addition to these personal pleas, Cyprian's letter to Sergius and Theodore also contains a solemn protest against the assumption of the metropolitan see in Moscow by Michael-Mityai,[30] who, before receiving an episcopal consecration, had adopted the metropolitan's dress and pastoral insignia, pretending that Alexis had appointed him as his successor.[31] According to Cyprian, Michael occupied the position of metropolitan-elect (1) through a false interpretation of the last will of Alexis, (2) through blunt inter-

---

[30] Cf. below the discussion on the identity of Mityai and on the circumstances of his appointment.

[31] Golubinsky (*Istoriya*, pp. 230–1), Kartashev (*Ocherki.*, p. 235) and other historians interpret this letter as witnessing the fact that Alexis indeed appointed Michael as his successor (as Theognostos did for Alexis himself). We have seen already (cf. above, pp. 204–5) that Alexis at the end of his life was, on the contrary, supporting the monastic party. Moreover, Cyprian explicitly describes this information as a calumny on Alexis (*chto kleplyut mitropolita, brata nashego, chto on blagoslovil ego na ta vsya dela, to est lzha*) and affirms that the text of the Last Will of Alexis is in his possession for presentation to the patriarch in Constantinople (*ed. cit.*, cols. 180–1). Furthermore, he quotes canonical arguments against the very *possibility* of bishops appointing their successors, but he does not – on the contrary – accuse Alexis of having performed the act itself. We shall see below that the appointment of Michael resulted from an arrangement between Dimitri and the pro-Genoese regime in Constantinople.

vention of the prince in the affairs of the Church, which requires that bishops be elected by an episcopal synod, and not by civil authorities, (3) through bribery and simony. This last accusation, of particular importance for the understanding of the events, is supported by the angry exclamation: 'These people place their confidence in money and the Genoese' (*tii na kuny nadeyutsya i na Fryazy*). Indeed, an agreement was reached between Moscow and the pro-Genoese regime in Byzantium, immediately after the death of Alexis: the agreement, which certainly involved a monetary donation by the Russians and the mediation of Genoese bankers – whose role will become even clearer as our discussion goes further – stipulated, through letters sent by Patriarch Macarios, that Cyprian was not to be accepted in Moscow and that a separate metropolitan 'of Great Russia' (distinct from the metropolitan 'of Kiev, Russia and Lithuania') be consecrated in the person of Michael-Mityai.[32] Against the plan of Patriarch Philotheos, which he wanted to realize in the person of Cyprian, of having a single metropolitan of Russia acceptable to all the political rulers of his domain, Moscow, with Genoese help, was now setting up a separate metropolitanate 'of Great Russia'. As Olgerd in 1355, so Dimitri in 1378 was opposing the unity of the metropolitanate in the name of local political interests!

Cyprian meanwhile, emphatically calling himself metropolitan of all Russia[33] and claiming to be the only legitimate successor of Alexis in Lithuania, as in Moscow,[34] solemnly excommunicated those who opposed his canonical rule and proclaimed his intention to plead his cause in Constantinople with the patriarch and the synod.[35]

---

[32] Speaking of Patriarch Macarios, the *Act* of 1389 affirms: "Ἅμα τε γὰρ ἐγνώρισεν ἐκεῖνον ἀποθανεῖν, καὶ παραυτίκα γράφει πρὸς τὴν Μεγάλην ῾Ρωσίαν, μηδαμῶς παραδέξασθαι τὸν Κυπριανόν, ἀλλὰ παραδίδωσιν τὴν ἐκκλησίαν ἐκείνην διὰ γραμμάτων πρὸς τὸν ἀρχιμανδρίτην ἐκεῖνον Μιχαήλ, ὅν ἐγνώρισε δι᾽αἰδοῦς ἔχειν τὸν εὐγενέστατον ῥῆγαν, κῦρ Δημήτριον, καὶ πλὴν τῆς χειροτονίας αὐτῷ πᾶσαν τὴν ἀρχὴν ἐγχειρίζει τῆς ἐκκλησίας ἐκείνης, καὶ γράμμασιν ἐκεῖνον ὁπλίζει ὡς ἂν ἐνταῦθα παραγενόμενος μητροπολίτης ἀποκαταστῇ τῆς Μεγάλης ῾Ρωσίας, MM, II, 120–2: unfortunately, the Acts of the patriachate of Macarios (who was formally deposed in 1379) are not preserved.

[33] 'I, by the will of God and the election of the great and holy synod, with the blessing and confirmation of the ecumenical patriarch, have been appointed metropolitan for the entire land of the Rus" (ed. cit., col. 173).

[34] 'Since my brother died, I am bishop in this place, the metropolitanate is mine' (*ibid.*, col. 180).

[35] *Ibid.*, col. 186. In response to Cyprian's letter, Sergius and Theodore expressed their loyalty to him, as the legitimate metropolitan; cf. Cyprian's third letter to them, written in Kiev, on 18 October 1378 (ed. Prokhorov, *Povest'*, p. 202).

Unfortunately, he could not expect much support from Macarios and Andronicus IV.

Travelling through Kiev, Moldavia and Valachia (the usual way by the Volga on the Don rivers through Sarai and Caffa, would imply danger of interception by the Mongols and the Genoese),[36] Cyprian was a victim of robbery, crossing the Danube. He then visited his motherland, Bulgaria, where he was warmly greeted by the Bulgarian Patriarch Euthymius, and the population of Trnovo.[37] The visit to Bulgaria, in addition to being a reunion between Euthymius and Cyprian, former Athonite monks, now invested with the highest hierarchical positions in the Church, may have had a diplomatic significance also: special links between Bulgaria and Lithuania seem to have existed throughout the fourteenth century, as can be seen from the consecration of Metropolitan Theodoret in Trnovo (1352) and from the appointment of the Bulgarian Gregory Tsamblak as Metropolitan of Kiev (1415). The Bulgarians traditionally supported the progress of Orthodoxy in Lithuanian lands and understood that this progress was impossible if the metropolitan of Kiev gave one-sided support to Muscovite policies. Clearly, there existed common grounds for consultation with Cyprian.

Cyprian arrived in Constantinople in April–May 1379.[38] Again showing courage, he faced directly a pro-Genoese government and a hostile patriarch, with whose explicit connivance he had just been so brutally expelled from Moscow. However, it appeared – at least for a time – that providence was acting in his favour: on 1 July 1379, John V and his son Manuel, with the Sultan Murad's approval and Venetian help, re-entered the city, while Andronicus IV, taking his mother Helena and grandfather John-Joasaph Cantacuzenos as hostages, fled to Genoese Galata.[39] Patriarch

---

[36] On the routes between Russia and Constantinople and the political and economic implication of adopting one or the other, see Tikhomirov, 'Puti'.

[37] His visit to Bulgaria is described in detail by Gregory Tsamblak in his funeral oration to Cyprian (Ed. B. Angelov, *Iz starata*, pp. 185–7; cf. commentary on that text in Sokolov, *Arkhierei*, p. 478).

[38] In his *Encomion* of St Peter, Cyprian, with his usual chronological accuracy, specifies that he remained in Constantinople thirteen months (*ed. cit.*, col. 1644). On the other hand, we know that he left the capital very suddenly *before* the consecration of Pimen, which occurred in June 1380 (MM, II, 16); Cyprian's name figures in the presence list of a synodal act of June 1380, which is *signed* by Pimen, as metropolitan (MM, II, 7–8). One should suppose, therefore, that the synodal session, the departure of Cyprian, and the consecration of Pimen, followed by the signing of the Act, all occurred almost simultaneously, in a matter of days, in June 1380.

[39] On these events, see Barker, *Manuel II*, pp. 33–6.

Macarios, an appointee of Andronicus, was 'immediately' deposed from his see by the Synod. Cyprian had the moral satisfaction of taking part in the session and of signing the decree of deposition.[40] In another *Act* of the patriarchate, dated September 1379, and issued before a new patriarchal election could yet be performed, one sees the signature of Cyprian, as 'metropolitan of all Russia' ('Ο ταπεινὸς μητροπολίτης πάσης 'Ρωσίας Κυπριανός):[41] this clearly indicates that he made his claim to assume power over the entire metropolitanate, as successor of Alexis, as plain in Constantinople as in Moscow, and that the legitimacy of the claim was recognized, at least for a time, at the patriarchate in 1379.

Cyprian himself gives a dramatic description of the situation in Byzantium in 1379–80: 'I could not leave', he writes, 'because of the great trouble and violence which oppressed the Queen of cities: the sea was controlled by the Latins, while the land was possessed by the God-hating Turks.'[42] In fact, until May 1381, Genoese and Venetians fought each other across the Golden Horn, with each Italian party having its own Palaeologan emperor to support and with Sultan Murad acting as ultimate arbiter.

It is under such conditions that the delegation from Moscow, bringing to Constantinople a candidate for a separate 'metropolitanate of Great Russia', in conformity with an agreement reached with Patriarch Macarios and Andronicus IV, also arrived in Constantinople. In the midst of a series of incredible imbroglios, the affairs of the Russian Church were now to be settled by a new patriarch, Neilos Kerameus, enthroned, after a rather long vacancy of the patriarchal throne, in May or June, 1380.[43]

---

[40] He recalls the fact in his *Encomion* of Peter (VMC, 21 December, col. 1644): 'Patriarch Macarios, by the judgement of God and of the Catholic Church, was deprived of his hierarchical rank and submitted to excommunication and seclusion, as a heretic. Together with other bishops, I was present at that council and signed the act of his deposition.' Cf. a description of this deposition by eighteen bishops with accusation of (an unspecified) heresy, in the act which briefly restored Macarios to the patriarchate in 1390 (MM, II, 143).

[41] MM, II, 6.

[42] *Encomion* of St Peter, VMC, 21 December, col. 1644; cf. below, App. 9, p. 301.

[43] The date can be established on the basis of contemporary patriarchal documents. A patriarchal act, dated September 1379, was issued while the patriarchal see was still vacant. The patriarchal confirmation of the *Act* by Neilos, upon his election, is given in June 1380 (MM, II, 6–7; cf. Darrouzès, *Régistre*, pp. 372–3). The chronology is confirmed by the Act of 1389 which specifies that the consecration of Pimen (June 1380) took place as Neilos 'was just entrusted with the leadership of the church' (MM, II, 121). The date given in most publications for this enthronement ('late 1379') must therefore be corrected to May–June 1380.

2. MITYAI, PIMEN, AND CYPRIAN

The colourful personality of Michael-Mityai emerges on the historical scene in the period between the election of Cyprian as metropolitan (1375) and the death of Alexis (1378). There is no doubt that Mityai's career in Moscow is connected not only with the strictly ecclesiastical issue of the unity of the Metropolitanate of Russia, but also, quite prominently, with the clashing political ideologies represented by Cyprian on the one side, and the violently anti-Lithuanian 'boyar' party in Moscow, which saw no future in maintaining political, cultural and ecclesiastical ties with the southern and western areas of the former Kievan realm, and was, therefore, defending a form of Muscovite separatism, based upon the familiar pattern of loyalty to the Tatars. It is to that party that the person of Cyprian was utterly unacceptable, even if he was supported by influential monastic personalities, like St Sergius himself.

We have seen earlier that, upon his arrival in Moscow in June 1378, Cyprian found Mityai-Michael,[44] acting as metropolitan-elect. The episode of Mityai is so extraordinary and, at the same time, so important in Russian history, that, in addition to regular mentions under appropriate years in the chronicles, it served as a subject for a separate story (*povest'*), which, in at least three major versions, was also included in the same chronicles.[45]

A vicar (*namestnik*) of Metropolitan Alexis in Moscow, Mityai was a secular priest, originally from Kolomna. Contemporary texts describe him as physically and intellectually very imposing. For several years, he was 'the spiritual father of the Grand-prince and of the senior *boyars*' and was appointed *pechatnik* ('carrier of the seal') of the Grand-prince, which certainly denotes political, as well as ecclesiastical responsibilities. He was highly unpopular in those circles, particularly monastic, which were in constant correspondence with Cyprian and the patriarchate, and which supported the ideology promoted by Patriarch Philotheos. No wonder

---

[44] The name *Mityai*, which sounds like a diminutive of Dimitri, is unusual in designating a cleric. Its use in the contemporary sources may denote ironic disapproval of his ambitions. It may have been a family name, however. Mityai's monastic name was Michael and he is referred to by this name in the acts of the patriarchate.

[45] According to recent studies on the *Povest' o Mityae* by G. M. Prokhorov, the original version is found in the *Rogozhskaya* Chronicle (PSRL, xv, Moscow, 1965, cols. 124–31), whereas the third expanded, and less reliable version is that of the *Nikonovskaya* (PSRL, xi, St Petersburg, 1897, pp. 35–41.) Cf. Prokhorov, 'Letopisnaya', pp. 238–54, who also gives a new edition of the *Povest'* (*Povest'*, pp. 218–24), reproducing the text of *Rog*.

that the *Povest'* mentions that Mityai also 'was hostile to monks and abbots'.[46] We have seen earlier that the old Metropolitan Alexis, in his later days, seems to have sympathized not only with Cyprian personally, but also with St Sergius and the monks. He, therefore, opposed the appointment of Mityai as his successor. However, in 1376, the metropolitan condoned his monastic tonsure and immediate appointment as 'archimandrite' of the monastery of the Saviour (*Spassky*) in Moscow. This was a clear step towards promotion to the episcopate.

When Alexis died on 12 February 1378, Michael-Mityai and the Muscovite party which supported him were enjoying the full sympathy of Grand-prince Dimitri. Action was swiftly taken to assure Michael's appointment to the see of metropolitan. By request from Moscow, the pro-Genoese Patriarch Macarios authorized the candidacy of Michael to a separate see 'of Great Russia', distinct from the metropolitanate 'of Kiev and Lithuania', which was already occupied by Cyprian. The exchange of letters took several months.[47] Meanwhile – perhaps unsure of the results of his correspondence with Constantinople – Mityai tried to obtain from the Grand-prince and the Russian bishops his consecration as bishop. This, perhaps, was an attempt to follow the model set by Theognostos, who in 1353 had consecrated Alexis bishop of Vladimir, a few months before his own death, in order to make his candidacy stronger within the patriarchate. But Mityai, unable to obtain the same preferential treatment from Alexis, tried to find canonical arguments which would allow his consecration in the absence of a metropolitan.[48] Unfortunately for him, Byzantine canon law did not allow the consecration of bishops without confirmation by the metropolitan of the province. However, it provided the possibility for a synod of bishops to ordain a metropolitan, without necessarily seeking the approval of

---

[46] Cf. *Rog.*, col. 125.

[47] A total of eighteen months elapsed between the death of Alexis (February 1378) and Mityai's departure for Constantinople in July 1379 (*Rog.*, cols. 127–8).

[48] 'Even before going to Constantinople, [Mityai] planned to be consecrated a bishop in Russia. As he thought these things, he once told the Grand-prince: I read the book known as the Nomocanon, which contains the canons of the apostles and the fathers, and found a chapter that it is proper for five or six bishops, assembled together, to consecrate a bishop. So now, let Your Majesty quickly give the order to all the bishops of the whole province of Russia, to assemble and to consecrate me as a bishop'. *Rog.*, cols. 126–7. Canon 1 of the 'Holy Apostles' requires two or three bishops for an episcopal consecration; according to Canon 4 of Nicaea, however, new bishops are elected by all the bishops of a province and *confirmed by the metropolitan*. These texts were easily available in Slavic translations of the *Nomocanon* (cf. Žužek, *Kormčaja*.)

one patriarch. In practice, if Mityai had been consecrated in this way, the Church of 'Great Russia' would have become *de facto* independent not only of the metropolitan 'of all Russia', but also of the patriarchate, following in this the example of the Bulgarian and Serbian Churches (whose independence was recognized by Constantinople after they had assumed it themselves) and anticipating similar acts of independence which, in the next century, would be accomplished in western Russia (consecration of Gregory Tsamblak in 1415) and in Moscow (consecration of Jonas in 1448). The fact that Mityai envisaged ecclesiastical independence for 'Great Russia' alone is clearly shown in the composition of the council of 'the province of Russia' which he envisaged: five or six bishops, i.e. precisely the bishops of 'Great Russia',[49] with the exclusion of the bishops of the west and south-west, who, in any case, were under the control of Cyprian. The case was clearly one of 'Great Russian' separatism from the original united Metropolitanate of Kiev *and all Russia*.

The plan of Mityai did not materialize for two reasons. On the one hand, a positive reply eventually arrived from Patriarch Macarios in Constantinople, accepting the principle of a separate 'Great Russian' metropolitanate,[50] so that the desired goal could be achieved without challenging the canonical authority of the patriarchate. On the other hand, in Russia itself, Mityai faced the stern opposition of the monastic, 'pro-Byzantine' party, whose spokesman, among the bishops, was Dionysius of Suzdal. A former abbot of the monastery 'of the Caves' (Pechersky) in Kiev and consecrated to the see of Suzdal by Metropolitan Alexis in 1374, at the time of the greatest diplomatic successes of Cyprian, Dionysius is praised, by the chronicles, as a holy and learned man.[51] In 1378–9 he refused to recognize Mityai as metropolitan-elect and vetoed his plans to set up an independent 'Great Russian' metropolitanate. Faced with the wrath of the Grand-prince, Dionysius obtained the protection of the great 'elder' St Sergius. The latter certainly shared Dionysius' distaste for Mityai, but was apparently ready to accept whatever decision was forthcoming from Constantinople. As for Dionysius, who adopted a more

---

[49] The 'Great Russian' part of the metropolitanate included, by 1378, the six dioceses of Novgorod, Rostov, Suzdal, Sarai, Ryazan and Tver (cf. above Ch. 4 (p. 78)). The diocese of Vladimir belonged to the metropolitan himself.

[50] Cf. *supra*, p. 211.

[51] Cf. *Troits.*, p. 396; cf. G. M. Prokhorov, 'Kharakteristika Dionisiya Suzdal'skogo' in *Kul'turnoe nasledie drevnei Rusi* (Likhachev Festschrift), Moscow, 1976, pp. 86–8; also *Povest'*, pp. 66–74.

extreme attitude, he decided to fight Moscow's separatism in Constantinople itself: escaping from Moscow without the knowledge of either the Grand-prince or his sponsor, St Sergius, he took the Volga route towards Byzantium.[52] At the same time Mityai-Michael, together with an imposing Russian delegation, also began his journey towards Constantinople, taking the route of the Don. The delegation included a great number of archimandrites, abbots, priests, deacons and monks, the dean (*protopop*) of the Moscow clergy, the senior *boyarin*, as the Grand-prince's ambassador and eight *boyare* of the metropolitan's court. The embassy carried with it the metropolitan's own treasury and garderobe and also open letters of credit, with the Grand-prince's seal, allowing it unlimited access to funds in Constantinople.

When the party left at the beginning of July 1379,[53] the Muscovite authorities were unaware of the changes which were occurring in Constantinople on 1 July: the return of John V and the deposition of Patriarch Macarios. Had they known, it is quite possible that they would have proceeded with Mityai's plans to set up a 'Great Russian' metropolitanate independently of the patriarchate, instead of seeking Constantinople's approval.

On its way to Byzantium, the delegation paid a visit to the Golden Horde and spent some time enjoying the hospitality of Mamai.[54] From the nominal khan Tulyak Michael-Mityai received a *yarlyk*, sanctioning privileges to the Russian Church,[55] as represented by 'Great Russia'.

However, the grand design of the Muscovites was aborted by a series of quite unforeseen circumstances, worthy of a modern suspense-story.

[52] Cf. the description of these episodes in the original version of the *Povest' o Mityae* (*Rog.*, cols. 127–8). The later interpolated version (*Nik.*, p. 38) attributes to Dionysius the ambition of becoming metropolitan himself. However, such plans seem anachronistic on the part of Dionysius, in 1379. In 1383, in a changed situation, Dionysius will indeed be appointed administrator of the metropolitanate (cf. Prokhorov, 'Letopisnaya', pp. 250–1; *Povest'*, pp. 79–80; for a contrary and, in our opinion, inaccurate interpretation of Dionysius' intentions in 1379, see Grekov, *Vostochnaya Evropa*, pp. 117–18).

[53] *Rog.*, col. 128.

[54] The text of the *Provest'* (*Rog.*, col. 129) is interpreted by I. B. Grekov as meaning that Mityai was 'detained' by Mamai. This author also accuses Mamai of responsibility for the death of Mityai (*op. cit.*, p. 119). However, his conception which presupposes that the Muscovite party which was promoting Mityai's consecration was holding a nationalist anti-Tatar policy is untenable (cf. the generous *yarlyk* granted by Mamai to 'metropolitan Michael', following note); cf. Prokhorov, *Povest'*, pp. 84–5.

[55] *Lvov.*, pp. 198–9.

Having taken a boat in Caffa, the Russian delegation was already in view of Constantinople, when the metropolitan-elect suddenly died. His body was buried in Galata, an important detail, which shows exactly the political dimensions of the whole project: Galata was not only a Genoese possession, but also, in 1379–80, served as refuge to Andronicus IV. The city was in the midst of civil war, and the Muscovites were friends of the usurper, and not of his father John V, who occupied the city of Constantinople itself.

The *Povest'* gives a vivid description of the events which followed. 'When Mityai died, [the members of the Russian delegation] entered a state of strife and indecision. They were confused as it is written: they were confused and agitated like drunken men, and all their wisdom disappeared [cf. Ps. 107.27]'.[56] Indeed, the powerful candidate for the metropolitanate was dead, and the patriarchal throne of Constantinople was vacant with the deposition of Macarios. The Genoese power was challenged by Venice and John V, and, in addition, Metropolitan Cyprian himself was at hand in the city and admitted as full member of the Synod with the title 'Metropolitan of all Russia'.[57]

One can only imagine the intrigues and pressures of all sorts which preceded the settlement of Russian ecclesiastical affairs by Patriarch Neilos and his synod in June 1380. Considering the background of the new patriarch – a former monk, endowed with a certain talent as a preacher and the author of an *Encomion* in honour of the great theologian of Byzantine Hesychasm, St Gregory Palamas[58] – one would have expected, under his patriarchate, a return to the policies of Patriarch Philotheos. But, clearly, Neilos possessed neither the personality, nor the freedom of action of his predecessor. He was entirely indebted to Emperor John V for his election and could not be expected to solve Russian problems independently of the political situation which prevailed in Byzantium. In June 1380, when he took his decision, the war between Venice and Genoa, John V and Andronicus IV, was still

---

[56] *Rog.*, cols. 129–30.
[57] Cf. his signature with that signature in Greek in an act issued before June 1380, MM, II, p. 6.
[58] On Neilos, see particularly H. Hennephof, *Das Homilien des Patriarchen Neilos und die chrysostomische Tradition. Ein Beitrag zur Quellengeschichte der spätbyzantinischen Homiletik*, Leiden, 1963; and I. Dujčev, 'Le patriarche Nil et les invasions turques vers la fin du XIVe siècle', *Mélanges d'archéologie et d'histoire de l'Ecole française de Rome*, 78 (1966), pp. 207–14. The *Encomion* of Palamas (cf. PG, CLI, cols. 655–78) adds no substantial information to the original *Life* of Palamas by Patriarch Philotheos Kokkinos.

raging, and neither side could envisage a total victory: the compromise which would end the war in 1381 was already on the cards in 1380, and John V was not in a position to withstand the political pressure of the Genoese and the financial offers of the Muscovites. The Russian delegation used to the full the open credit bestowed upon it by Grand-prince Dimitri. According to the *Povest'*, 'the Russians, acting in the name of the grand-prince, borrowed silver from the Genoese and the Turks [*u Fryaz i Besermen*] with an interest which keeps growing until today. They made promises and distributed gifts right and left, barely satisfying everybody.'[59]

As a result, the synodal act of June 1380 follows a narrowly Muscovite interpretation of the events: Metropolitan Cyprian is presented as a 'second Roman' (cf. above, Chapter 7) and as an agent of Lithuania. His consecration in December 1375 is interpreted as a result of deception, of which Patriarch Philotheos himself fell victim. The Act finally proclaims the decision of the Synod to accept the proposals of the Muscovite ambassadors and to consecrate one of the three archimandrites, who accompanied Mityai-Michael to Constantinople, named Pimen, as metropolitan.

How did the candidacy of Pimen come about, to replace that of Mityai? The version found in the Russian *Povest' o Mityae* and in the Greek synodal act of 1389 affirms that the ambassadors, using blanks furnished by the Grand-prince, forged the nomination of Pimen, whom Patriarch Neilos, knowing nothing about the death of Mityai, considered as the real nominee of Dimitri.[60] But this version is certainly unacceptable: the name and person of Mityai was known in Constantinople through the previous correspondence between Moscow and Patriarch Macarios. Furthermore, can one imagine that Cyprian and Dionysius of Suzdal, both present in Constantinople in 1380, would not have informed the patriarchate of such a naive substitution?[61] Clearly, the forgery version is a deliberate device to clear the memory of Patriarch Neilos, of Emperor John,[62] and of Dimitri of Moscow, and to

[59] *Rog.*, col. 130; the Russians will remain indebted to the Genoese until 1389, see below, p. 236.

[60] *Rog.*, *ibid.*; MM, II, p. 121. The latter text is particularly apologetic and, therefore, unconvincing; cf. the rhetorical question about the supposed ignorance of Neilos: 'How could his good and divine soul, unfamiliar with any evil, and full of every virtue, suspect such an evil deceit?'

[61] Cf. Golubinsky, *Istoriya*, p. 245; Sokolov, *Arkhierei.*, p. 503–4.

[62] The *Povest' o Mityae* was composed in 1381–2, probably by Cyprian himself who was then recognized by Dimitri as 'Metropolitan of all Russia' and needed the approval of the authorities in Constantinople (cf. Prokhorov, 'Letopisnaya', pp.

place the blame for the disastrous consequences of Pimen's consecration upon Pimen himself and the Russian ambassadors, whose
mistake has been to follow the existing instructions of Dimitri too
faithfully, at a moment when spectacular changes in Moscow's
policies were forthcoming.

Taken on its face value, however, the consecration of Pimen,
seen with the eyes of Patriarch Neilos in 1380, was a fully understandable compromise between the various pressures which were
exercised upon him and could be seen as serving best the interests
of the patriarchate under the circumstances. In spite of all the
pressures and bribes, Neilos did not fulfill the promise of Macarios
to establish a *separate* metropolitanate 'of Great Russia': Pimen
was consecrated as 'Metropolitan *of Kiev and Great Russia*'. At the
synod, a discussion took place 'whether it was legitimate to consecrate Pimen as Metropolitan of Great Russia without making him
also Metropolitan of Kiev, which is, from the beginning the
metropolis of all Russia'.[63] The question was resolved negatively:
the title of Kiev remained with Pimen, whereas Cyprian was
restricted to 'Lithuania and Little Russia'. Furthermore, Neilos
formally maintained the unity of the metropolitanate by stating
that, upon the death of Cyprian, Pimen would become metropolitan 'of all Russia'. He also decided, however, that in the
future, such metropolitans would be appointed 'by request from
Great Russia'.[64] In fact, Neilos attempted a return to the system
which existed at the time of Theognostos and Alexis, with an additional and permanent privilege granted to Moscow to 'request'
new metropolitans. In terms of political realities, which prevailed
in 1380 in Russia and the strength of Lithuania, the system was no
longer realistic, but, at least, the division of the metropolitanate
desired in Moscow was not formally condoned.

Clearly, Cyprian could not be happy with the arrangement. He
attempted to stand by the decision of Philotheos which made him
the sole metropolitan of all Russia after the death of Alexis. At the
synod, his point of view received the forceful support of the Metropolitan of Nicaea, Theophanes, eminent Palamite theologian and

12-13). The act of Patriarch Anthony (1389) adopts the same version, in an
attempt to preserve, wherever possible, an appearance of consistency in the
handling of Russian affairs by John V and the patriarchate.

[63] MM, II, 16.

[64] *Ibid.*, p. 18. This point finds confirmation in the fact that the acts of patriarchal
chancery under Neilos continued to mention a single 'metropolitanate of Kiev
and all Russia' (cf. the act of 1382 elevating Dionysius of Suzdal to archbishop,
RIB, col. 200).

friend of both Cantacuzenos and Philotheos.[65] However, precisely because Neilos could not avoid the appointment of a Muscovite candidate, he was also forced to endorse the view that the appointment of Cyprian by Philotheos before Alexis' death was uncanonical. Eventually, both Theophanes and Cyprian formally accepted the view of the 'majority' of the Synod, but Cyprian left for Kiev before Pimen's consecration took place, obviously disappointed with his new title, recognized by Neilos: 'Metropolitan of Lithuania and Little Russia'.[66] The Act of 1380 says nothing about *his* right to succeed Pimen, in case of the latter's disappearance, and Cyprian, familiar with the situation in Russia, must have accepted the idea that the metropolitanate would have, in fact, to remain divided between himself and Pimen, the first 'Great Russian' metropolitan.

But even more unexpected developments were soon to follow, radically changing again the fortunes of the competitors and determining the fate of Eastern Europe in a totally new way.

3. THE BATTLE OF KULIKOVO

It is quite possible that the very sudden departure of Cyprian from Constantinople[67] was not only due to his disappointment with the decisions of Patriarch Neilos, but also to confidential information received from Russia, where momentous events were in the making.

As we have seen earlier (pp. 183–4), the years between 1374 and 1380 were a period of diplomatic manoeuvring and military skirmishes between the Horde of Mamai and the Grand-principality of Moscow. Neither side trusted the other. Moved by fear of Tatar reprisals and also by vested economic interests, the boyar party in Moscow and the Genoese diplomats were ready to restore the old pattern which existed in the time of Ivan Kalita, of Moscow playing the role of the Horde's main ally in Russia. The

---

[65] *Ibid.*, p. 16; cf. M. Jugie, 'Theophane III de Nicée', DTC, xv, 2, Paris, 1946, cols. 513–17; Meyendorff, *Introduction*, p. 415; Beck, *Kirche*, pp. 746ff. Theophanes was also familiar with Slavic affairs and was instrumental in healing the schism between Constantinople and the Serbian church: in 1368, the Serbian prince John Uglješa calls him 'my lord, my father, the intercessor and healer of my soul', MM, i, p. 563.

[66] The names of Cyprian and Pimen figure both, with their respective titles, in a synodal act of June 1380: Cyprian in the presence list (MM, ii, 7) and Pimen among the signatories (*ibid.*, 8). The latter's signature, in Slavonic (which denotes that he knew no Greek) was obviously given after Cyprian's departure from Byzantium.

[67] 'He fled secretly, without telling anything to anyone', MM, ii, 16.

appointment of Mityai and his visit to Mamai was an expression of this policy. But Dimitri was also solicited by partisans of closer relations with Lithuania and of a confrontation with Mamai. He was extricated from his dilemma by Mamai himself, who took the decision to solve the problem militarily, after the failure of diplomacy in the case of Mityai. Mamai was menaced from the East by the conquests of Tamerlane (Timur-lenk), who had succeeded in 1370 in placing a legitimate Juchid (Mamai did not belong to the dynasty), Tokhtamysh, on the throne of the Golden Horde. Controlling only the western parts of the former territory of the Horde, increasingly suspicious of Dimitri's intentions, he had no time to lose. He therefore set in motion a powerful and most dangerous anti-Muscovite coalition which included the Genoese of Caffa, Prince Oleg of Ryazan, and, most importantly, Grand-prince Jagiello of Lithuania.

Faced with the impending menace, Dimitri appealed to the moral authority of St Sergius and, publicly receiving his blessing for the impending struggle, he also hastily succeeded in setting up an alliance of Russian princes, which included two sons of Olgerd of Lithuania, older half-brothers of Jagiello, Andrew of Polotsk and Dimitri of Bryansk.[68] The decisive battle took place on 8 September 1380, on the upper Don, less than 200 miles south of Moscow, and is recorded in the sources as the battle 'beyond the Don' (*Zadonshchina*), or the battle on the field of Kulikovo. For the first time since the Mongols conquered Russia, a Russian army repulsed a major Tatar onslaught. The battle was also something of a political paradox: the Grand-prince of Moscow, whose principality had risen, earlier in the century, largely because it had then played the role of the major Tatar ally and client among Russian principalities, was now the leader of national liberation. After winning so many political victories over its adversaries, Moscow now succeeded in a military triumph of incalculable symbolic significance. But the victory could be won not only because of Dimitri's military superiority, but also because Grand-prince Jagiello of Lithuania, Mamai's ally, failed to join the Tatar armies. On the day of the battle, his army stood at a relatively short distance from Kulikovo (one day's march).

[68] Dimitri of Moscow may have envisaged a confrontation with Mamai, as early as the Fall of 1379 (cf. Prokhorov, *Povest'*, pp. 101–5). For the sources and the immense bibliography on the battle of Kulikovo, see particularly M. N. Tikhomirov, V. F. Rzhiga and L. A. Dmitriev, eds., *Povesti o kulikovskoi bitve*, Moscow, 1959; and D. S. Likhachev and L. A. Dmitriev, *Slovo o polku Igoreve i pamyatniki kulikovskogo tsikla*, Moscow–Leningrad, 1966; cf. also Vernadsky, *Mongols*, pp. 255–63.

There does not seem to be any doubt on whose side lay the sympathies of the Genoese: a Genoese contingent fought on the Mongol side at Kulikovo. However, Dimitri also took ten *Suro-zhane* (merchants connected with Surozh-Sougdaia) as observers of the battle (*videniya radi*).[69] He obviously did not want to break commercial relations with Crimean merchants in case of victory and, in case of defeat, their intercession would have been helpful with Mamai. He may also have known that the Genoese authorities of Caffa were already in touch with Khan Tokhtamysh, Mamai's powerful competitor, and were ready to switch their diplomatic and commercial connection towards an eventual new ruler of the Horde.[70] This cynical political realism of the Italian merchants provided a bloody conclusion to the battle on the Don. Mamai, after his defeat by the Russians in September 1380, faced Khan Tokhtamysh on the river Kalka in the spring of 1381: utterly crushed, he sought refuge in Caffa with his Genoese allies, but was murdered there upon arrival.

There is no echo of all these events in contemporary Byzantine sources. The miserable internal squabbles between members of the Palaeologan dynasty and the exploitation of these squabbles by Venetians, Genoese and Turks, must have absorbed the attention of the ruling Byzantine circles in the crucial years 1379–81. The only personality who, on the one hand, was in a position to speak on behalf of Byzantine religious and political interests, and who, on the other hand, was fully acquainted with the background of the events and of their implications for the future of the Byzantine 'Commonwealth', was Metropolitan Cyprian.

Most historians dismiss the information found in later versions of the chronicles about the blessing received by Dimitri of Moscow from Metropolitan Cyprian before the battle,[71] and some authors suspect Cyprian himself of having personally edited the chronicles accordingly.[72] Indeed, the accounts of direct advice given to Dimitri by Cyprian are legendary. Cyprian was not in Moscow in 1380. As we have seen earlier, he had left Constantinople in June of that year, as Metropolitan of 'Lithuania and Little Russia', and

---

[69] See *Povesti o kulikovskoi bitve*, p. 55. On the importance of their presence and their possible Italian or Greek identity, see the unpublished Master's thesis by Douglas Andrews (*The Merchants of Surozh, Moscow and the Crimea during the fourteenth century*, Columbia University, N.Y., 1976), who kindly allowed me to read his manuscript.

[70] On this point, see Yu. K. Begunov, 'Ob istoricheskoi osnove Skazaniya o Mamaevom poboishche', in *Slovo o polku*, pp. 521–3.

[71] *Nik.*, p. 53; cf. Vernadsky, *Mongols*, p. 259.

[72] See particularly M. N. Tikhomirov, *Srednevekovaya Moskva v XIV–XV vekakh*, Moscow, 1957, pp. 267–70.

must have immediately gone to Lithuania. However, one may surmise that he certainly saw Grand-prince Jagiello soon after his arrival. His ties with the Lithuanian princely family were long-standing and went back to his mission of 1373–4 and his tenure as metropolitan in 1376–8. If the baptism of Grand-prince Olgerd, under the Christian name of Alexander, before his death (1377) is indeed a historical fact, it could not have occurred without the participation of Cyprian. With the sons of Olgerd, who were Orthodox Christians, Cyprian must have been in close touch. Jagiello – whose Orthodox name was Jacob – remained his friend in later years when he became King of Poland.[73] On the other hand, as his letter of 1378 to St Sergius shows,[74] Cyprian also remained loyal to the idea of Muscovite 'primacy', in spite of the treatment he had received from Dimitri. Finally, his hatred for the Genoese, inherited from Patriarch Philotheos, could only have been made more acute after his recent sojourn in Byzantium. One can be sure, therefore, that, if Jagiello asked him for his advice on the issue of whether he should march together with Mamai – Mityai's sponsor! – and his Genoese allies against the armies of Dimitri, where two members of the Lithuanian dynasty were also serving, his answer could only have been negative.

There is, of course, no hard evidence that his advice was either sought or given. But the hard facts are nevertheless that Jagiello, at the last moment, failed to join forces with Mamai and, that, immediately after the battle of Kulikovo, Dimitri sharply changed his attitude towards Cyprian. This could not have happened if his success at Kulikovo had not convinced the Muscovite Grand-prince that the policies of friendship with Lithuania, defended by Cyprian, were tangibly justified. On the other hand, as a person, Cyprian enjoyed the full support of the monastic party, whose leader, St Sergius, had publicly endorsed the struggle with Mamai.

So 'during the same winter [1380–1], the Grand-prince Dimitri Ivanovich sent his spiritual father, Theodore, Abbot of Simonov-sky [a nephew of St Sergius] to Kiev, calling for Metropolitan Cyprian and asking him to assume his metropolitanate in Moscow. He sent him before the beginning of Great Lent. In the year 1381, on the Thursday of the sixth week after the Great Day [of Easter], on the feast of the Ascension of the Lord,[75] the most holy Cyprian, [by appointment] from Constantinople, came from Kiev to

---

[73] Obolensky, *Philorhomaios*, p. 94; on the christianity of Olgerd and his sons, see below, p. 241, note 59.
[74] Cf. above, p. 203.   [75] In 1381, Ascension Day fell on May 24.

assume his metropolitanate in Moscow. The Grand-prince Dimitri Ivanovich received him with great honour and the whole city came out to meet him. On that day, there was a great banquet at the prince's palace to honour the metropolitan, and they rejoiced greatly.'[76] In addition, according to a Byzantine synodal act, Dimitri formally apologized to Cyprian 'for his past transgressions against him', putting the blame upon 'the letters of the former patriarch',[77] i.e. the arrangement by which the pro-Genoese Patriarch Macarios (1376-9) authorized the appointment of a separate metropolitan 'of Great Russia'.

The unfortunate Pimen, meanwhile, remained in Constantinople until after a peaceful settlement was concluded between John V and his son, Andronicus IV, in May 1381. In the Autumn of the same year he finally arrived in Russia. Arrested in Kolomna, deprived of, his insignia and servants exactly as Cyprian was in 1378, he was successively imprisoned in several towns, dutifully enumerated in the chronicle (Okhna, Pereyaslavl', Rostov, Kostroma, Galich, Chukhloma and Tver).[78] Some of the ambassadors who in Constantinople had arranged his consecration were executed.[79]

The sudden benevolence shown by Dimitri towards Cyprian in 1381 would be fully understandable, if one knew for sure what distinguished service was rendered in the crucial year 1380, by Cyprian to the Grand-prince. We have already suggested that a direct influence on Jagiello is the most likely hypothesis, which would explain why the later tradition of the events, enshrined in the Nikon chronicle, associated Cyprian with the symbolic victory over Mamai, side by side with St Sergius, and established his reputation as a patron of the liberation of Russia from the Mongol yoke. The canonization of the Grand-prince Alexander Nevsky, defender of Orthodoxy against the Western Crusaders and ancestor of Dimitri, effected by the new metropolitan in 1381,[80] was another occasion to cultivate the prestige of Moscow in a way which was congenial to the Lithuanians, still constantly faced with the challenge of the Livonian Order. Even in this canonization, the unity of the 'two Russias' seems to have been at the centre of Cyprian's concerns.

---

[76] *Rog.*, cols. 141-2; *Troits.*, p. 421. Cf. also the connection between the battle of Kulikovo and the return of Cyprian in an appendix to the poem *Zadonshchina* by the monk Sofony in *Slovo o polku*, p. 550.

[77] MM, II, 122.   [78] *Rog.*, col. 132.   [79] MM, II, 122.

[80] Cf. N. Serebryansky, *Drevne-russkie knyazheskie zhitiya*, Moscow, 1915; cf. also I. V. Grekov, 'Ideino-politicheskaya napravlennost' literaturnykh pamyatnikov feodal'noy Rusi kontsa XIV v.', *Pol'sha i Rus'*, Moscow, 1974, p. 394.

10

Lithuania turns westwards

The Battle of Kulikovo placed Moscow in an unprecedented position of leadership in Russia. Not only did its victory over the hated Tatars enhance its military prestige, but also the re-establishment of a metropolitan in Moscow, who was in a position to travel in Lithuania and exercise jurisdiction over the entire country, including the western and south-western dioceses, created a situation which had not existed since the times of Theognostos. Moreover, Metropolitan Cyprian did not owe his power to the Tatars, but was a long-standing champion of an anti-Tatar alliance. The immediate consequence of the new situation was an agreement, in 1381, between Dimitri and Prince Oleg of Ryazan, who had acted as an ally of Mamai and who later escaped to Lithuania: with the metropolitan's blessing, Oleg renounced his oath of allegiance to Jagiello of Lithuania and accepted the position of 'younger brother' of Dimitri.[1]

The rise of Moscow's power was bound to provoke jealousies. Whatever the reasons for his non-intervention in the Battle of Kulikovo, the Grand-prince of Lithuania was still not ready to condone Moscow's leadership in Russia. The formal switch of allegiance accomplished by Oleg was only one of several developments which could certainly not be to his liking. Meanwhile, a pro-Muscovite movement made progress in Lithuania itself, and, eventually, contributed to a bitter internal struggle between members of the ruling dynasty, a struggle which involved the interests and future of the Orthodox Church in Lithuania, as well as Lithuania's relations with both Moscow and Byzantium.

In October 1381, Jagiello, who had been designated Grand-prince by his father, Olgerd, was forced to recognize the supremacy of Olgerd's brother Keistut, who occupied Vilna. Keistut, a bitter enemy of the Teutonic Order, was partisan of an alliance with Dimitri of Moscow. Jagiello, on the contrary, soon obtained

---

[1] On this agreement, see Grekov, *Vostochnaya Evropa*, pp. 144–5.

powerful support from the Order – signalling his future pro-Western orientation – and also undertook diplomatic contacts with the new Khan Tokhtamysh, ruler of the Golden Horde, who in 1381 granted him a yarlyk, recognizing Jagiello as Grand-prince and implying the reaffirmation of an at least nominal Tatar supremacy over Lithuania.[2] Eventually, Keistut was defeated and killed, by order of his nephew (autumn 1382), and Jagiello re-established his rule over the Grand-principality. This event marked a temporary end of the hopes for an alliance between Moscow and Lithuania against the Teutonic Order in the West and the Tatars in the East.

It is, therefore, in military and diplomatic isolation that Moscow had to face the forceful return of the Mongol armies.

As we have seen earlier, Tokhtamysh, a descendant of Chingis Khan, defeated Mamai in battle in 1381 and, supported by the friendship of Timur (Tamerlane), who had control over the Asiatic parts of the Mongol Empire, re-established for a time a powerful Mongol grip over Russia. Dimitri of Moscow tried to appease him with gifts and diplomatic gestures, but in vain. In August 1382, the Mongols occupied and destroyed the city of Moscow itself, from which both the Grand-prince and Metropolitan Cyprian had escaped. Most Russian principalities, including particularly Ryazan and Tver, cooperated with the new ruler. It appeared that the victory of 1380 had been totally in vain and that Russia had returned to its dependence on the Horde, as it had existed in the first half of the century. In reality, however, the Mongol empire lacked the internal unity and dynamism of the past and the Russians had acquired enough military and political potential to remember the symbolic value of the Battle of Kulikovo: the process leading to independence was only delayed, but not interrupted by the catastrophe of 1382.

I. FURTHER INSTABILITY IN THE METROPOLITANATE

A shrewd diplomat, highly dedicated to the idea of the united metropolitanate, Cyprian was involved twice, during his long career, in actions which were questionable from the canonical point of view. The first of these actions was his appointment as 'Metropolitan of Kiev, Russia and Lithuania' in 1375 during the lifetime of Alexis. However, this action was sanctioned – as a case

---

[2] Cf. Vernadsky, *Mongols*, pp. 263–4.

of 'extreme *oikonomia*' by the authority of the respected Patriarch Philotheos and practically accepted by Alexis himself (cf. above, pp. 204–5), but still it provided a pretext for Cyprian's enemies in their arguments against him at the Synod of Constantinople in the spring of 1380. The second, and – formally – even more questionable action was accomplished by Cyprian without any support from the patriarchate and upon a simple invitation of Grand-prince Dimitri: his assumption of the metropolitanate in Moscow in May 1381. However scandalous and inappropriate from his point of view, the consecration of Pimen, as 'Metropolitan of Kiev and Great Russia' was an accomplished fact, which he himself – being in Constantinople – had acknowledged by accepting the title of 'Lithuania and Little Russia'. In 1381, however, as political circumstances underwent a sudden change, he took Pimen's place, as the latter was sent to prison by Dimitri.

The official version, adopted by the Grand-prince, was that Pimen was not his original candidate.[3] But circumstances changed again with the sack of Moscow by Tokhtamysh. The policy of uniting Russian principalities against the Tatars had failed. Upon his return to his destroyed capital, Dimitri had no other choice – and perhaps no other desire – than to return to a policy of loyalty to the Horde. This allowed him at the end of 1382 to be recognized by Tokhtamysh as Grand-prince of Vladimir, although his old competitor, Michael of Tver, was also well received in the Horde: the old Tatar tactic of dividing Russian princes in order to control them better, was thus fully reinstated.[4] On the other hand, the Genoese were quick to re-establish a firm alliance with Tokhtamysh in order to secure their settlements in the Crimea and their commercial interests in Sarai: the Genoese archives contain the texts of these treatises concluded between the authorities in Caffa and the representatives of the khan in 1380, 1381 and 1387.[5] In 1381, also, their friend and client Andronicus IV was recognized at Constantinople as co-emperor and heir of John V,[6] so that appropriate pressures upon Patriarch Neilos and his synod

---

[3] Cf. Act of 1389, MM, II, 122.
[4] A good review of the situation in Vernadsky, *op. cit.*, p. 269; Grekov, *op. cit.*, pp. 165–6.
[5] Cf. the specific promises of faithfulness and loyalty to 'the emperor' (*a lo imperao*, i.e. the khan) with 'his friends being our friends, his enemies our enemies' and the commitments not to accept enemies of the emperor, or 'those who turn their faces away from the emperor' (Silvestre de Sacy, 'Pièces diplomatiques tirées des archives de la République de Gênes', *Notices et extraits des manuscrits de la Bibliothèque du Roi*, XI, Paris, 1827, p. 54a); cf. Yu. K. Begunov, *op. cit.*, pp. 521–3.
[6] Nicol, *The Last Centuries*, pp. 292–3.

were inevitable, against any policy of disloyalty to the khan in Russia.

In such circumstances, the next episode in the career of Metropolitan Cyprian is fully understandable. Dimitri had no use for a metropolitan, who could not, as Cyril, Maximus, Theognostos and Alexis, play the role of an authoritative representative of Byzantium, and be recognized as such by the khan. In fact, Cyprian's canonical standing in the patriarchate was shaky, and politically he was *persona non grata* with both Tokhtamysh, the Genoese and the Genoese-controlled authorities in Constantinople.[7] As Tokhtamysh approached Moscow, Dimitri seems to have panicked. 'Hearing that the *tsar* himself (i.e. the khan) marches upon him with his entire might, he did not go to battle, neither did he lift his hand against the *tsar* Tokhtamysh, but he retired in his own city of Kostroma.'[8] Cyprian stayed longer in Moscow, but eventually also abandoned the city. Being the only metropolitan of the fourteenth century who never visited the Golden Horde, he was not anxious to face Tokhtamysh and foresaw no future for himself in a Tatar-dominated Muscovy. He thus fled to Tver. Briefly returning to Moscow in the autumn of 1382, after the sack of the city, he saw the arrival of the Tatar ambassador, Karach, who brought the khan's 'mercies' to Dimitri and, in fact, sanctioned the latter's capitulation. Cyprian then immediately left for Kiev. In a matter of days, the grand-prince 'brought Pimen out of confinement upon the metropolitan's see with honour'.[9] For the first time, a separate 'Metropolitan of Great Russia' was in power in Moscow.

It appears that the first year of Pimen's tenure was relatively successful. Being *persona grata* with Tokhtamysh, he was able to

---

[7] Patriarch Neilos was sending letters to Dimitri demanding the acceptance of Pimen (MM, II, 122).

[8] *Troits.*, p. 423. Historians who like to preserve the reputation of Dimitri as a political and military leader prefer to think that, in leaving Moscow, he was busy marshalling resistance to the Tatars (cf. for instance, Grekov, *op. cit.*, p. 159).

[9] *Ermol.*, p. 129; cf. also *Troits.*, p. 425. The *Ermolinskaya* chronicle also reports that Dimitri was angry at Cyprian 'because he did not withstand the siege'. This remark may simply witness to the political and personal disagreement between Dimitri and Cyprian, for the Grand-prince – who had also left Moscow – was hardly in a position to give Cyprian lessons on valour. Cf. the more general statement found in the *Nikonovskaya Letopis*, whose account goes back to the historical compilation of 1408, prepared by Cyprian himself before his death: 'The great prince Dimitri Ivanovich did not desire (the presence of) Cyprian, Metropolitan of all Russia and nourished hostility towards him.' The account then relates the triumphal reception of Cyprian in Kiev – the 'mother of the Russian churches' (PSRL, XI, Moscow, 1965, p. 81). The view of P. Sokolov (*Arkhierei*, pp. 529ff.) according to which Dimitri stood for the candidacy of Cyprian during the entire 1381–2 period is untenable.

consecrate Sabbas as a new bishop for Sarai, in the winter of 1382–3,[10] and, one year later, the great missionary, St Stephen of Perm, also received episcopal consecration from him.[11] Stephen was close to the monastic circles of St Sergius, and St Sergius himself, who had always been a supporter of Cyprian, seems to have accepted Pimen's regime without major protests: in any case, he remained loyal to Dimitri and close to his court.[12] But two other representatives of the monastic party, the respected Bishop of Suzdal, Dionysius, and St Sergius' own nephew, Theodore, Abbot of Simonovsky, staged a fierce campaign against Pimen which eventually led to his downfall. However, their campaign was not on behalf of Cyprian – perhaps because they knew that he was personally unacceptable to Dimitri and that, canonically, his rights over Moscow had been superseded by Pimen's since 1380 – but on behalf of their own interests and ambitions, supported, in the case of Dionysius, by the political separatism of the princes of Nizhni-Novgorod. Actually, the confusion created by their actions and trips to Constantinople was so great, that the available sources do not allow us to discern the various factors of the situation, which certainly included political pressures, personal idiosyncrasies, corruption in Constantinople, as well as issues of canon law. The crisis was further prolonged by the distance which separated Moscow from Byzantium, where decisions concerning the administrative status of the Russian Church continued to be made and to which all the interested persons travelled repeatedly.

A resolute foe of Mityai's candidacy, Dionysius of Suzdal, had already gone to Constantinople to fight the latter's appointment in 1379. He returned from the Byzantine capital only in January 1382. One can be sure that – together with Cyprian himself and Theophanes of Nicaea – he accepted the majority decision taken by the synod of Patriarch Neilos in appointing Pimen. Indeed he received great honours from the patriarchate: his diocese of Suzdal was elevated to the rank of an archbishopric, with extended jurisdiction over Nizhni-Novgorod and Gorodok, and he himself was honoured with the right of wearing a *polystavrion*,[13] a distinction which the Archbishop of Novgorod Basil had previously received from Metropolitan Theognostos,[14] but which had been denied to

---

[10] *Troits.*, p. 425.

[11] *Ibid.*, p. 427; on Stephen, see above Ch. 6.

[12] In 1385, he baptized Dimitri's son Peter and also fulfilled a diplomatic mission with Oleg of Ryazan, convincing him to accept peace with the grand-prince (*Troits.*, p. 429).

[13] *Troits.*, p. 426; cf. also MM, II, 137–8. [14] Cf. above, Ch. 4, p. 84.

his successors. Enhancing the prestige of the princes of Nizhni-Novgorod, Dionysius was now a semi-independent prelate, ranking only after the metropolitan and the Archbishop of Novgorod.[15] Such honour may have been bestowed upon him also in recognition of his constant activity as a learned transmitter of Byzantine religious and cultural riches to Russia.[16] In 1381, from Constantinople, he sent the monk Malachias 'the Philosopher' to Russia with two exact copies of the famous icon of the Hodeghetria, which were placed in the main churches of Suzdal and Nizhni-Novgorod.[17] In 1382 again, he brought with him relics of Christ's passion and of many saints.[18] He was also sent, as a special patriarchal legate, to refute the heresy of the *strigol'niki*, carrying special letters on the subject by Patriarch Neilos to the cities of Novgorod and Pskov.[19] Upon his arrival in Moscow, Dionysius wrote to Grand-prince Dimitri, announcing his elevation, but also humbly apologizing for his opposition to him (and to Mityai) in 1379.[20] There is no doubt that, willingly or unwillingly, he was at that time, reconciled with the metropolitanate of Pimen.

However, in June 1383, Archbishop Dionysius, accompanied by Theodore, Abbot of Simonovsky, the Grand-prince's father confessor, left for Constantinople again. The chronicles indicate – obscurely – that they were sent by Dimitri 'in connection with the administration of the metropolitanate of Russia'.[21] The Greek synodal document of 1389 is much more specific: it relates that Dionysius and Theodore brought from Moscow a full-fledged indictment of Pimen, including letters signed by Dimitri and other Russian princes, accusing Pimen of having obtained the metro-

---

[15] His new prestige is particularly emphasized in *Rog.*, cols. 147–8.

[16] The patriarchal act bestowing upon him the dignity of an archbishop is preserved only in a Slavic version. The text praises Dionysius for his knowledge of Scripture and of canon law (RIB, cols. 199–204).

[17] *Rog.*, col. 142; *Troits.*, p. 422. On Malachias, see E. E. Granstrem, 'Chernets Malakhia filosof', *Agiografichesky Ezhegodnik* (1962), Moscow, 1963, pp. 69–70.

[18] *Rog.*, col. 148; *Troits.*, p. 426.

[19] *Novg.*, pp. 378–9 (Engl. tr., p. 159); cf. the letters of Neilos to Novgorod (in Greek, MM, II, 31–4), to Pskov (in Slavonic, RIB, cols. 191–8). On the heresy of the *Strigol'niki*, see N. A. Kazakova and Ya. Lur'e, *Antifeodal'nye ereticheskie dvizheniya na Rusi XIV-nachala XVI veka*, Moscow–Leningrad, 1955; A. I. Klibanov, *Reformatsionnye dvizheniya v Rosii v XIV-pervoi polovine XVI vv*, Moscow, 1960; for an excellent survey, cf. Fedotov, *Religious Mind*, II, pp. 113–48.

[20] Text first published in PS, 1866, March, pp. 247–50, and republished in Prokhorov, *Povest'*, pp. 202–3. According to Prokhorov, however, the letter should rather be attributed to Cyprian and dated 1381 (*ibid.*, pp. 193–7). This does not modify the well-established facts, witnessing to the reconciliation between Dionysius and the ruling circles of Church and State in Moscow in 1382.

[21] *Troits.*, p. 426.

politanate by fraud. The sources do not indicate directly what were the motivations of Grand-prince Dimitri when he removed his support of Pimen and sponsored the mission of Dionysius. One may suppose, however, that his goal was the restoration of a united metropolitanate, under Moscow's political control, as it existed in the times of Peter, Theognostos and Alexis. Since Pimen was clearly not in a position to be accepted in Lithuania, and since Cyprian was unacceptable to Dimitri, a third solution – that of a metropolitanate headed by Dionysius, a man well-known in Constantinople and generally respected in Russia – seemed to be a realistic possibility, which required, however, the formal deposition of both Pimen and Cyprian. As we have seen above, the accusation of direct fraud against Pimen was probably unjustified and, although the document of 1389 forcibly endorses it (since it endorses the point of view of Cyprian), it also rather confusedly puts the blame on 'the deposed patriarch' (ὁ χρηματίσας πατριάρχης) Macarios, on the Russian ambassadors of 1379–80, and on Archbishop Dionysius. 'All this was only words and appearances on the part of Dionysius, for in secret, he was plotting something else; having hypocritically deceived everybody with false words, under the pretext of restoring the diseased and endangered Church of Russia, he himself insidiously assumes the whole power.'[22]

In fact, the synodal text of 1389 reflects an utterly confused situation for which the real responsibility belonged to Grand-prince Dimitri, the ambitious Russian churchmen, and a Greek patriarchate, hopelessly weakened – since the removal of Philotheos – by internal political feuds, external pressures and degrading corruption. It also reveals a painful split in the monastic party in Russia: Cyprian, on the one hand, and Dionysius and Theodore, on the other, were all friends or disciples of St Sergius and originally shared the same ideology of Orthodox unity and Byzantine imperial tradition. By 1383, they were competing with each other for power and honours, as Byzantine Hesychasts had done also during the struggle between Patriarchs Philotheos and Callistos in 1353–64.

The drafter of the synodal document of 1389 seems to recognize his own intellectual dishonesty in his attempt at describing the events without mentioning the forces which were really responsible for all the confusion in the ecclesiastical affairs of Russia.

---

[22] MM, II, 123. The text seems to imply that Dionysius made two trips to Constantinople in 1382–3 which is difficult to imagine chronologically.

After having stated the decision taken by Neilos with imperial approval – two Greek envoys, Metropolitans Matthew of Adrianople and Nikandros of Ganos accompanied by a large staff of imperial and patriarchal officials[23] would go to Russia to investigate the accusations against Pimen, depose him if necessary, and install Dionysius as metropolitan – the act recognizes that the decision made the Russians 'furious', so that they 'uttered insults against us and added sarcasms, accusations and murmurs', but immediately and apologetically responds: 'The Russians are the ones who deserve [the accusations], for they invented frauds, plotted deceit, rejoiced in evil and indulged in thousands of evil deeds through the ambassadors which they sent to us. And now they accuse us of all this!' Clearly, the scandalous episodes (of 1380–4) did much to destroy trust and solidarity, which were the conditions for the survival of the Byzantine 'Commonwealth'! But the departure of the Byzantine commission of inquiry was far from being the end of the story.

Archbishop Dionysius, who, in anticipation of Pimen's (and Cyprian's?) deposition, was entrusted by Neilos with the task of administering the metropolitanate,[24] travelled to Kiev on his way to Moscow. But he never reached his ultimate destination: in Kiev he was put under arrest by the local Prince Vladimir Olgerdovich, who was obviously opposed to the new schemes for the administration of the metropolitanate. Dionysius died in confinement in Kiev on 15 October 1385 and was buried at the Pechersky monastery where he had been an abbot. He was eventually venerated as a saint.[25] Meanwhile, the Byzantine commission went to Moscow, endorsed the accusations against Pimen, and had him deposed. But the unfortunate prelate decided to fight back. Dressed in civil clothes, he escaped from the Russian capital on 9 May 1385, and, by way of Sarai, appeared in Constantinople to seek justice. He

---

[23] Cf. *Troits.*, p. 428, 435; act of 1389, MM, II, 123.

[24] The Russian chronicles affirm that he was 'appointed Metropolitan of Russia' but also still give him the title of 'archbishop' (cf. for example *Rog.* col. 149; *Troits.*, p. 429). The appointment is not mentioned in the act of 1389 (but only a *desire* of Dionysius to assume the metropolitanate). Actually, it was formally unfeasible *before* a canonical deposition of Pimen and Cyprian. One should assume therefore that there was only a conditional arrangement for Dionysius to assume administrative powers in Russia during the canonical proceedings against Pimen and Cyprian, but that he was not formally appointed metropolitan.

[25] *Rog.*, cols. 150–1; *Troits.*, p. 429. D. Obolensky rightly rejects the gratuitous hypothesis of E. Golubinsky (*Istoriya*, p. 223) supported by A. Kartashev (*Ocherki*, p. 332), that Cyprian was involved in provoking Dionysius' death (*Philorhomaios*, p. 92, note 59). On the extraordinary personality of Dionysius, see also Prokhorov, *Povest'*, p. 176.

must have received some support from powerful friends – presumably Tatar and Genoese – for upon his arrival his protests against the unusual procedures taken against him (a deposition without hearing!) were accepted by Neilos and he was allowed to celebrate as bishop.[26] Thereupon, the Greek metropolitans who had been to Russia returned. They were accompanied by Cyprian, who had been convoked by a patriarchal letter, and forced to face an inquiry,[27] presumably on the issue of his arbitrary arrival in Moscow in 1381.

One may only imagine the problems and pressures now faced by the Byzantine authorities! The debates and intrigues lasted years. Pimen and Cyprian struggled for influence at both the imperial and patriarchal courts until 1389. More astonishing still is the role of Theodore of Simonovsky, who, in 1384, having returned from Constantinople to Moscow with the title of 'great archimandrite' and the status of a patriarchal *stavropeghion* granted to his monastery,[28] came back to Byzantium again in 1387,[29] bringing more accusations against Pimen. At that time, he was also enjoying the friendship and confidence of Cyprian.[30] However, 'as the judgement concerning [Pimen's status] was delayed, due to certain circumstances of the moment [διά τινα καιρικά συμβάντα], until such time as a canonical synod would gather upon patriarchal initiative',[31] Theodore suddenly entered into an understanding with Pimen. One may imagine that this sudden shift of Theodore – the nephew and close disciple of St Sergius – was motivated by his failing to obtain any firm decision from Neilos and his synod: indeed, in the absence of a synodal judgement, Pimen was unquestionably the canonical metropolitan 'of Kiev and Great Russia'. He was also accepted as such, in northern Russia, by everyone, including Theodore's spiritual father, St Sergius,

---

[26] *Troits.*, p. 428; MM, II, 124: the chapter in the document of 1389 does not even attempt to hide the contradictions in the patriarch's attitude.

[27] That Cyprian was also under canonical indictment is indicated in MM, II, 98–9.

[28] *Rog.*, col. 150; cf. also particularly, Pachomios, *Life of St Sergius*, ed. Tikhonravov (repr. L. Müller, 1967), p. 127: 'the holy patriarch Neilos . . . established the monastery Simonovsky to belong to the patriarchate . . . and not to be dependent in any way upon the metropolitan'. This description fits exactly the canonical status of *stavropeghion* in the Byzantine practice (cf. Beck, *Kirche*, pp. 84ff., 129ff.).

[29] According to the act of 1389, he arrived during the trip which Cyprian took to Lithuania in 1387 (cf. MM, II, 124 and 98–9).

[30] Cf. a letter of Cyprian to Theodore, written in 1385–6 (Prokhorov, *Povest'*, pp. 171–81).

[31] MM, II, 124–5. The Turks were gradually occupying the entire Balkan peninsula and, locally, Byzantine factions and Italian merchants were in continuous competition; Pimen certainly enjoyed the protection of his Genoese creditors.

whereas the other competitor, Dionysius, was dead and Cyprian remained *persona non grata* in Moscow. One may conclude that Theodore – aside from possible personal considerations or ambitions – could well have been concerned with the normal course of ecclesiastical affairs in Russia, which needed a metropolitan and had been neglected for several years by incomprehensible delays at Constantinople. Thus, he considered that further struggle against Pimen was futile and harmful.

Reflecting the official point of view which prevailed after 1389, the synodal act of that year gives the agreement between the two men a very negative interpretation. 'Pimen and Theodore, having agreed with each other, exchanged mutual promises and oaths and arranged certain unholy agreements and schemes. They escaped from Constantinople and secretly moved to the East', i.e. into Turkish-occupied territory. Refusing to comply with official orders of the emperor and the canonically required three successive summons by the patriarch, they were deposed and excommunicated *in absentia* by a synod, which suddenly was able to obtain the canonical plenum. Furthermore, Pimen – with the probable participation of local Greek bishops in Turkish-occupied Asia Minor – consecrated Theodore as Archbishop of Rostov. Both refused to recognize the sanctions imposed by the Synod. Since, in any case, Patriarch Neilos died soon afterwards (1 February 1388),[32] leaving the patriarchate vacant for almost a year, they returned to Moscow in June 1388.[33] Pimen was again fully acknowledged as metropolitan and presided over the consecration of several bishops: Theognostos of Ryazan (15 August), John of Novgorod (17 January 1389) and Paul of Kolomna (22 May).[34] One may surmise that he received at least some diplomatic support from the traditional friends of the metropolitanate 'of Great Russia': Mongols, Genoese and Turks. As for Theodore, no one doubted the legitimacy of his consecration. Eventually, he headed the list of Russian bishops, which accompanied Cyprian as he solemnly returned to Moscow in the spring of 1390,[35] and served at his archbishopric until his death on 28 November 1394.[36]

Pimen, however, was not so lucky. Worried about his relationship

---

[32] Cf. H. Hunger, 'Das Testament des Patriarchen Matthaios I (1397–1410)', BZ, 51, 1958, p. 308.

[33] MM, II, 125–6.

[34] *Novg.*, p. 382; *Troits.*, p. 433; *Rog.*, pp. 154–5.

[35] *Troits.*, p. 435. Cf. also the highly respectable role attributed to Theodore in both versions of the *Life* of St Sergius, *ed. cit.*, pp. 52–4, 124–8.

[36] *Troits.*, p. 445.

to the patriarchate and having learned that the new Patriarch Anthony, enthroned in Constantinople in January 1388, had confirmed his deposition, he left for a third and last journey to Constantinople on 13 April of that year,[37] described in detail by Ignatius of Smolensk, one of the clerics of bishop Michael of Smolensk who was accompanying the metropolitan,[38] and in a newly published letter of Patriarch Anthony. The numerous inconsistencies and contradictory decisions taken during the patriarchate of Neilos could have given Pimen the hope that Anthony's decision was not final either. On his way, Pimen stopped in Ryazan, where a meeting of Russian bishops, obviously organized in advance, was taking place, including the local bishop of Ryazan,[39] as well as Sabbas of Sarai, Theodore of Rostov, Euphrosyn of Suzdal, Isaaky of Chernigov and Daniel of Zvenigorod. Their personal attitudes towards Pimen are not quite clear, but, eventually, not only Pimen, but also Theodore, Euphrosyn and Isaaky set out for Constantinople in the obvious hope of resolving the question of the metropolitanate once and for all.[40]

Travelling by boat on the Don river, Pimen and his party were stopped in Tana (Azov) by the Genoese (*Fryaze*), who claimed from the metropolitan the reimbursement of his debts. One can only presume that the debts went back to the financing of his consecration in 1380[41] and, probably, also to other cases of financial dependence upon the Genoese merchants by the 'Great Russian' party in Moscow. The Genoese extracted a substantial sum from Pimen (*dovol'nu mzdu vzemshe*) and let him go. It is during the stay in Azov that Pimen broke his temporary alliance with

---

[37] *Troits.*, p. 433. This departure on Tuesday of the Holy Week was a very sudden event. According to the Russian sources, Dimitri was opposed to the journey, but he did not use his power to prevent it. The Grand-prince was obviously, content with Pimen's regime – whether or not it was canonically sanctioned by Constantinople – as he would have been content with Michael-Mityai, as metropolitan of 'Great' Russia only. There are no grounds for the belief, expressed by Prokhorov (*Povest'*, pp. 183–3), that Pimen was faced with opposition in Moscow.

[38] A new critical edition of the *Khozhdenie Pimena* by Ignatius, with English translation and detailed commentary by George Majeska is scheduled to appear in the collection of the Dumbarton Oaks Studies.

[39] The name of the bishop of Ryazan is Theognostos, according to the independent text of the *Khozhdenie*. According to the version found in the chronicles, his name is Jeremiah, 'the Greek'. The contradiction may be explained by the existence in 1389 of two bishops in Ryazan: Theognostos, consecrated by Pimen in 1388 and Jeremiah, consecrated by Cyprian (or directly by the patriarch?), cf. Sokolov, *Arkhierei*, pp. 562–3.

[40] Cf. on that Sokolov, *Arkhierei*, pp. 560–2.   [41] Cf. above Ch. 9, p. 219.

Theodore of Rostov: the latter was arrested and beaten in a Genoese jail, and his belongings were confiscated.[42] Unwilling to support Pimen any more, Theodore managed to reach Constantinople independently and joined the party of Cyprian.

After crossing the Black Sea and stopping in Sinope, Pimen finally arrived in the vicinity of Constantinople at the end of May 1389. There he learned, through envoys sent into the city, that the new Patriarch Anthony was adamant in enforcing the decree of deposition taken against him by Neilos in late 1387 and which had been confirmed in February 1389.[43] Finding himself in a seemingly hopeless situation, Pimen did not despair: he remained in Turkish-held Astrabike and then moved to Chalcedon. Turks and Genoese were eminently hospitable to him. Also he must have been expecting radical political changes in Constantinople: the defeat of the Serbs in June 1389 at Kossovo Polje made a speedy capture of Constantinople itself an immediate possibility. On the other hand, Pimen may have learned that Turks and Genoese were preparing another overthrow of the elderly Emperor John V in favour of his grandson, John VII, son of Andronicus IV. This last event actually took place in April 1390 and was followed by a brief restoration of the deposed Patriarch Macarios, who had supported in 1376–9 the creation of a separate metropolitanate 'of Great Russia'.[44] The monk Ignatius of Smolensk, who remained in Byzantium until that date, describes the events in detail.

However, Pimen was not lucky enough to see them. Having vainly demanded justice from Patriarch Anthony through the intermediary of Bishop Michael of Smolensk, he received three successive canonical summonses from the Synod, in accordance with the requirements of a regular procedure of deposition, being accused by Cyprian and Theodore. He refused to appear and was then deposed *in absentia*.[45] Being apparently in a state of psychological depression, he died on 10 September 1389, in Chalcedon and was buried in Galata, the Genoese stronghold, where the body

---

[42] This information is found in a synodal act of patriarch Anthony, dated September 1389, preserved in a Slavic version and published by Prokhorov (*Povest'*, p. 227).

[43] MM, II, 127.

[44] Cf. the act of reinstatement of Macarios, MM, II, 142–7; curiously, the drafter of this act of reinstatement is named as the *rhetor* Michael Balsamon, whom we already know as the author of the *Encomion* of the Lithuanian martyrs of 1347 (cf. above, pp. 187–8), may have been, at the patriarchate, a representative of the most deliberately pro-Muscovite and anti-Lithuanian circles.

[45] Act of Anthony, ed. Prokhorov, *Povest'*, pp. 226–6.

of Michael-Mityai had also been laid to rest, in 1380.[46] If he had survived a little longer, he would have stood a good chance of being reinstated as metropolitan by Macarios.

But what were the activities of Metropolitan Cyprian during these stormy episodes in the life of his competitor?

We remember that he had been summoned to Constantinople and had arrived there, together with the two Greek Metropolitans Matthew of Adrianople and Nikandros of Ganos, in the autumn of 1385. He was also placed under indictment by Patriarch Neilos, presumably for his arbitrary assumption of the metropolitanate in Moscow in 1381. But, as we have also seen, Neilos and his synod were dragging out the procedures indefinitely, probably because both Pimen and Cyprian enjoyed powerful protection. In the case of Pimen this protection came from Dimitri of Moscow, the Golden Horde, the Genoese and the Turks. As for Cyprian, he seems to have enjoyed favour with Emperor John V, who, in his later years, returned to the views defended earlier by his father-in-law, John Cantacuzenos, and by Patriarch Philotheos. His son Andronicus IV and grandson John VII were now using against him the same Genoese connection which he, in the past, had used against Cantacuzenos, so that it was inevitable for the old emperor to find some support with the Venetians and some comfort in the stable institutions of the Orthodox Church. It is remarkable how utterly forgotten were now his trip to Rome in 1369–70 and conversion to Roman Catholicism! The protection accorded to Cyprian by the emperor would explain not only the passivity of Patriarch Neilos and his synod in 1385–8, but also Cyprian's presence – with the title of 'Metropolitan of Russia' – at sessions of the synod.[47] He resided at the monastery of Studios, whose rich library of Greek and Slavonic manuscripts satisfied his need of intellectual stimulation. His use of the title of metropolitan

---

[46] On the sojourn of Pimen in the vicinity of Constantinople, on his death and place of burial, see particularly G. Majeska, *op. cit.*; the Russian chronicle sadly notes: 'Certain people stole his belongings' (*Troits.*, p. 435). The Act of Anthony states more candidly that Pimen's money, considered as illegitimately acquired, was transferred to Cyprian and Theodore of Rostov (Prokhorov, *Povest'*, p. 228).

[47] A metropolitan 'Ρωσίας appears twice in synodal presence lists under Patriarch Neilos: in October 1385 and in May 1387, cf. MM, II, 57 (for the date see Darrouzès, *Régistre*, p. 377), 96. In the second case, the incumbent is certainly Cyprian, since Pimen, in May 1387, was in Russia. In October 1385, both Pimen and Cyprian may have been in Constantinople; however, Emperor Andronicus IV, Pimen's protector, had died in June of that year, and it is unlikely that Pimen would have occupied a voting position in the Synod after that date. The incumbent mentioned in the act of 1385 must therefore be no other than Cyprian.

'of all Russia' indicates that, in his mind, it had always been his, since the death of Metropolitan Alexis, by virtue of the decision of Patriarch Philotheos. This is shown again on an autograph manuscript of the *Ladder* of St John Climacus, in a Slavic version, copied by Cyprian himself with the following inscription: 'In the year 6895 [1387], 24 April, the present book was completed at the monastery of Studios by Cyprian, the humble Metropolitan of Kiev and all Russia.'[48] It is after Cyprian completed this work on 29 May 1387, that Emperor John V officially requested the synod to suspend the canonical procedure against him for a year, in order to give him an opportunity to fulfil a diplomatic mission on the emperor's behalf. The synod unanimously granted the sovereign's request, on the condition that Cyprian would abstain from interfering in the ecclesiastical affairs of 'Great Russia'.[49] This decision clearly indicates that Cyprian – even if formally indicted – remained in excellent standing with the court of John V and that he still claimed jurisdiction over the whole of Russia. This claim could not be sustained only because of Grand-prince Dimitri's support for Pimen. As to the nature of the diplomatic mission entrusted to Cyprian, one may surmise that it was connected with the dynastic union between Poland and Lithuania, which occurred in 1386 and which was jeopardizing the future status of the Orthodox Church in the western regions of Russia.[50]

As Cyprian returned to Byzantium, Patriarch Neilos died (1 February 1388).[51] The long vacancy of the patriarchal throne ended with the election of Anthony (January 1389),[52] a man devoted to the old ideology of imperial unity, and a friend of John V. One of the first acts of Anthony's patriarchate (February 1389) was to confirm Cyprian as 'Metropolitan of Kiev and all Russia' (forgetting all indictments against him), and to depose Pimen. All the previous patriarchal decrees which had gone contrary to the policy defended by Cyprian, were either declared illegitimate if they were taken by the deposed (χρηματίσαντος) Patriarch Macarios, or annulled, because the Russian envoys of

---

[48] The manuscript, which used to belong to the monastery of the Trinity–St Sergius is now at the Lenin Library, Moscow (Fund No. 152); cf. Vzdornov, 'Rol' masterskikh', p. 189.
[49] MM, II, 98–9.
[50] Cf. Obolensky, *Philorhomaios*, p. 93; there is no reason whatsoever to believe, as I. V. Grekov does (*Vostochnaya Evropa*, pp. 186–8), that Cyprian was held responsible for the union between Poland and Lithuania. One would rather think that he was sent to western Russia to salvage the interests of the Orthodox Church.
[51] Cf. above, n. 32.   [52] MM, II, 112.

1379–80 had supposedly led Patriarch Neilos into error when he consecrated Pimen.[53] Appropriate credit was also given to Emperor John V for his newly discovered dedication to the unity of the Russian metropolitanate and support given to Cyprian. ('Before anyone else [this unity] was approved by the most powerful and holy emperor, the preserver and supporter of what is just and proper.')

As of February 1389, however, there were still substantial obstacles standing in Cyprian's way: the opposition of Grand-prince Dimitri and the presence of Pimen in Moscow. These obstacles soon disappeared: Dimitri died on 19 May 1389,[54] and Pimen on 10 September of the same year. The Russian bishops and clergy who had accompanied Pimen to Constantinople rallied to Cyprian. No questions were raised about consecrations and ordinations performed by Pimen as he was deposed by Patriarch Neilos, not even in the case of Theodore of Rostov. Another of Pimen's appointees, Euphrosyn of Suzdal, was confirmed in the privileges which had been bestowed upon his unhappy predecessor and spiritual father, Dionysius: he was also given the title of archbishop and jurisdiction over Nizhni-Novgorod and Gorodets.[55]

Finally, on 1 October 1389, Cyprian departed for Russia, having distributed a substantial sum of money in gifts to Byzantine officials.[56] Avoiding the eastern route which passed through Mongol-occupied areas, he went through Belgorod (Akkerman) and Kiev, and, in 1390, on the third Sunday of Lent (6 March), arrived in Moscow. The chronicle gives the following description:

'In the year 6898 [1390], Cyprian, the metropolitan, came from Constantinople to Russia; accompanying him were two Greek metropolitans: one was named Matthew of Adrianople, and the other, Nikandros of Ganos[57] – and also Theodore, archbishop of

---

[53] The long synodal act of February 1389 (MM, II, 116–29) also gives the history of the events in Russia since 1353. Its account is generally more accurate than that of the act of Neilos of 1380 (MM, II, 12–18), at least in the sense that the contradictory aspects of Byzantine politics are rather frankly recognized.

[54] *Troits.*, p. 434.

[55] MM, II, 137–8 (July 1389). Euphrosyn changed camps even before Pimen's death; on Euphrosyn, see Sokolov, *Arkhierei*, p. 548, as opposed to Golubinsky (*Istoriya*, p. 301, n. 4), who supposes that Euphrosyn was consecrated in Constantinople. On Dionysius as 'spiritual father' of Euphrosyn, see MM, II, 192–3 (note the use of the term καλογηρώς instead of γέρων).

[56] Cyprian and Theodore of Rostov left a promissory note for 1000 old Novgorodian rubles, dated 8 September 1389, to the imperial διερμενευτής, Nicholas Notaras (text in AI, I, No. 252, p. 473).

[57] The same two Greek prelates had gone to Russia in 1385 to pass judgement on Pimen and returned together with Cyprian.

Rostov, Euphrosyn, bishop of Suzdal, Michael, bishop of Smolensk, Isaaky, bishop of Chernigov, and Jeremiah the Greek, bishop of Ryazan. Cyprian came to Moscow from Kiev to assume his metropolitanate during Great Lent, on the Sunday of the veneration of the cross. And the grand-prince Basil Dimitrievich met him, together with his mother, the grand-princess, and his brothers and the boyars . . .'[58]

There seems to be no doubt that, in 1390, Cyprian was able to gather around his person practically unanimous support, which included the former friends of Pimen. As we have seen in the case of Theodore of Rostov, the exercise of canonical 'economy' allowed for the recognition of all consecrations performed by Pimen, at the time when he was formally deposed. Cyprian's impressive learning, his intellectual and diplomatic ability, his closeness to the monastic circles and to the great St Sergius, allowed for a very favourable comparison with the two candidates, Michael-Mityai and Pimen, whom Grand-prince Dimitri had promoted as heads of a separate 'metropolitanate of Great Russia'. Under Cyprian, the entire Metropolitanate of Kiev and all Russia was again reunited, and will soon include again even the distant dioceses of Galicia. By virtue of his strong personality, he will be able to remain, at least for a time, a powerful spokesman for the perennial ideas of the Byzantine Commonwealth. However, the radical change which had occurred in the political and religious situation of the Grand-principality of Lithuania in 1386 modified the conditions under which the metropolitan 'of all Russia' was to exercise his ministry and paved the way for future and more permanent tensions.

2. THE UNION OF KREWO

During the reigns of Gedymin and Olgerd, the Grand-principality of Lithuania had grown into a major multi-ethnic power, whose population, in its vast majority, identified itself as *Rus'*. The pagan religion of the Grand-prince had increasingly become an anachronism. Later Russian Chronicles identify all the twelve sons of Olgerd as Orthodox Christians, and himself as baptized and tonsured a monk before his death in 1377.[59] However,

---

[58] *Rog.*, cols. 157–8.
[59] The sons of Olgerd's first wife, Mariya Yaroslavna of Vitebsk, bore Christian names: Andrew, Dimitri, Constantine, Vladimir and Theodore. The sons of his second wife, Ul'yana, daughter of Alexander Mikhailovich of Tver, preferred to

Olgerd's ambition to become the unifier of Russia was challenged by Moscow, which was also receiving the authoritative support of Byzantium and of the Orthodox Church. Meanwhile, on its western borders, Lithuania was constantly menaced by the Teutonic Knights and competed with Poland for the control of 'Little Russia', i.e. essentially Volhynia, since Galicia was solidly in Polish hands already. On the other hand, Jagiello's own personal rule had been first and forcefully challenged by his uncle Keistut. Keistut's son Vitovt (Witold) inherited his father's ambitions after the latter's murder by Jagiello (1382). As we have seen earlier, some of Jagiello's advisers – including Metropolitan Cyprian – pushed for an alliance with Moscow. One of the most suggestive expressions of this pro-Muscovite political line in Lithuania was the project of a marriage between Jagiello and a daughter of Dimitri of Moscow.[60] The project, which would have changed the course of history, was never realized. After the sack of Moscow by Tokhtamysh (1382), Grand-prince Dimitri resumed a posture of loyalty to the Golden Horde and Cyprian lost his power over 'all Russia'. In any case, Jagiello's personal ambition and anti-Muscovite feelings were hardly compatible with similar ambitions of Dimitri and parallel anti-Lithuanian sentiments in Muscovite ruling circles. One fully understands, therefore, that he responded with interest to the possibility, suddenly offered to him, of assuming the Polish crown: as king of Poland, he would receive unquestionable personal predominance over the other princes of the house of Gedymin, and would become the ruler of a vast monarchy, uniting Poland and Lithuania; by effecting the required conversion to Roman Catholicism, he could hope, as his grandfather Gedymin did, to receive protection from the papacy against the Teutonic Knights.

Negotiations with the Poles began in secret as early as 1383 and resulted in a document, drafted on 14 August 1385, in Krewo, near Vilna: Jagiello was to marry Jadwiga, the eleven-year-old daughter of Louis of Hungary (d. 11 September 1382), who had already been crowned 'king' of Poland on 15 October 1384, and become king himself. He also promised his own conversion, that of his brothers and relatives and that of all nobles and dignitaries to

use traditional Lithuanian pagan names, but all bore Christian names, as well: Jagiello-Jacob, Skirgiello-Ivan, Koribut-Dimitri, Lugwen-Simeon, Wigund-Alexander. Cf. Yu. K. Begunov, D. S. Likhachev and L. A. Dimitriev, eds. *Slovo o polku,* p. 513

[60] Cf. document published by L. Cherepnin, 'Dogovornye i dukhovnye gramoty Dmitriya Donskogo', *Istoricheskiya Zapiski,* 24, 1947, pp. 247–50.

Roman Catholicism. He pledged to 'reunite forever his own lands of Lithuania and Russia to the crown of the kingdom of Poland'.[61]

In February 1386, a series of spectacular ceremonies took place in Cracow: on the 15th, although an Orthodox Christian, Jacob-Jagiello was rebaptized and received the Roman-Catholic name of Ladislas (Władisław); on the 18th, he married Queen Jadwiga; on 4 March, he was crowned king.[62] The new regime did not formally suppress the feudal divisions which characterized the political structure of Lithuania: the various Russian and Lithuanian princes, who recognized the suzerainty of Jagiello as Grand-prince, now pledged allegiance to him as king.[63] Of Jagiello's brothers and cousins, only Vitovt, Skirgiello and Svidrigiello were rebaptized, whereas the other Gediminovichi remained Orthodox.[64] Jagiello's brother Skirgiello was appointed the king's representative in Lithuania.

This is not the place to analyse the new political situation in detail, but simply to point to the consequences of the Union of Krewo for the interests of the Byzantine heritage and the Orthodox Church, which was the most powerful spokesman for that heritage in Eastern Europe. These consequences are obvious: under the suzerainty of a Roman Catholic monarchy, cultural, political and economic pressures were soon exercised – especially upon Russian and Lithuanian nobility – to adopt Polish ways and attitudes. State privileges were limited to Roman Catholic nobility. Moreover, as we have seen earlier, the practice adopted in the fourteenth century by militant Roman Catholicism in Central and Eastern Europe – particularly by the Hungarian and Polish kings – to assimilate 'schismatics' with pagans and, therefore, rebaptize Orthodox converts showed that the Orthodox population of Lithuania could not expect much in terms of preservation of its religious and cultural identity.[65] The new religious zeal of King

[61] *Terras suas Litvaniae et Rusiae coronae regni Poloniae perpetuo applicare*, in *Akta Unii Polski z Litwa, 1385–1791*, ed. S. Kotrzeba-W. Semkowicz, Krakow, 1932, p. 2.

[62] For a general survey of these events and their background, see, for example, Z. Wojciechowski, *L'Etat polonais au Moyen-Age*, Paris, 1949, pp. 124–31; O. Halecki, 'From the Union with Hungary to the Union with Lithuania: Jadwiga, 1374–1399' in *The Cambridge History of Poland to 1696*, Cambridge, 1950, pp. 196–200.

[63] *Akta Unii*, Nos. 16–34, pp. 12–31.

[64] 'The other princes of Lithuania, brothers of Prince Jagiello, since they had previously received baptism by the rite of the Greeks, could not be persuaded to repeat, or more exactly, to supplement their baptism', Dlugosh, *Historia Polonica*, x.

[65] Ch. 3, pp. 66–7; the Polish practice of rebaptizing the Orthodox was reported to the Council of Constance in 1417, where no action was taken. The practice was, however, condemned by the bull *Altitudo divini consilii* of Pope Alexander VI in 1501 (cf. K. Chodynicki, *Kościół Prawosławny a Rzeczpospolita Polska (1370–1632)*, Warsaw, 1934, pp. 82–3).

Jagiello is recognized by all historians, even by those who consider the Union of Krewo as a highly positive development: Jagiello, writes O. Halecki, 'carried through the promised conversion of his [Lithuanian] nation . . . At Wilno . . . , he founded a Catholic cathedral, granted generous privileges to the bishop [in 1387], created a series of parishes and forbade future mixed marriages between the Lithuanians, who were all expected to become Roman Catholics, and the Orthodox Ruthenians, who were allowed to profess their own religion.'[66]

In 1383–5, when the Union of Krewo was in preparation, Metropolitan Cyprian was on Lithuanian territory, but, apparently, had no opportunity to exercise any influence on events. In 1387, however, one can be almost certain that his mission to western Russia was connected with plans to counteract the effects of Jagiello's marriage and apostasy from the Orthodox faith. Cyprian established contacts with Vitovt and prepared an alliance between him and the Grand-principality of Moscow. Visiting Kiev in 1387, he met Dimitri's oldest son and heir, Basil Dimitrievich, who had been sent to the Golden Horde as a hostage in 1382, but who had escaped (or been freed) in 1385. Basil's long stay in Lithuanian territory (1385–7) was certainly a preparation for his future alliance with Vitovt, patronized by Cyprian. In any case, in 1387, through the intermediary of the 'elder *boyarin*' of Moscow, Basil was called back by his father and arrived in Moscow in January 1388 accompanied by officials from Lithuania.[67] All this suggests serious negotiations, which resulted, on 9 January 1391, after Cyprian's return to Moscow, in a solemn marriage between Basil, who had succeeded his father as Grand-prince of Vladimir, and Sophia, daughter of Vitovt.[68]

Vitovt, later Grand-prince of Lithuania, was until his death in 1430, the main champion of Lithuania's independence and nourished vast projects of expansion.[69] His initial competition with his cousin, Jagiello, forced him to seek temporary refuge with the Teutonic Order. There he was baptized a Roman Catholic,

---

[66] *Op. cit.*, pp. 201–2; see also 'From Florence to Brest (1439–1596)', Rome, 1958, pp. 22–3.   [67] *Rog.*, col. 153.

[68] Ibid., p. 159. On the negotiations and the role of Cyprian, see Grekov, *Vostochnaya Evropa*, pp. 189–95. The Russian chronicler, in a surprisingly casual way, reports that Sophia 'possessed the good habit of her father: she was never tired of fornication' (*Tver.*, col. 445).

[69] On Vitovt, see particularly A. Barbashev, *Vitovt i ego politika do Gryunval'dskoi bitvy (1410)*, St Petersburg, 1885; cf. Pfitzner, *Grossfürst Witold von Litauen, als Staatsmann*, Brünn, 1930; also surveys in F. Dvornik, *The Slavs in European History and Civilization*, New Brunswick, N.J., 1962, pp. 223–9; O. Halecki, *ibid.*, pp. 210–31.

but later became an Orthodox under the name of Alexander. In 1386, he was rebaptized, together with Jagiello, into Roman Catholicism. In 1392, the Polish king was forced to recognize his autonomy, as master of Lithuania. In close alliance with his son-in-law, Basil of Moscow, Vitovt dreamt of ending the Mongol yoke over Russia and of realizing Olgerd's dream of a Russia united under Lithuanian auspices. Having welcomed the exiled Tokhtamysh, he marched against Timur, but was defeated in 1399 at the river Vorskla. This major disappointment forced him to content himself with his status of autonomy in the framework of the Polish-Lithuanian Commonwealth, under the symbolic leadership of King Jagiello. Together, the two cousins inflicted a bloody defeat upon the Teutonic Order at Tannenberg, or Grunwald (1410). But rapprochement with Jagiello meant conflict with Moscow. Thus Vitovt attempted, as did Olgerd in the past, to detach the Orthodox dioceses of his realm from the jurisdiction of the Metropolitan of Kiev, residing in Moscow (cf. the consecration of Gregory Tsamblak, 1415–19). But Vitovt's separatism proved ultimately short-lived and, in the fifteenth century, the Polish-Lithuanian Commonwealth evolved in the direction of a monolithic Roman Catholic monarchy.

3. METROPOLITAN CYPRIAN AND THE STRENGTHENING OF BYZANTINE CONNECTIONS

The Union of Krewo radically changed the configuration of forces in Eastern Europe. The history of the long and stormy tenure of Vitovt clearly shows that Lithuania could no longer lay claim to the inheritance of the Kievan realm: the cultural and religious implications of its belonging to the Polish crown had eliminated it as a serious competitor to Moscow. However, the activities of Metropolitan Cyprian, as head of the Church 'of all Russia', also prevented a development of narrow Muscovite patriotism, which had made an appearance during the reign of Dimitri. The metropolitan was strongly concerned with the fate of the Orthodox Church in Lithuanian and Polish territories and always cultivated the concept of a 'Russia' which included Halich, Vladimir-in-Volhynia, Lutsk, Smolensk, as well as Novgorod, Moscow and Vladimir-on-the-Klyazma. This unity, for him, was primarily an ecclesiastical unity, which could be preserved and strengthened only if peace and, if possible, alliance existed between Moscow and Lithuania. It was, therefore, natural for him to seek the establishment of family ties between the houses of Ivan Kalita and Gedymin. At the same time, as an appointee of the patriarchate of Constantinople, he maintained the idea that Orthodox Christians everywhere were to preserve their loyalty to the wider and universal Christian Commonwealth with its centre in Byzantium. His own personal loyalty to it provided him with at least a symbolic recourse to a superior authority. Unfortunately Constantinople could rarely offer him any real help, or administrative direction: Cyprian was personally a more experienced and able leader than any of the Byzantine patriarchs since the death of Philotheos Kokkinos. The prestige of the 'Queen of cities' remained largely symbolic, but Cyprian knew how to use symbols brilliantly.

Upon arrival in Moscow, he was quickly able to reconcile his own supporters with those of Pimen. In June 1390, in Tver, he presided over the deposition of Bishop Euthymius of Tver, an appointee of Alexis: in this action he was seconded not only by the two Greek metropolitans who had accompanied him from Constantinople, but also by Bishops Michael of Smolensk and Stephen of Perm, two appointees of Pimen.[70] Cyprian consecrated his protodeacon, Arsenius, as Bishop of Tver.

In three other cases during his early years as metropolitan in Moscow, he requested the direct support of the patriarchate of Constantinople: these were cases related to ecclesiastical affairs in Novgorod, Suzdal and Galicia. In all three cases, the local bishops had used the administrative instability of the previous years to achieve a measure of independence from the metropolitan, by obtaining privileges directly from the patriarchate. Cyprian intended to put some order to that.

The title of archbishop and the right to wear a *polystavrion* had been granted to a previous head of the church of Novgorod, Basil Kalika.[71] These were cherished external symbols of a de facto autonomy of the diocese of Novgorod, which also, as we have seen earlier, used the practice of choosing the archbishop by lot, after an election of three candidates by local clergy and laity.[72] However, one of the remaining signs of Novgorod's ecclesiastical dependence upon the metropolitan was the latter's right to receive appeals against the judgements of the archbishop. This right was refused to Pimen in 1385 by the Novgorodians, who formally

---

[70] *Tver.*, col. 445; *Nik.*, pp. 124–5; cf. Golubinsky, *Istoriya*, pp. 302–6.
[71] Cf. above, p. 84.
[72] The practice is described in detail for the election of John in 1388, before his consecration by Metropolitan Pimen, *Novg.*, pp. 381–2 (Engl. tr., pp. 161–2).

swore no longer to accept the metropolitan's judgements. This attitude implied substantial financial loss for the metropolitan's treasury, but Pimen's own shaky position prevented him from challenging the Novgorodians. Cyprian, on the contrary, even before leaving Constantinople in 1389, obtained from Patriarch Anthony and his synod, a stern note to Novgorod, requesting compliance with the traditional practice.[73] After his arrival in Moscow, he visited Novgorod early in 1392, but faced a humiliating rebuttal. The republic had just concluded a profitable commercial arrangement with the Teutonic Order and decided to face up to the metropolitan's displeasure and even excommunications.[74] Cyprian immediately complained to the patriarch through a special envoy, Demetrios the Athenian, whereas the Novgorodians also sent their ambassador, Cyril, to Constantinople, calling for the recognition of their autonomy. The Novgorodians even threatened conversion to the Latin Church.[75] The response came in the form of two severe letters from Patriarch Anthony. Both were brought in the autumn of 1393 by a Byzantine delegation, which included Michael, Archbishop of Bethlehem, and Alexis Aaron, a member of the immediate staff of Emperor Manuel II.[76] Addressing John of Novgorod as a simple 'bishop' (ἐπίσκοπε τοῦ Μεγάλου Νοβογραδίου) and strongly asserting his universal authority (ἡ σύνοδος . . . προνοουμένη . . . τῶν ἀπανταχοῦ τῆς οἰκουμένης χριστιανῶν), the patriarch confirms the sanctions taken by Cyprian against the Novgorodians and calls them to repentance.[77] If the Novgorodians had any serious

---

[73] The synodal act is not preserved, but is mentioned in *Nik.*, p. 124.
[74] Details on both the agreement with the Germans and the conflict with Cyprian in *Novg.*, pp. 384–5 (Engl. tr., pp. 164–5); *Nik.*, pp. 126–7.
[75] Θέλομεν γενέσθαι Λατῖνοι, MM, II, 178.
[76] On the missions of Michael of Bethlehem to Russia see D. Obolensky, 'A Byzantine Grand Embassy to Russia in 1400', *Byzantine and Modern Greek Studies*, 4, 1978 (Essays presented to Sir Steven Runciman), pp. 127–8, and 'A late Fourteenth-Century Byzantine Diplomat: Michael, Archbishop of Bethlehem', *Mélanges I. Dujčev*, ed. S. Dufrenne, Paris, 1979, pp. 26–43; on Alexis Aaron, see E. Trapp, et al., eds., *Prosopographisches Lexikon der Palaiologenzeit*, Vienna, 1976, p. 1. On the title of οἰκεῖος, which belonged to Alexis Aaron, see G. Weiss, *Joannes Kantacuzenus*, pp. 143–5 (with references to previous literature). The instructions to Michael by the patriarch (MM, II, 171–2) provide important information about the handling of official documents in late Byzantium (see I. Medvedev, 'Reviziya vizantiiskikh dokumentov na Rusi v kontse XIV v.', *Vspomogatel'nye istoricheskie distsipliny*, VII, Leningrad, 1976, pp. 289–97).
[77] MM, II, 181–7 (first letter); II, 177–80 (second letter). The first letter was already signed (September 1393), when the Novgorodian ambassador Cyril arrived: his arguments necessitated the drafting of the second letter (cf. A. Pavlov, RIB, VI, app., cols. 253–4).

plans to 'become Latins', they had no opportunity for doing so: not only was their territory soon invaded by a Muscovite army, because of 'the charter which Great Novgorod had written not to be summoned by the metropolitan to Moscow' (a reference to the Novgorodian pledge not to accept the metropolitan's judgements), but the newly arranged alliance between Basil and Vitovt made possible the permanent presence in the republic of princes of both ruling families. The Novgorodians returned the incriminated 'charter' to Cyprian, who lifted his sentence of excommunication.[78] However, during his new and long visit to Novgorod, in the company of a patriarchal ambassador, on Easter of 1395, Cyprian was still unable to obtain his judicial rights: this time, however, he abstained from issuing new canonical sanctions.[79] Timur was menacing Moscow, and no political and military help could be expected from Basil. Archbishop John was repeatedly convoked to Moscow, and was even held in seclusion there for three years, but the stubborn Novgorodians were able to maintain their liberties. As late as 1429–31, the metropolitan's judicial rights were still unsuccessfully claimed by Cyprian's successor, Photius.[80] The extraordinary powers of Cyprian with the princely courts of Moscow and Vilna, and the prestige of the ecumenical patriarchate were thus successfully challenged by the freedom-loving commercial republic of Novgorod.

The second case, when Cyprian caused a direct involvement of Byzantium in the affairs of Russia, concerned the diocese of Suzdal. Clearly unhappy with the privileges obtained from Patriarch Neilos by Dionysius of Suzdal in 1382 and confirmed in 1389 for his successor Euphrosyn, namely the inclusion in the diocese of Suzdal of the important cities of Nizhni-Novgorod and Gorodets, Cyprian reported to Constantinople that the claim of Dionysius in 1382 was unfounded, that Nizhni-Novgorod and Gorodets had never been formally attached to the diocese of Suzdal, that Dionysius was entrusted with governing that area only on a temporary basis by Alexis and obtained confirmatory letters from Patriarch Neilos only because in 1382 there was no 'general united metropolitanate' (ἐπεὶ οὖν μητροπολίτης οὐκ ἦν 'Ρωσίας καθολικός). Consequently, Nizhni-Novgorod and Gorodets were now to be returned to the diocese of the metropolitan.[81] As a result, Michael

---

[78] *Novg.*, pp. 385–6 (Engl. tr., pp. 165–6); *Nik.*, p. 155.
[79] *Novg.*, p. 387 (Engl. tr., p. 167).
[80] Cf. Golubinsky, *Istoriya*, pp. 318–19, 394–5.
[81] MM, II, 192–4. E. E. Golubinsky considers these claims of Cyprian blatantly

of Bethlehem and Alexis Aaron were entrusted with an investigation which resulted in a decision favouring the metropolitan. With great persistence, Cyprian was establishing himself as truly the 'catholic metropolitan' of Russia, as Theognostos had been before him, gradually suppressing the centrifugal trends which appeared during the troubled times of Alexis and Pimen.

Finally, Cyprian also requested Constantinople's support in handling the old problem of the separate metropolitanate of Galicia. The see became vacant in 1391.[82] At that time, the Orthodox Church in Galicia was hard pressed by Roman Catholics: the metropolitan's residence was moved outside of Halich, where a Latin bishopric had been established.[83] The patriarchate appointed a hieromonk Symeon as administrator of the metropolitanate, with competence over Moldavia as well. The Moldavian Orthodox hospodars Balitsa and Dragus are specifically designated as protectors of Orthodox affairs in Galicia and Moldavia,[84] in preference to the Roman Catholic King Jagiello. The troubles of the Church in that area were further compounded by the activities of an adventurer, Paul Tagaris, who profited from the great confusion of the times, travelled in Palestine, Syria, Asia Minor, Georgia and the Balkans, and ordained bishops, claiming to be Patriarch of Constantinople.[85] Tagaris 'consecrated'

untrue (*ibid.*, p. 321). However, the original synodal texts issued in 1382 and 1389 are not preserved, but only described in MM, II, 137–8. This description strongly affirms that Dionysius claimed the two towns as 'parts of his diocese' (ὅτι εἰσὶ ταῦτα ἐνορία τῆς ἐκκλησίας αὐτοῦ), that he obtained a document (γράμμα) to this effect from Neilos, and that the same rights were confirmed for Euphrosyn by a document (σιγίλλιον) of Anthony, in which Euphrosyn was named 'archbishop of Suzdal, Nizhni-Novgorod and Gorodets'. On the exact meaning of the terms γράμμα and σιγίλλιον, see Darrouzès, *Régistre*, pp. 181–203.

[82] Cf. the mention of its vacancy for two years in a document of October 1393 (MM, II, 181). Most historians assume that Metropolitan Anthony, appointed by Philotheos in 1371 (cf. above, p. 192), lived until that date. However, the name of Anthony is not mentioned in the documents concerning 1391, and sources indicate that another incumbent was in charge of Galicia, at least since 1381 (cf. above, Ch. 9, n. 11).

[83] Cf. above, Ch. 8, n. 60. On the affairs of the metropolitanate of Galicia in 1391–3, see D. Obolensky, 'A Late Fourteenth-century Byzantine Diplomat', pp. 29–31.

[84] MM, II, 157–8; on the ecclesiastical connections between Galicia and Moldavia, see above, Ch. 8, p. 193.

[85] Cf. his confession before Patriarch Anthony in 1394, MM, II, 224–30; cf. Darrouzès, *Régistre*, p. 385; cf. also R.-J. Loenertz, 'Cardinal Morosini et Paul Tagaris, patriarches', REB, 24, 1966, pp. 224–56; D. M. Nicol, 'The Confessions of a bogus Patriarch: Paul Tagaris Palaiologos, Orthodox Patriarch of Jerusalem and Catholic Patriarch of Constantinople in the fourteenth century', *Journal of Ecclesiastical History*, XXI, 1970, pp. 289–99 (repr. in D. M. Nicol, *Byzantium: its Ecclesiastical History and Relations with the Western World*, London, Variorum, 1972).

Symeon to the episcopate, an episode for which the latter had
to repent.[86] Clearly, distance and political obstacles prevented
administrative supervision of the area from Constantinople: under
such circumstances, the desire of Cyprian to re-establish over
Galicia his own authority as Metropolitan of Kiev and all Russia
is understandable. But in 1391 he immediately faced a competitor:
the Bishop of Lutsk, John Baba[87] was named Metropolitan of
Galicia by King Jagiello, over the protests of the neighbouring
Bishop of Vladimir-in-Volhynia. Cyprian wrote to Constantinople
about the situation and John himself rushed to Byzantium in 1393.
'Halich was given to me by the king', he said to the synod, 'who is
the local sovereign; I lacked only a patriarchal blessing.'[88] The
intruder was rebuked and deposed by the patriarch and by
Cyprian. The latter, during his stay in Lithuania in 1396, consecrated a new bishop of Lutsk, Theodore.[89] But John apparently
had been still receiving Jagiello's support in Galicia for several
years. In 1397, however, Patriarch Anthony appointed Michael of
Bethlehem – about whom we now learn that he was familiar with
the Slavic language – as administrator of both Galicia and
'Mavrovlachia'.[90] He also asked King Jagiello to expel John Baba
from Galicia, and to recognize the temporary authority of
Michael of Bethlehem with the option of nominating another
candidate for the Metropolitanate of Galicia. Meanwhile, Cyprian
had made attempts to annex Galicia to the Metropolitanate of
Kiev, and even to administer the see of Mavrovlachia. On these
two points, he faced a rebuke from Anthony, who confirmed the
decision of Patriarch Philotheos taken in 1370: both provinces,
Mavrovlachia and Galicia, are to be administered by primates
appointed in Constantinople, and not from Kiev or Moscow.[91]

Cyprian must have been disappointed by the unrealistically

---

[86] MM, II, 158.

[87] His name is mentioned in a latter of Patriarch Anthony to Cyprian, MM, II, 284.

[88] MM, II, 181.   [89] *Troits.*, p. 448.

[90] MM, II, 278–80 (ἔχει μετ' αὐτῶν κοινωνίαν καί οἰκειότητα ἀπὸ τῆς ἰδίας
διαλέκτου καί γλώττης); cf. D. Obolensky, *ibid.*, p. 128, note 23.

[91] MM, II, 283–4. The ecclesiastical affairs in 'Maurovlachia', or Moldavia were even
more confused than in Galicia. Episcopal consecrations had been performed there
by the Metropolitan of Galicia. In 1394, however, a Greek, Jeremiah, was appointed
metropolitan by Constantinople, but was rejected by the local princes. A compromise solution was found only in 1401, when Joseph, one of the bishops previously consecrated in Halich and rejected by the patriarch, was appointed
metropolitan by Patriarch Matthew (MM, II, 528–30); cf. Arseny, *Izsledovaniya:
monografii po istorii Moldavskoi tserkvi*, St Petersburg, 1904, pp. 13–26; V. Laurent,
'Aux origines de l'église de Moldavie', REB, 5, 1947, pp. 158–70; and D. Obolensky,
op. cit., pp. 38–40.

conservative attitude of Patriarch Anthony. Was he not better able to promote the Church's interests in Eastern Europe than the patriarchate? In any case, the patriarchal decision on Galicia remained a dead letter: the 'metropolitanate' disappears from the records, whereas, in 1414, *bishop* John of Halich – who, manifestly, was deprived of the title of metropolitan – participated in a synod, sponsored by Vitovt, to elect a separate Metropolitan of Kiev, Gregory Tsamblak.[92] Clearly the powerful figures of Cyprian and his successor, Photius, while being great defenders of Byzantium's moral prestige, were now able to assert their power over Galicia, even in opposition to the formal wishes of the patriarchate.

This spirit of initiative and *de facto* independence, coupled with faithfulness to the *symbolic* significance of the Byzantine imperial system, is best illustrated by the relationship of Metropolitan Cyprian with Jagiello and Vitovt. Characteristically, during the sixteen years of his tenure of the metropolitanate in Moscow (1390–1406), he never travelled either to the Golden Horde, or to Constantinople, but he made two long stays on the territory of the Kingdom of Poland, in 1396–7 and 1404–5.[93] His primary concern was obviously to maintain the Orthodox faith there, and he pursued this goal with broad and, sometimes, daring schemes, using his personal acquaintance with the Polish king and the Grand-prince of Lithuania, who continued to respect him in spite of their conversion to Roman Catholicism.

Unthinkable during the reign of Dimitri of Moscow, a peaceful visit of Grand-prince Basil to Lithuanian-occupied Smolensk, where he was met by Vitovt, took place on Easter 1396. Cyprian accompanied the Muscovite Grand-prince and consecrated a new bishop in Smolensk.[94] Other pressing business was awaiting

[92] *Nik.*, p. 223; on these events see also Tikhomirov, *Galitskaya Mitropoliya*, pp. 127–39.
[93] Golubinsky, *Istoriya*, pp. 334–40; Obolensky, *Philorhomaios*, p. 94, notes 67 and 68.
[94] *Troits.*, p. 447. Bishop Michael of Smolensk who, as we have seen earlier, had played an active role in the ecclesiastical diplomacy of the period, by that date no longer occupied the see. In spite of his appointment by Pimen in 1383 and his having travelled with the latter to Constantinople in 1389, Michael, a former monk of the Simonovsky monastery, that stronghold of Byzantine influence in Moscow, had readily switched to support of Cyprian. Nevertheless he soon resigned his see, while remaining a close advisor of the new metropolitan. In 1396–7 he accompanied the metropolitan to the Lithuanian-occupied areas and resided with him in Kiev. It was there that he commissioned the copying and illuminating of a luxurious Psalter by the metropolitan's protodeacon, Spiridon. The Psalter is a fine example of Russian art, inspired by contemporary Byzantine models. Bishop Michael died in Moscow in 1402 (cf. L. Lavrovsky, 'Istoriko-kriticheskaya proverka kataloga Smolenskikh episkopov', *Smolenskie eparkhial'nye Vedomosti*, 1898, No. 14,

Cyprian in the western and southern areas of his ecclesiastical territory. Religious and political tensions had grown since the Union of Krewo. The metropolitan's vicar in Kiev, the Athonite monk Thomas, was even implicated in the murder of Prince Skirgiello in the winter of 1397. Skirgiello, brother of King Jagiello and a convert to Rome, had lost his power in Lithuania and received Kiev in compensation, where he replaced the Orthodox Prince Vladimir Olgerdovich.[95] He may have fallen victim of Orthodox fanaticism, or it may have been a result of political intrigue, but Cyprian, who was in Lithuania at that time, seems not to have been personally affected by this episode and even, as we have seen earlier, continued to use his connections with the king to establish his power over Galicia, and even Moldavia, where ecclesiastical affairs were in turmoil. It is also at that time, again in agreement with King Jagiello, that he initiated the extraordinary project of holding 'in Russia' – i.e. most certainly Lithuania – an ecumenical council for the reunion of the Churches.

The interminable and sad story of the various attempts at negotiating the union of the Churches of Byzantium and Rome in the Palaeologan period cannot be told again here. The general pattern was that the popes demanded unconditional ecclesiastical union, as a condition for military aid against the Turks. This demand was accepted by the emperors Michael VIII and, for a brief period (1369–70), John V, but the desired help failed to materialize. The vast majority of Byzantine opinion, whose main spokesman had been Emperor John Cantacuzenos and the Palamite monastic party, looked with scepticism at these hasty political attempts to reach a union, and proposed the convening of a Council at which both sides could freely defend their views. The popes, however, rejected the idea of a Council which would question the position of the Roman Church in doctrinal matters.[96] When he proposed to hold a council 'in Russia', Cyprian was therefore in full conformity with the views of his mentor, the late Patriarch Philotheos Kokkinos, and of the hesychast milieus of Byzantium. Furthermore, the crushing defeat at Nicopolis (September 1396) of King Sigismund of Hungary, who had responded to appeals for

pp. 780–1; V. Maykov, 'O vladyke Mikhaile, upomyanutom v zapisi litsevoy Psaltiri 1397 goda', *Sbornik statei pamyati L.N. Maykova*, St Petersburg, 1902, pp. 99–107; G. Vzdornov, *Issledovanie o Kievskoy Psaltiri*, Moscow, 1978, p. 31.)

[95] Cf. Golubinsky, *ibid.*, p. 337; Grekov, *Vostochnaya Evropa*, pp. 205–6.

[96] Cf. Meyendorff, 'Projets', pp. 149–77; for a general review of the Union attempts, see J. Gill, *Byzantium and the Papacy, 1198–1400*, Rutgers University Press, New Brunswick, N.J., 1979.

help by the Byzantines, must have created a feeling of understandable urgency: unless the Christian world was united against advancing Islam, the fate of Constantinople was sealed. Indeed, in the same year 1396, Sultan Bayezid began a direct siege of the city, which was to last eight years, so that the convening of a council in Constantinople was out of the question, and 'Russia' could appear as an acceptable location.

The project is known to us only through two letters of Patriarch Anthony to King Jagiello and to Cyprian respectively, dated January 1397.[97] The response of Constantinople was negative: Russia was not an appropriate place for holding an ecumenical council, and, in any case, the siege of Constantinople was to be lifted first. The patriarch further urged Jagiello to join in a new Crusade with Sigismund of Hungary, who, after Nicopolis, had visited Byzantium and left the city with the promise of marching again in March. He also encouraged Cyprian to exercise his influence upon his 'great friend', the Polish king (φίλος σου πολύς ἐστιν ὁ κράλης).[98]

What appears in this exchange is, on the one hand, the unrealistic and tragic helplessness of the ruling circles in Constantinople and, on the other hand, the new assurance of the Metropolitan of Kiev, who held a high opinion of his own Church and envisaged it as a natural meeting-place of Christendom. In the imaginative mind of Cyprian – which also proved unrealistic – the unpleasant fact of Jagiello's conversion could itself be turned into an advantage for the Orthodox world by making possible the reunion of a council between East and West on the territory of the Polish Kingdom, where Orthodox and Roman Catholics were now coexisting. Together with the leading theological circles of Constantinople, Cyprian undoubtedly thought that, at such a Council, the victory of Orthodoxy over Latin 'innovations' was, at least, a possibility, and that, therefore, the disadvantageous situation of Orthodoxy in the Kingdom of Poland – as also elsewhere – could be reversed.[99] Standing above the local political interests of

---

[97] MM, II, 280–2, 282–5. Large extracts translated into English in Barker, *Manuel* II, pp. 150–2.

[98] MM, II, 283.

[99] The fact that such views were indeed held by leading Byzantine theologians is shown, for example, in a letter of Patriarch Philotheos to the Archbishop of Ohrid (1367): 'We agreed with the pope's envoys that, if our teaching appears at the council as better than those of the Latins, they will come to us and adopt our confession; before God, we dare to say that this will happen indeed' (MM, I, 492). The Byzantine delegates who sailed for Ferrara in 1438 also hoped to 'win' the arguments with the Latins.

Moscow, Lithuania and Poland, Cyprian was thinking in universal terms, in the great tradition of the Byzantine mind.

During the crisis, which prevented him from assuming the metropolitanate in Moscow (1381–9), he seems to have received the active personal support of Emperor John V.[100] In the person of the old emperor and, after his death (16 February 1391), in that of his brilliant son, Manuel II (1391–1425) who 'had all the capacity for becoming one of the greatest of Byzantine Emperors in many respects'[101] Cyprian continued to see the symbolic head of the Christian *oikouméne*, without whose leadership the union of Christian forces against Islam was impossible. It appears that the election of Patriarch Anthony and the subsequent reappointment of Cyprian in 1389 had been effected with the direct participation of Emperor John V: the synodal document of 1389 repeatedly proclaims that 'the most powerful and holy emperor' is concerned about the unity of the Metropolitanate of Russia under Cyprian and that he issued a special chrysobull to that effect.[102] It is in that context that one should understand the famous letter to Grand-prince Basil of Moscow by Patriarch Anthony written and brought to Moscow by Michael of Bethlehem in 1393.[103] According to information which had reached the patriarch (undoubtedly through Cyprian) the Muscovite Grand-prince had opposed the liturgical commemoration of the Byzantine emperor by the metropolitan. 'You hinder', the patriarch writes, 'the metropolitan from commemorating the sacred name of the emperor in the diptychs . . . and you say that "We have a church, but neither have an emperor, nor do we reckon one".' He continues by recalling the role of past emperors in calling councils and defining the order of the Church, and he finally proclaims: 'Up to this day, the emperor has had the same election [χειροτονίαν] by the Church and the same position and is prayed for in the same way; he is also anointed with the great chrism[104] and is elected emperor [χειροτονεῖται βασιλεύς] and autocrator *of the Romans, that is of*

---

[100] Cf. above, p. 239.   [101] J. Barker, *ibid.*, p. 393.

[102] MM, ii, 127, 128. The text of the chrysobull of John V is not preserved, but it must have been similar to the chrysobull of John Cantacuzenos on the same subject, issued in 1347 (MM, i, 268–70).

[103] M, ii, 188–92; the relevant passages are translated by J. Barker, *ibid.*, pp. 106–9.

[104] The anointment of the emperor with the holy chrism was of relatively recent origin. It was initiated in Nicaea, in emulation of the Latin emperors of Constantinople (G. Ostrogorsky, 'Zur Kaiseralbung und Schilderhebung in spätbyzantinischen Krönungsceremoniell', *Historia*, 4, 1955, pp. 246–56). On the controversy about chrismation of emperors, which occurred in the thirteenth century, see J. Meyendorff, 'Ideological crises', pp. 8–13.

all Christians; and in every place and by every patriarch, metropolitan and bishop the name of the emperor is commemorated, wherever there are Christians . . . Even the Latins, who have no communion whatsoever with our Church, give to him the same subordination, as they did in past times, when they were united with us. To a much greater extent Orthodox Christians owe this honour to him. Christians should not despise him simply because [at present] the gentiles have encircled his residence . . . For Christians, it is not possible to have a Church, and not to have an emperor, for the empire and the church have a great unity and commonality, and it is impossible to separate them. Christians reject only the heretical emperors, who were raging against the Church and introducing doctrines which were corrupt and foreign to the teachings of the apostles and the fathers. But [at present] the most powerful and holy emperor [Manuel II] is, by the grace of God, quite orthodox and very faithful; he is the champion and defender [δεφένστωρ] and advocate of the Church, and no bishop can abstain from mentioning him.'

But was this famous text – which is always, and justifiably quoted as a remarkable reaffirmation of Byzantine political and religious universalism – caused by a brisk upsurge of Russian separatist feelings, as the literal meaning of Anthony's prose might make us believe? On the part of Basil, such a sudden ideological shift was highly unlikely. It was his father Dimitri who had repeatedly challenged the pro-Byzantine policies of Cyprian and the monastic party; furthermore, Dimitri's dealings with the Greeks, during the confused years 1378–89, must have rather discouraged him from looking up to Byzantium as the centre of the Christian universe. But Basil had just accepted Cyprian and condoned his policies: he was also enjoying Constantinople's support against Novgorodian rebelliousness and Lithuanian hostility. It is therefore much more likely that Basil had not innovated, but rather had expressed a mild protest against an innovation *introduced by Cyprian*.

In order to fully support such an interpretation of the letter, one would certainly need a full study of the Slavonic liturgical books used in Russia since the tenth century. But some facts are known: several Russian manuscripts of the *Sluzhebnik (Euchologion)* of the twelfth and thirteenth centuries contain mentions of 'our right-believing prince' only.[105] The practice continues in the fourteenth century, without mention of the emperors, and is found for example

[105] Cf. b. Gorsky–K. Nevostruev, *Opisanie Slavyanskikh rukopisei Moskovskoi sinodal'noi biblioteki*, III, p. 2; cf. D'yakonov, *Vlast'*, p. 24, n. 2.

in a copy of the rite for the blessing of water on 1 August.[106] Cyprian himself in his letter to Sergius and Theodore written in June 1378, declares that, at solemn services, he uses *diptychs* (proclamations of 'many years') where the name of Dimitri of Moscow, not the emperor's, is first.[107] However, in Cyprian's personal copy of the *Sluzhebnik*, prepared in 1397, stands the mention of 'our most pious and most faithful emperors'.[108] Furthermore, in a letter to the clergy of Pskov, contemporary with the *Sluzhebnik*, Cyprian specifically mentions – together with other *new* liturgical practices which he was introducing in Russia, in conformity with those of Constantinople – instructions 'how to mention the Orthodox emperors, together with the great princes . . . , as we do here at the metropolitanate'.[109] These facts seem to show that Cyprian was innovating, when he was introducing the mention of the emperors in the diptychs and that the practice never attained general acceptance. However, they also indicate that Cyprian, supported by the patriarch, was able to overrule the Grand-prince's objections and that his decision to introduce the mention of the emperors stood firm in Moscow, at least for a time.[110]

One can fully understand why the reference to the supreme and universal authority of the Byzantine emperor was important for Cyprian after 1390: it provided him with a symbol of impartiality between Basil, Vitovt and Jagiello. His most essential goal was to preserve personal and immediate control over the whole of his metropolitanate. During his first stay in Lithuania (1375–8), he could afford to mention first the name of Grand-prince Dimitri, because Olgerd was still formally a pagan. After 1386, however, was it possible to mention the Muscovite Grand-prince before *King*

---

[106] Mansvetov, *Kiprian*, p. 53. G. M. Prokhorov signals the existence of a parchment *menaion* for December, which he dates to 1380–90, which contains a note, possibly by Cyprian himself, specifically denying the existence of 'emperor and patriarch' in Russia; the proclamation of 'many years' is addressed to the princes and to the 'Metropolitan of Kiev and all Russia' only, Prokhorov, *Povest'*, p. 119.

[107] RIB, vi, col. 181.

[108] Dmitriev, 'Rol'' i znachenie', p. 225; A. Gorsky–K. Nevostruev, *op. cit.*, pp. 13–14; however, in the same *Sluzhebnik* of Cyprian, the order of preparation of holy gifts (προσκομιδή) does not contain the mention of the emperors, but mentions only 'our pious and God-loving prince and all our pious princes' (Mansvetov, *ibid.*, p. 33).

[109] RIB, vi, col. 239.

[110] Although Cyprian's successor, Metropolitan Photius (1408–81) was a Greek and certainly shared Cyprian's views on the role of the Byzantine emperors in the Christian world, one is surprised *not* to find the mention of the emperors in an official *Order* for the election of bishops, dated 1423 ('Again we pray for our pious and Christ-loving prince', RIB, vi, col. 441).

Jagiello without gravely offending the latter? Also, and in any case, Jagiello, now a Roman Catholic, could not be mentioned as 'most pious and most faithful' sovereign. On the other hand, however, Cyprian's plans for Church union could be compromised by a deliberate, and therefore, offensive omission of Jagiello's name. Was it not logical, therefore, to establish a less controversial commemoration of the Orthodox emperor of Constantinople – whose nominal universal primacy, as Patriarch Anthony himself stated, was recognized by the Latins themselves – and thus reaffirm the metropolitan's independence from 'local' princes, as well as his hopes for the eventual triumph of Orthodoxy at an ecumenical council convoked and presided over in Russia or Lithuania by the emperor of 'New Rome'?

The religious and political ideology which Cyprian tried to express by establishing the imperial commemoration in Russia is also reflected visually in an extraordinary iconographic monument: the 'major' *sakkos* (equivalent to the Western dalmatic) of Metropolitan Photius (1408–31), successor of Cyprian. This remarkable piece of Byzantino-Russian embroidery offers, on its front side, surrounding a scene of Christ's Descent into Hell, the frontal full-length figures of Emperor John VIII Palaeologus (1425–48) and his first wife Ann (d. 1417), daughter of Basil Dimitrievich, and, on the other side, Grand-prince Basil (1389–1425) and his wife Sophia, daughter of Vitovt.[111] The composition clearly emphasizes the marital links between the Palaeologan, the Lithuanian and the Muscovite princely families, established by the marriage of John VIII and Anna (1414), but it also affirms the supremacy and universality of the Byzantine Empire. Moreover, the importance of that supremacy for the local Russian situation is further underlined in the composition by the quite unexpected image of three saints, represented between the pictures of Basil and his daughter Anna. These three saints are the 'martyrs of Vilna', Anthony, John and Eustathius, executed by Olgerd in 1347 and canonized by Patriarch Philotheos in 1374.[112] The message brought by the

---

[111] On the *Sakkos* of Photius, now preserved at the Kremlin Armoury in Moscow, see Bank, *Vizantiiskoe iskusstvo*, p. 287. (Tr. pls. 300–4, and p. 329). D. Obolensky presents convincing arguments, dating the *sakkos* between AD 1414 and 1417. John VIII was officially 'crowned' co-emperor in 1421, but Byzantine sources also indicate that he had been invested with a *pilos* (imperial head-gear) and 'proclaimed' emperor (ἀναγόρευσις) as early as AD 1401–8 ('Some Notes concerning a Byzantine portrait of John VIII Palaeologus', *Eastern Churches Review*, IV, 2 (1972), pp. 141–6.)

[112] Cf. above, Ch. 8, pp. 187–8.

iconography of the *Sakkos* becomes clear: loyalty to the Byzantine Commonwealth is a condition for the maintenance and progress of Orthodox Christianity in the whole of Russia, both in Muscovy and in the Lithuanian-held territories. This was precisely the programme which Metropolitan Cyprian tried to promote, especially during his first visit to Lithuania in 1396–7, and which was inherited also by his successor Photius.

We know less about the second visit of Cyprian to the western parts of his metropolitanate in 1404–6. We learn however that he was received with great honours by Vitovt in Vilna[113] and was present, for two weeks, at a special meeting of Jagiello and Vitovt in Milolyub.[114] Upon Vitovt's insistence, he was also obliged to depose the Bishop of Turov, Anthony, accused of pro-Tatar (and presumably, anti-Latin) policies; but he apparently refused to admit the latter's guilt and provided him with shelter in Moscow.[115]

Clearly, Cyprian was maintaining a policy of diplomatic appeasement towards the Roman Catholic rulers of his western territories, and was successful in preserving good relations with them, but he was also in constant touch with Constantinople, which increasingly needed his help without offering much support to his own needs and plans. Thus, from the draft of a letter by Patriarch Matthew to Cyprian (1400), we learn that Emperor Manuel II and the patriarchate had repeatedly appealed to the Muscovite Grand-prince for financial help, and that Michael of Bethlehem, accompanied this time by two other important Byzantine officials, was again going to Russia with the purpose of fund-raising.[116] The letter announces the recent reconciliation of Manuel II with John VII and also Manuel's departure for the 'regions of France', in search of help. Solicitous and undignified, Matthew bestows extraordinary praises on the Metropolitan of Kiev: 'O most beloved brother, since you exerted yourself in the past, as a man who loves the Romans, exert yourself now and instruct and recommend counsel to all that they should do as we suggest and require. And assure them that giving for the sake of guarding the holy city is better than works of charity and alms to the poor and ransoming captives.'

One wonders whether a similar set of priorities for Christian

---

[113] *Nik.*, p. 191. [114] *Ibid.*, p. 192. [115] *Ibid.*, cf. Golubinsky, *Istoriya*, pp. 340–1.
[116] A complete English translation of the text in Barker, *Manuel II*, pp. 202–4; on the embassy, see D. Obolensky, 'A Byzantine Grand Embassy to Russia in 1400', *Byz. and Modern Greek Studies*, 4, 1978, pp. 123–32, where some pertinent corrections to Barker's translation and interpretation are given (cf. notes 13 and 16).

giving has ever been uttered by a prelate before, but one can suppose that, as they have occasionally been in the past, the Russians were generous again in helping Constantinople besieged by Bayezid. In any case, the temporary salvation of the city came from the victory of Tamerlane over Bayezid in Angora (1402), not from either Western or Russian help.

In addition to his role in temporarily securing the unity of the metropolitanate, Cyprian's main historical contribution was that of being the most active, the most consistent, and the most competent transmitter of Byzantine theological, liturgical and literary traditions to Russia.[117] But in terms of his place in the history of Russia, his greatest achievement may have been the editing of a comprehensive 'all-Russian' compilation (*svod*) of chronicles, which envisaged the histories of the various principalities, which often kept separate chronicles, as the history of a single nation, heir to the ancient Kievan realm of Vladimir and Yaroslav, but also a part of the Byzantine 'Commonwealth'.[118] The compilation, which was ready in 1408, after the metropolitan's death, faithfully reflects the views which also appear in Cyprian's letters and which were expressed in his activities as metropolitan: the Grand-principality of Moscow, as the most reliable centre of the Orthodox faith, enjoys primacy among Russian principalities, but it does not possess any monopoly, either cultural, or political. The merits and achievements of the principalities of the west and south-west, and, indeed, the role of the Grand-princes of Lithuania, also receive proper recognition and credit. Similarly the shortcomings, mistakes and crimes committed by either the Muscovite or the Lithuanian leaders are generally acknowledged with fairness.

In his epic struggles for the unity of his metropolitanate, Cyprian may have made occasional mistakes, but he always remained an independent man. With consistency and shrewdness, he used the 'Byzantine connection' as a means of preserving this independence, which was so often threatened from the East, as well as from the West. He also remained faithful to the traditions of Byzantine monastic Hesychasm, not only by introducing in Russia the Constantinopolitan text of the *Synodikon* of Orthodoxy – a liturgical

[117] Cf. the discussion of this aspect of Cyprian's activities above, in Ch. 6.
[118] See particularly Priselkov, *Letopisanie*, pp. 128–40; M. D. Priselkov also produced a reconstructed text of Cyprian's compilation, which was known as the *Troitskaya letopis* and which was destroyed in the Moscow fire of 1812 (M. D. Priselkov, ed., *Troitskaya letopis. Rekonstruktsiya teksta*, Moscow–Leningrad, 1950). Priselkov's work serves as foundation for the numerous modern studies on the chronicles, particularly by D. S. Likhachev, and several of his colleagues and disciples.

celebration held on the first Sunday of Lent – which included the solemn endorsement of the theology of St Gregory Palamas and a condemnation of his adversaries,[119] but also by personally copying works of monastic spirituality: his autograph copy in Slavic of the *Ladder* of St John Climacus and of the works of Pseudo-Dionysius have been preserved.[120] Also, the Russian Hesychasts of the sixteenth century, who struggled for the principles of monastic poverty (*nestyazhanie*) against the party of the 'Possessors', liked to refer to Cyprian's *Instructions* to Abbot Athanasius, where he formally condemned monastic ownership of vast domains and serfs, as an inadmissible corruption of the monastic ideals, and referred to his own experiences as a monk on Mount Athos.[121]

During the last years of his life, he lived mostly in his country retreat of Golenishchevo, pursuing a life of scholarship and prayer, and avoiding Moscow even on the occasion of episcopal consecrations.[122] He died in his retreat on 16 September 1406.[123]

[119] Cf. the critical edition of the *Synodikon* by J. Gouillard in *Travaux et Mémoires*, 2, Paris, 1967; in 1395, Cyprian, writing to the clergy of Pskov, specifically states: 'I sent you the correct text of the Synodikon of Constantinople, which we also follow here (in Moscow) in commemorating (the Orthodox) and cursing the heretics: you should also conform yourself to it' (RIB, vi, col. 241); cf. Obolensky, *Philorhomaios*, p. 773.

[120] Cf. detailed description in Vzdornov, 'Rol' masterskikh', p. 189; A. I. Klibanov, *op. cit.*, p. 326; Dmitriev, 'Rol' i znachenie', p. 224.

[121] RIB, vi, cols. 263–5.

[122] Cf. the consecration of Bishops Hilarion of Kolomna and Metrophanes of Suzdal in Golenishchevo, *Nik.*, p. 194.

[123] Golubinsky, *Istoriya*, p. 355.

Conclusion: dreams and reality

More than the history of any other European country, the history of Russia has been treated in the light of generalized theories. The various schemes used by historians inevitably include the issue of 'influences' coming from Byzantium, from the Mongols and from Western Europe. In each case, however, the ideas of any given author are shaped by his particular understanding and evaluation of the Byzantine, the Mongol and the Western European civilizations respectively. Thus in the case of the Byzantine 'influence' upon Russia, each historical approach depends upon the given author's own view of Byzantium and its political system. V. Val'denberg, for example, in a well-documented study, shows that the Muscovites inherited from Byzantium the idea that imperial power is *limited* and subject to the superior religious values protected by the Church.[1] R. J. H. Jenkins, however, holds a different view of Byzantium, and, therefore, of Byzantine influence in Russia. For him, Byzantium stands for imperial absolutism, which was adopted both by the Russian tsars and the modern Soviet leaders. 'The modern Russian state', he writes, '. . . merely carries on the tradition of tsarist days . . . The age-old structure is essentially the same' and 'this structure is, very recognizably, the Byzantine Palace of the Third Rome.'[2]

Similar contradictions appear among historians concerning the Mongol impact on Russia. Whereas some see in the Tatars only enemies, who galvanized national resistance and thus created a national consciousness,[3] others, on the contrary, following the founder of modern Russian historiography, N. M. Karamzin, believe that 'Moscow owes its greatness to the khans.' The Mongol

---

[1] *Drevnerusskiya ucheniya*, pp. 132–69.

[2] *Byzantium. The Imperial Centuries. AD 610–1071*, London, 1966, p. 4.

[3] 'The Russian State with Moscow at its head was created not with the assistance of the Tatars, but in the process of a hard struggle of the Russian people against the yoke of the Golden Horde', B. D. Grekov and A. Yu. Yakubovsky, *Zolotaya Orda i eë padenie*, Moscow–Leningrad, 1950, p. 256.

rule, as viewed by the so-called 'Eurasians', served as a pattern for Russian statehood: the khans replaced the universal empire of Byzantium[4] and later Russian tsars were nothing but successors of the khans, as they ruled over much of the same territories.[5] Others still, recalling the building of the Moscow Kremlin by Italian architects in the fifteenth century and the influx of Western ideas, insist upon the breaking-up of the Byzantine inheritance in Muscovite Russia and the adoption of political and cultural patterns more akin to Machiavelli than to Greek patristics.[6]

I do not intend to discuss these various points of view, which all reflect various aspects of an inevitably complex historical process. In reference to the Byzantine impact on the Russian civilization, however, one has only to keep in mind that belonging to a supranational and potentially universal community of Orthodox Christians, headed by Constantinople, was a culturally essential and politically important factor in the events of the fourteenth century. This belonging was expressed in the liturgy and hymnography of the Church, and in the powerful administrative apparatus directed by the Metropolitan of Kiev and all-Russia. Byzantine clerics and diplomats constantly visited Russia and Russian pilgrims and merchants travelled through to Byzantium and other centres of the Middle East. Of the literary documents, religious or secular, available to Russians, the vast majority were translated from the Greek. Byzantine artists were decorating Russian churches and taught local artists. Clearly, Byzantine medieval civilization was part of the very texture of Russian life, whereas the Mongol domination was always felt as a hated 'yoke', existing de facto and imposed by force, even if it could occasionally be used as a tool against other, particularly Western, enemies. In any case, the Mongols never became a consciously accepted cultural model. The use of the term *tsar* to designate the Mongol khan, as well as the Byzantine emperor, is, in itself, not indicative of any real sense of loyalty to the Golden Horde. The Slavonic biblical usage applied the term to the kings of Babylon, Chaldea and Egypt as well. What made the real difference between 'tsars' is the recogni-

---

4 Cherniavsky, '*Khan* or *Basileus*', pp. 65–79.
5 'The feeling among many Turkish and Mongol tribes that the Russian tsar was the successor of the Mongol khans created a favourable situation psychologically for the extension of the tsar's rule over these tribes', Vernadsky, *The Mongols*, pp. 388–9. Vernadsky also emphasizes the historical dependence of the Muscovite state centralization on the Mongol principles of administration.
6 Cf. particularly G. Florovsky, *Puti Russkago Bogosloviya*, Paris, 1937.

tion of the Greek emperor, as the only and universal 'Orthodox' and 'Christ-loving' sovereign.[7]

In attempting to understand the transmission of political theories and ideas from Byzantium to Russia, it is important to realize that neither in Byzantium nor in Russia were political ideas static and unchanging. Only confusion can result, if, for instance, one accepts the presupposition that Byzantium was always and uniformly governed by a regime of 'caesaropapism'. The concrete cases of Justinian I imposing his decrees on the 'Three Chapters', or Michael VIII forcing union with Rome upon Greek clergy were admittedly cases of caesaropapism but these cases were presented to the Russians by their Byzantine mentors, the stern hesychast monks, as obvious abuses.

Abundant evidence is, indeed, available, and was quoted in the preceding chapters, to show that the monks, while remaining by and large faithful to imperial ideology, were also, in practice and in theory, opposed to caesaropapism. They contributed to the formulation of the Byzantine imperial idea along the more practical lines of a 'Commonwealth' of Orthodox nations, acknowledging the ideal supremacy of the emperor. Furthermore, the Turkish threat seems to have led at least some of them to believe that the Slavic nations, and particularly Muscovite Russia, would be able to continue to act as bulwarks of Orthodox Christianity, as Byzantium had done for centuries. This was certainly the meaning of such symbolic gestures as the bringing to Russia by Dionysius of Suzdal of exact copies of the famous icon of the Virgin Odeghitria, traditionally considered as protectress of Constantinople (1382);[8] the translation into Slavic of prayers, addressed specifically to that icon by Patriarch Philotheos Kokkinos;[9] the solemn transfer to Moscow from Vladimir by Metropolitan Cyprian of the Byzantine icon of the 'Virgin of Vladimir', to which the people attributed the miraculous salvation of Moscow from the armies of Timur (Tamerlane) in 1395.[10] Moreover, one would not imagine that the symbolism of the Byzantine imperial and Russian princely portraits on the *sakkos* of Photius could have been devised without at least some implicit admission of a possible *translatio imperii* to Moscow.[11]

---

[7] Cf. the very suggestive description of the universal order in the *Life* of St Stephen of Perm by Epiphanius the Wise; see above Ch. 6, p. 137.
[8] Cf. above, Ch. 10, p. 231.
[9] Prokhorov, 'Gimny', p. 148.
[10] *Mosk.*, pp. 222–5.
[11] Cf. above, Ch. 10, p. 257.

The Russians certainly learned well the lesson about a perennial empire, which Patriarch Anthony had expressed in its most explicit form – 'It is not possible for Christians to have a Church without an Emperor' – but no one taught them that the emperor was in total and unconditional control of the Church. In his letter to Grand-Prince Basil, Patriarch Anthony admitted that Christians should indeed 'reject' those emperors who became 'heretics' and introduced 'corrupt doctrines'.[12] Thus, obedience to the emperor was strictly conditioned by his orthodoxy, and the Russians were certainly in a position to know not only about the heretical emperors of the past, frequently mentioned in liturgical texts (e.g. the troparion to the martyrs of the iconoclastic period who 'destroyed Kopronymos with the sword of faith'), but also about Michael VIII Palaeologus and John V who had formally accepted the Latin faith. Furthermore, civil interference in church administration was also, at least in principle, condemned. One of the most consistent aspects of the rule of Metropolitan Cyprian in Russia was his concern for independence from civil authority, whether Muscovite or Lithuanian: without independence, he would have been unable to maintain his administrative control over a politically divided country. In 1378, having just been humiliated and molested by Dimitri of Moscow, he wrote to St Sergius and to Abbot Theodore, quoting the canons which prohibit the intervention of secular princes in episcopal elections.[13] Even after his permanent establishment on the metropolitan's seat in Moscow, in his semi-autobiographical *Life of Peter*, he still opposes Erastianism, which has been, in his view, the origin of the candidacy of Geronty, supported against Peter in 1305–8 by the Grand-prince of Vladimir, Michael Yaroslavich of Tver.[14] On the other hand, in patriarchal letters sent to their country, the Russians read more often about the authority of the ecumenical *patriarch*, defined in terms reminiscent of Western papism, than about the power of the emperor.[15] All this suggests that Byzantium's covenant with Russia in the fourteenth century, as expressed by the hesychast monks controlling the patriarchate, was not caesaropapism, but rather the idea of a strong, unified Church,

---

[12] MM, II, 192.

[13] RIB, vi, col. 178; cf. full translation of his letter below, App. 8, pp. 292–9.

[14] VMC, 21 December, col. 1635; cf. Dmitriev, 'Rol' i znachenie', p. 247. Cf. also similar reference to canons condemning caesaropapism in the encyclical of Metropolitan Photius against the election of Gregory Tsamblak (1416) in RIB, vi, cols. 341–2.

[15] Cf. *supra*, Ch. 5, pp. 112–18.

transcending national allegiances and political boundaries. To the Russians, the Byzantine emperor was presented as a supporter, not a master, of this Church.

For several decades following the final installation of Cyprian (1390), Muscovite Russia remained faithful to that covenant. Cyprian's successor, Photius (1408–31), a Greek, endowed with political sense and a strong personality, also succeeded in enforcing the policy of unity. He faced challenges not from the Grand-prince of Moscow, but from Vitovt of Lithuania, who dreamt of assuming the plans of Olgerd. After the death of Cyprian, he attempted to replace him with his own candidate, the Greek bishop of Polotsk, Theodosius, but was rebuked by Constantinople.[16] In November 1415, Vitovt supported the move of western-Russian bishops to elect a separate metropolitan, directly challenging the jurisdiction of Photius and of the patriarchate over his domain. The motivation for this action was found in an unnamed misdeed of Photius, probably connected with taxation and fund-raising. The metropolitan received from 'the Council of bishops of the metropolitanate of Kiev' the solemn announcement that they no longer recognized him as a bishop.[17] An official synodal act signed by the bishops of Polotsk, Chernigov, Lutsk, Vladimir-in-Volhynia, Peremyshl', Smolensk, Kholm and Turov, gathered in Novgorodok, declared that Photius 'neglected' his flock in Lithuania by living in Moscow, while only collecting taxes in the western dioceses; that Grand-prince Vitovt had unsuccessfully tried to obtain a separate metropolitan in Constantinople; that ecclesiastical independence from Constantinople had been practised under Grand-prince Izyaslav of Kiev[18] and was an accomplished fact in the case of the Bulgarians and the Serbs; and finally that ancient canons authorize the bishops of every province to elect their own metropolitan. Even more importantly, the act – after proclaiming that the metropolitanate of Kiev will continue to recognize the Patriarch of Constantinople as 'patriarch and father', as well as the other Orthodox patriarchs – formally raises against Constantinople the accusation of simony and caesaropapism, referring to the sad precedents of the fourteenth century.

'We turn away in disgust, because we cannot support the violence done by the emperor to the Church; for indeed, the holy ecumenical patriarch and the divine synod of Constantinople can-

---

[16] Cf. *Akty otnosyashchiesya k Zapadnoi Rossii*, I, No. 25, p. 36; cf. RIB, VI, col. 329.
[17] RIB, VI, cols. 307–10.
[18] The reference is to the election of Metropolitan Clement Smolyatich (1147–55).

not appoint a metropolitan according to the canons, but follow the emperor's [Manuel II] will. Nowadays, the gift of the Holy Spirit is bought and sold, as this was done for the church of Kiev by his [Manuel's] father [John V], in our own days, in the case of Metropolitan Cyprian, and in those of Pimen, Dionysius and many others. Concern was not given to the honour of the Church, but to much gold and silver.' Consequently the Russian bishops refuse to accept a metropolitan 'appointed for money by an emperor who is a layman, and not by the will of the patriarch and by decision of an authentic apostolic synod'.[19]

The candidate elected in Novgorodok as Metropolitan of Kiev and all Russia (but without jurisdiction over Moscow) was Gregory Tsamblak, a Bulgarian and a close disciple and admirer of Metropolitan Cyprian.[20] Gregory and his supporters – as well as Grand-prince Vitovt – justified the election of a separate metropolitan in Lithuania as an act as legitimate as the appointment of Cyprian in 1375. But the circumstances and the intentions were clearly different. The movement which brought Gregory to power was clearly more 'separatistic' than the shrewd and essentially 'unifying' policies of Patriarch Philotheos in 1375: Tsamblak could never hope to achieve jurisdiction over the whole of Russia. On the other hand, Metropolitan Photius could not, as Alexis could, be accused of 'neglecting' the western dioceses, and of being a tool of Muscovite policies. He had visited Lithuania and Galicia in 1412 and returned there – after the disappearance of Gregory – in 1420–1, 1423, 1427, and 1430. Not Photius, but Tsamblak was a tool of a civil power, which was not even Orthodox. In spite of his grandiose projects for Russia, Vitovt was a vassal of the Polish king, his cousin Jagiello, so that his domain lay clearly outside of the Byzantine 'Commonwealth'. In fact, Tsamblak became involved in ambiguous projects of Church union. With an impressive retinue of clergy, he visited the Council of Constance. But the rather cool reception which he received there on the part of Latin clergy and princes[21] was another proof that a metropolitan of Kiev, appointed by the will of a Roman Catholic ruler and without the blessing of Constantinople, could hardly contribute on his own to union negotiations between the Churches of the East and the West.

---

[19] RIB, vi, cols. 309–14.
[20] The widely accepted view that Gregory was Cyprian's nephew has been recently convincingly challenged, cf. above, Ch. 9, n. 8.
[21] On this visit, see J. Gill, *The Council of Florence*, Cambridge, 1958, p. 25.

Violently denounced by Photius, who insisted again on the unity of the metropolitanate,[22] and excommunicated by Patriarch Joseph II of Constantinople,[23] Gregory soon disappeared from the scene (1419) and Photius re-established his jurisdiction over all the dioceses, including even the Polish-held Galicia. The episode of Tsamblak's election in Novgorodok was, however, a significant event pointing to the gradual loss of prestige suffered by Byzantium in Russia. For the first time, a representative council of bishops openly accused Constantinople of corruption and caesaropapism, and called for an independent, or 'autocephalous' Church in Russia. One can be sure that similar views and aspirations had existed also in Moscow, especially at the time when Michael-Mityai unsuccessfully tried to assume the metropolitanate in 1378–80, but Moscow's secessionism was eventually checked by Dionysius of Suzdal and, later, by Metropolitan Cyprian. Similarly, the powerful figure of Photius prevented ecclesiastical independence to be asserted in Lithuania. But the dream – patiently cultivated by Patriarch Philotheos and Metropolitan Cyprian – of a united Orthodox world recognizing the symbolic political leadership of the Byzantine emperor and the centralized ecclesiastical administration of the patriarchate was crumbling and losing credibility.

The Grand-principality of Moscow upheld the dream most consistently, and for a surprisingly long period. The Muscovite government did not even try to ensure that the Byzantines fulfil the promise made by Patriarch Neilos in 1380: that the metropolitan be appointed upon nomination from Great Russia only.[24] Not only was Cyprian's successor a Greek, appointed directly from Constantinople, but also, upon the death of Photius (1431), the candidate of the Muscovite Grand-prince, Bishop Jonas of Ryazan, was turned down, and the Muscovites accepted another Greek (or Hellenized Bulgarian), Isidore.[25] This policy of strict loyalty to Byzantium was certainly an achievement of Metropolitan Cyprian's personal and lasting prestige, which profited his successors as well. It was also the result of the Byzantine support given to Moscow against its competitors, and of the religious and cultural ties, which were so strongly reinforced in the fourteenth century.

[22] In an encyclical addressed to all the bishops, clergy and princes of Russia, Photius proclaimed that there was one metropolitan in Russia since Russia's baptism under Vladimir and that this system of Church government was to be preserved until the end of time (RIB, VI, col. 318, 326–7).

[23] RIB, VI, cols. 357–60.   [24] MM, II, 18.

[25] A separate Metropolitan Gerasimus appeared again in Lithuania in 1434–5.

Furthermore, after the conversion of the Lithuanian rulers to Latin Christianity, Moscow was the only real claimant to Byzantium's inheritance in Russia, and this Byzantine connection provided the metropolitan with additional moral power to keep his control over the western dioceses, threatened by the Polish Roman-Catholic rule.

However, the connection was now at the mercy of a development which would give further credence to Moscow's growing sense of self-sufficiency. The development took the form of a major historical event: the Union of Florence, signed and promoted by Isidore, Metropolitan of Kiev and all Russia (1439), the appointee from Byzantium.

Even then, however, the Muscovite reaction came in a diplomatically mild form. Having originally authorized the administrative and financial obligations involved in the travel of a large Russian delegation, headed by Isidore, to Florence,[26] Grand-prince Basil II did nothing until Isidore's return (1441). Even after finally expelling him, he formally requested Constantinople to authorize an election of a new metropolitan in Russia,[27] and waited for seven more years before proceeding with the election of Metropolitan Jonas, without the blessing of Constantinople (1448). The negative reaction of the Muscovite Grand-prince found clear and sufficient justification in what the Russians had learned from their Byzantine teachers: an emperor, or a patriarch who betrays the Orthodox faith is no longer to be accepted as a legitimate authority. But other diplomatic and political aspects of the situation were also considered in Moscow and explain Basil's diplomatic game. Administrative loyalty to Constantinople was the guarantee of the metropolitanate's unity: the Muscovite authorities must have hesitated to appoint a metropolitan independently before checking the reaction of the Orthodox clergy and people in Lithuania. This reaction was generally hostile to Isidore, not only for purely doctrinal reasons, but also because of the still lingering 'Great Schism' in the West. King Władisław III of Poland had sided – at least until 1443 – with the Council of Basel against the pope and offered no help to Isidore, because he was an envoy of Eugenius IV. Thus, Church union was not immediately enforced in Polish and Lithuanian territories. Elected by Russian

---

[26] On this, see particularly A. Ya. Shpakov, *Gosudarstvo i tserkov' v ikh vzaimnykh otnosheniyakh v Moskovskom gosudarstve ot Florentiiskoi unii do uchrezhdeniya patriarshestva*, I, Kiev, 1904, pp. 43–8.

[27] RIB, VI, cols. 525–36.

bishops in Moscow in 1448, Bishop Jonas was formally invested with the traditional title of 'Metropolitan of Kiev and all Russia', and obtained formal recognition by King Casimir IV of Poland as the metropolitan of the entire Russian church (1451).[28] The documents of the period clearly suggest that a permanent break with Constantinople was not considered as inevitable in Moscow and that, if the decree of Florence was rejected in Byzantium, the old *status quo* could have been restored.

These last vestiges of the dream fell apart with the fall of Constantinople (1453), the appointment of Gregory Bolgarin as 'Metropolitan of Kiev and all Russia' by the Uniat ex-patriarch Gregory Mamme (1458), exiled in Rome, and the recognition of the 'Uniat' metropolitan by the Polish king. Moscow's reaction was inevitable. In a letter to the bishops of Lithuania and Poland, Metropolitan Jonas solemnly proclaimed that the sack of the 'Queen of cities' by the Turks was a punishment for the betrayal of Orthodoxy in Florence.[29] At this point the 'Byzantine Commonwealth' formally ceased to exist and the nationalistic and separatistic trends, which had appeared both in Moscow and in Lithuania, were vindicated by history itself. It is true that union with Rome did not last long in Kiev: already in 1470 Metropolitan Gregory Bolgarin switched his canonical allegiance to the Orthodox patriarch in Turkish-held Constantinople. But the division between the metropolitanates became permanent. When Metropolitan Jonas died (1461), his successor, Theodosius, was elected 'Metropolitan of all Rus'' without the title of 'Kiev': he was appointed 'for the house of the most-pure Mother of God, near the grave of the holy great wonder-worker Peter, the metropolitan' (i.e., in Moscow), whereas Russian bishops were required to pledge allegiance to him, as their legitimate primate, and to renounce 'Gregory, excommunicated from the holy Catholic church, who calls himself Metropolitan of Kiev'.[30] Thus, the Muscovite metropolitan had de facto renounced a claim to 'Little Russia', as belonging to his jurisdiction. In later years, the newly consecrated

---

[28] RIB, vi, cols. 563–6. However, the dioceses of Halich and Peremyshl' were excluded of his jurisdiction. They will be attached by Pope Pius II to the metropolitanate of Gregory Bolgarin in 1358 (cf. Tikhomirov, *Galitskaya mitropoliya*, pp. 147–8).

[29] RIB, vi, col. 623.

[30] RIB, vi, cols. 684, 689; cf. the de-facto recognition of the new state of affairs by the patriarch of Jerusalem, Joachim, who in 1464 asked Metropolitan Theodosius and 'the council of the Church of Great Russia' to perform the episcopal consecration of his *protosyggelos* Joseph as Metropolitan of Caesarea Philippi (RIB, vi, cols. 925–40).

Russian bishops were also asked to pledge not to receive metropolitans 'appointed in Constantinople, in the dominion of ungodly Turks, by a pagan tsar'.[31] 'Great Russia' with Moscow as its capital and the grave of St Peter, the 'Wonder worker' as its major sanctuary, was now seen as the last refuge of true Orthodoxy.

The problem of the Byzantine inheritance, as it developed in the following centuries of Russian history has been often discussed by scholars. Our own study is limited to the events of the fourteenth century and the particular impact of Byzantine civilization and policies upon Russia during that period. It is clear that these events were decisive in the following ways.

(1) Byzantium contributed decisively to the fact that Moscow and not Vilna (or perhaps Tver) became the capital of the Russian Empire. This statement is not meant to diminish the importance of the geographic and economic factors – which are known in the classical description of V. O. Klyuchevsky – or the role played by the Tatar administration, or the personal achievements of Ivan Kalita and his successors, or any other factor which contributed to the rise of Moscow. But, in the fierce competition which opposed Moscow to the Grand-principality of Lithuania, which – throughout the fourteenth century – controlled a much wider part of Russia, including the august old capital, Kiev, and certainly a more numerous population which identified itself as *Rus'* and enjoyed, under Lithuanian rule, greater independence from the hated Mongol yoke, the religious and political sanction, coming from the Byzantine patriarchate and empire, made an essential difference and swung the balance in Moscow's favour.

Nineteenth-century Russian historiography – and particularly the ecclesiastical historians – tended to understand the transfer of the metropolitan's seat from Kiev to Vladimir and Moscow, as a natural and organic development and to present the attempts at establishing separate metropolitanates in Galicia and Lithuania as flagrant usurpations, initiated by 'foreign' Polish and Lithuanian rulers and supported by the corruption and venality of the Byzantines. This view may give the partial explanation of some concrete incidents, but it certainly does not provide any adequate description of the historical situation as a whole. It suffers from an

---

[31] RIB, vi, col. 451, n. 3; col. 683, n. 2; cf. Makary, *Istoriya*, vi, p. 40. These extreme formulae, directed against the jurisdiction of Constantinople, were are action against the appointment of Spiridon Satana, as Metropolitan of Kiev, by the patriarchate. Spiridon was recognized neither in Moscow, nor in Kiev and died in monastic retirement, with a certain fame as a scholar and hagiographer (cf. A. Ya. Shpakov, *op. cit.*, pp. 229–44, and bibliography).

obvious anti-Byzantine bias and presupposes that, for all practical purposes, the borders of the Muscovite Grand-principality corresponded to the limits of 'Russia', as such. In fact, for Byzantium, the situation in Russia presented a difficult choice between 'two Russias', and if, as we have repeatedly noted, the Muscovite grand-princes may occasionally have been quite generous in replenishing the empty treasury of the Greek emperors and of ecclesiastical officials, there is no sufficient reason to believe that Byzantine support was given always and only to the highest bidder. Actually, we do not know whether Moscow's bids were really much higher than Lithuania's. But we do know of other factors which, throughout the fourteenth century (except for a brief period under the reign of Patriarch Callistos, in 1355–61) have certainly contributed to Byzantium's choice. The Grand-prince of Moscow was an Orthodox Christian, and, as such, more eligible than the pagan rulers of Lithuania to inherit the tradition of ancient Kiev. Of course, Olgerd, the 'fire-worshipper', was also offering to adopt Byzantine Christianity, but the constant competition of Latin missionary expansion in Lithuania (which almost succeeded under Olgerd's father Gedymin) were a disquieting element and made Moscow appear as a definitely more secure residence for the metropolitan 'of all Russia'. Furthermore, northern Russia appeared as more receptive to Byzantine religious and cultural influence: monasticism, religious art and literature were prospering under the aegis of Ivan Kalita and his successors, in ways unknown in southern and western Russia since the age of Yaroslav of Kiev. Finally, and most significantly, Moscow's loyalty (until around 1370) to the Golden Horde coincided with the Byzantine diplomacy of the early Palaeologan period, based upon friendship with the Mongols. This policy was also in the interests of the Genoese merchants, who controlled trade on the Black Sea and the commercial routes leading from the Mediterranean to the Orient through Sarai. Respected by the khans, the metropolitans of Russia, appointed by Constantinople and frequently visiting the Horde, were convenient diplomatic agents for the maintenance of Byzantine interests in Eastern Europe. Their mission could most conveniently be fulfilled from Moscow.

The de facto preference given to the northern principalities by the Byzantine ecclesiastical policies in Russia were bound to provoke problems in Lithuanian- and Polish-held areas. These problems were of a double nature: the pastoral needs of the local Orthodox dioceses could not be filled appropriately by a primate residing in distant and politically hostile territory, and the political interests of the Lithuanian Grand-prince and the Polish king were jeopardized, especially in extreme situations, for example, when Metropolitan Alexis assumed actual charge of the Muscovite government. However, the patriarchate did not succumb to these centrifugal pressures: the Byzantines knew well that the division of the metropolitanate implied the weakening of each of its parts and the eventual control of the Church by local interests. The shrewd policies of Patriarch Philotheos Kokkinos and Metropolitan Cyprian succeeded in temporarily suppressing both Lithuanian and Muscovite separatisms, symbolized respectively by Roman 'of Lithuania' and, later, Michael-Mityai and Pimen 'of Great Russia'. These policies allowed a new solidarity – and, at times, even alliance – between Moscow and Lithuania, which contributed to the victory of Kulikovo and the gradual disintegration of Tatar power in Russia. Unfortunately, the Polish-Lithuanian Union of Krewo (1385) and, later, the Union of Florence, made unity with Moscow practically impossible. The hopes of Metropolitan Cyprian for a unified *Rus'*, so well enshrined in his compilation of chronicles, was not fulfilled: the historical realities of the two following centuries led to the gradual bifurcation of the 'Great Russian' and 'Ukrainian' cultures and nationalities.

(2) In spite of the unfavourable political circumstances, the intellectual, ideological and spiritual impact of the Byzantine religious movement, generally known as Hesychasm, left a long-lasting mark in Russia. Without solving the problem of the relationship which existed in Byzantium between the victory of Palamite theology in 1351 and the so-called artistic 'Renaissance' of the Palaeologan period, it is possible to affirm that, in Russia, the great renewal of art, expressed in the works of Theophanes the Greek and Andrei Rublev, is undoubtedly connected with the monastic circles which, around St Sergius, got their inspiration from Hesychasm. Furthermore, the Russian monastic movement took remarkably strong proportions: its role in the social history of northern Russia is well known, but its obvious and immediate connections with Byzantine tradition is not always fully recognized by historians. Patristic, ascetical, hagiographic and liturgical texts were translated in great numbers – with or without the mediation of Southern Slavs – and continued for centuries to be copied and read in Russia.

The new availability of a living spiritual tradition, not only in the form of texts translated from the Greek, but also expressed in

272

the actual example of numerous monastic communities, in new and creative artistic forms, in the beginnings of a native literature and in newly discovered concerns for social implications of Christianity, clearly show the various dimensions of the Byzantine hesychast inheritance in northern Russia.[32] Because of this inheritance, Muscovy became not only a powerful and frequently oppressive empire, but also the country of St Sergius, Andrei Rublev, and St Nilus Sorsky.

Metropolitan Cyprian was particularly – and legitimately – associated with Hesychasm, not only because he introduced in Russia the disciplinary, doctrinal and liturgical practices adopted in Constantinople by his mentor, Philotheos, but particularly because he sternly preached against ownership of feudal domains by monasteries: his *Instruction* on this point to the Abbot St Athanasius Vysotsky,[33] was to be widely used in the sixteenth century, during the famous dispute between 'Possessors' and 'Non-Possessors'. St Nilus Sorsky, leader of the 'Non-Possessors' and most prominent teacher of Hesychasm in Russia, undoubtedly stands in the spiritual lineage of the fourteenth-century Hesychasts. The same can be said of later representatives of the same tradition in Russia.

(3) The Russians received the notion that culturally, politically, and religiously, they were a part of a wider, universal community. The universality of the emperor of Byzantium – as distinct from the local, or national competence of the other rulers, including the Grand-prince 'of all Russia' – was affirmed in official letters arriving from Constantinople, and acknowledged in locally-composed documents, as for example, the *Life* of St Stephen of Perm by Epiphanius the Wise.[34] However, these universalistic notions were not accepted without resistance. Especially after 1370, a 'nationalistic' and self-affirmative trend manifested itself in Moscow, as the patriarchate of Constantinople abandoned a policy of uncon‐ ditional support of Muscovite interests in favour of a more even‐ handed attitude, which recognized the needs of the Orthodox Church in Lithuania as well as Muscovy. Understandably, this same separatistic trend felt itself vindicated after the scandal with Isidore. With the independent election of Jonas (1448) and the final division of the metropolitanate, the Church of Moscow be‐ came de facto a national Church. Its primate became much more dependent upon the Grand-prince, since he was his appointee.

[32] On this point, see Prokhorov, 'Keleinaya literatura', pp. 317–24.
[33] RIB, VI, col. 263. [34] Cf. above, p. 137.

But nationalistic mentality never succeeded in suppressing totally the ideas of universality and of ecclesiastical independence which were so strongly promoted by Patriarch Philotheos, by Metropolitan Cyprian and by the Hesychasts of the fourteenth century. Representatives of these ideas – primarily monastics and some *literati* – had little access to power in the State or in the Church, but they never ceased to have a significant impact on society.

We have noted earlier that symbols, which could be interpreted as preludes to a *translatio imperii* to Russia, were sometimes used in the fourteenth century. However, no official *translatio* ever occurred. Even after Florence and the fall of Constantinople, the Muscovite Grand-prince did not formally claim the succession of the emperors. Not even the marriage of Ivan III with Zoe-Sophia, the niece of the two last Byzantine *basileis* and the granddaughter of Manuel II – which was clearly intended to make an eventual claim to succession more credible – did lead to the claim itself. Significantly, the claim was implied in letters from the Venetian Senate,[35] but not in any Muscovite document of the period! The ideas found in the famous letters of the monk Philotheos of Pskov, written to Grand-prince Basil III in the early sixteenth century and formulating the idea of Moscow, 'the Third Rome', were never formally endorsed by the Muscovite State. Moreover, when Ivan IV was finally crowned and assumed the title of *tsar*, he asked for – and obtained – a sanction of the Eastern Patriarchs, captives of the Turks, and refrained from taking the title of 'emperor of the Romans', becoming 'tsar of all Russia' only. What a contrast with the South-Slavic empires of Bulgaria and Serbia!

Of course, in the fifteenth and sixteenth centuries, the Middle Ages were over and Western cultural and political ideas – which came to Russia together with the Italian-educated princess Zoe-Sophia and which were symbolized in the rebuilding of the Moscow Kremlin by Italian architects – made Byzantine political philosophy partially obsolete for the Russians. But one should also note that this philosophy was never simply discarded. Quite to the contrary, it still provided the official framework of political thinking: as late as 1588, Boris Godunov, the shrewd prime-minister of Tsar Theodore Ivanovich, made the attempt at convincing the visiting patriarch of Constantinople, Jeremiah II, to remain in Russia. If the patriarch had accepted, there is no doubt that the scheme of a

---

[35] *Quando stirps mascula deesset imperatoria, ad Vestram Illustrissimam Dominationem jure vestri faustissimi conjugii pertineret* (Senato, Secreti, XXVI, 50, quoted in A. Ya. Shpakov, *op. cit.*, I, p. xviii.)

'Third Rome' would have been officially realized, and proclaimed. But Jeremiah preferred to return to the Phanar, while succumbing to Russian pressure in establishing a 'patriarchate of Moscow'. This new patriarchate did not claim universal primacy and eventually settled – in spite of its immense wealth, prestige and power – with the fifth place in the order of Orthodox patriarchs.

This deliberate ideological self-limitation of the Russians can be explained by a variety of considerations. In no way did it prevent the Russian empire from spectacular growth, as a *national* state. But precisely because of this national character of the Muscovite tsardom, some deep-seated consciousness kept reminding its leaders that the 'Roman' (and Byzantine) political ideology excluded the right of any nation, as nation, to monopolize the leadership of the universal Orthodox Christian Commonwealth. Since the Muscovite state always defined itself in national terms, it could claim no right to a real *translatio imperii*. The example of the Nicaean state of the thirteenth century can serve as a model for this inner dialectic: expelled from Constantinople, it is not in virtue of its resurgent 'Hellenism' that Nicaea maintained the standard of the Christian *oikouménè*, but because it still claimed to be 'Roman' and looked for the restoration of its power in the only real 'New Rome', Constantinople.

In Muscovy, the 'universalist' consciousness was maintained and voiced by the monastic circles, which had been trained in it by the influx of Byzantine ideas and spirituality in the fourteenth century. It expressed itself in literature. D. S. Likhachev, explaining the elaborate and flowery style known as *pletenie sloves*, notes that it represents a concern for 'the universal, the absolute and the eternal' to be found in 'the particular, the concrete and the temporal' events described in the texts: the method used was to imitate Greek models, since – in a peculiar genealogy of sacred languages, described by the Bulgarian 'philosopher' Constantine Kostenetsky – the Slavic tongue is only a child of Hebrew, its father, and of Greek, its mother.[36] It is precisely because Russia was only a 'nation', and not a 'third Rome', that the Russian Church (often in opposition to the brutal integrationism of the Muscovite government) found it legitimate to spread Orthodoxy among *other* nations: the missionary activity of St Stephen of Perm – praised by Epiphanius the Wise, the great promoter of Byzantinism and 'weaving of words' in Russia – consisted in assuming the

---

[36] Cf. Likhachev, *Nekotorye zadachi*, pp. 110–12, 117.

model of Sts Cyril and Methodius and in translating Scriptures and the liturgy into the language of the Finnish Permians. His example was to be followed by many Russian monks and churchmen until modern times.

The same universalist consciousness found defenders among the hesychast 'Non-Possessors' of the sixteenth century, who maintained Metropolitan Cyprian's advocacy of monastic poverty, but also – spurred by Maximus the Greek – challenged the administrative independence of the Russian Church from Constantinople, which, in their opinion, had been usurped. Subsequently, in the seventeenth century, a most powerful expression of the 'provincial' and nationalistic trend of Russian Orthodoxy was shown in the schism of the 'Old Believers', who protested the introduction by Patriarch Nikon of practices adopted from the 'corrupt' Greeks.

Under a slightly different form, the tradition of Byzantine Christian universalism was used as a recourse by those who were unhappy with the dependence of the Russian Church upon civil authority. In the circles close to Archbishop Gennadius of Novgorod (1484–1504) – who was neither a Hesychast nor a 'Non-Possessor', but had become familiar with Western patterns of Church–State relations – there emerges the curious and extremely popular *Legend of the White Cowl* (*Skazanie o belom klobuke*) a peculiarly Russian variation of that extraordinary document, which played such a large role in Western and Eastern medieval institutional concepts, the *Donation of Constantine*.[37]

According to the Russian *Legend*, Pope Sylvester of Rome received a white cowl as a gift from Emperor Constantine after the latter's conversion. The symbolic and miraculous value of the cowl was neglected in Rome, after the reign of the Emperor *Karul* (i.e. Charlemagne, the imitator of anti-Byzantine religious polemics in the West) and the tenure of Pope Formosus (891–6, frequently mentioned as the initiator of the schism). The cowl was then sent to Constantinople by the last Orthodox pope and was received by Emperor John Cantacuzenos and Patriarch Philotheos, who, foreseeing the forthcoming fall of the New Rome, sent the cowl to Archbishop Basil Kalika of Novgorod (1330–52). The conclusion resolves itself in the theme of the 'Third Rome': 'All the kingdoms

---

[37] Cf. particularly N. N. Rozov, 'Povest' o Novgorodskom belom klobuke kak pamyatnik obshcherusskoi publitsistiki XV v', TODRL, IX, 1953, pp. 178–219 (analysis of the various versions and editions; dating; bibliography). The *Legend* has also been recently studied by Labunka (unpublished dissertation, Columbia University, N.Y., 1975).

will be reunited into the one kingdom of Russia', where a patriarchate will also be established.

Neither the chronological and historical inconsistencies, nor the more important issue of Novgorodian local pride, reflected in the *Legend*, are directly relevant to our theme, but the fact that the heroes of the myth on a mystical connection between Roman primacy, Constantinople and Russia are no other than John Cantacuzenos, Patriarch Philotheos Kokkinos and a powerful Novgorodian archbishop of the fourteenth century is quite significant. Fully acknowledging the medieval and Byzantine notion that Empire and Church are inseparable, the *Legend*, following the *Donation*, credits Constantine with the initiative of singling out the Bishop of Rome and granting him the white cowl. Furthermore, it attributes not only to Philotheos but also to John Cantacuzenos a role in the transfer of the cowl to Russia. But, in Russia itself, the recipient is not a prince but an archbishop, Basil of Novgorod, who, as we have seen earlier, had been granted the right to wear a *polystavrion* (a *phelonion*, or chasuble with crosses) by Metropolitan Theognostos.[38] In order to emphasize this privilege, granted specifically to an ecclesiastic, the *Legend* proclaims that the miraculous white cowl is 'more honorable than an imperial crown'. There is no doubt that, in this affirmation, lies the real message which the authors intend to convey: the Byzantine inheritance associated with Cantacuzenos, Philotheos and fourteenth-century Hesychasm is an inheritance of a mystical nature, whose recipient in Russia is the Church, rather than the state. Tsar Ivan IV was fully aware of that aspect of the *Legend*, which was unpleasing to him, and, in 1564, bestowed the right to wear the white cowl upon the metropolitan of Moscow, as head of the imperial Russian Church.[39] After 1589, the privilege was kept by the patriarchs of Moscow. But since the white cowl, according to the *Legend*, signified a supremacy of the priesthood over the empire, it remained unwelcome to the increasingly secularized Russian state. Peter the Great, after suppressing the patriarchate, considered that the safest way of destroying the symbolism of the cowl was to make it into a rather common piece of ecclesiastical

[38] Ch. 4, p. 84; Archbishop Basil Kalika did, indeed, wear an elaborate white cowl which was discovered in his tomb (N. N. Rozov, *op. cit.*, pp. 191–2). The cowl may have been considered as a distinction accompanying the *polystavrion*. His successor, Moses, is also represented with a white cowl on the frescoes in Volotovo.

[39] Cf. Sokolov, *Arkhierei*, pp. 292–5. Sokolov, however, considers the *Legend* to be a document of the seventeenth century, which is untenable in the light of the research done by Rozov and, later, Labunka, on the manuscript tradition.

attire: he granted the right to wear a white cowl to all the metropolitans of the Russian Church.

The growth of a powerful national empire, the development in the Ukraine of separate cultural patterns, with strong Polish influences, the secularization of the Russian state under Peter and Catherine – not to speak of the more recent developments which marked the twentieth century – are the 'realities' of Russian history. In terms of political ideology, the concepts generated by Russia's belonging to the Byzantine Commonwealth and promoted by Patriarch Philotheos, Metropolitan Cyprian, St Sergius of Radonezh and St Stephen of Perm were nothing but dreams. However, dreams, when they are rooted in powerful spiritual forces, possess the peculiar property of providing the life of nations – and indeed human society as a whole – with patterns of judgement, norms of behaviour and historical meaning. The revivals of monastic spirituality in nineteenth-century Russia, the universal appeal of religious art – which achieved its apex with Theophanes and Rublev – and, in general, the continuous vitality of Orthodox Christianity, in a country where religion is banished from the mainstream of society, are all making the fabric of Russian civilization incomprehensible outside of its Byzantine background. In order to understand the problems fully, the events of the fourteenth century, which saw the birth of modern Russia (since the Kievan period is rather its pre-history) provide the essential key.

Appendices
Some translated sources

The translated sources presented below represent a selection of characteristic documents, reflecting the relations between Byzantium and Russia in the fourteenth century and frequently used in the preceding chapters. Nos. 1–9 are integral translations of the Greek, or Slavonic originals. No. 10 contains selections of the synodal documents of 1380 and 1389.

I

Emperor John VI Cantacuzenos restores the unity of the metropolitanate of Kiev and all Russia (August 1347)

(Original text in Zachariae, *Jus*, III, pp. 700–3; RIB, VI, app., cols. 13–19; also in MM, I, pp. 267–71, as part of the Synodal Act of Patriarch Isidore on the same issue.)

Since the time when, by the grace of Christ, the nation of the Russians accepted the knowledge of God, the most holy dioceses found in the region of Little Russia, known as Volhynia – i.e. the dioceses of Galicia, Vladimir, Kholm, Peremyshl', Lutsk and Turov – depended, as well as the most holy dioceses of Great Russia, upon the most holy metropolitanate of Kiev, which is presently held by its most sacred Metropolitan Theognostos, *hypertimos* and exarch of all Russia.

However, during the recent time of confusion,[1] those who governed the affairs of the empire and also the man who unworthily presided over the Church,[2] profited from the instability of the times and had no other concern than to fulfil their own appetites. They reversed the normal order of the political and ecclesiastical affairs, threw chaos and confusion practically everywhere and caused every possible harm and damage to the souls and bodies of Christians. Among the novelties introduced by them was that they separated the aforementioned dioceses of Little Russia from that most holy metropolitanate of Kiev and placed them in the dependence of the high-priest of Galicia, having promoted him from bishop to metropolitan.

This action abolished a situation which had been established by custom from of old in the entire country of Russia. All the Christians inhabiting it refuse to have two metropolitans as their pastors and consider [the division of the metropolitanate] as intolerable and hateful. They desire, as was said before, that the practice which they knew from of old remain untouched and unchangeable and make every effort to

---

[1] The 'time of confusion' (καιρὸς τῆς συγχύσεως) referred to here is the period of civil war in Byzantium (1341–7).

[2] Patriarch John Calecas (1333–47), a supporter of the anti-Palamites, deposed in 1347.

reverse the innovation. Actually, the same novelty had been undertaken at other times, but it was abolished and reversed immediately,
because, as we said, the Christians of Russia refused to condone the
abolition of a situation to which they were accustomed.

The most noble Grand-prince of Russia, the very beloved nephew of
Our Majesty, Lord Symeon, presently reported about it to Our Majesty
and, in a petition endorsed also by the other Russian princes, requested
that, by a chrysobull of Our Majesty, the said dioceses be restored to
the said most holy metropolitanate of Kiev, as before.

Our Majesty, therefore, judging that this petition of his is just and
blessed, being in conformity with the aforementioned custom, prevailing from past times until today, and also [knowing] the exceptional
virtues and God-pleasing life of the most sacred Metropolitan of Kiev,
hypertimos and exarch of all Russia, who was deprived [of his rights],
consents, orders and defines by issuing the present decree, sealed with
gold, that the most holy dioceses in the said Little Russia – Galicia,
Vladimir, Kholm, Peremyshl', Lutsk and Turov – be submitted again
to the aforementioned most holy metropolitanate of Kiev, since, as was
shown earlier, they were illegitimately given to [the bishop] of Galicia
during the aforementioned time of confusion; and also that the incumbent of the said most holy metropolitanate of Kiev should accomplish
in those dioceses whatever the divine and sacred canons prescribe the
metropolitans to accomplish in the dioceses which are submitted to
them and whatever the same most sacred Metropolitan of Kiev – who
was deprived [of his rights] – was accomplishing there, consecrating
and enthroning bishops, judging and investigating ecclesiastical affairs,
whenever necessary, and doing other things, prescribed by the divine
and sacred canons; and that the God-loving bishops of those most holy
dioceses should pay proper obeisance to the same most sacred Metropolitan of Kiev, *hypertimos* and exarch of all Russia, the Lord Theognostos (and to those metropolitans who would succeed him) as to their
First Bishop, and be submitted to all his words and instructions, tending
to the progress of Christians living there, or related to other issues of
ecclesiastical and canonical life and order.

Consequently, in virtue of the present chrysobull of Our Majesty, the
aforementioned most holy dioceses of Little Russia shall be henceforth
submitted to the most holy metropolitanate of Kiev – which was
deprived [of its rights] – and to its present incumbent the most sacred
metropolitan, *hypertimos* and exarch of all Russia, Lord Theognostos.
As was said before, their ecclesiastical affairs shall be judged, investi-
gated and properly solved by him. He shall also and after him his
successors, accomplish there whatever is proper and canonical. And
this order shall be preserved forever, in conformity with ancient custom, as was shown before, so that the most holy dioceses [of Russia]
shall remain under one metropolitan.

Our Majesty has published on this matter the present chrysobull and it was forwarded to the region of the aforementioned metropolitanate of Kiev, so that this issue may be solved.

Issued during the month of August of the present fifteenth indiction of the year 6855, with the signature of our pious and God-established sovereignty.

2

Patriarch Philotheos affirms his universal authority and supports Metropolitan Alexis as regent of Muscovy (June 1370)

(Original in MM I, pp. 520–2; RIB VI, app. cols. 109–13.)

Very noble princes of all Russia, beloved and desired sons of our Humility in the Holy Spirit! Our Humility wishes you all health and happiness for your souls, strength and prosperity for your bodies, success and luck in all your life's affairs, an extension of your power and an increase of the honours you receive, and every other good and saving thing from God Almighty.

Our Humility knows well and for a long time the purity of your faith and of your piety, which, in times past, in the beginning, you received from our most holy, catholic and apostolic Church of God and which you preserve, as you received it, without blemish, pure and unchanging, since you are Orthodox Christians. Since this is indeed the most exalted of all good things, Our Humility never ceases to pray that you keep this faith in yourselves and that you grow further in your faith in God and in your piety.

You will indeed obtain those things, if you render the appropriate fear, honour, submission and obedience to the most sacred Metropolitan of Kiev and all Russia, *hypertimos*, the beloved brother and concelebrant of Our Humility in the Holy Spirit, whom God, through our hands, has granted to you; if you love him and that which he tells you – the authentic sons of the Church – as you ought to love God himself.

Since God has appointed Our Humility as leader of all Christians found anywhere on the inhabited earth, as solicitor and guardian of their souls, all of them depend on me, the father and teacher of them all. If that was possible, therefore, it would have been my duty to walk everywhere on earth by the cities and countries and to teach there the Word of God. I would have had to do so unfailingly, since this is my duty. However, since it is beyond the possibilities of one weak and mightless man to walk around the entire inhabited earth, Our Humility chooses the best among men, the most eminent in virtue, establishes

283

and ordains them as pastors, teachers and high priests, and sends them to the ends of the universe. One of them goes to your great country, to the multitudes which inhabit it, another reaches other areas of the earth, and still another goes elsewhere, so that each one, in the country and place which was appointed for him, enjoys territorial rights, an episcopal chair and all the rights of Our Humility.

And since you have there, as my representative, the most sacred Metropolitan of Kiev and all Russia, a venerable, pious and virtuous man, endowed with all qualities, able by the grace of Christ to feed the people and lead it to saving pastures, capable of consoling distressed souls and strengthening shaking hearts – as you well know, since you experienced his superior character and his holiness – you owe him the same great honour and obedience, as you would be obliged to render to myself, if I was present there. For he is invested with our rights and he is my representative, so that the honour, the submission and the obedience which are rendered to him, passes on to Our Humility and, through us, is finally directed to God Himself.

Therefore, as true sons of the Church of Christ, nourishing the right faith and piety in your souls, you must obey your father, pastor and teacher, whom, through us, God has granted you. You must love him, as you love me, and consider his words as words of God. If you act accordingly and if you are thus disposed towards the Church of God and towards your most sacred metropolitan, you will, first of all, receive your reward in this present life, having acquired God as your ally and helper in whatever need. He will grant you increase of power, long life, abundance of riches, success in all good things, untroubled, painless existence and bodily health. Also, in the future life, you will receive the kingdom of heaven, the inheritance and the enjoyment of eternal good things. And from Our Humility, you will get many great praises, gratitude and prayers to God.

May His grace and mercy preserve you, standing fast in the right and pure faith, obedient to the father and teacher of your souls, so that you may remain without sickness, happy and above any grievous occurrence.

With a mark of the venerable hand of the patriarch: on the month of June, eighth indiction.

3

Enemies of Moscow excommunicated by patriarchate (June 1370)

(Greek original MM, I, pp. 523–34; RIB, VI, app., cols. 117–20.)

In as much as the very noble princes of Russia have all agreed by covenant, making awesome oaths and kissing the honourable and life-creating cross, together with the very noble Grand-prince of all Russia, Lord Dimitri, to the effect that they would all together take arms against those who are foreign to our faith, the enemies of the cross, who do not believe in our Lord Jesus Christ, but practise the evil and blasphemous worship of fire;

and in as much as the Grand prince, in accordance with those oaths and agreements which he made with them, despised his own life, considered that loving God, making war for Him and struggling against His enemies is more precious than anything, and was waiting for them in readiness;

and in as much as they, having no fear of God and no respect for their oaths, but betraying those oaths and the cross, which they had kissed, were not faithful to the mutual agreements and promises, which they had promised, but rather allied themselves with the impious Olgerd, who made war against the Grand-prince, killed and destroyed many Christians;

and in as much as, for these reasons, the princes were excommunicated by the most sacred metropolitan of Kiev and all Russia, the beloved brother and concelebrant of Our Humility in the Holy Spirit, since they had despised and betrayed the commandments of God and their own oaths and covenants;

having learned all this, Our Humility thought that the princes have committed a great sin against Christians and also holds them excommunicated, since they have acted against the sacred community of Christians. They will receive pardon from Our Humility, when they act in accordance with agreements and oaths, and take arms against the enemies of the cross together with the Grand-prince; when they come and fall down at the feet of their metropolitan and request him to write about it to Our Humility. When the metropolitan writes to us here that they had returned and repented truly and in good faith, they will also receive pardon from Our Humility.

These men should know that excommunication is a separation and a total estrangement from the holy Church of God, and they should repent truly and in good faith, so that they may receive from Our Humility a pardon for what they have done.

With a mark of the venerable hand of the patriarch: on the month of June, eighth indiction.

4

The threat of King Casimir of Poland (1370)

(Greek text in MM, I, pp. 577–8; RIB, VI, app., cols. 125–8.)

To the Primate, the most sacred patriarch of Constantinople of the ecumenical council: greetings and very respectful petition from your son, King Casimir of the land of Poland and Little Russia, and from the princes of Russia, who believe in the faith of Christians, and from the boyars of the Russians, respectful petition.

We request from you our high priest. Today the whole land is ruined without law, because the law is reduced to chaos. From times immemorial, Galicia was known everywhere as a metropolitanate, and, from times immemorial, it was the throne of a metropolitanate. Niphon was the first metropolitan having received your blessing; the second metropolitan was Peter; the third metropolitan was Gabriel; the fourth metropolitan was Theodore. All these occupied the aforementioned throne of Galicia.

The princes of Russia were our relatives, but these princes left Russia [=Galicia, occupied by Casimir, *Ed.*] and the country was widowed. Henceforth I, King of Poland, took over the land of Russia. And now, O holy father, patriarch of the ecumenical councils, we request from you our own high-priest, because, by the grace of God and with your blessing, together with our princes and boyars, we elected a worthy, good man, whose life is pure and whose heart is humble – the very sacred bishop Anthony, and [we are sending him to you] for this purpose to receive your blessing.

For God's sake, and for ours, and for the sake of the holy Church, bestow your blessing upon that man, so that the throne of that metropolitanate may not remain vacant. Consecrate Anthony as a metropolitan, so that the law of the Russians may not be reduced to chaos, so that it may not disappear.

And if the grace of God and your blessing are not bestowed upon that man, do not complain against us afterwards. We will be forced to baptize the Russians into the faith of the Latins, if there is no metropolitan in Russia, for the land cannot remain without a law.

5

The protest of Olgerd

(Greek text in MM, I, pp. 580–1; RIB, VI, suppl., cols., 135–40.)

From the king of the Lithuanians, Olgerd, to the patriarch, respectful greetings.

You sent me a letter with your servant Theodore, saying that the metropolitan [Alexis] is complaining to you against me. He says: 'King Olgerd has attacked us.' I did not start the attack. The attacks came first from him. They did not renounce the kissing of the cross [i.e., a pledge of allegiance, or friendship], which they offered me and they did not send back the documents used in the oaths. They attacked me nine times. They convoked my wife's brother, prince Michael, covering themselves with oaths, and the metropolitan made him free of all fear, inviting him to come and to leave at will, and they arrested him. And they arrested my son-in-law, Prince Boris of Nizhni-Novgorod and confiscated his principality. They attacked my son-in-law, Prince Ivan of Novosil', and his principality: they arrested his mother and took away my daughter, in spite of the oaths which they gave them. In spite of their oaths, they took from me the following cities: Rzheva, Sishka, Gudin, Osechen, Goryshevo, Ryasna, Velikie Luki, Klichen', Vseluk, Volgo, Kozlovo, Lipitsa, Tesov, Khlepen', Fomin Gorodok, Berezuesk, Kaluga, Mtsenesk. All these are cities, and they took them all, in spite of the kissing of the cross, and they did not send back the documents used in the oaths. We did not bear that much, and we attacked them, and unless they set things right with me, I will not bear with them even now.

With your blessing, their metropolitan blesses the bloodshed until this day. Not even our fathers knew such metropolitans as this metropolitan! He blesses the Muscovites to commit bloodshed. He never visits us. He never goes to Kiev. And when someone kisses the cross to me and then escapes to them, the metropolitan frees him from his allegiance. Did it ever happen in the world, that one would be freed from allegiance after kissing the cross? My servant, Ivan of Kozelsk, kissed the cross to me, with his mother, his brothers, his wife and his children, promising to remain with me, but he fled, taking the mother, the brothers, the wife and the children, and metropolitan Alexis freed him from his kissing-of-the-cross . . . Ivan Vyazemsky kissed the cross, then fled, betraying those who pledged for him, and the metropolitan freed him from his kissing-of-the-cross. Basil the *nagubnik*[3] kissed the cross in the presence of a bishop, so that the bishop pledged for him, but he betrayed the bishop's pledge, and fled, and the metropolitan freed him from his kissing-of-the-cross. And many others fled, and he frees them from their oath, that is, from the kissing-of-the-cross.

The Metropolitan should have blessed the Muscovites to help us, since we fight the Germans on their behalf. We invite the metropolitan to visit us, but he never comes to us. Give us another metropolitan for Kiev, Smolensk, Tver, Little Russia, Novosil' and Nizhni-Novgorod!

---

[3] On the probable meaning of *nagubnik*, the title of a Lithuanian state official, see RIB, VI, app., col. 139, note 4.

6

Philotheos: evenhandedness is a condition of unity (1371)

(Greek text in MM, I, pp. 320–2; RIB, VI, supp., cols., 155–60.)

Most sacred Metropolitan of Kiev and all Russia, *hypertimos*, beloved brother and concelebrant of Our Humility in the Holy Spirit, grace and peace from God be with Your sacredness.

I received your letter, sent with your servant Avvakum, and I read what you write and report in it. Let it be known to you that, even before [I received it], I arranged to send you a reliable personal envoy: indeed, the Grand-prince of the Lithuanians sent me a letter, where he wrote important things, and I thought it proper to send my envoy to Your Sacredness with a letter from Our Humility, from which you will learn exactly what the Grand-prince of Lithuania wrote.

As my envoy was leaving, a monk came with a letter from the Grand-prince of Tver, Michael. I received the letter and read what he wrote. For he also wrote important things and, in addition, he asked for a trial between him and yourself: Your Sacredness would be called here before the synod and he would send his boyars, so that a trial may take place.

How can I refuse him a trial? So I wrote to Your Sacredness, through the aforementioned envoy, as you will learn yourself from my letters. If possible, you should come here, or, if that is not possible, you should send your boyars, and he will send his, so that a trial may take place. But now, as your servant Avvakum came, I also learned from your letter, and also personally from him, what you write and what you request.

So, imitating Christ the Peacemaker, I now write and call upon you: there is nothing good, as it appears to me, in the scandals and conflicts which happened between you and the prince of Tver, Michael, and in the fact that you both come to trial. Rather, as his father and teacher, you should try to make peace with him. If he made mistakes, you, as his father, forgive him and accept him again as your son, and have peace with him, as also with the other princes. And he also, as I write to him, must repent and seek forgiveness. These appear to me as good and proper steps to take: let it be so, without further debate. But if you refuse and request a trial, I do not object, but beware of the possible heavy consequences.

As I said before, Our Humility wrote a letter to the prince of Tver, Michael, and I am sending it with your servant Avvakum. When it comes into your hands, give it to my envoy, whom I sent there previously. Give him also one of your servants, as translator, so that he may go with him to the prince of Tver to show him my first letter, and also the second one, which I am now writing about peace, so that he may also talk to him, calling him to repentance and to peace. I have confidence that he will not act otherwise, but follow my directions.

Your Sacredness certainly knows that, when we performed your consecration, we consecrated you as Metropolitan of Kiev and all Russia: not of a portion, but of all of Russia. But now I hear that you visit neither Kiev, nor Lithuania, but remain in one place, leaving the rest without pastoral care, without supervision, without fatherly instruction. This is offensive and foreign to the tradition of the sacred canons. The right attitude for you is to visit the whole land of Russia, to have love and fatherly disposition towards all the princes, to love them all equally, to show them the same and equal disposition, good-will and love. You should not love some and accept them as your sons, whereas you do not love others. Rather, consider them all as your sons and love them all equally. Then they also will render you favour, love, full and complete submission, whereas you will receive God's help.

Let it be known to you that I also wrote to the Grand-prince of the Lithuanians, asking him to love and honour you according to the ancient custom, as the other princes of Russia also do. I also asked him that when you travel to his region, he must show you honour, devotion and great love, so that you may travel throughout his lands without difficulty. And you also try, as far as possible, to have love and good disposition towards him, as towards the other princes, because the people of God, named after Christ, which happens to be under his rule, needs your supervision and teaching. It is, therefore, an absolute necessity that there be love between you and him: you must see both him and the people of God, to teach it. Do this with every possible zeal and without any further discussion.

For the rest, Our Humility wrote to you more extensively through my servant John: you will learn it without fail.

7

After the death of Alexis: Cyprian and his monastic friends. Letter 1 to St Sergius (3 June 1378)

(Slavic text in PS, 1860, May, pp. 84–5 and Prokhorov, *Povest'*, p. 195.)

A blessing in the Holy Spirit to the beloved sons of Our Humility, the venerable Abbots Sergius and Theodore. I pray God that you pursue the salvation of your souls, together with the brotherhood given to you by God. Instruct them in the ways of salvation. I hear of you and of your virtue, how you despise all worldly pursuits and concern yourselves only with the will of God: I thank God greatly for this and I pray Him, that He may grant us to meet together and to receive the pleasure of a spiritual conversation. Let it be known to you: I have arrived in Lyubutsk on Thursday 3 June, and I am on my way to see my son, the Grand-prince, in Moscow. I am coming bringing peace and blessing, as once Joseph when he was sent by his father to his brothers [cf. Gen. 45]. Whatever some say about me, I am a bishop, not a military man. I bring a blessing, as the Lord, who sent his disciples to preach, teaching them saying. 'He that receiveth you receiveth me' [Mat. 10.40; John 13.20]. So be ready to see me, wherever you see fit. I am looking forward to seeing you and being consoled with a spiritual consolation. May the mercy of God and the holy Mother of God, and my blessing be with you.

8

Cyprian faces Moscow's separatism.
Letter 2 to St Sergius (23 June 1378)

(Slavic text, PS, 1860, pp. 85–102, 448–62; also in RIB, vi, app. cols. 173–86 and Prokhorov, *Povest'*, pp. 195–201; paragraphs and marginal sub-headings are mine. J.M.)

Cyprian, by the grace of God, metropolitan of all Russia, to the venerable elder, the Abbot Sergius and to Abbot Theodore, and to any other, who shares your views.

1. You and the whole Christian people are aware of what happened to me: something which no bishop, since the beginning of the Russian land, ever suffered. The whole universe knows that I, through the will of God, through election of the great and holy synod, through the blessing and installation by the ecumenical patriarch, was appointed metropolitan of the entire land of the Rus'. Thus I went to the Grand-prince with fully open heart and good will. But he sent envoys instructing them not to let me pass. He blocked the roads, placing military detachments and officers, giving them instructions to treat me harshly, up to the point of even putting us to death mercilessly. But I, being rather concerned with his dishonour and the fate of his soul, went through by another road, placing my hope in my openheartedness and the love I nourished for the Grand-prince, his princess and his children. But he assigned a torturer, the cursed Nicephorus, to watch over me. Is there any evil against me, which he left undone? Blasphemes, insults, derision, thefts, hunger! He locked me in the dark, naked and hungry, and I am still sick from that dark cold place. In addition to the great harm they did to my servants, letting them go, riding emaciated horses, without saddles, with bast bridles, they drove them out of the city having stolen all their belongings, including shirts, knives and leggings. Not even shoes and hats they left them!

Dimitri dishonours Cyprian

2. Thus, was there nobody left in Moscow concerned about the soul of the Grand-prince and his inheritance? Did everyone stay aside passively? The Grand-prince is told that the horses are returned, but he does not know that out of forty or so horses, not one is in good shape, but all are exhausted, lamed and worn out, because they raced on them where they wished, and now they are lost.

Perhaps, laymen are fearful of the prince, since they have wives and children, properties and wealth, and they do not want to lose them (as the Saviour said himself: 'It is easier for a camel to go through the eye of a needle, than for a rich man to enter into the Kingdom of God', [Mat. 19.24]). But you, who have renounced the world and the things of the world, and who live for God alone, why did you remain silent, seeing such evil? If you are concerned about the soul of the Grand-prince and all his inheritance, why did you remain silent? You should have torn apart your garments and 'spoken before princes' without fear: if they had listened to you, it would have been well; if they had killed you, you would be saints. Do you not know that the sin of the people falls on the princes, and the sin of princes – on the people? Do you not know Scripture which says that the curse of fleshly parents falls on children's children? How much more, the curse of spiritual fathers 'uproots the very foundations' [cf. Ecclesiasticus 3.9] and leads to perdition. Why do you content yourself with silence, when you see the holy place blasphemed, according to Scripture which says: 'The desolating sacrilege standing in the holy place' [Dan. 11.31; 12.11, Mat. 24.15]? Is this the way for the prince and the boyars to venerate the metropolitanate and the graves of holy metropolitans? Is there nobody who read the divine canons? Do you not know what is written in them?

Bishops do not appoint successors

3. Canon seventy-six of the Holy Apostles reads: 'A bishop should not allow a brother, or a son, or another relative, or a friend to appoint whoever they want to the episcopal dignity; it is not right to appoint heirs of one's episcopacy and make God's gift into human preference. The Church of God cannot be made dependent upon heirs. If anyone does it, such an appointment is null and the perpetrator is to be excommunicated.' Listen also to the commentary on this canon:

The high priestly power is to be considered a grace and a gift of the Holy Spirit. How can anyone dare to transmit a spiritual grace as a lot to someone else? This is why bishops are not allowed to ordain and install whomever they wish as their successors in their churches. Indeed, those who have no right to leave to whomever they wish the properties which they acquired during the course of their episcopate (but only that which they received as an inheritance from relatives, according to Canon thirty-two of the Council of Carthage), how could such men transmit episcopacy itself, to others, as successors of their pastoral authority, leaving them as administrators of the affairs of the poor and granting to whom they wish, out of human preference, or friendship, or because of blood-relationship, the things which were consecrated to God? If any such gift occurs, the action is invalid according to the canons, and the perpetrator is to be excommunicated. For it has been ordained that bishops would be appointed by synods.[4]

[4] Cf. the original Greek text of Canon 76 of the Holy Apostles and its commentary by Zonaras in Rhalles-Potles, II, pp. 97–8; Canon 32 of Carthage, *ibid.*, III, pp. 386–7.

Also Canon twenty-three of the Council of Antioch says: 'Even at the end of his life, a bishop is not permitted to establish another as his successor.'[5] This was also forbidden to the Israelites: for Moses was considered guilty, because he elevated Aaron and his sons to the priesthood, so that if God had not affirmed their priesthood by a sign, they would have been deprived of it.[6]

4. Look also at Canon twenty-eight of the Holy Apostles, which says: 'If a bishop or a priest or a deacon acquires the high priestly dignity for money, let him be deposed, as well as the one who ordained him, and let him be cut away from holy communion completely, as Simon Magus by me, Peter.'[7] The thirtieth Canon of the same Holy Apostles says the same: 'If a bishop acquires the high priesthood with the help of civil authorities, let him be deposed and excommunicated, as well as those who cooperated with him.'[8] And let us note this: when is a priest punished twice or, according to St Gennadios, Patriarch of New Rome, even three times [for the same crime]? Listen to the commentary on the same canon [twenty-eight of the Holy Apostles]:

Against simony and Caesaropapism

In Canon twenty-five, it has been said: one should not condemn twice for the same crime.[9] But here and in both canons [i.e. Canons 29 and 30], the punishment is indeed double because of the greatness of the evil committed and the heaviness of the sin. For there is no greater evil than to buy a divine gift either with money, or with the power of the prince, or to sell it: indeed, the gift of the Holy Spirit is then considered as a servant, as it is written in the encyclical letter of Tarasius, the most holy patriarch of Constantinople, to the pope of ancient Rome, Hadrian: Macedonius and other enemies-of-the-Spirit will fare better than these [simoniacs], for they blasphemed against the Holy Spirit by making Him a servant of the God and Father, whereas these make Him their own servant. For anyone who sells, or buys, wants to be the master of what he buys and then acquires it for a piece of silver. Such sins are not forgiven. For this reason those who buy and sell the high priestly dignity with money or the power of the prince, are both deposed and excommunicated, and completely expelled from the Church. The epistle of the holy patriarch Gennadios even condemns them to anathema. It says: let such a man be excommunicated and deprived of every priestly dignity and service, and let him be cursed and anathematized, whether he bought the grace of the Holy Spirit, or whether he sold it, if he is a cleric; if he is a layman, let him be cursed.[10]

So, you hear the canons and commandments of the holy Apostles and holy fathers. What Christian, who accepts for himself the holy name of Christ, would dare to speak otherwise? For Scripture also says that: 'Anything which is innovated, or accomplished, or planned

---

[5] Rhalles-Potles, III, pp. 165–6.   [6] Numbers 16. 1–50.

[7] Rhalles-Potles, II, p. 37; cf. Act 8.21.

[8] Rhalles-Potles, II, p. 37 (the Greek text has two var.).

[9] Rhalles-Potles, II, p. 32.

[10] Commentary on Canon 30 of the holy Apostles by Zonaras (Rhalles-Potles, II, pp. 37–8).

against the traditions of the Church, the teachings and proclamations of the holy and ever memorable Fathers, let it be anathema.' And also after a while: 'To those who neglect the sacred and divine canons of our blessed fathers, who confirm the holy Church and, adorning the whole Christian community, direct it towards divine piety, let them be anathema.'[11]

Mityai

5. If such is the case, how is it possible that, in your city, a monk occupies the metropolitan's seat, wearing a hierarchical robe [*monatiya*] and cowl [*klobuk*]; on his head, there is a hierarchical veil [*peremonatka*] and he carries a staff? Did one ever hear of such an evil thing? Certainly it is written in no book. Since my brother [metropolitan Alexis] is dead, I am high priest after him: the metropolitanate is mine. There is no way in which he could appoint a successor after his death. Is it conceivable that one would invest someone with high priestly garments before his ordination, since no one is allowed to wear them except high priests? How does he dare to stand on the high priestly place? Is he not afraid of God's punishment? And he also does something fearful, terrible and full of awesome consequences: in the holy sanctuary, he sits on the *synthronon*! Believe me, brothers, it would have been better for him not to be born. And if God suffers it and is not sending punishment, it is because he prepares such people for eternal suffering. And why do they utter calumnies against our brother, the metropolitan, that he blessed him for all these actions? This is a lie. Indeed, Canon thirty-four of the Holy Apostles and Canon nine of the Council of Antioch, which is in accordance with it, say: 'Bishops should do nothing apart from their primate, except each one in his own territory, and the primate [should do nothing] in the absence of the others, for the sake of unity.'[12] Or do you ignore what happened upon the metropolitan's death? I have seen the letter which the metropolitan wrote, when he was dying and that letter will be with us at the great Synod.

Cyprian, in Lithuania, worked for unity

6. And let this be known to you: I have received the high priesthood two-and-a-half-years ago and, since I entered Kiev, two years and fourteen days before today, which is 23 June, no single word against the Grand-prince Dimitri came from my mouth, neither before my consecration, nor after it; I have not spoken against his princess, or against his boyars, and have not made agreements with anyone to give preference to anyone more than to him. I am not guilty against him either in action, or in word, or in thought. Rather, I prayed God for him, for his princess and for his children. I loved him with my whole heart and I wished well to him and to all his domain. And if I heard anyone

[11] Both texts are from the *Tome of Union* (920), Rhalles-Potles, v, p. 10.

[12] The text quoted here by Cyprian is the synopsis of canon 34 of the Apostles by Aristenos (Rhalles-Potles, II, p. 47; cf. the full text, *ibid.*, p. 45; Canon 9 of Antioch, III, pp. 140-1.) The implication of Cyprian is that Alexis could not have – even if he had wished to – appoint Mityai as his successor against the wish of other Russian bishops, particularly Dionysius of Suzdal.

making evil remarks against him, I hated that man. And wherever I celebrated a solemn liturgy, I ordered that the ceremonial acclamation of 'many years' be sung to him first, and then to others. Whenever I discovered prisoners, coming from his domain, I arranged, wherever I could, their liberation, buying them away from the pagans. In Lithuania, I found some citizens of Kashin, who were held for two years in a dungeon and, for the sake of the Grand-princess, I bought them out, as I could, and let them go to her brother-in-law, the prince of Kashin.

What faults did the Grand-prince find in me? How am I guilty against him, or his domain? I was going to him to give him my blessing, to him, to his princess, to his children, to his boyars, and to his entire domain, and to live with him in my metropolitanate, as did my brothers [the former metropolitans] with his father and grandfather, the Grand-princes. I also intended to present him with precious gifts. He accuses me of having gone first to Lithuania: but what evil did I commit, while I was there? Let no one accuse me for what I have to say. Because [when I was in Lithuania], I liberated many Christians from bitter bonds. Many who ignored God, recognized the true God because of us and came to the Orthodox faith through holy baptism. I erected holy churches, I confirmed Christianity, I restored ecclesiastical domains, wasted for many years, in order to appropriate them for the metropolitanate of all the Rus'. Novgorodok, in Lithuania, was lost for a long time, but I restored it, and obtained the tithe and villages for the metropolitanate. For how long in the land of Volhynia, did the diocese of Vladimir remain empty, without a bishop? But I consecrated a bishop and restored the area. Similarly, villages belonging from times immemorial to St Sophia [in Kiev] were lost to princes and boyars, but I am suing for them and will restore them, so that, after my death, God's justice would be secured.

7. Let it be known to you that our brother, Metropolitan Alexis, did not see fit to send any bishop to Volhynia, or to Lithuania, or to call anyone to him, or to supervise ecclesiastical affairs, or to teach, or to admonish anyone, or to punish the guilty bishop, archimandrite, and abbot, or to teach a prince, or a *boyarin*. Since there was no supervision by the metropolitan, each bishop was careless and did what he wished, whereas priests, monks and all Christians were like animals without a shepherd.

Dimitri wants
division

But now, with the help of God, the affairs of the Church are restored through our efforts, and the Grand-prince should have received us with joy, since this would have been to his own honour. I am trying to re-unite lost areas to the metropolitanate and want to make things firm, so that they may remain forever, for the honour and majesty of the metropolitanate. But the Grand-prince plans to cut the metropolitanate in two! What advantage would be gained through such a plan? Who are his advisors? What are my faults before the Grand-prince? I trust in God that he will find no fault in me whatsoever. In any case, even if

I had a fault, the prince cannot rightfully judge hierarchs. I have a patriarch, who has primacy over us, and I have the great synod. The Grand-prince should have reported my faults, and they would have issued legitimate judgement. But now he dishonoured me without a reason, he deprived me of my goods, he imprisoned me and held me hungry and naked, while my monks were held in another place and my servants elsewhere. He held me in a dark place, ordering that my servants be sent out naked with dishonourable words. And who can recount the blasphemies, which they uttered against me? Is this the reward which the Grand-prince gives me for my love and goodwill?

Listen to what the holy council says – the council called 'first-second' – which met in the church of the Word and Wisdom of God, that is at Saint Sophia; Canon three of that holy council says: 'If a layman, usurping power, despising divine and imperial decrees, and mocking the awesome ecclesiastical customs and laws, dares to strike a bishop, or imprison him, either for a cause, or having made up a cause, let him be cursed.'[13] This is what I suffered now. The curse of the holy council applies when one accuses a bishop who committed a fault. But which fault did they find in me, when they locked me in one room with guards, so that I could not even come out to go to church? Then, in the evening of the second day, they led me out, as I did not know where they were taking me: to be killed, or to be drowned. To dishonour me even more, the guards and the cursed Nicephorus, the general, who were leading me out, were clothed in the clothes of my servants and were riding their horses and their saddles.

Excommunication of the rebels 8. Listen, O heaven and earth and all Christians, what Christians have done to me, what they have done to a patriarchal envoy, insulting the patriarch, and the emperor, and the great council. They called the patriarch a Lithuanian, and also the emperor, and the most venerable ecumenical synod. To the best of my ability, I wished that this evil would subside. God knows that I loved Grand-prince Dimitri with a pure heart, and I wished him well, ready to give my life. But, since they inflicted such an indignity upon me and upon my episcopate, through the grace given me by the most-holy and life-giving Trinity, in accordance with the canons of the holy fathers and the divine apostles, all those who were involved in my arrest, imprisonment, dishonour and ridicule, all those who plotted these acts, let them be excommunicated without blessing by me, Cyprian, Metropolitan of all Russia, and cursed according to the canons of the holy fathers. And anyone who would dare to burn the present letter, or hide it, falls under the same [curse].

As to yourselves, venerable elders and abbots, answer me quickly,

---

[13] Cyprian makes a confusion between the two 'Photian councils': the 'first-second' Council of Constantinople (859–61) and the 'great council of St Sophia' (879–80). The quotation is from Canon 3 of the latter (Rhalles-Potles, II, p. 710).

what is your opinion, for I withdrew my blessing from that place [Moscow]. And I am travelling to Constantinople, seeking protection from God, the holy patriarch and the great synod. Whereas these people rely on money and the Genoese, I rely on God and my right.

This letter was written by me on 23 June, in the year 6886, first indiction. The dishonourable treatment by these people is giving me greater honour in the whole earth and in Constantinople.

9

Constantinople in 1379: the Encomion of
St Peter by Cyprian

(Slavic text, VMC, Dec. 21, cols. 1942–46; cf. the shorter version in Prokhorov, *Povest'*, pp. 214–15.)

Before that time, by means unknown to me, but through ways known to God, I, a humble man, was elevated to the exalted throne of this metropolitanate of the Rus' by the most holy and marvellous Philotheos and the holy synod around him. But as I came to the land of the Rus', some contrary events took place because of my sins. In the course of the third year of my tenure, I took the road to Constantinople again. As I reached the city after many troubles and temptations, hoping to find some consolation, I found instead a great disorder in imperial and patriarchal affairs. At the patriarchate of Constantinople, the throne was illegitimately occupied by the insane Macarios, who had dared to usurp the exalted patriarchal throne without a synodal election and the sanction of the Holy Spirit, simply by the will of the emperor. Before his usurpation, the throne of the great ecumenical patriarchate of Constantinople was adorned by that most holy and blessed patriarch Philotheos, who fed the flock of Christ beautifully for many years, who fought against the heresy of Akindynos and Barlaam and who destroyed their evil doctrines and heresies by his divine teachings, who also with his spiritual words conquered the heretic Gregoras[14] and put down completely his false doctrine and writings, and who also anathematized those heretics.

The blessed patriarch Philotheos himself wrote many divine books for the confirmation of the Orthodox. He also composed *Encomia* and many different canons.

However, the emperor [Andronicus IV] who then reigned in the above-mentioned city of Constantinople, did not want this holy and great man, admirable in deed and word. Using false and calumnious accusations, he removed him from the hierarchical throne and imprisoned him in a monastery. Then, in accordance with his own evil habit, he chose a certain insane Macarios, who was mentioned already

[14] The Slavic text has *Grigoriya* (Gregory), but the needed correction is obvious: on the treatises of Philotheos against Gregoras, see Meyendorff, *Introduction*, p. 405.

and who was completely deprived of reason. Against ecclesiastical tradition and order, he installed 'a desolating sacrilege in the holy place' [Dan. 11.31; 12.11; Mat. 24.15], as described in ancient Scriptures: Jacob was expelled, whereas Esau, who was hated before he was born, is brought in [cf. Gen. 25; Mat. 1.2–3; Rom. 9.13]. So Arcadius, having listened to his wife, imprisoned John Chrysostom, and made the criminal Arsacius a successor to his throne.

But the admirable Philotheos, a man of God and a honey-producing tongue, never ceased, in the midst of such sufferings and mishaps, to glorify and to thank God. After a year, he fell asleep in blessedness, delivering his soul to the living God and was counted in the list of patriarchs, whose life he emulated, since he lived in a God-pleasing manner and ended his life in holiness. We will speak again elsewhere of this blessed patriarch.

Meanwhile, the emperor who did him evil, was suddenly deposed, and lost his life miserably,[15] whereas Macarios, the patriarch appointed by him, by a judgement of God and of the Catholic Church, was deprived of his hierarchical dignity and condemned to deposition and imprisonment as a wrong-believing heretic. Together with the other bishops, I was present at that synod and have signed the act of his deposition.

At that time, I remained in the imperial city, named Constantinople, for thirteen months. I could not go out of it, because the imperial city was beleaguered by much disorder and trouble: the sea was held by the Latins, whereas the earth and dry ground was controlled by the God-hating Turks. And as I was blocked in such a way, I became unbearably sick, so that I was almost dead. As soon as I regained consciousness and recovered my intellect, I began to call upon the help of the holy hierarch Peter, saying the following prayer: 'O servant of God, who pleased the Saviour! I know that you have great access to God, and that you can, O hierarch, help the bereaved and the sick, whenever you wish: if your will is that I reach your throne and venerate your grave, O venerable teacher and good instructor, give me help and relief from my illness.'

Believe me, my children: at that very hour, by the prayers of [Peter], the miracle-worker, the speedy intercessor, the unbearable pain ceased, and I regained health, as if I was never sick, and, after a few days, I left the imperial city. Through the help of God and of His friend Peter, the miracle-worker, I crossed the sea and reached the land of the Rus'. I came and venerated his miraculous grave, as the Grand-prince of all Russia, Dimitri, the son of the Grand-prince Ivan [II], and of the glorious Grand-prince Ivan [I, Kalita], received us with joy. For such

---

15 Andronicus IV died in June 1385, after repeated armed conflict with his grandfather John V. The shorter version of the *Encomion* does not contain the reference to the emperor's death, saying only that 'he miserably destroyed the empire' a possible reference to the events of 1376–9 (ed. Prokhorov, *Povest'*, p. 215).

were the ways of the great hierarch and miracle-worker, such were his labours and efforts, which pleased God from his youth and from his very young age, and for which God glorified him, granting him this reward.

Here is our word of praise, which we, as we humbly can, address to you, O admirable among the hierarchs who preceded you and whom you imitated as a busy apostle, ceaselessly caring about the flock entrusted to you, about the spiritual sheep of Christ, whom He redeemed by his blood, in his ultimate mercy and goodness. And you, O hierarch, you have 'kept the faith', as the great apostle says, and 'finished the race' [2 Tim. 4.7] and, in gladness, you enjoy the perpetual light of the Trinity. Having received heavenly wisdom, you were carried to the top of the temple and deservedly led to the throne of the Almighty. So, we pray you, holy hierarch, look down on us and direct us from on high according to your mercy. You know how difficult is this present life, for, in times past, you also experienced its labours, O blessed one. But since the land of the Rus' acquired you as its intercessor, and since the glorious city, named Moscow, possessing your venerable relics, preserves them eagerly, as a treasure, and since – as if you, our bishop and intercessor, were still alive – our glorious Orthodox princes, coming every day, venerate them with warm faith and receive blessings together with all the Orthodox, sending up glory to the life-giving Trinity, make that we all receive that glory in Christ our Lord Himself, to whom be glory, honour and majesty together with His Father, who is without beginning, now and ever and unto ages of ages, Amen.

IO

Byzantine wavering

The two patriarchal acts of 1380 and 1389, representing two contradictory attitudes of Constantinople towards Russian affairs, are
preserved in a mutilated form in the patriarchal registry published in
MM (cf. Darrouzès, *Régistre*, pp. 253–4, 373, 380). The passages translated
below represent the essential parts of the two long documents.

A. MOSCOW'S SEPARATISM PARTIALLY VINDICATED BY PATRIARCH NEILOS IN 1380

(MM, II, pp. 12–18; RIB, VI, suppl., cols., 165–83.)

. . . Many years have passed since the late Lord Alexis had been sent
from Russia as God-loving bishop of Vladimir, and was consecrated
here Metropolitan of Kiev and all Russia. Soon afterwards, the late
Grand-prince of Moscow and all Russia Ivan [II], as he was dying,
entrusted to the metropolitan not only his son, the presently reigning
Grand-prince of all Russia, Dimitri . . . but also the responsibility and
guardianship of the whole government . . . He did not trust anyone
else, since [Moscow] was challenged by many enemies, and many,
who hated the Grand-prince, sought his power . . .[16] The metropolitan
sought in every way to save the child and to preserve the country and
the government for him. Whereas the other princes chose to keep quiet
and to preserve peace, the fire-worshipping prince of the Lithuanians,
always ready to attack and destroy another country and conquer every
city, but finding no way to penetrate Great Russia, did not keep quiet,
but showed fiery anger against the metropolitan and sought to hurt
him in the worst way . . . [*Here follows an account, very hostile to Lithuania,
of the appointment of Roman and the events of 1355–75.*]
    Many accusations were then forged against the metropolitan [Alexis],
so that the most-holy and ever-memorable Patriarch Lord Philotheos,
ignorant of the treachery and the deceit, sent the present metropolitan
of the Lithuanians and of Little Russia [Cyprian], as an arbiter
between the two parties, so that he might reconcile them according to

---

[16] The beginning of the document is mutilated and the translation reflects only the
general meaning of the passage.

justice and reestablish peace between them. But Cyprian, forgetting
the instructions of his superior, used all his energies to capture that
church for himself and all his imagination in order not to fail in his
project. First of all, he took leave of his colleague, who had been sent
with him there, as a security, so that none of his actions might become
known; then he cringed to the prince of the Lithuanians and to his
friends: they united and got so closely together, that they considered
Cyprian as a new Roman and sent a petition, asking that he be
appointed metropolitan. If this does not happen, they wrote, they
would obtain one [metropolitan] from the Latin Church. Of these
letters, Cyprian himself was both author and sender. On the one hand,
he was offering his support to Metropolitan Alexis, convincing him to
stay at home and not to expect any trouble, since he, Cyprian, had
assumed all concern for his interests; on the other hand, he was acting
differently, showing himself to be not his friend, owing him much
gratitude for the many services Alexis had rendered him, but his
greatest enemy, forwarding false libels, full of many accusations and,
in every way, seeking to have him deposed.

After all these intrigues, Cyprian was secretly consecrated as Metropolitan of Kiev and of the Lithuanians, realizing his plans. He took
over a part of the Church, as the metropolitan his friend was still alive,
and received a synodal act concerning the other part [i.e. Great Russia],
so that he would not miss that either. He also requested the full deposition of the old metropolitan, as everyone was deceived and believed his
forgeries . . . [*Byzantine ecclesiastical officials sent to Russia bring reports
unfavourable to Cyprian.*]

Throughout the province of Russia, there was much murmuring,
division and great popular unrest, but it calmed down when Metropolitan Alexis sent counsels and advice both general and personal. Also
letters are written to our most holy and great Church of God [from
Moscow], complaining about the cloud of sorrow covering their eyes,
in connection with the consecration of Metropolitan Cyprian, asking
for sympathy and compassion and requesting help of the divine synod
against the unjustified dishonour which befell them. The ambassadors
of our own Church who returned from there reported the same things
to the synod and were supported by many other witnesses also coming
from there.

As these letters were written, Metropolitan Cyprian did not remain
inactive, but made every effort to reach Great Russia and take hold of
it, especially when Metropolitan Alexis departed to God in grand old
age. But since his great efforts were not successful and he was not
accepted there, he took the road of Constantinople and appealed to the
sacred and great synod, under the deposed patriarch [Macarios] who
preceded us, requesting help in his endeavour to govern Great Russia.
But as he found here circumstances inconsistent with his goal, he sat
waiting and nourishing empty hopes.

After some time, as the Church [of Constantinople] was still widowed, ambassadors from Great Russia came, bringing letters, requesting that the most pious hieromonk and archimandrite Pimen, whom they brought with them, be appointed metropolitan, and claiming loudly that the consecration of Cyprian had occurred against canons. As soon as Our Humility, by a judgement of God, ascended the exalted throne of patriarchs, they came to us, entrusted us with the letters, reported the views and the demand of Grand-prince Dimitri of all Russia, who had sent them, and asked that their petition be fulfilled. And as Metropolitan Cyprian was also coming to ask for Great Russia in addition to Kiev, Our Humility, considering that the demand and petition of the ambassadors was just and thinking that his consecration, which occurred during the lifetime of Metropolitan Alexis, was un-canonical, decided that his case was to be the subject of canonical judgement and investigation, so that, if it is found to be canonical and legal, it would be accepted and no further debate would take place, and if not, Cyprian would be deprived of what he pretends to possess.

He requested that a few [documents][17] be examined, as part of his defence. After a few days, he came to the sacred synod and said that he was not seeking to be judged, but was only requesting to receive that which the synod, in a written decision, had determined as being his, if that appears to be just. If not, he was ready to be content with that part [of Russia] for which he was ordained and that he had already re-nounced the rest. He said this and, apparently, doubting that anything good would come of a debate, even if it takes place in his presence, on the issue of the petition coming from Great Russia, he secretly fled, without talking to anyone.

After that there was a first debate on the question of whether or not Pimen should be consecrated as Metropolitan of Russia, and a second on the issue of how such a consecration can take place, except if he receives the title of 'Kiev', since Kiev was from the beginning the capital of all Russia. Many arguments were exchanged at the synod, and it appeared as necessary and legitimate for us to consider favourably the just petition of such a big nation: there should be an election and they should receive as high-priest the man they are asking for.

Through the very venerable great chartophylax, the Metropolitan of Nicaea – since he was residing in the imperial city and was prevented by sickness from attending the sacred synod – was also invited to give his opinion on the question, but he refused, saying that he accepted the decision taken concerning Metropolitan Cyprian [by Philotheos in 1375] as legitimate.

[*After a protracted debate between the synod and the Metropolitan of Nicaea, Theophanes, the latter finally accepts not to oppose the majority's will.*]

---

[17] *Lacuna* in the text; one may presume that the documents included the authentic last will of Alexis, mentioned in Cyprian's letter to St Sergius (cf. above, pp. 210, 296).

[The synod then] decided and decreed, first, that Pimen should be consecrated metropolitan 'of Great Russia', and, second, that he should be given the title of 'Kiev', according to the ancient custom of that metropolitanate, since it is impossible for a high priest to be metropolitan 'of great Russia', if he is not first called metropolitan 'of Kiev', which is the Catholic church of all Russia and the primatial see.

As to Cyprian, he should have been expelled not only from Kiev, but from every part of Russia, since he took over that Church by deceit and was consecrated uncanonically, as we have said above, at a time when the legitimate metropolitan, the late Alexis, was still alive and was deprived of his own Church, in his absence and without judgement, in opposition to the exact meaning of the sacred order of the Church. However, we use condescension in his case, since he secretly left and is not present here to be properly judged according to the canons, and we declare that he is metropolitan only of Little Russia and the Lithuanians. As to the [synodal] decree, to which he refers, we declare that it is null and void, because it was not issued according to the canons.

Therefore, since the very venerable hieromonk Pimen was elected and consecrated as true metropolitan 'of Kiev and Great Russia', by the grace of the Holy Spirit, through Our Humility by a vote of the sacred synod of the aforementioned most sacred metropolitans around us, with the good will and consent of the most powerful and holy emperor, it is proper that his title be 'Metropolitan of Kiev', according to ancient custom, and that he also controls Vladimir and the whole of Great Russia, as the late Metropolitan Alexis did before him . . .

[*A standard list of canonical duties of the metropolitan follows.*]

And if Cyprian, the Metropolitan of Little Russia and the Lithuanians dies before him, [Metropolitan Pimen] shall assume responsibility also for Little Russia and the Lithuanians and shall be the pastor of the Lord's Christian people, which is found there, strengthened by the grace of the All-powerful God; he shall then alone be proclaimed Metropolitan of Kiev and all Russia, as long as he is alive, and, after him for all times, there will be a high priest of all Russia, according to ancient custom, whenever [or whoever?][18] they request [it] from Great Russia.

The present synodal act shall be entrusted for safety to the most sacred Metropolitan of Kiev and Great Russia, beloved brother in the Holy Spirit and concelebrant of Our Humility, as it was written in the month of June of the year 6888.

By the venerable patriarchal hand: Neilos, by the grace of God Archbishop of Constantinople, New Rome, and ecumenical patriarch.

[18] The var. ὅνπερ ('whoever') is suggested by A. S. Pavlov in RIB, v, app., col. 183, for ὅταν which is in the text.

B. UNITY RESTORED AND CYPRIAN VINDICATED BY
PATRIARCH ANTHONY (1389)

(MM, II, pp. 116–29; RIB, VI, suppl., cols. 193–227.)

From the beginning, since the Russians became Christians and submitted themselves to our great, catholic and apostolic Church of Christ, the entire province of Russia has been placed under the pastorship and administration of a single metropolitan . . .

[*Cf. the translation of the following paragraph above, Chapter 4, pp. 75–6; the text continues with a very critical evaluation of the exclusively pro-Muscovite policies of Metropolitan Alexis.*]

Irritated and desirous to put an end to this situation, the princes [of the anti-Muscovite camp] sent a great embassy to that holy patriarch [Philotheos in 1375] and to the divine and sacred synod with letters asking and praying that another high priest be given to them, who would visit them, and guide them and teach them the saving things, profitable to their souls. They claimed that this was their last attempt; if it failed, they would appeal to another Church, which, for a long time, has stood away from the right doctrines and is foreign to the Orthodox Church of the Christians.

What should have been the reaction of that great man of God and authentic patriarch? He would neither divide Russia into two metropolitanates, nor neglect a nation so numerous, which had been left for so many years without high-priestly supervision and sanctification, and which was asking to obtain those from him with words full of goodness, justice and true supplication. So concentrating within himself, gathering himself up in the Spirit, and also convening the great high priests and obtaining their advice and true counsels, he chose a middle road. On the one hand, in order that such a numerous nation would not remain without bishops, and would not be given to total destruction and spiritual ruin by joining another Church, he used extreme economy [οἰχονομία], condescended to the demand of the plaintiffs and consecrated the above-mentioned Lord Cyprian as metropolitan 'of Kiev, Russia and the Lithuanians', that is of those parts, which the Metropolitan Lord Alexis had left without supervision for many years. On the other hand, in order to maintain the old status of Russia, so that it would still remain in the future under one metropolitan, he issued a synodal decree stipulating that, after the death of the Lord Alexis, the Lord Cyprian should take over the whole of Russia and be the one metropolitan of all Russia.

[*The arrangement should have worked, if not for the unfortunate actions of the deposed Patriarch Macarios*][19] who as soon as he learned about the death [of Alexis] immediately wrote to Great Russia, ordering them not

[19] *Lacuna* in the text.

to accept the Lord Cyprian, and, in formal letters, delivered that Church to that archimandrite Michael, whom he knew as a favourite of the Grand-prince, Lord Dimitri, entrusted him with full power in that Church, although he had not received episcopal consecration and charged him in writing to come here and be appointed Metropolitan of Great Russia . . .[20]

Meanwhile, the Grand-prince of Moscow, Lord Dimitri, as soon as his spiritual father and regent, the Metropolitan Lord Alexis, died, out of veneration and submission to the latter and nourishing a remnant of hatred against the Lord Cyprian, finding unexpected additional support in the letters of the deposed patriarch [Macarios], sent that archimandrite Michael, to be consecrated Metropolitan of Great Russia. However, divine judgement followed his every step: before reaching the imperial city, as he was still on his boat in the Black Sea preparing to disembark in the morning, he died. However, this event did not discourage the rascally ambassadors: for the misfortune of that Church, they agreed on a mischievous plan, concocted false documents and established a certain hieromonk, named Pimen, as their own pastor, giving promises and making oaths to one another that no one of them will ever reveal the truth. They appear before the most holy and ever memorable patriarch, Lord Neilos, who has just taken the leadership of the Church, and show him the [false] letters. He, ignoring the mischievous plan, believed the letters to be authentic (how could such a good and divine soul, which never tasted any evil and was full of every virtue, suspect such a deceit?) through synodal decision, consecrates Pimen as Metropolitan of Russia.

Here are the good results of the evil initiatives contained in the letters of the deposed patriarch [Macarios]! For he is the real culprit of all these events. It is from his letters and from information concerning the Latins that the Russians took courage to send the ambassadors and to concoct false documents saying that, whatever happens, they would not accept the Lord Cyprian, a man who had been nominated by the prince of the Lithuanians, their worst enemy.

[*The document further recounts contradictory information reaching Constantinople concerning Pimen, the brief return of Cyprian to Moscow in 1381, and the activities of Archbishop Dionysius of Suzdal.*]

After so many accusations were raised against Pimen, the synod, with the consent of the patriarch and the concurrence of the most powerful and holy emperor, considered it proper to send two high priests, one ecclesiastical official and one imperial officer, who would make an inquiry about Pimen and depose him if they find out that indeed he had been consecrated on the basis of deceit and forged documents. The delegation received power to expel him from the Church and install Dionysius instead.

[20] *Lacuna* in the text.

This decision greatly disturbed the Russians and they were driven mad against the Catholic Church: they uttered many insults, blames and accusations against us all and murmured against us. However, they themselves are the ones who deserved all this, because they forged lies, plotted deceit, rejoiced in wickedness and accomplished thousands of evil deeds through the ambassadors whom they sent to us. Of all these things, they accused us in return. However, none of these unfortunate events had any other origin than the ambassadors who came from Russia. Quarrelling with each other, splitting in two parties and, often, divided in three opposing groups, bringing out contradictory letters, accusing each other and fighting each other, they created divisions and conflicts, while the Church did not know on whose side was the truth. They should hide and keep silence, instead of throwing insults at the Church!

[*Here follows the account of the death of Dionysius, the return of Pimen to Constantinople, where he was first vindicated, then condemned, after his agreement with Theodore of Simonovsky and their joint flight into Turkish-occupied territory.*]

Therefore, Our Humility, after consultation with synodal colleagues, the metropolitans and *hypertimoi* of Heraclea, Cyzicus, Nicomedia, Ouggrovlachia, Nicaea, Monembasia, Attaleia, Adrianople, Serres, Selymbria, Gothia, Sougdaia, Varna and Derkos, decided and decreed that the synodal deposition of Pimen by our predecessor, the most holy and ever memorable Patriarch Lord Neilos, has occurred canonically and justly and should in every way be maintained [*a listing of arguments supporting the decision*].

Whereas therefore, Pimen had been deposed earlier and since his deposition is now maintained through a synodal decision of Our Humility, so that he has no further ground for a defence, it having been shown early, that henceforth there would be only one legitimate metropolitan of all Russia;

whereas, more than to any other, this is acceptable to our most powerful and holy emperor, the leader and defender of that which is just and proper;

whereas, unquestionably, there lies the glory of the whole Church and of all Christians;

whereas, on the other hand, the most sacred Metropolitan Lord Cyprian already possesses that part [of the metropolitanate] in which he resides, and he also has a decision of the most holy and ever memorable patriarch, Lord Philotheos, which makes him, after the death of Lord Alexis, to be the one and only Metropolitan of all Russia,

We all unanimously maintain the said decision, and we restore him – as if for a new beginning – and we annul anything which came in between, that is the scandals, the uncertainties, the conflicts, the struggles, and the evils caused by these, and we consider those as having never taken place, judging that they resulted from [unhappy] times and circumstances, and also from original pretexts, described earlier. Neither the Lord Philotheos nor the Lord Neilos, who lived blessed lives and departed in an even more blessed way to the Lord, we consider as willing participants in such divisions, but as neither responsible, nor guilty of the accusations and reproaches levelled against them by some people. By the present synodal decision, we restore the Lord Cyprian, as Metropolitan of Kiev and all Russia, in practice and in title. He will hold the metropolitanate in its entirety until the end of his life; he shall consecrate bishops in the dioceses which from the beginning were submitted to the metropolitanate; he shall ordain priests, deacons, sub-deacons and readers, and fulfil the other duties which belong to the practice and title of a legitimate metropolitan of all Russia. His successors, all the metropolitans of Russia, will possess the same rights, succeeding each other after each one's death, and this order shall be kept unchanged from now until the end of time, as it is confirmed by a venerable chrysobull of the most powerful and holy emperor. This our present decree and restoration of previous order shall never be revoked either by us or by our successors, since the facts themselves have convinced us how great an evil is separation and division of that Church in many parts, and how great an advantage there is in having one metropolitan govern that province.

For this reason, the present synodal decree of Our Humility was delivered to the most sacred Metropolitan of Kiev and all Russia, *hypertimos* and beloved brother and concelebrant of Our Humility in the Holy Spirit, Lord Cyprian, and to the Church of Russia, so that it may belong to it, as exclusive and eternal security, in the month of February, of the present twelfth indiction of the year 6897.

By the venerable patriarchal hand: Anthony, by the grace of God Archbishop of Constantinople, New Rome, and ecumenical patriarch.

[*The patriarchal signature is followed by that of seventeen metropolitans.*]

Index

Index

Anthony, Patriarch of Constantinople (1389–90, 1391–7), 12, 75, 76, 103, 116, 118, 137, 200, 220, 236, 237–40, 247, 250, 253–5, 257, 264, 307–8

Antioch, Patriarchate of, 30, 110, 115, 116, 137, 180

Appanage system, 15

Arabs, 3, 20, 29, 31, 102, 122

Archangel Michael, church of, in the Kremlin, 141, 143

Arctic Ocean, 5, 83

Aristarches, S., 9

Aristenos, Byz. canonist, 75, 110

Aristotle, Aristotelianism, and the Byzantines, 98, 101, 104, 139

Armenia, Armenians, 5, 17, 49, 206

Arsen'ev, S. V., 132

Arsenius, bishop of Tver, 246

Arsenius, Patriarch of Constantinople (1261–7), 113–4, 139

Arseny, 250

Art, Byzantine, in Russia, 19–21, 23–4, **138–44**, 272–3; see also Palaeologan Renaissance

Arta, capital of Epirus, 32

Asen I, Bulgarian ruler (1186–96), 32

Asia, 30, 33, 35, 37, 137, 173

Asia Minor, dioceses of, 73, 74, 77, 110, 235

Astrabike, town of, 237

Athanasius, bishop of Sarai, 82

Athanasius, bishop of Vladimir-in-Volhynia, 82, 165

Athanasius II, Patriarch of Alexandria, 43

Athanasius I, Patriarch of Constantinople (1289–93, 1303–11), 92–4, 112–14, 123, 124, 139, 149, 150, 152, 153

Athanasius of Vysotsk, St, 131, 202, 260 273

Athos, Mt, monasteries of, Athonite monks, 21, 24, 96–8, 102, 104, 109, 110, 115, 123, 125, *128–30*, 178, 202, 212, 252, 260

Austria, 41

Avars, 29

Avignon, 59

Avvakum, envoy of Metropolitan Alexis to Constantinople, 188, 290

Azov, city of, see Tana

Azov, Sea of, 29

Balard, M., 162, 178

Balitsa, Moldavian hospodar, 249

Balkans, the, 5, 140; and Byzantium, 4, 14, 17, 31–4, 36, 47, 77, 113, 129, 130, 164, 166, 177, 179, 206, 234

Balsamon, Michael, *rhetor*, 188, 237

Balsamon, Theodore, Byz. canonist, 74, 75, 85

Baltic Sea, region of, 16, 48, 53–5, 145, 147; trade route from, 3, 9, 49

Bank, A. V., 257

Barbashev, A., 244

Barker, J. W., 212, 253, 254, 258

Barlaam 'the Calabrian', philospher, 52, 97–100, 142, 143, 176

Bari, town of, 26

Baron, S. H., 14

Barsanuphius (Varsonofy), bishop of Sarai, 150

Basel, Council of, 268

Basil, bishop of Tver, 196

Basil, brother of Grand-prince Daniel of Galicia, 41

Basil, Bulgarian Archbishop, 33

Basil II, Byz. Emperor (976–1025), 4, 12, 14, 112

Basil I, Grand-prince of Moscow (1389–1425), 12, 69, 103, 116, 118, 137, 241, 244–5, 248, 251, 254–7, 264

Basil II, Grand-prince of Moscow (1425–62), 268

Basil III, Grand-prince of Moscow (1505–33), 274

Basil (Gregory) Kalika, Archbishop of Novgorod, 82, 84, 127, 189, 230, 231, 246, 276–7

Basil, *nagubnik* of Olgerd, 289

Batu, Mongol Khan, 29, 37–40, 44, 48, 56

Batyushkov, P. M., 146

Baumgarten, N. de, 26

Bayezid, sultan, 253, 259

Beccos, John, see John Beccos

Beck, H. G., 83, 142, 143, 221, 234

Begunov, Yu. K., 223, 228, 242

Bela IV, King of Hungary (1235–70), 40

Belobrova, O. A., 135

Belgorod, diocese of, 78, 240

Benedict XII, Pope (1334–42), 66

Beneshevich, V. I., 75

Berdibek, Mongol Khan, 181, 185

Berezuesk, city of, 288

Berke, Mongol Khan, 56

Bessarion, Byz. humanist, 105, 106, 139

Black Sea, 2, 3, 9, 36, 48–51, 70, 145, 158, 159, 162, 172, 174, 187, 205, 237, 158, 159, 162, 172, 174, 187, 205, 237, 271, 308; trade, *see* trade, areas, Black Sea

Index

Blastares, Matthew, 117
Bogomils, Cathars, 137
Bogoyavlensky, monastery in Moscow, 132
Bohemia, 62
Boissonade, J. F., 149
Boleslav (Yuri), prince of Galicia-Volhynia, 63, 65, 95, 154
Boojamra, J. C., 113
Boris I, Bulgar Khan (852–89), 13
Boris, prince of Nizhni-Novgorod, 135, 194, 288
Boris and Gleb, Kievan martyr-saints, 25
Boris Godunov, Russian Tsar (1598–1605), 274
Bosnia, 66
Bosphorus, 4, 35, 161
Bosphorus, 'Cimmerian', 50, 51
Bratianu, G. I., 49
Bréhier, L., 87, 111, 112, 113
Bremen, city and metropolitan see of, 53, 54
Brest, city and principality of, 59
Bryansk, city and diocese of, 78, 145, 170, 186
Buda, city of, 66
Bulgakov, S., 134
Bulgaria, Bulgarians, 3, 5, 7, 12, 13–15, 17, 18, 20, 21, 22, 30–4, 40–2, 46, 48, 51, 55, 66, 70, 75, 77, 92, 106, 109, 115, 119, 120, 124, 125, 128–30, 132, 164, 165, 169, 171, 173, 179, 194, 200, 201, 212, 216, 274
Burunday, Mongol general, 56
Byelorussia, Byelorussians, 8, 59, 163

Caffa, city of, **48–51**, 141, 159, 212, 218, 222, 223, 228
Callipolis (Gallipoli), city of, 173
Callistos, Patriarch of Constantinople (1350–3, 1354–63), 99, 106, 114, 115, 120, 127, 129, 130, 134, 164, 165, 168, 171, 178–81, 199, 200, 232, 271
Cappadocian Fathers, 125
Carolingian Empire, 13, 14
Carpathian Mountains, 9, 37, 199
Casimir III the Great, King of Poland (1330–70), **62–7**, 93, 94, 154, 155, 157, 159, 160, 162, 163, 191–4, **287**
Casimir IV, King of Poland (1447–92), 269
Caucasus area, 29, 34, 37
Cavallini, Byzantine art compared to, 138
Cembalo, city of, 51
Central Asia,
  and the Mongols, 37

Central Europe, and Byzantium, 4, 47
Chalcedon, city of, 141, 237
Chalcedon, Council of (451), 73, 74, 110, 111, 142
Charlemagne, Frankish King, later crowned Emperor (768–814), 13, 14, 276
Charles of Anjou, Norman King of Sicily, 35, 36, 59
Charles IV, King of Bohemia, Holy Roman Emperor (1346–78), 62
Cherepnin, L., 242
Cherniavsky, M., 69, 118, 137
Chernigov, town of, 38, 77, 78, 145, 168, 184, 265
China, Mongol conquest of, 37, 38, 182; trade route to, 2, 49
Chingis Khan, Mongol ruler (1206–27), 15, 29, 36, 37–8, 182, 227
Chodynicki, K., 243
Chora, monastery of the, 138, 139
Chrysostomos, 83
Chukhloma, town of, 225
Chud' Lake, battle of (1242), 44, 54
Cimmerian Bosphorus, 50, 51
Circassians, 69
Čiževskij, D., 136
Clement III, Anti-pope (1080, 1084–1100), 28
Clement, Metropolitan of Kiev (1147–1155), 20, 40, 87, 89, 265
Clement V, Pope (1305–14), 58, 159
Clement VI, Pope (1342–52), 66, 105, 175
Clucas, L. M., 109, 114
Cluniac monks, monasticism, influence in the Western church, 107, 109
Conrad IV, German Emperor (1259–1254), 31
Conrad of Masovia, Polish duke, 54, 61
Constance, Council of, 266
Constantine V Kopronymos, Byz. Emperor, iconoclast (741–75), 264
Constantine VII Porphyrogenetos, Byz. Emperor (913–59), De administrando imperio, 4, 9, 10
Constantine IX Monomachus, Byz. Emperor (1042–55), 6, 16
Constantine Kostenetsky, 128, 129, 275
Constantine I (the Great), Roman Emperor (324–37), 11, 30, 73, 178, 276–7
Constantine, son of Olgerd, 241
Cosmas Indicopleustes, 18
Cracow, city of, 62, 65, 193, 243

313

Index

Index

321

Index

324

Index